# Sir Arthur **Bliss**

## Standing out from the Crowd

Paul Spicer

ROBERT HALE

First published in 2023 by
Robert Hale, an imprint of
The Crowood Press Ltd
Ramsbury, Marlborough
Wiltshire SN8 2HR

enquiries@crowood.com

**www.crowood.com**

**British Library Cataloguing-in-Publication Data**
A catalogue record for this book is available from the
British Library.

ISBN 978 0 7198 1633 8

All plate images supplied by the author.

Every reasonable effort has been made to trace and credit
illustration copyright holders. If you own the copyright
to an image appearing in this book and have not been
credited, please contact the publisher, who will be pleased
to add a credit in any future edition.

Typeset by Simon and Sons

Cover design by Maggie Mellett

Printed and bound in India by Parksons Graphics

# CONTENTS

*Preface*                                                                                    5
*Acknowledgements*                                                                           7

**Chapter One:** The Curtains Open                                                           9
**Chapter Two:** The Nation Arming                                                          26
**Chapter Three:** The Diaghilev Effect                                                     50
**Chapter Four:** *A Colour Symphony*                                                       72
**Chapter Five:** Love Via the Stage: The 'Volcanic Anglo-American'                         81
**Chapter Six:** Towards *Morning Heroes*: 1927–1930                                       103
**Chapter Seven:** Things to Come: New Paths                                               123
**Chapter Eight:** Strings, Travel Guides and Checkmate                                    146
**Chapter Nine:** An American Interlude                                                     167
**Chapter Ten:** The Dance Resumes: The BBC, *Miracle in the Gorbals* and *Adam Zero*      188
**Chapter Eleven:** Towards Grand Opera and Beyond                                          212
**Chapter Twelve:** Master of the Queen's Musick                                            232
**Chapter Thirteen:** Musical Diplomacy, *The Lady of Shallot*, and Opera for Television    253
**Chapter Fourteen:** Unblessed *Beatitudes*                                                278
**Chapter Fifteen:** Australian Interlude and a Vision of Retrospect                        305
**Chapter Sixteen:** The Curtains Close                                                     333

*Endnotes*                                                                                  371
*Bibliography*                                                                              377
*Index*                                                                                     379

# Preface

I was approached to write this book as soon as my biography of Sir George Dyson had gone to press in 2014. When asked, I realized how little I knew about Bliss, and how unfamiliar I was with his music. What I did know generally failed to excite me, and I felt so agnostic about the project that I seriously questioned whether I was the right person to undertake it. However, I then realized that I could turn this into a positive by making the music pass certain critical tests. I am certainly no apologist for Bliss. This is an issue for many biographers who work too hard to persuade their readers that so-and-so's music has the divine spark, questioning why concert promoters and recording studios are not lining up to programme his or her music.

Writing this preface after having finished the main text of the book, I am now in a position to evaluate the whole oeuvre and to weigh up Bliss's character. I can ask the question posed in the first chapter as to whether we know Bliss any better for listening to his music. He certainly wasn't going to help us by opening himself up to scrutiny. In his second *Desert Island Discs* programme in 1972, which should be a light-hearted but fairly candid canter through his life, enthusiasms and loves, he simply sounded tetchy at being submitted to questioning by Roy Plomley. He eased up somewhat as the programme unfolded, but he gave the impression of the whole interview being a rather disagreeable necessity. This was a good example of the protective shield he presented to the world. The *Times* obituary noted 'his handsome military bearing' and reminded readers that he served as an officer in the Grenadier Guards in World War I. He never lost that military bearing, which also made him appear unapproachable to strangers. It was also in that terrible, wasteful war that he lost the brother he loved so much, a loss that coloured so many of his works throughout his life.

Living as we do in an informal age of personal revelation when even members of the Royal Family wash their dirty linen in public, the guarded persona of well-known people whose lives encompassed the two World Wars seems like a foreign country. Bliss's conducting manner is similarly unemotional, like Boult's – efficient, accurate and putting the onus on the players to make the music come alive, the detailed work done in rehearsal. One is reminded of Boult's comment after seeing André Previn conducting rather wildly on one occasion: 'I wonder what he did in rehearsal?' It was a different world. So, Bliss's comment suggesting that if we want to get to know him then we should listen to his music tells us that it was only when he expressed himself through music that he put his innermost thoughts on display. The skill is in the reading.

Bliss's output of composition can be loosely divided into five periods: the pre-war juvenilia, the post-war *'enfant terrible'* works, the 1922 *Colour Symphony* and the beginnings of maturity, the high maturity works from 1929, loosely starting with *Pastoral* and *Serenade,* through *Morning Heroes* and onwards, and finally, the 'Indian summer' works of the last seven years (*Angels of the Mind, Cello Concerto, Metamorphic Variations* and *The Shield of Faith*). It is an engaging journey that, given my initial agnosticism, found me becoming more and more involved and wondering what the next musical revelation would be. The final period is, to my mind, the most interesting and shows Bliss writing deeply personal works which have a searingly emotional core. The extraordinary thing is his desire to go on composing – and composing better than ever – in these last years all through his serious final illness. His famed energy levels never really faltered, right to the end.

Bliss himself felt he would be a poor subject for a biographer as he had no perversions, extra-marital affairs, or the need to pep himself up with drugs. He was, to all intents and purposes, a very ordinary, normal, and deeply committed husband to his remarkable wife, Trudy, who outlived him by thirty-three years, dying in 2008 aged one hundred and four. It is therefore of real interest to understand how this 'normality' is reflected in his music. My instinct is to say that what becomes apparent as the years progress is a deepening of the emotional core which mirrors the deepening of the bond between him and Trudy. This would seem to furnish us with an explanation for the outstanding works of his 'Indian summer' and a warmth of expression which, whilst certainly not absent from earlier works, positively glows in these final works.

During the writing of this book, I had serious conversations with a number of deeply committed Bliss aficionados, wanting to know what it was that spoke to them so strongly about his music. But as my own investigation developed it became clear there were going to be a number of works which stayed with me for life, showing with absolute clarity the journey I had travelled. This also begged the question as to why, as a British music specialist, I did not know these remarkable works earlier in my life. This, then, is at the heart of the writing of this book. I want the reader to share my journey of exploration, and to join me in the excitement of discovery. I want them to get to know this remarkable man, to listen, and to share my new found enthusiasm for this music with another generation of music lovers who, like me, will find the sheer variety, colour, vibrancy, drama, and the deep well of emotional undercurrent irresistible.

# Acknowledgements

A number of people have been key to the writing of this biography to whom I am deeply indebted. Karen Sellick, Bliss's younger daughter, was a source of huge encouragement throughout, and especially as the book was nearing completion when she was very ill. One of her daughters read a number of chapters to her during her final illness. Very sadly, Karen died before she could see the whole text, but it was partly her very positive reaction to what she was read which spurred me on with greater confidence to complete the book. She was a very special person and I was privileged to be able to speak to her often. It was good, too, to be able to meet her elder sister, Barbara, at the start of the research back in 2014, and to gather some of her memories of her father before her death early in 2020.

Perhaps the most helpful of all has been my old friend, Andrew Burn, Chairman of the Bliss Trust, who has such a long-standing association with, and knowledge and love of Bliss's music. He not only helped me with factual information through the many programme notes and articles he has written for recordings, concerts and periodicals, but perhaps more importantly was a sympathetic ear and sounding board when my early agnosticism over Bliss's music threatened to boil over. His calm, wise counsel was what eventually helped me to see the light. I also want to thank the Bliss Trust, especially Elizabeth Pooley, for their generous sourcing of many scores that have been so important to read as Bliss's life progressed. The Trust has also provided generous financial support for the photographs and images used in the book. Both Elizabeth Pooley and Andrew Burn were extremely helpful in assisting with all aspects of the photographic material.

I also acknowledge, with thanks, the black and white photographs that have been supplied from the Bliss Archive at Cambridge University Library. They can be identified by the acronym 'CUL' by each photograph.

Giles Easterbrook, a founding member of the Bliss Trust, and fount of knowledge of all things relating to Bliss, has been a constant companion in the enormous amount he has written about so many of Bliss's works. It was therefore with the greatest sadness that we learned of his early death in late August 2021 just as the first draft of this book was delivered. His spirit hovers over all these pages.

Robert Milnes, another Bliss trustee and a good friend of Trudy Bliss, has been extremely helpful in providing personal information otherwise not in the public domain. Monica Darnbrough has provided me with reams of concert reviews, articles and cuttings from the *Times* throughout the writing process which has been such a help in saving time when, already seven years into the writing of the book, time was of the essence to the ever-patient publishers.

I must put on record the great help I received from Robert Clark relating to Bliss's First World War period. Another important contact who proved a mine of information was Professor Jonathan Elkus, who I met at the University of San Francisco at Berkeley where his father, Albert, had headed the Music Department and invited Bliss to be a visiting Professor around the time of the outbreak of World War II. The Music Librarian, John Shepherd, was also very helpful in allowing me to see the large quantity of Bliss-related material held there. It was valuable to see where Bliss worked and see the Hertz Hall where Bliss's ballet *The Lady of Shalott* was premiered. Relating to this, the staff at the Museum of Performance and Design of San Francisco Ballet proved most helpful in providing programmes and photographs relating to this premiere and subsequent performances. Caroline Williams also helped with her research into Trudy Bliss's family in America, as did Paul Jackson of the University of Winchester, who did a great deal of research around Santa Barbara and was very helpful in pointing me to important locations there.

Lewis Foreman has, as ever, proved a mine of information and a source of privately made recordings where no commercial alternative currently exists. Pianist Mark Bebbington, who recorded all Bliss's piano music for Somm Recordings, was very kind in loaning me all his Bliss piano scores and giving me very helpful opinions on various works from the perspective of the professional pianist. The indefatigable John Smith of the Royal Birmingham Conservatoire kept me plied with references to Bliss, which he found in many different sources. Bill Sneddon was also very helpful with his remarkable research into the details of Bliss's father's various marriages.

I would like to place on record my gratitude to the librarians at the Cambridge University Library who were so helpful to me on my numerous visits to the Bliss archive there. Nothing was too much trouble for them. Finally, and most importantly, I must place on record my grateful thanks to the British Academy/Leverhulme Foundation for the research grant I was awarded, aided by staff at the Royal Birmingham Conservatoire, which helped in particular to fund my American research.

This book, like the other biographies I have written, has taken a long time to finish because of a busy professional life, which had to take precedence because it pays the bills. That it has been finished at this point in the summer of 2021 is thanks to the Covid-19 pandemic and lockdowns that enabled me to focus on it almost entirely for some eighteen months – together with composition, which provided much-needed contrast to the writing of words. This balance of work seems to me to have its equivalent in the essence of music, light, shade and contrast of mood, all of which are at the heart of this story.

# Chapter One

# THE CURTAINS OPEN

'If you want to know about me, listen to my music'. So said Bliss towards the end of his life. Bliss's friend, the poet Robert Nichols, quoted an aphorism by F.H. Bradley in his preface to *Such Was My Singing:* 'It is good to know what a man is, and also what the world takes him for. But you do not understand him until you have learned how he understands himself.'[1] So here is another side to Bliss's desire for us simply to get to know his music. We need also to know what Bliss *wants* us to know through what he writes of himself in his music. And is this to be taken as the real deal? Does Bliss understand *himself* and is he speaking the truth to us through his music? Are there gestures or characteristics that regularly appear which are intended to make us feel a certain way about him? As I am to tell you the story of his life I want, as a biographer, to be certain that I am being told the truth. How can a biographer translate Bliss's desired 'listening' into the written word? A challenge, certainly. But the more the immersion in his music, the more the traits of personality emerge, and the more complex yet the task becomes. There is a detective story here and we are urged to examine the clues to the mystery through the pages of Bliss's music. There will be no Agatha Christie-like dénouement in a stylish drawing room at the end, but the course of this narrative will hope to lay bare the essential elements which will lead the reader to want to go and investigate Bliss's music for themselves – surely the desired outcome for any musical biography.

But before we can start dusting for fingerprints, we have to amass our facts, see where Arthur Bliss came from and understand what early childhood influences set him up for the possibility of the noteworthy career that was to develop.

Bliss was a hybrid in being born of an American father and an English mother. This conceptual duality remained of the utmost significance throughout his life, even being mirrored in his own marriage to an American. Bliss's father, Francis, known as Frank (1847–1930), was a seventh generation American born in Brooklyn, Long Island, but whose family for all the previous generations had lived in Springfield, Massachusetts, to where the first of the Blisses to live in the USA emigrated from Rodborough, near Stroud in Gloucestershire in the seventeenth century. He was the second of four children born to Elijah and Mary Bliss. Elijah (1816–1899) is recorded as having had a number of different jobs through his career, and at various times was described as an importer, a merchant, an oil and cloth manufacturer, and a 'secretary'. He was obviously quite well-to-do if the last address at which Frank lived with them was anything to go by: 111, Sixth Avenue, Brooklyn, a large brownstone house typical of the area. After his wife's death in 1884 aged 61, Elijah moved to London for his remaining years. He sailed from New York and arrived in Liverpool on 8 May 1891, three months before Arthur's birth.

Frank Bliss's first wife was Lillie Pancoast, who he married in 1884 but who died two years later. They had one son, George born in 1885, Bliss's half-brother, who was educated at Haileybury College and who died in 1927, aged only forty-two. Frank's second wife was Celestine Adrienne Leture, who he married in Brooklyn on 19 October 1875. It is not clear when she died, although we know Frank was a widower when he married Agnes Davis on 6 November 1890. They had three children, Arthur Edward Drummond (b.1891), Francis Kennard (b.1892), and James Howard (b.1894). However, Agnes was only to survive until Arthur was four years old. Arthur remembered her in his autobiography *As I Remember* as an ardent music lover and that 'she must have been a good amateur pianist, if the volumes of her music that I have, all marked with her phrasing and fingering, are sufficient proof.'[2]

Frank Bliss had come to the UK as a representative of John D. Rockefeller's Standard Oil Company in 1896. They lived in Barnes, a prosperous and leafy suburb bordering the Thames in south London. Their house, called Hawthornden, was in Queen's Ride overlooking Barnes Common, and would later be destroyed in the Blitz. Agnes died in Nice, France, on 18 March 1895 and was repatriated to be interred in the cemetery at Mortlake, close to Barnes. Whether because Hawthornden had too many personal memories to bear, or because with the children still so young it seemed the appropriate moment for a change, Frank decided to buy a house in Holland Park, Bayswater. No. 21 is a very substantial detached house in one of the most desirable parts of London, which Arthur described as 'very big and magnificent'[3] and it was their home for the more than a quarter of a century.

'Big and magnificent' might also describe Frank Bliss – not that he was tall; a passport application noted that he was a little over 5' 8" with a 'healthy' complexion and a moustache, but he was a distinguished-looking man with a strong personality and a firm set of principles. He was also a 'man who loved fine things and was a discriminating collector.'[4] Arthur soaked up the essence of these beautiful things all around him and felt them to be 'an imperceptible but abiding form of education'. In a moving tribute he went on to say that 'I was supremely lucky not only in having such a father, to whom indeed I owe all that I may have myself achieved, but also having one who by his own ability and hard work was able to give me the perfect environment in which to spend the years of my youth.'[5]

There is no doubt as to the good fortune Arthur and his brothers had in being born into such a wealthy, loving and supportive environment, but there was never any question that this privilege might be abused or taken advantage of as the boys were expected to work out their own destiny with the same application that their father had shown in achieving his success.

Are there any clues from these earliest days as to the direction Bliss's music might take in due course, especially his strong dramatic instinct? He recounted being fascinated by clocks – so fascinated, indeed, that his concerned father felt moved to remove or cover them: rhythm, pulse and chiming quarters. A performance of Ravel's *L'Heure Espagnol* years later would bring it all back. A fascinating mechanical Chinese vase at home would play music while a tea drinking mandarin complete with drooping moustaches would appear and retract as if by magic. 'Glittering splendour'[6] witnessed watching Queen Victoria's Diamond Jubilee was another early impression, together with experiencing John Philip Sousa's famous band: 'Was it the immaculate white kid gloves that Sousa drew on before raising his baton, with something of a Beecham panache, which attracted me most or the drilled precision with which various groups of his band, cornets, trombones, woodwind, acknowledged in turn the applause? I forget, but I wish I could re-hear how he performed those marches of his.'[7] Add to this his father's habit of telling his boys stories from Homer's *Iliad* and the *Odyssey* when out walking and, aged about eight, the intimidating dancing lessons he had to undergo with the venerable Mrs Wordsworth, described later in Bliss's life by the great Dame Ninette de Valois as 'formidable'. The process of growing into our skins is the process of gathering and filtering experiences. The key is which of those experiences remain as stimulants to feed the creative mind.

Music was an essential part of the household routine and all three boys were encouraged to learn instruments. Arthur, being the eldest, perhaps naturally took his mother's instrument, the piano; Kennard played the clarinet, and Howard, the cello. The three boys played chamber music together in the spacious surroundings of their own home, or as photographs show, their grandmother's (Agnes's mother) house in Mortlake. The boys used to love Sunday visits to their grandparents, partly because the garden bordered the river. On Boat Race days there was the thrill of seeing the competing Oxford and Cambridge eights striving to reach the finishing point first. The result was announced by either dark blue (Oxford) or light blue (Cambridge) papers floating down into the garden, thrown from a hot air balloon at the conclusion of the race.

Schooling had begun in 1898 at the Norland School in Holland Park Avenue. This was followed two years later at the pre-preparatory Wilkinson's School in Orme Square near to Holland Park. Then, in 1902, Arthur was sent to Bilton Grange School, a preparatory school very close to Rugby to which all three boys in their turn would go. These schools were fairly grim places and Bliss described Bilton Grange as having 'Dickens-like horrors.'[8] It is therefore of little surprise to find that it was the 'self-effacing and dedicated music master' who provided the antidote to the general brutality in the form of an introduction to Beethoven and his piano Sonatas, and on leaving, a gift of the two volumes of Schubert's Sonatas which Bliss kept in use throughout his life.

Beethoven proved to be a very powerful stimulant to the young Bliss who, wound up to fever pitch in his desire to know more about this maverick genius, had a recurring dream in which he was to have a lesson with Beethoven himself. In his imagination Beethoven was living in a derelict hut by the Thames and Bliss ran through the streets to get to him only to be stopped by sinister playing from a band in whichever way he turned. Flinging himself forward he got to the hovel where Beethoven awaited only to be told by a 'veiled figure' that 'The master is dead'(!) The boy certainly had a vivid imagination – perhaps another early fingerprint.

At Bilton Grange, Bliss discovered an essential personality trait: 'I had quickness and facility, but not the faculty of concentration.'[9] Allied to this was a much later self-assessment: 'I admit to being a bad subject for the camera, as I am too for the portrait painter and the sculptor. My temperament demands activity, not a passive role: I only feel myself in action.'[10] These traits are two sides of the same coin. And further: 'If my music is to make any impression it must move on, and not be static; that is the very essence of my own character.'[11] And now, perhaps, a second fingerprint has emerged from our detective's dusting. The essential first lesson in the art of concentration came into sharp focus when at Bilton Grange Bliss tried and failed to play a piece of Handel from memory. As he put it, in the process of learning the music 'the next page of the score was always more interesting than the one in front of me, with its instant difficulties to overcome.'[12] Never again, even when conducting his own music, did he trust his memory. Another side to this was Bliss's habit of revising works sometimes several times. Perhaps the next page always being 'more interesting' led him to hasty conclusions which needed rectifying later, something, as we will see, which was to be counterproductive to the acceptance of some of his scores.

Prizes for French, maths and music showed an early academic aptitude, and school concerts were never without a contribution from the young Bliss (or his brothers when they arrived). Drama at the school was another extra-curricular activity in which he participated, but sport was not, at least according to the school records, much in evidence at this stage. Significantly, he met E J Dent, of King's College, Cambridge, an old boy of the school, who visited for a weekend, attending concerts on both the Saturday and Sunday evenings, and playing the piano himself. He was to become a good friend and mentor of both Arthur and Kennard later on when they went up to Cambridge.

Bilton Grange, whilst undoubtedly a tough regime, was a civilized school with a sizeable proportion of its boys learning musical instruments and singing (there were three choirs). A feature of Sunday evenings was an informal concert which gave the boys an opportunity to show off their skill and have a goal for their practising.

In common with a fair proportion of the boys at Bilton Grange, Bliss went on to Rugby School, just a few miles away. He started there on 28 September 1905 in W.N. ('Spitter') Wilson's house. Wilson obtained his nickname because of his propensity to spit when talking. In trying to overcome it he often made a sound which to the boys sounded like 'ob'. This led to a probably apocryphal remark often quoted at the time 'Little boys should be (ob)seen and not heard'!'[13] Wilson was also responsible for the management of an 'Army Class' that prepared boys for entrance to the

Army Colleges at Woolwich or Sandhurst, which was seen as a very significant change in the balance of the curriculum dominated by Classics.

Music in the public schools at this time was a peripheral, extra-curricular activity and, as Bliss put it, 'In my time any boy who showed a determination to become a musician was *rara avis*, to be treated with a good deal of condescension, if not worse. All teaching and practising had to be squeezed in after school hours and in very inadequate premises.'[14] The Director of Music was the remarkable Basil Johnson, who remained at Rugby until 1914, when he moved to Eton – succeeded at Rugby by George Dyson. Bliss was fortunate in having such an able, supportive and dedicated master to lead him forward. As he remembered: 'He fought hard for increased opportunities. I owe him many happy hours of a Sunday afternoon at his house playing on two pianos with friends and gaining in this way knowledge of classical symphonies.'[15] And at last we come to the first mention of a Bliss composition performed at the Johnson's house. 'Somewhat unusual, it was a quartet for piano, clarinet, cello and timpani, written for my brother Kennard and myself, with the addition of two friends who played the cello and drums in the school orchestra. Still under the spell of Beethoven it consisted of variations in the somber key of C minor. The small invited audience recoiled each time the timpani were thwacked and finally could not restrain their laughter: perhaps a good preparatory lesson against some future audience reactions.'[16] Howard had not joined the school at this point or he would have undoubtedly been the cellist in the performance. The choice of instruments obviously reflected the experience he had in playing chamber music with his brothers at home.

A forward-thinking young temporary music master standing in for a sick colleague introduced Bliss to the music of Debussy and Ravel trying to subvert Bliss's hero-worship of Beethoven who, along with the other great composers of the past, the evangelizing teacher wished to consign to the dustbin of history. 'At fifteen years of age I was immediately captivated by the French masters. I loved the delicious sounds and poetry of Debussy and the cool elegant music of Ravel – no beetling brows and gloomy looks here, but a keen and slightly quizzical look at the world.'[17] · This was the first modern music Bliss had encountered and its effects would be clear to hear in his first serious works. He met Ravel in 1919 and told him how influential his music was on him at such an early age and was met with a classic Gallic shrug, which to Bliss showed that it was not a view shared by the new young composer turks snapping at Ravel's heels. 'My affection for his music has never wavered. Some of his work may consist of trifles, but they are trifles fashioned with all the imagination and finish of a Fabergé ornament.'[18]

There are two other pieces dating from his time at Rugby. One is an arrangement of Tchaikovsky's *March and Valse des Fleurs* for clarinet and cello first performed on 17 January 1908, and the other, a much more substantial sounding *Trio for piano, clarinet and cello* which was first performed on 19 January 1909. He was obviously keen to use his Christmas holidays productively both in writing and being able to rehearse the music with his brothers before term started.

The opening of the new Temple Speech Room at Rugby on 3 July 1909 by King Edward VII was a great occasion in the history of the school, and in young Bliss's life to date. The Speech Room was designed by the great Victorian architect Sir Thomas Jackson who had been the architect for the enlargement of Butterfield's impressive school chapel in 1896. When a distinguished previous Headmaster, Frederick Temple, who had risen to become Archbishop of Canterbury, died in 1903, it was felt that a suitable memorial would be a new school hall large enough to accommodate the rising numbers in the school. It was designed with an 'Albert Hall' style of stage with tiered choir seating rising to an organ which occupied most of the width of the wall above. An impressive building indeed and one in which, in his last year at the school, Bliss was to perform several times, undoubtedly the most important of which was singing in a performance of Elgar's *Dream of Gerontius* in April 1910.

The growing importance of Elgar's music to Bliss was recounted when he wrote: 'My musical life during the years at Rugby was enriched by a growing love for the music of Elgar. I had heard the *Enigma Variations* on several occasions, and in my last year at Rugby I took part in a performance of *Gerontius*, which put the seal on my fervent admiration. The summers we spent so close to the Malvern Hills made much of his music seem an intimate utterance of our own pleasures.'[19] Holidays were pleasantly varied and mostly in England at this time, 'Christmas in London, Easter by the sea, generally near Swanage, and for the summer months my father used to rent some house in the beautiful counties of Worcestershire, Shropshire or Herefordshire.'[20] But these local places were balanced, once the boys were a little older but still at school, by two wonderful skiing holidays at Territet in Switzerland. However, for all the excitement of the ski slopes, Bliss preferred the summer holidays spent in England. They spent five holidays in Cradley Rectory in Herefordshire, Bliss enjoying being able to drop into the church next door and play the organ, and also developing a passion for microscopy encouraged by the local curate. So engrossing did this become that Bliss's father bought him his own microscope. 'This miniature and magic world of beauty provided the perfect anodyne for the frustrations and failures of creative efforts.'[21]

'Creative efforts', whether frustrating or successful, are very often encouraged in the young by contact with an influential person – perhaps by the hero-worship of a major composer. In Bliss's case this was undoubtedly Elgar. He tried, unsuccessfully, to elicit a signed photograph from his hero when at school, and didn't manage to actually meet him until 1912, when he was two years into his Cambridge studies. Once that meeting had taken place, although turbulent later on, their relationship flourished and was particularly supportive when Bliss was on the frontline in France. Elgar sent Bliss a copy of his *Cockaigne* overture to France in the first week of the battle of the Somme. It was signed and had 'Good luck' inscribed in the flyleaf. When the war had ended, Elgar invited Bliss to come to hear a playthrough of his new Violin Sonata. There was a full house of distinguished people including Bernard Shaw and Landon Ronald. W.H. Reed, for many years leader of the London Symphony Orchestra and a close friend of Elgar's, played the violin, and Elgar himself played the piano. Bliss turned the pages and recalled: 'Was my disappointment due to the far from brilliant performance or to the belief that its musical substance had little in common with the genius of his earlier masterpieces? I hope I sat quiet, as if absorbed.'[22]

Bliss's time at Rugby was coming to an end in 1909 but another long-lasting influence was to come from a rather unexpected source and demonstrate the serendipitous nature of teaching. Rupert Brooke's godfather, Robert Whitelaw, was, according to Bliss, an inspired teacher and a real eccentric who positively quivered with excitement when declaiming 'famous passages from *King Lear* and *Oedipus Rex*.'[23] Bliss would go to Whitelaw's house to have his Latin or Greek verse corrected and marvelled at his teacher's passion for barrel organs. 'Outside in his drive there was usually one hired, or, if he was lucky, two, grinding out tunes from the Italian operas... I have never heard anyone except Whitelaw who could handle words, especially Greek or Latin, under a sound barrage... Certain Verdi tunes are now debarred from my enjoyment.'[24]

At the end of his time at Rugby, Bliss decided that he should take the opportunity of learning – or at least being exposed to a stringed instrument and he took some holiday lessons with the distinguished German violinist Wilhelm Sachse who had been teaching one of his half-brothers. Bliss decided to try his hand at the viola but never progressed as Sachse would always prefer to get him to accompany Brahms violin sonatas during his lessons instead. This may say more about Bliss's potential on the viola as Sachse perceived it especially with only a few weeks of tuition in prospect than anything else, but, as Bliss commented, he learned the great Brahms sonatas this way. Bliss's later work with Lionel Tertis on the Viola Sonata written for him would teach him far more than he ever gathered from Sachse in his short period of tuition.

Bliss started at Pembroke College, Cambridge in the autumn of 1910. It was in every sense a whirlwind of experiences. After the hothouse, closed environment of public school, university was a sudden breath of fresh air – not that in those days there weren't some school-like restrictions, but essentially it was an adult environment and it was possible to rub shoulders with like minds and to extend experience through exposure to brilliant young people and older teachers. The two people he related to most strongly were Charles Wood and Edward Dent (of Bilton Grange memory). With Wood he studied counterpoint and fugue. Despite a seemingly conservative way of teaching Bliss grew to admire and like his teacher greatly. His conservatism, however, extended to his musical tastes, and on taking him to hear the British premiere of Schoenberg's *Five pieces for Orchestra* in the Queen's Hall Wood had to be disowned for laughing hysterically during the performance!

Wood was one of the first students at the newly founded Royal College of Music in its original building on the west side of the Royal Albert Hall in London. He studied with Stanford and Parry before moving to Selwyn College, Cambridge and then to a teaching post at Gonville and Caius College, becoming its first Director of Music in 1894. He lost a son in the first World War, just as Bliss was to lose his younger brother, Kennard.

It was Edward Dent who was to prove an abiding friend and influence, not only to Arthur Bliss, but to his younger brothers, as we shall see. Bliss described him as 'the most stimulating influence, bringing into a somewhat provincial backwater a keen breeze from musical Europe. He gave generously of his time to young musicians, and a visit to his house might lead to playing through an act of a Mozart opera, with Dent singing most of the parts in Italian, or a heated discussion about contemporary music.'[25] One of the great attractions about Dent for Bliss was his recent return from a long period spent in Europe and a resulting friendship with Ferruccio Busoni whose playing, as Bliss noted, like Liszt's was given added authority through the creative side of their personalities. His interpretations were as stimulating as they were unorthodox. An example of this which Bliss referred to was Busoni's use of the pedal in Bach's *Chromatic Fantasy and Fugue*. 'In the Fantasy... his arrangement allowed of a mysterious blurring of colours, far more orchestral in sound than the keys of the piano seemed capable of giving. He was a unique phenomenon among the great players I have heard, and I am grateful that even at second hand I had a chance to glimpse something of his ideals.'[26]

One figure at this time who had been at Cambridge between 1892–5 was Ralph Vaughan Williams whose quiet musical revolution was sweeping through the musty corridors of the establishment. Bliss took part in one of the earliest performances of the *Sea Symphony*. He was also present at the first performance of *On Wenlock Edge* given by the tenor Steuart Wilson, with the extraordinary W. Denis Browne (also a casualty of the first War) playing the piano. Bliss does not recall who the string players were, but he remembers with absolute clarity RVW himself sitting at the front dressed in tweeds and smoking a pipe: 'a massive man with a magnificent head.'[27]

Bliss's recollections of his Cambridge years are few and far between, and we are left with the impression that a very good time was had by all and that study was something of a necessary evil. Occasional mentions of new music are there: a society that Bliss founded with some friends, modestly called 'The Gods', was formed to play through their new works in what Bliss described as 'a mood of mutual admiration'. He admitted to a 'reluctance to concentrate, except haphazardly, on the central core of my being, my music. Life with a very large capital L was too delicious just to breathe in, and I think that I mortgaged the immediate future by this dilettantism, just when I should have closed the doors on a good slice of life and locked myself in with my work.'[28]

One of the earliest extant works we have from this time is a piano piece composed in his first year at Cambridge (1910) called *May-Zee*. Its dedication is slightly pretentiously written in French: 'Composée et Dediée à son amie MW'. We assume that the 'M' of the initials is the 'Maisie' of the title. Perhaps she was one of those who made Cambridge 'just too delicious to breathe in' – who knows? However, this accomplished short piece shows a rather socially restricted salon-style waltz. It has elegance and style, and a degree of virtuosity is needed to bring it off in performance. It was published by Gould and Company.

Two years further into his studies at Cambridge came a wholly different piano *Intermezzo*, a more mature conception; introspective in nature, more substantial, and showing a far more interesting, reflective side to Bliss's creative nature. It was published by Stainer & Bell at the same time as his first *Suite for Piano*, dedicated to his father and published by Joseph Williams. The *Suite* is a much more extensive and interesting work, and is the first multi-movement work we have. It isn't surprising, perhaps, that all the earliest works are for piano: Bliss was an accomplished pianist, and these early pieces, which he must have played himself, show a real feel for the instrument and some of its possibilities. Stylistically it is still rooted in Edwardian England, with Brahms hovering over his shoulder. There is nothing here to hint at what will come so vividly into focus after the War. But every composer's progression is fundamentally different. The *Suite* is still a significant work, with its central *Ballade* being a big-boned movement lasting nearly eight minutes. What is revealed as these pages unfold is an obviously extrovert temperament which has a tender core. This is a real fingerprint. For while the means of expression and the style in which he will express himself develops out of all recognition, the underlying personality which needs to express itself is there to be read in embryo in these pages. What is interesting about the relatively immature piano writing of these movements is how much of the music is located in the centre of the piano keyboard. He doesn't venture much to the extremes, which gives the music a rather 'boxed in', thick textured feel and shows how this music will have been written at the piano. Even the *Scherzo* is rather lumpen in this way, with the small helter-skelter run from the top of the piano right at the end feeling like a sudden moment of freedom.

The next work, *Valses Fantastique*, written the following year in 1913, is a far more interesting conception and shows a considerable leap forward in stylistic invention. There is no doubt that the French school is beginning to weave its magic web around his creative mind. Ever since being introduced to Debussy and Ravel at Rugby he had obviously been trying to process this 'cool elegant music', as he called it. Here, in this new work, there are the first signs that his collar was being loosened, his brow unbeetled, and his view more quizzical (to use his descriptions of Ravel). The work is in four movements and was later withdrawn along with the two works already discussed, although two movements of the *Valses Fantastique* were used right at the end of his life for *A Wedding Suite* for piano celebrating the wedding of his half-sister, Enid in 1974.

The pianistic writing in the *Allegretto Amabile* first movement is very considerably advanced from the earlier works, and shows the influence of Ravel (whose *Valses nobles et sentimentals* had been published two years earlier). The movement opens as if nothing had changed, but soon the clouds seem to part. While he finds it difficult to assume Ravel's degree of French nonchalance and grace, there is a real feeling that he wants to lighten his mode of expression. The second movement, *Poco piu andante*, continues the journey, and the third movement, *Poco lento e molto espressivo,* is the closest he comes to Ravel's impressionistic world. It is also notable that he now moves out of the centre of the piano keyboard using a far greater expanse of the instrument. The fourth movement, *Introduction – moderato,* grows out of the previous movement and shows yet more harmonic advances, bringing the work to a beautifully dreamy and impressionistic conclusion.

Only recently formed at Cambridge, The Apostles had been another, far more influential society than the more inward-looking 'Gods'. At that stage all were male, but it later became the Bloomsbury Group when it moved to London and included Virginia Woolf and Vanessa Bell. This highly subversive group of free-thinkers rejected Victorian values, and were influenced themselves by the revolutionary philosophical ideas of Bertrand Russell and G.E. Moore. They encapsulated the new thinking in his summary that 'one's prime objects in life were love, the creation and enjoyment of aesthetic experience and the pursuit of knowledge.'[29] They promoted a new informality and freedom of expression which were cemented by the huge social changes which flowed as a reaction to the Great War so soon to engulf Europe.

Bliss was not genetically disposed to sign up to the whole package of ethics espoused by this group, but he was of the new generation for whom deference to the older generation was not an automatic right; it had to be earned. His father's rock-like New England principles were deeply embedded in Bliss's psyche and would not be abandoned at a whim, or even after three years of relatively wild Cambridge experiences. Moving to the Royal College of Music in 1913 to study briefly with Stanford he found the experience disheartening to the extent that he preferred 'to forget the hours I spent with Stanford: they were not many and from the first moment when he scrawled on my manuscript "he who cannot write anything beautiful falls back on the bizarre", I felt the lack of sympathy between us. He was a good teacher when in the mood: I felt that instinctively, and certain maxims, such as "Let in air to your score", linger in the mind as truisms to be followed, but his own disappointments as a composer perhaps affected his outlook and he had a devitalising effect on me.'[30] Crucially, he went on, 'at the age of twenty-two I was too old to conform, and like my brother Kennard, a hero-worshipper of Berlioz, I regarded the defiant attitude of the great Hector towards the Paris Conservatoire as the only right one for a student.'[31]

One of the most salutary experiences of the RCM on the young Bliss was his exposure to the greatest compositional talents among the students of his generation, Herbert Howells key amongst them (notably Stanford's favourite student). Bliss's recollection of Howells is interesting: 'His quickly written scores, showing a beautiful resolute calligraphy, with their technical maturity simply disheartened me. I had to learn one of the most painful lessons in life, that there are others who are born with more gifts than oneself: no amount of self-confidence can at heart convince one to the contrary.'[32] And yet Bliss was to go on to have a far more successful career – at least on the face of it and in the mainstream – than Howells. But, as an aside, perhaps where Howells's loss of his son Michael at the age of nine to polio was an almost debilitating leitmotif throughout his life which he hoped, though failed, to exorcise through the writing of *Hymnus Paradisi*, Bliss did, to a greater extent, exorcise the ghost of his dead brother through the writing of his own requiem to Kennard, *Morning Heroes*, and to move on.

One of the great experiences of his RCM time was going to the Drury Lane Theatre with his closest friends of the time, Howells, Arthur Benjamin and Eugene Goossens, to see the latest Diaghilev production of a Stravinsky ballet. Stravinsky was *the* man of the moment – even of the generation. Slightly later than the years we are currently investigating Bliss gave a lecture to the Society of Women Musicians on 2 July 1921. In this wide-ranging talk he took a look at music in various countries ending with Russia. Fascinatingly, he congratulates the Russians 'not only for what they have created, but also for what they have killed…'[33] He continues: 'Let us take a toll of some of their victims.

1. The oratorio composed especially for the provincial festival on the lines laid down by the Canon [sic] and Chapter.
2. The symphonic poem *á la* Strauss, with a soul sorely perplexed, but finally achieving freedom, not without much perspiring pathos.
3. The pseudo-intellectuality of the Brahms camp followers, with their classical sonatas and concertos, and variations, and other 'stock-in-trade'.
4. The overpowering grand opera with its frothing Wotans and stupid King Marks.

Give me such works as *Le Sacre du printemps, L'Histoire du soldat,* the *Sea Symphony* and *Savitri, The Eternal Rhythm* and *The Garden of Fand,* the Ravel Trio and de Falla's *Vide Breve, L'Heure espagnole* and the *Five Pieces* of Schoenberg, and you can have all your Strauss *Domestic* and

*Alpine* symphonies, your Scriabin poems of Earth, Fire and Water, your Schreker, your Bruckner, and your Mahler.'[34] Ouch! A young man's exhortation indeed, and notable that before long he would be writing his own sonatas, concertos and a grand opera. His final word in this outburst was reserved for the Germans as a whole: 'I fear I cannot say a good word of German music: it is to me anathema, not because it is Teutonic, but because to my mind it is at the same time ponderous and trivial, or, in the jargon of present-day science, boundless, yet finite.'[35] This from a man who idolized Beethoven and loved playing the Brahms violin sonatas with his viola teacher. But this, also, from a man who had just lost a much-loved brother to the Germans in the conflict we will come to in the next chapter.

We are getting slightly ahead of ourselves in our timeline, but whether or not these opinions were those of hot-headed youth there is no doubt that they were sincerely held and also acted upon in his own compositions of those years, as we will see in Chapter Three.

Bliss's developing relationship with Elgar had grown a real reciprocity so that the Elgars took a serious interest in Bliss's first foray into the medium of the string quartet. He noted 'The Elgars were very sympathetic friends to me during the following years [after his initial meeting]. When the war came, she [Lady Elgar] wrote to me in France:

> Dear Mr Bliss,
> I must send you a few lines to tell you I had great pleasure on Friday as I was able to hear your Quartet. I did so wish you could have been present too as it was, at least it seemed to me, beautifully played and was received with much warmth of applause... I much wished that Sir Edward could have heard it... the music seemed so full of eager life and exhilarating energy and hope, and the writing for the instruments so interesting, and producing delightful effect, some beautiful cello sounds in the first movement for instance. I shall hope to hear it again... I hope your leave will really come before long and we hope you will let us know and come and see us as soon as possible...'[36]

The Quartet in A major was written in 1914 and given its first performance on 7 July that year in the Blisses' home in Holland Park, played by Nettie Carpenter and Eugene Goossens (violins), Ernest Young (viola) and Howard Bliss (cello). Its first public performance was given in the Aeolian Hall by the Philharmonic Quartet: Arthur Beckwith and Eugene Goossens, Raymond Jeremy and Cedric Sharpe, on 25 June 1915.

The quartet played it regularly after this. Bliss dedicated the work to his Cambridge friend and mentor, E.J. Dent. Dent, in reply complained that '*all* young composers embarrassed him by putting his name at the head of their earliest and most immature chamber works(!)'[37] In the way that the *Valses Fantastique* was such a step forward from earlier piano works, this quartet shows just how grounded Bliss's compositional technique was by now and it is of little surprise therefore that he found Stanford's strictures unsympathetic. There is also little doubt that Stanford would have found 'modern stinks' to excoriate in this new work from his student and it could well be that Bliss would have found that more encouraging than the small details of criticism which Stanford might have tried to circle with his famous blue pencil. But this work actually falls after Bliss's time with CVS.

What comes across in this first instrumental work is the freedom of the individual lines – a hallmark of a real composer. Never mind that the language is not yet formed into a personal style. The music of this quartet is very much of its time and the influence of Vaughan Williams (with some almost direct quotations from *On Wenlock Edge* composed only three years earlier) looms large not only in the mood and character of some of this music but also in its use of instruments and textures. It is a shame that Bliss didn't have the confidence to keep the quartet in his list of works because, early as it is, it has some real inventiveness and a sense of command in its compositional processes. Playing for some twenty minutes, it is also a substantial chamber work.

Written around the same time and seen through Novello's presses by his father, like the string quartet while Bliss was on active service, was a Piano Quartet in A minor written for and dedicated to the pianist Lily Henkel and her Quartet. Bliss remembered that it 'was given a public performance in Bath while I was there (recuperating after being wounded) at Prior Park, and the event was considered by my commanding officer sufficiently noteworthy to have the cadet corps officially represented at the concert! So his second-in-command stoically came into Bath with me, and sat through what turned out to be the first serious concert he had ever attended – an endearing example of protocol duly observed.'[38]

The Piano Quartet is another substantial work in three movements lasting just under twenty minutes. The two outer movements are built on classic formal (Sonata) lines but are interrupted by a tiny two-minute scherzo. It is a lovely foil to the intense seriousness of the first movement and has some of the most interesting scoring of the whole work. In fact, this little movement feels like a fingerprint, so much more natural does it feel as an expression of Bliss himself. The brevity which defies convention also feels like an attempt to break loose from the very obvious stylistic shackles of the other movements. His friend, the poet Robert Nichols, wrote very interestingly about originality in the autobiographical preface to *Such Was My Singing*, his collection of poems written between 1915 and 1940:

'Goethe remarks: "People are always prating on about originality, but what do they mean? As soon as we are born the world begins to work on us, and this continues to the end. What can we call our own save energy, strength and will? Could I give an account of all that I owe to great predecessors and contemporaries, there would be but small balance in my favour [39]... Perhaps what those who demand "originality" of the poet actually desire is to feel the presence of a distinct personality. If so, they are in good company. For the same poet said to Eckermann: "Personality is everything in art and poetry".' [39,40]

In the present writer's opinion this applies absolutely to Bliss. For there is a very clear and powerful personality at work which is not necessarily reflected by a wholly original voice – but then how many composers can we name who are original in the way Goethe means?

The only other works of which we know, or think we know, that were written in 1914 are a lost *Rhapsody* for clarinet and piano. and a song, *Tis time, I think, by Wenlock town*, setting a poem by A.E. Housman. The rhapsodic piano part of the song would certainly place it at this time or even slightly earlier. The thickness of the piano textures seems to place it closer to the *Intermezzo* of 1912 perhaps, but the manuscript (it was not published) gives no real clue. It has a poignant ending powerfully observant of Housman's final verse and finally repeating the words 'Wenlock Edge' almost as a final glance over the shoulder:

Oh tarnish late on Wenlock Edge,
Gold that I never see;
Lie long, high snowdrifts in the hedge
That will not shower on me.

This is a substantial song and shows Bliss's instinctive feeling for vocal line. That is different from a memorable melodic line – something to which we will return a number of times during the course of this narrative. It is no surprise that Bliss amassed a considerable list of songs in his output during his life, of which this was the first. It was obviously a medium he enjoyed.

Another song possibly from this time – perhaps 1915 – is *The Hammers* setting an onomatopoeic poem by Ralph Hodgson which starts:

Noise of hammers once I heard,
Many hammers, busy hammers,
Beating, shaping, night and day,
Shaping, beating dust and clay
Saw the hammers laid away.

The pounding of the hammers in Bliss's setting is reminiscent of Honneger's famous representation of a steam train in *Pacific 231* of 1923 and Mossolov's *Iron Foundry* of 1927 but evidently predating both. George Dyson's *The Blacksmiths* of 1934 also sets a fantastical alliterative medieval poem about the noise of an iron foundry. All these pieces show the power of music to describe visceral energy, and of all the works so far discussed, this perhaps comes closest to Bliss's own feelings about himself as being a man of action, energy and drive, a major fingerprint which is possibly his defining characteristic. Perhaps most interesting of all in this setting are the very final bars which are inconclusive, leaving a question mark hanging in the air reflecting the final line: 'silent hammers of decay'.

One final recollection from Bliss of this time points up an important personality trait which emerged earlier. He elected not to live at home whilst studying at the RCM, despite the closeness of his father's house to Kensington, because there were too many servants in the house. 'I must not only *be* alone, but *feel* that I am.'[41] He compared himself to his friend Darius Milhaud who could work in a crowded room and he wished he had that facility of concentration. But as we saw in his fateful concert all those years earlier at Bilton Grange this was not something which was going to change. Conditions needed to be right for him so he could work effectively and marshal his concentration.

Chapter Two

# THE NATION ARMING

From the houses then, and the workshops, and
    through all the doorways,
Leapt they tumultuous—and lo! Manhattan arming.
To the drum-taps prompt,
The young men falling in and arming;
The mechanics arming, (the trowel, the jack-plane, the
    blacksmith's hammer, tost [sic] aside with precipitation;)
The lawyer leaving his office, and arming—the judge
    leaving the court;
The driver deserting his wagon in the street, jumping
    down, throwing the reins abruptly down on the
    horses' backs;
The salesman leaving the store—the boss, book-keeper,
    porter, all leaving;
Squads gathering everywhere by common consent, and
    arming;
The new recruits, even boys—the old men show them
    how to wear their accoutrements—they buckle
    the straps carefully;
Outdoors arming—indoors arming—the flash of the
    musket-barrels;
The white tents cluster in camps—the arm'd sentries
    around—the sunrise cannon, and again at sunset;
Arm'd regiments arrive every day, pass through the
    city, and embark from the wharves;

(How good they look, as they tramp down to the river,
   sweaty, with their guns on their shoulders!
How I love them! how I could hug them, with their
   brown faces, and their clothes and knapsacks cover'd with dust!)
The blood of the city up—arm'd! arm'd! the cry
   everywhere;
The flags flung out from the steeples of churches, and
   from all the public buildings and stores;
The tearful parting—the mother kisses her son—the
   son kisses his mother;
(Loth is the mother to part—yet not a word does she
   speak to detain him;)[1]

Here is part of Walt Whitman's *Drum-Taps* written in 1865 describing the start of the Civil War in America. Bliss stated that he felt that this poem was the only one he had encountered which had any relation to the feeling of his own time. Whitman spent three years on the battlefields helping wounded soldiers and wrote viscerally and movingly about it. Essentially, however, he was not anti-war, feeling that the conflict was democracy in (violent) action which was necessary to secure the outcome of a perceived freedom through independence. The feeling he engenders is one of outraged compassion. One of the most passionate of all the poems from *Drum-Taps* is the third section *Beat! Beat! Drums!* which Vaughan Williams set so memorably in his plea-for-peace choral work *Dona nobis pacem* (1936):

Beat! beat! drums!—blow! bugles! blow!
Through the windows—through doors—burst like a ruthless force,
Into the solemn church, and scatter the congregation,
Into the school where the scholar is studying,
Leave not the bridegroom quiet—no happiness must he have now with his bride,
Nor the peaceful farmer any peace, ploughing his field or gathering his grain,
So fierce you whirr and pound you drums—so shrill you bugles blow.[2]

Here Whitman reinforces the image of the ordinary man being torn from his domestic existence into the whirlwind of destruction made somehow heroic by the beating of the drums and the calling of the martial bugles.

Bliss's innate sense of duty, honour and national pride inculcated as much by his father as by his very traditional schooling (he had been in the Rugby Officers Training Corps) sent him along to the Recruiting Office.

As he said 'My action was purely automatic, sparked off by a feeling of outrage at the cause of the war, of a debt owed, and added to this was the spirit of adventure and the heady excitement which the actions of my own contemporaries engendered.'[3] But he then went on to say that 'Since then the ever-deepening horrors of wars have made the very word the most hideous in our language, but at that time its vague unknown possibilities made it remote from realistic definition.'[4]

Bliss's recollection was of signing up in early August 1914 and being assigned to a Dockers Battalion. However, the Dockers Battalions were not established at this stage and so his memory is faulty on this point. Recruiting in the first days and weeks was a chaotic process and it is therefore of no surprise that he was 'abruptly switched' on 31 August to the Inns of Court Training Corps (ICOTC) which was part of the Territorial Force (TF). The TF was the forerunner of the Territorial Army and had been created from the Volunteer Force and Imperial Yeomanry in 1908. These volunteer soldiers trained at weekends or at a summer camp. The TF was designed for the defence of Britain, while the British Expeditionary Force (BEF) was sent overseas. The TF was 'embodied' or 'mobilized' on the outbreak of war.

The unit Bliss initially joined, the ICOTC, was one of the more unusual in the British Army. Its only role was to train officers, with many who had joined before the outbreak of war transferring to the TF London Regiment. Prior to the war, it had three infantry companies and one cavalry squadron. Bliss enlisted at 10 Stone Buildings, Lincoln's Inn, London, the unit's headquarters, was allocated the regimental number 1051 and his rank was Private (Pte). This was Bliss's only regimental number, as officers didn't have regimental numbers during this period.

Bliss served with the ICOTC between 31 August and early September, when he was discharged on appointment to a commission. On the formation of 'Kitchener's Army' (or the 'New Army' as it was officially called) on 3 September, the ICOTC was under great pressure to provide more officers than realistically they were able to train. They faced various problems including lack of equipment. But Bliss's experience with this unit was short lived as he was commissioned as a Second Lieutenant after only a month and sent to the 13th (Service) Battalion, Royal Fusiliers. He served with this Battalion until he was wounded on 7 July 1916. His own recollections of the early days with the Fusiliers in Shoreham, Sussex began with the comment that 'I was in charge of a platoon of recruits as raw and as unacquainted with matters military as I was.'[5] Two incidents were used as illustrations: 'War seems to stimulate rain, for it certainly rained without ceasing during that winter in Shoreham. In billets it was well enough, but under canvas often intolerable. One evening a new draft of youngsters arrived and I was on duty. They had of course all volunteered for service, with all that it implied in willingness and in loss of normal life (think back to Whitman above). No arrangements had been made for them; perhaps indeed they were not expected, but there they were, and no bedding or blankets for them – just a couple of sodden tents with their soaking tent boards. Spare dry blankets etc. were safely locked away in the Quartermaster-Sergeant's stores. These I was told could not be issued without a chit from the Adjutant. 'Where was the Adjutant?' 'In London!' I decided it was a case of my draft seizing them by force or risking a couple of pneumonia cases. We seized them. The next morning was officially a grim one for me.

The second incident was on a night manoeuvre; and I thought my very cleverness would ensure at least promotion. I was ordered to take a patrol through the 'enemy' outposts and bring back a report on their positions. It happened to be a full moon that night, which made secrecy difficult, so I commandeered a hay cart that was moving in the direction we had to take and hid my few men in it – to make the disguise even securer, caps were exchanged with the farmer and his son. In this way I was able to make a good get-away and a fairly accurate report. To my surprise, I was given to understand that if I played the fool in this way I had better go elsewhere. As all of us realized, we were simply wasting time these early months in play-acting – no proper uniforms, no proper rifles, elderly retired officers instructing us in methods long discarded.'[6]

One of the most remarkable sources for Bliss's battalion is Guy Chapman's *A Passionate Prodigality* in which Bliss is mentioned several times. Chapman's recollection of Shoreham was equally colourful:

'It was not so much the circumstances; the dull little south coast watering-place in winter; the derelict palazzo, the headquarters, facing on one side the tumbling grey sea and on the other an unkempt field; it was not the men in shabby blue clothes and forage caps with their equipment girt about them with bits of string: it was the obvious incapacity and amateurishness of the whole outfit which depressed. The 13th had been broken off from a swarm of men at the depot some three months earlier, and from then left almost completely to its own devices.'[7]

The battalion with whom Bliss now served had thirty officers and 977 other ranks divided into four companies. The roster of other elements makes sobering reading given how the hostilities were to develop: thirteen riding horses, twenty-six draught horses, eight heavy draught horses and nine pack horses, two machine guns, one horse-cart, twelve two-horse carts, three two-horse wagons and nine bicycles.[8] The 13th Battalion would have been plagued by lack of equipment during its first months in existence. In addition, there were few qualified instructors.

Training continued in Shoreham or Worthing and Bliss reported some progress in the efficiency of the operation leading to their departure for France on 30 July 1915, sailing on the *Golden Eagle* and arriving at Boulogne around 2am the next day. This innocent sounding statement hid grim realities. Guy Chapman, the junior subaltern, was sent to the bottom of the ship where he sat trusting he would not be sick. 'The men lay tightly pressed together, rows of green cigars, and a great odour of sweaty, dusty humanity clotted between the decks... At last, I rose and kicked out the subaltern who was due to relieve me. I climbed wretchedly to the bows. Two destroyers flirted playfully round and about us, making signals at intervals. Someone began to talk of submarines. I didn't care. I looked down into the sea and was very ill. In my misery, I hardly noticed our entrance to the harbour, and was nearly the last to leave the boat. As I staggered onto the quay, burdened with a pack weighing 53 lbs., a rifle, a revolver, field-glasses, a prismatic compass, 120 rounds of rifle ammunition and 24 of revolver, my newly nailed boots shot from under me and I clattered on the pavé.'[9]

After a long wait for all equipment to be unloaded they marched to a rest camp about a mile and a half outside the city. Late on 31 July, the Battalion boarded a train for Watten where it arrived early on 1 August. Bliss noted in his diary, 'After seeing my platoon under cover, I turned into a barn and slept. Later I took a turn around the village, typical of the many we were subsequently going to make our temporary home – an old Flemish church, the house perhaps of the curé or monsieur le maire, and a collection of farms, outhouses, barns. In these the men were quartered, lying just as they had flopped down, anyhow and anywhere, exhausted and asleep.'[10]

Arduous marching started at 3.30 in the morning in order to avoid the heat of the August sun. Bliss's company was at the rear and he wryly noted that however slow the forward march might appear to be those in the rear were always having to run to keep up. Eventually the march brought the company to Armentières, some 100 kilometres from Boulogne, having come via Bailleul where Bliss had been billeted with another officer in a house where the housekeeper regaled them with stories of English officers who had stayed there and met a variety of gruesome injuries or ends. A good night was enjoyed despite her efforts to ensure otherwise.

The task at Armentières was digging defence lines east of the town. The Germans had enterprisingly stationed themselves in factory chimneys in Lille and as Bliss observed 'there are few more unnerving experiences than leading a slow-moving column of men from A-B, knowing that over a stretch between these two points we are observed and present an easy target to the enemy's guns.'[11]

Reading Bliss's diaries underlines a point that he made after reading the letters he and Kennard wrote home and which his father had beautifully typeset: 'I find most of mine make dull reading. It was not so much the censoring that prevented a vivid account as a natural reluctance to let those at home know how bad conditions often were.'[12] Bliss's brother Howard was excused active service due to ill health. Always of skinny build (as Bliss's daughter Karen remembered), she felt he probably had a weak heart which prevented him from serving.

On 19 August Bliss's company was in the firing line for the first time and his diary brings to life the general misery of it all: 'Heartily dislike rest billets – always shelled, and men killed in latrines. Mess in small smelly estamninet (café), flies a plague – cannot use better place, as l'Abbé insists we shall rape the women.

Sept. 4th – marched to Hannescamps – arrival 2.30a.m. and took over from the French. No guides, and trenches in a ghastly state – nothing but cesspools and open latrines, dug-outs very verminous. Cleaning up and fatigue parties ad nauseam.

Sept. 30th – sleep all morning – read *Julius Caesar* – wrote to Elgar and Parry – had rat hunt that night – they attacked at 9p.m. with intense bombardment of clay, then charged! A and I completely demoralized.'[13]

So, it continued. They remained in the frontline, rotating in and out of the trenches around Hannescamps, eleven miles southwest of Arras and using a long communication trench called Lulu Lane. On 8 November Bliss noted, 'Wicked day to relieve trenches: Lulu Lane under water: had practically to swim down: men fell into sump pits up to their shoulders: lost our cooker. C.O. sends round an alcoholic pledge to be signed! Refuse.'[14]

The driving rain, the blowing gale, everyone soaked to the skin, terrible skin boils, people dying from enemy fire and also from accidents when cleaning rifles all paint a picture of abject misery. The desensitizing effect of this led Bliss to write that 'a butterfly alighting on a trench parapet, a thrush's songs at "stand to", a sudden rainbow, become infinitely precious phenomena, and indeed the sheer joy of being alive was the more relished for there being the continual possibility of sudden death.'[15]

Bliss's Battalion remained in this area until the middle of February 1916. On the 12th they marched to Bailleulmont where they remained for a month before moving on to Doullens, twenty-two miles west of Hannescamps and near to Arras. Here the Battalion was inspected by both Field Marshal Haig and Lord Kitchener. At the end of June Bliss was Mentioned in Despatches, appearing in Haig's despatch of 30 April 1916 and published in the London Gazette. As the citation doesn't exist, we can only surmise that the award could have been given either for sustained good work or for a single act of bravery or consideration.

During all this time there was precious little opportunity for music making. In March the Company had a respite from the frontline and Bliss was able to do some piano playing – playing the only piano in the village belonging to the Curé, whose colleague in the next village lived with him and used at one time to be a Professor of Music. Bliss frequently wrote to his father asking for more gramophone records to be sent which he could play on the portable machine he had with him. Because they were 78s the music was often extracts from larger works such as the slow movement of Debussy's string quartet. Records were sent along with 'whisky, brandy, port, cigarettes, honey, asparagus, vermijelli for vermin, Harrogate rock candy and Fullers sweets, the *Times* "broadsheets" and Elgar's *Falstaff*, tins of calorite and a pair of Mallock-Armstrong ear-defenders, anti-boil remedies and a special "trench" pipe, a medal from a Mother Superior and the libretto of Stanford's opera *The Critic*. How all these and similar gifts to brother officers reached the frontline was one of the war's miracles.'[16]

Now came the battle of the Somme. Chapman recalled that, just before they were bussed to that frontline, Bliss had been involved in a particularly nasty engagement:

'The British had already begun to take over the village [Hannescamps]. The crossroads were placarded as Piccadilly Circus (we were a completely London brigade), and the ruins of the large farm at the corner naturally became Leicester Square...

One afternoon as we were sitting in the Leicester Lounge (you know; at the corner of Leicester Square), we were jolted by four terrific explosions almost over our heads... Just above Piccadilly Circus, a salvo had burst among a working party of the Loyals. Blood and limbs seemed to be strewn about the road. Mangled bodies lay silent or groaning... Arthur Bliss, very white and resolute, was holding a man's arm which fountained blood, while its owner stove to control the screams his torn body wanted to utter. Stretcher bearers came and the road was cleared...'[17]

On 6 July the battalion was taken in buses to the frontline trenches. The war diary for the battalion records: '7.20am. – An intense artillery bombardment opened on the German positions, lasting until 8 am when the attack commenced on both flanks. Our orders were not to attack until orders from the brigade were received or until the flanks were well advanced. As communication with the brigade broke down and the situation seemed favourable, the order was given to attack at about 8.25am... Each Company was attacking in two waves (½ Company in each). All Lewis guns came on in one wave at the rear. Bombing sections covered both flanks... Very little resistance was met with... Here No.2 Company was slightly held up, so were the King's Own. But about 25 men and 2 Lewis guns were detached from No.4 Company in the second line to support this party and finally the opposition was overcome... Very few casualties were suffered in the actual attack, but while holding the new position, we were hammered by the artillery considerably.'[18]

However, Bliss *was* a casualty. It seems possible that he was wounded shortly after the Battalion left the trenches. The Bapaume Road links Bapaume to Albert, and on the map, it is the road the Battalion was all over around 9.30am. This meant that Bliss was probably out in no-man's land for the best part of an hour before he was rescued:

'As we climbed out of the trench at 8.30 a.m. and advanced in a long extended line, we knew which alternative was the right one. They were waiting. I saw men falling on either flank and then I felt as though I had been struck a heavy blow on the leg by an iron bar. I fell in the mud and crawled to some hole for shelter. Later in the day when the battalion got astride the Bapaume Road, stretcher bearers, those brave and welcome adjuncts to any attacking force, found me and took me down to the First Aid Post.

A tetanus injection, and then I was in an army ambulance jolting down the road to the reserve posts. Below me in a bunk lay a mortally wounded friend whom I had last seen in Cambridge days.'[19]

Mercifully, Bliss's wound was relatively slight but it meant returning to England and a period of recuperation. The first medical board to assess Bliss's wound and general state was assembled at Caxton Hall, Westminster on 27 July 1916. They recorded:

'The Board find that a bullet entered the left leg penetrating the muscles and bringing in its track a good deal of clothing.

Entrance wound inner side lower 1/3rd left leg: exit wound posterior aspect lower 1/3rd left leg.

Both wounds became septic and a considerable amount of clothing was extracted from the track of the bullet.

The officer is still distinctly anaemic and limps on crutches.'

Bliss's wound was recorded as 'severe not permanent' and the period, that he would be incapacitated for military duty as two and three-quarter months. On the board's other page it was recorded that he wasn't likely to be fit for General Service for 3 months from the date of the medical board but that he could undertake light duties at home in about two months.

But far worse news was to come all too soon. On 31 July Kennard had written to Bliss for his birthday and after hearing about his wounding:

'I very much doubt if this letter will reach you on your birthday, but it may make a good attempt. Well, and I suppose you are looking forward to returning to the front, aren't you? Isn't the joy of sacrifice and the lust for honour hot within you again? Away with the life of ease and idle pleasure! Why waste money on an opera ticket, when you can present the Empire with a hand grenade? I have no gift to bring you! Whilst you are petted and in luxury I nobly am spending sixteen hours out of twenty-four in sleep, four out the remaining eight in food, and the other four in novels, chess, and military discussion (armchair variety)... I no longer hear the guns down south. There is also a rumour of 'leave' starting shortly. Can it be that the 'Great Offensive'...? But no! ... And so, farewell, and fervent wishes that next year's August 2nd will find the wound (in your brain) healed, never to re-open.'

Understandable cynicism and incredible irony given that so soon, on 28 September, Kennard would be shot dead. He was serving with the 459th Howitzer Battery 59th Brigade Royal Field Artillery. Gunner Moses Idwal Valentine wrote to Frank Bliss to say:

'I was with Lieut. Bliss that day as his signaller. The infantry had advanced, and Mr Bliss went forward as Forward Observing Officer. We reached the advanced infantry about 2 p.m., but being unable to observe clearly from there Mr Bliss went forward about thirty yards. The enemy were shelling heavily, and about 3 o'clock a heavy shrapnel burst close overhead and he fell without a sound. A piece of shrapnel had pierced his head, and I started to dress his wound; but his death must have been instantaneous.

I carried him back to the trench; and, being rather shaken, I laid him in a sheltered place out of the way of the advancing infantry, where later a party recovered his body. Thus, you will see that my being with Mr Bliss was part of my duty, for which I have been more than amply rewarded by being awarded the Military Medal. I am only too proud to have shown any respect to a brave officer, who had endeared himself not only to me, but to every man in the battery.'[20]

Kennard was buried in Aveluy Communal Cemetery Extension at Mesnil-Martinsart.

Kennard was a remarkably gifted young man who Arthur loved deeply. After following him to Bilton Grange and Rugby, Kennard won a classics scholarship to King's College, Cambridge. Arthur wrote movingly about him in his autobiography: 'As the years passed, I came to realize more and more what a poignant loss to the family Kennard's death had been. Poet, painter, musician, he was the most gifted of us all, and to *me* his rebellious nature would have been a stimulant, his caustic comments a sharp corrective through those years when I was struggling on my own for musical expression.'[21]

That 'rebellious nature' perhaps also saw its outlet in a different way which is worth recounting as Kennard had struck up a close relationship with his Cambridge mentor E.J. Dent. Dent was an influential musician of his day and one of the leading Cambridge musicians. He was also part of a circle of gay Cambridge men. It was Dent who brought Siegfried Sassoon and Gabriel Atkin together when Sassoon was in Cambridge for his officer training in 1915. Kennard's letters from the front to Dent show that there had obviously been at best shared 'sympathies' expressed and they throw a rather moving light on an unexpected side of his personality. In Hugh Carey's autobiography of Dent he states that 'Casualties strike hard, none more than the death of Kennard Bliss, the artist brother of Arthur Bliss; but Dent could endorse the feeling that for a man of his sensitivity and integrity instantaneous death was almost better than surviving in such awful surroundings.'[22] Which leaves one wondering what he felt about Arthur Bliss and his extended involvement in these 'awful surroundings', but then as much as he admired and respected Arthur, the close 'bond' established with Kennard was missing.

In his letters to Dent, who was obviously a close confidante at Cambridge, Kennard expresses in colourful terms his attraction to one or two young men whom he describes in such glowing terms that it is hard not to come to the conclusion that, although herded together with nothing *but* young men, he is obviously extremely attracted to the male form. Here are a few extracts:

'Last August I joined a ridiculous Territorial Battalion in which I remained for 10 months – as an officer's servant: so charming a young man – a clerk from Cricklewood: shy, and with the timid pride of a stag: a lovely master. But he left, so I took a commission in the Field Artillery. I hate being an officer, and I am no mechanic, so I doubt if I get my name in the papers until a bullet gives me a fleeting notoriety that I never craved.' [Sadly prescient...]

The next letter is more revealing:

'In reality my life is most unmilitary: I have virtually laid down the soldier's rifle for the housemaid's mop, and become in a word an officer's servant. "Never ask me whose!" You can guess! The adorable lieutenant whom I mentioned, I believe, to you. I persuaded his former man to go abroad and stepped into his place. He is in reality a very dull young man, a member of the Church of England Missionary Society, and engaged to be married. Equality with such would be impossible. As I couldn't make him my servant, I became his and devote myself to preserving his physical perfection for the delight of my eyes. He is really superbly built and moves always with a wonderful grace: he is a model master who makes me inevitably a model servant. Without him life would be insupportable.'

And the next:

'... And if I have not much idea of military smartness I have at least the one quality that makes a soldier invincible! I adore my officer. You have no idea what raptures he excites in me – a young, brown-eyed, brown-skinned subaltern with an amazing perfect figure and carriage, and a large Adam's apple. What more do you want? I follow him every-where with my eyes. My squad is very much out of sympathy with such a sentiment, manly young suburban "nuts proud" of their just-conscious puberty.'

And another, full of loaded meaning:

'The other day an elegant subaltern came up to me and asked me if I had seen a brown dog with a white coat on wandering about. I hadn't, but in the course of conversation I happened to mention Madingly, and he said, "I suppose you were from King's". I said "And you of course from Trinity". It turned out that he was Ryder, whom I remember by name as being a friend of my friends. He described himself as a "hanger-on to the intellectuals"... He was very charming and mannered in a most unmis-takable way. One of Fletcher's crèches (a word he used of course) whose Bach [sic] was worse than his bite. It is quite delightful meeting one of the "pleasant creatures" again. He told me he knew Humphrey very well by reputation. (What did he mean? My heart sank).'

And one more:

'You remember me mentioning a telephonist of rare beauty to you. I am with him now. He has just cooked my breakfast up at the Observation Station. I had a cruel snub from him the other day. My servant got wounded, and I asked him to take on the job. He begged to be excused as he felt he 'would take no interest in the work'. Oh, but I was depressed that evening! It was a thorough anti-bellum feeling. Still, he bears me no ill-will. I played chess with him last night up here from 4am to 7, in an interval between two of our frequent and exasperating bombardments.'

As a postscript to this insight into Kennard's personal life, it is valuable to remember that he was a skilled artist and he sent his brother Howard a letter dated 22 August 1916 in which he related that he was 'decorating a large letter box for the Mess. I have painted on the front a yellow woman fantastically dancing on some red, green and brown cushions against a dark green cat at her feet. On one of the sides stands a tall and thin, sinewy negro (a sort of greeny-purplish colour – wonderful) on one foot, with arms taut outstretched at the top of some steps against a bright orange, yellow background, zig-zagged with emerald all wet and running together like shot silk, seen through two thin round arches of a dark, very luminous green. It is absolutely superb in harmony of colour. I have never done anything finer.

I enclose a study for the negro. The finished copy is more vigorous even than this, and the arms better drawn. But nothing equals the easy precision of the leg he's standing on, does it?

Bliss's last meeting with Kennard was noted in his autobiography when 'on June 1ˢᵗ he walked into our rest billets, as my company were indulging in bayonet-fighting exercise! I rode out to his mess a few days later, heard his gramophone (much Berlioz), saw his gun-emplacements and had a sumptuous meal. I wrote to my father 'Really, if he always dines as well – soup, lobster mayonnaise, roast beef and chips, asparagus, sweets, savoury, washed down with a good white wine and liqueur brandy, the R.F.A., gastronomically speaking, is a greatly superior place to the R. Fus. K is very contemptuous of his Major… This was the last time I saw Kennard, but before his death my brother Howard and I received some letters from him, and I was eager to preserve them, for his indomitable, independent and sardonic spirit shines through them.'[23]

But life had to move on as the war progressed and another medical board was assembled to assess Bliss's state with a view to returning him to active service. On 5 October they recorded 'The wound had quite healed. He is however showing signs of nervous weakness and a return to duty would probably result in a complete breakdown. The recent loss of a brother on active service has helped to cause this.' Further Boards kept track of his gradual improvement. On 9 November: 'This officer

still suffers from neuralgia (supra orbital). He has had successive crops of boils and is now about to undergo treatment by vaccine'.

It was probably at this time of enforced rest that Bliss wrote one of the very few works to be written during the war. *Pastoral* for clarinet and piano was, in a sense, inevitable as an Elegy for Kennard, the talented clarinet-tist, so recently lost and whose ghost would not be exorcised for another thirteen years or so with the writing of *Morning Heroes*. The emotional scars were still very fresh from this fundamental loss, and writing music was one way Bliss had of at least attempting to express his sorrow.

This is a serenely beautiful piece which was originally a set of two with a lost *Rhapsody* partnering it. Simple in form, just three sections with the outer built on the initial material, but rather more complex and

interesting than this might suggest. Its very understatement is part of what gives this innocuously named piece its power. *Pastoral* could equally be an elegy for the ravaged French countryside in which his brother was killed and Bliss himself was wounded. It is full of resonances and these two pieces must surely have been cathartic for however short a period for Bliss. Musically, interest lies in the lilting D major opening and its low clarinet solo coming up out of the depths of the piano accompaniment. Unexpected, however, is the C major start to the second idea which pulls the music forward and brings it to its *con passione* climax. D major is restored for the initial music's return though with a very different piano figuration. The clarinet part is exactly the same as the opening but given a very different context. Perhaps the most telling section of the piece is an overtly troubled start to the coda where the piano uses the second section melodic material in the bass which brings dark thunder clouds into the music for the first time before carrying it to a quiet open fifths ending – an unresolved feeling for decidedly unresolved emotions. It was premiered on 17 February 1918.

One other short composition to come from this time (the manuscript is dated October 1916) and decidedly different from the *Pastoral* is a song called *The Tramps* setting a poem by Robert Service (1874–1958) taken from his *Songs of a Sourdough* (1907). In the process of trying to pick up the pieces after his demobilization at the end of the war and to help kickstart his career he published a catalogue of seven of his songs of which five are now lost. *The Tramps* is not one of them, however, and whilst the music may be very different from the deeply personal work in Kennard's memory, its text is still brim-full of war resonances. 'Can you recall, dear comrade, when we tramped God's land together, And we sang the old, old Earth-song, for our youth was very sweet… Alas the road to Anywhere is pitfalled with disaster; there's hunger, want and weariness, yet, O we loved it so!'

The music is a straightforward marching song in essence, but as always, with interesting harmonic twists and interesting modulations which raise it to the level of art song where, in other hands, it could easily have settled as a music hall ditty. The final cadence is a cunning ruse to return to the original key.

Another piece of music we know about from this time is a Fugue for string quartet which has been lost. An academic exercise? A determination to keep his brain active and exercising by writing a technical challenge which he might have felt was becoming rusty? We will never know.

Another by-product of this period was of course letter writing, and given Bliss's later turbulent relationship with Elgar there is one particular letter which it is worth quoting here. He wrote to his old friend Herbert Howells on 26 August, 1916 from the Empire Hotel, Buxton, where he was recuperating:

'Elgar is a very curious person. – He combines an intense belief in himself and the sincerity of his emotions with a blind faith that what οἱ πολλοί [the hoi polloi] think and feel is right. He is a determined believer in expressing the HEART of the PEOPLE – hence "for the fallen". I have never heard nor seen it, but from your description I can guess what it portrays. I have seen Elgar in tears over it – and if you consider it as the expression of the man who as a child drove round in the baker's cart to get to grips with and help the poor people of Worcester, I think you can judge it rather more mildly. But still, enough of that. When I see Elgar, I think he is a master; when I sit in my arm chair and peruse his works, I think him a charlatan – que faire?'

Interesting reflections from a hot-headed young man, which certainly didn't dampen his enthusiasm for his connection with the Elgars – a man in Bliss's position could, and would, benefit greatly from such a friendship. We have seen already the warmth of the connection between them which was to continue through to Elgar's commissioning of the *Colour Symphony* in 1922.

In this period of recuperation Bliss naturally turned to composition and in particular to the completion of a 'fiddle sonata' which he had been working on and, according to a letter written to Edward Dent, his former Cambridge teacher and mentor, was struggling with. What we have is a single movement work which was obviously road-tested in run-throughs or perhaps a trial performance (the manuscript has obviously been used in this way) before Bliss started working on revisions. Following Kennard's death Bliss had no inclination for further work until after the war and he sent his manuscripts to Herbert Howells for safe-keeping. Howells, in turn, wrote a heart-felt and wide-ranging letter which detailed his feelings about various musicians who had been killed, had very near misses, and other war-related issues. He also wrote of his feelings about Bliss's Violin Sonata and the other works he had been sent. Of the Sonata he wrote this fascinatingly wide-ranging response:

'I can tell you that the Sonata movement pleases me very much ... [it] is the best of the bunch. I like its freshness, and its unforced energy... it is fresh air and sweet-smelling earth... the sort of music which the unknown creator of some of our best folk-songs might have done if he had suddenly launched into sophisticated (formal) music immediately after a trip which embraced some of the best of our rural counties, and during which he read exclusively French authors! And in this particular piece... there is a certain quality which, for me, adds a charm, but which, for many, would seem like a weakness. It reveals that strangely characteristic restiveness of your musical mind... When you come to write a symphony, you will use in your first movement enough material for sixteen Beethovens, or twenty-six Brahms... that's what Elgar has done in his symphonies. All the up-to-dates are doing it... For myself I love the prodigality of the moderns... and your indulgence in it is the quality in your music which some would count a weakness and others (myself included) an added charm. I am prodigal too: most of us are in our music, we seem averse to chasing a thought to its logical conclusion. There is no point in our pretending that we think as much as the older men did.

Thinking hard is undoubtedly productive of the greatest things... But no! Arthur; we <u>feel</u>, <u>feel</u>, <u>feel</u>... our music is essentially sensitive stuff... and I'm horribly convinced that the hyper-sensitive things are not durable.'[24]

A curious conundrum concerning this sonata appears in a letter written by Bliss to his father on 25 September, just after he had received Howells's letter. In it he writes: 'I also enclose a letter from Howells that you may like to read, and which please keep. He is one of the few people that when writing letters completely effaces self, and this one, when you read, you will see is all about his friends... You will see in Howells's letter that he is returning my music to you. When you open it, will you write on top of the violin sonata "To Lady Elgar".'[25] The curious thing is that the one extant score we have of this work has no dedication either written or erased and it begs the question as to whether or not there might somewhere be a second score of the work which was perhaps sent to Alice Elgar and has yet to come to light. What did materialize were several apparently unconnected pages of violin and piano music which the violinist Rupert Luck examined and realized were revisions for the existing sonata movement which had three points of extensive crossings out and into which the revisions fitted, were duly incorporated and recorded. It is a fascinating detective story. Whether Bliss intended the sonata to have additional movements or not is debatable but what we do have is a large-scale movement encompassing a wide emotional range, and about as far from the avant-garde Bliss we know so well and which was waiting in the wings only a very short time away. This really was the last gasp of English pastoral romanticism from his pen.

It is a highly pertinent question to ask why Bliss should affect such a sea-change in his musical style so soon after this work. While this sonata shows Bliss's capability with a large canvas there is very little which is memorable about it. In fact, all Bliss's early music is worthy but relatively dull. Howells's own Piano Quartet in A minor of 1916 has a cut and thrust, an inevitability, a melodic genius, and an instinctive feel for the interaction of instruments in chamber music which really vies with Ravel's Piano Trio. He is at one with his style which we know will develop from here but won't radically change. It is for us to ask if Bliss perhaps realized that he was never going to compete with such natural skill using this language (he addressed his letters to Howells, 'Dear Genius') and therefore only a complete change of approach, style and landscape might put him in a position where his voice would be heard above the clamour of the competition. It could also be that his naturally extrovert personality was simply not aligned to the kind of music he had been writing to this point and he realized that he needed a different kind of stimulus in the same way that he needed an external idea or *scena* to stimulate his imagination and get his creative juices churning. That, as we will see, would be provided by the Stravinsky/Diaghilev partnership. What also must not be underestimated is the hurricane of change following the end of the war and the feeling that all that had gone before was, to a large extent, irrelevant and that a new language was needed for new times.

Bliss had to wait for a medical board to pass him fit for Light Duties and he had a long, frustrating wait. It would not be until 15 February 1917 that another medical board found that he was 'now fit for light duty – no route marches'. He was found to be still unfit for General and Home Service for another six weeks. A final minute from Captain H. H. Hardy dated 18 February 1917 recorded:

'Will you please now order him to No.18 O.C.B. (Prior Park, Batt) with effect from 15.2.17, on which day he has passed fit L.D. (light duties), and joined that unit. He has four times vainly applied for a M.B. (Medical Board), and much time has been wasted.'

Bliss was attached to the No.18 Officer Cadet Battalion (O.C.B.) at Prior Park, Bath with effect from 15 February 1917. Officer Cadet Battalions had been created in 1916 and during the war, over 70,000 men were commissioned from them. The Battalion had an establishment of either 400 or 600 cadets and Bliss recorded:

'After being passed fit for duty, I was posted, as an instructor, to an officers' cadet battalion in Prior Park, Bath, the beautifully laid out eighteenth-century house and park designed by Ralph Allen...

The instruction consisted of drilling and physical training, map reading, signalling and surveying, work at the rifle ranges, exercises in trench warfare and lectures of various kinds.'[26]

While with the Battalion there were two more medical boards, both assembled at Bath War Hospital. The first on 14 March 1917 found that 'there is still some weakness of the left ankle' and that Arthur was unfit for General Service for a month, though he was recorded as fit for Home Service. Bliss's final medical board was held at Bath War Hospital on 18 April 1917 and recorded that 'he has completely recovered' and was fit for General Service.

Whilst at Prior Park Bliss had leisure to explore Bath, 'and I made full use of a room with a piano that I found near the Abbey. I now associate the hours in this room almost entirely with the music of *Götterdämmerung*. Apart from *Die Meistersinger* I had not yet seen any Wagner operas. *The Ring* existed for me only in a piano transcription.

I was deeply immersed in a romantic attachment, and Wagner's music seemed to provide just the right outlet for the emotions: in that little room in Bath, I stormed through the conflicts between Brünnhilde and Siegfried with much ardour.'[27] So much for his youthful rant about German music and Wagner related in Chapter One.

It seems extraordinary in the midst of all the seemingly uncontrolled mayhem of war that some semblance of normality could coexist with the constant leitmotiv of death all around. But not only does Bliss write of this early romantic attachment but he also, and far more significantly, writes of his first meeting with the poet Robert Nichols with whom Bliss said he had a 'close but uneasy friendship over the years.'[28] 'His was a complex personality compounded of many warring elements. Sometimes he would be wildly exuberant and excitable, at others he would sink into a black depression and self-pity. Always generous and loyal to his friends, he would then alienate them by some mad Quixotic action, embarrassing to both giver and taker… What kept our friendship alive was my respect for his creative gifts… At our first meeting in 1917, he entered like some attractive young faun in uniform, elated at the success of his first published poems.'[29]

There were other diversions whilst Bliss was at Prior Park as well as a rather unfortunate meeting with Rudyard Kipling who was collecting material for a new book about the training of the 'New Army' (*The New Army in Training*: December 1914). When Kipling visited, Bliss was with his troops engaged in target practice on a rifle range. On being introduced to meet Kipling ('a small man distinguished by thick overhanging eyebrows, keen eyes behind magnifying glasses, and a jutting chin')[30] the great man asked what he was doing with his men. Bliss relates that he was totally tongue-tied as the seemingly unimportant work of shooting rifles in a miniature range at cardboard cut-outs seemed to him to be simply 'too remote from any experience to be faced on the frontline. No words came from me, and Kipling walked away, beside the displeased Colonel, despairing, I suspect, of our military future.'[31]

While at the Officer Cadet Battalion Bliss decided to join the Grenadier Guards which was the most senior regiment of infantry in the British Army. It was also one of the most exclusive, its officers being drawn mostly from the upper classes. The Regiment suffered major casualties on the Western Front and was in constant need of new officers. Bliss applied for an appointment in the Special Reserve of Officers which he filled out on 16 March 1918. The Special Reserve of Officers was one route to obtaining a commission. Bliss stated on his application that he

wished to be appointed to the Grenadier Guards. His good moral character was certified by a Justice of the Peace of the County of London the
next day, the day he also passed his medical examination. Following an
interview on 18 March he was recommended as a suitable candidate. He
recalled:

'The months went by and, with new officers on sick leave coming as
instructors, it was getting time for me to go. I should like to have been
sent to rejoin what was left of my old regiment, but the chances seemed
very remote and so, acting on the suggestion of a friend who was in
the Grenadier Guards, I decided to join this regiment in London. I
say 'I decided' but it was not so easy as all that: first I had to have two
acknowledged sponsors and then seek a personal interview at Wellington
Barracks. If you were favourably viewed you could then find yourself
stationed at Chelsea Barracks. The situation was exactly as if a man who
had just taken his degree at Cambridge should by magic be transported
back to his preparatory school.

In spite of a year of active service in France and then months spent in
instructing others in military procedure, there I was again on the Square,
rifle in hand, listening with my fellow subalterns to the commands of a
regimental sergeant-major. There were lectures on the history and tradition of the Brigade of Guards, and minute regulations dealing with what
could and could not be done: the taboos were numerous…

The fifth summer of the war passed with frustrating slowness. I
seemed to be just marking time with instruction at Tidworth on bombing
and revolver shooting, varied by a riding course in Knightsbridge
Barracks: but at last, early in September 1918, I was ordered to France
to join the 1st Battalion, Grenadier Guards. I found myself taking a draft
out and on the way in France passing my old trenches near Monchy
au Bois and Adinfer, south of Arras, then down the Bapaume Road to
Langnicourt and our divisional H.Q.'[32]

Bliss had been a Captain (temporary) in his previous battalion but
entered the Guards as a Lieutenant again. Once Bliss was accepted, he
joined the 5th (Reserve) Battalion at Chelsea Barracks. This Battalion
did not serve abroad, and its sole task was to provide drafts for the
Grenadier Guards' four other battalions serving on the Western Front.
Bliss recorded his initial movements in France through letters and it is
fortunate that he did as there are no surviving battalion documents from
this period. He landed in France between 9 and 11 September 1918. He
was posted to the 1st Battalion and he wrote to his father in frustration
having been sent to hospital with suspected tonsillitis. He wrote, 'I am

angry about this, as I was to join my battalion this evening, and it looks bad to go ill on the eve of going into the line, but I can't help it.'[33]

Another letter to his father written from the No.2 General Hospital at Le Havre on 15 September recorded that it was not tonsillitis but an aggressive wisdom tooth which had to be cut out. He wrote: 'what a curse is laid on me that whenever I come to France, I have tooth-ache! Suffer so in England.'[34] On 24 September he left the hospital and wrote again to his father saying that he would be joining his battalion tomorrow.

The Battalion had been heavily engaged by the time Bliss joined it. The Commonwealth War Graves Commission recorded that between 1 October 1914 and 1 October 1918, the Battalion had suffered 1,214 in dead alone. If you added wounded and missing as well, the 1st Battalion Grenadier Guards had probably suffered more than 3,000 casualties by October 1918. Bliss was very fortunate that he wasn't posted to the 1st Battalion earlier in the year. He was recorded as arriving with two other officers and a draft of 143 other ranks on 30 September 1918 when the Battalion was just west of the Canal du Nord where they remained until 7 October. Bliss then wrote to his father on 10 October: 'The last two days have been spent on the move. Last night we messed in a billet that had only just been evacuated by the Germans. They had cleared out too quickly to raze the village to the ground, and we had the luxury of a roof over our heads and beds of a sort... In the billet in which I am writing my cook found for me a battered German cornet. I don't know whether I can add it to my kit, which is growing enormous. I am sitting at the moment on a ruined piano stool!'[35]

The battalion had moved on from Havrincourt on the east bank of the Canal du Nord on 8 October to Marcoing, five miles east. The next day they moved on again to Séranvillers-Forenville, another 6 miles east. The Battalion was now to the south of Cambrai. On 10 October, the Battalion continued its march east, this time by 9 miles, when it moved to Cattenières. During the fighting of 11 October, No.4 Company with which Bliss was serving remained on the eastern edge of Quiévy. On the 13th the Battalion was heavily shelled and, as recorded in the War Diary, one of the posts was rushed by a party of 80 Germans under cover of an intense Minenwerfer barrage and only one man escaped. At 6 pm, the Battalion was relieved and 'marched back by Companies to billets in Quiévy all ranks very tired and needing rest'. The war diary recorded that between 11 and 13 October, the Battalion suffered 3 officers wounded, 11 other ranks killed, 48 wounded and 17 missing. Bliss's luck was holding for the time being. He wrote to his father of these days: 'We have had a rather rough time lately, fighting a pursuing action, not knowing exactly where the Germans are. The villages we passed through were almost intact, proving a hasty but disciplined retreat. The few old peasants that were left welcomed us, crying hysterically. I feel well.'[36]

On 19 October, the Battalion marched to Saint-Vaast-en-Cambrésis where 'Ammunition, bombs etc. were handed out and a hot meal was given to the troops. The night was dark and pouring with rain'. (War Diary)

On 22 October, Bliss was gassed while the Battalion was on the line of the Solesmes Road. The war diary recorded that 'No.4 Company were rather seriously gassed losing Lieut. Bliss and Hall and 10 men, all gassed more or less slightly'. Bliss wrote to his father from the No.8 General Hospital in Rouen on 26 October:

'Since last writing I have been in two-night attacks and, during the second, had the ill fortune to swallow a gulp of gas. Hence the above address. It is very slight but means remaining quiet for a week or two, and I shall probably be sent to Trouville for a short recuperation... there is nothing to be anxious about.'[37]

In fact, his sick leave lasted for longer than he imagined and it wasn't until 11 December 1918 that he wrote in his diary that he was returning to Pau and Base H.Q. He spent Christmas Day guarding prisoners which he felt to be a 'very distasteful task, especially at that season.' But he went on to say that 'The German non-commissioned officers on the other hand had lost none of their arrogant parade-ground bearing towards their men, though they were unpleasantly subservient to any British officer whose duty it was periodically to have the prisoners counted. They bullied their wretched charges in true Prussian style, and stirred in me at any rate to retaliatory measures.'[38]

The Battalion remained at Cologne until after Bliss had left for Britain. Little of interest happened in these final weeks except for an inspection by the Prince of Wales who remained for lunch on 15 January 1919. The war diary ends on 16 February. Bliss's Protection Certificate was completed at the Officers' Dispersal Unit in London on 14 February 1919. He probably left the 1st Battalion by 10 February to journey back to Britain. The document recorded his medical category as A1, the highest, showing he had completely recovered from his 'gulp of gas'. Bliss's final connection with the Army was severed with this record from his Protection Certificate:

'The undermentioned Officer of the Special Reserve of Officers will be Disembodied [demobilized] with effect from 15 February 1919 unless he hears to the contrary from the War Office, on and after which date he will not be entitled to draw pay.'

Arthur resigned his commission on 29 January 1920 with the notification appearing in the 28 January 1920 *London Gazette*. To all intents and purposes, Arthur left the army when he was disembodied (the Special Reserve term for demobilization) on 15 February 1919.

In the midst of all this drama domestic life at home continued as a leit-motif to his surreal experiences in London and in France. Most dramatic of all was his father's re-marriage which came as a huge surprise to the family. Frank had met a lady who was local to him in Holland Park and who had been widowed early in the war. Ethel had two young children with her first husband and was to give Frank wonderful companionship, as well as a daughter (his only one), for the rest of his life. Arthur was asked to be his father's Best Man at the wedding in June 1918, a role he was very happy to play.

In his autobiography Bliss recounts another very personal experience from this time. Up to the point of his injury he felt that he was unassail-able. As he put it 'The bullet that bore my name had not been cast. The sense of my own vital individuality was too strong to allow the thought that a chance shell could in its haphazard way blot out *my* existence. The coming return to the same battlefields now made this brash confidence waver. The throw of luck had so far been all on my side, but as odds usually go, the cast should now be against me.'[39] As so often in these situations an appeal to a higher authority was the perhaps inevitable but also irrational solution. Bliss wrote that his father's own very deep-rooted sense of right and wrong made religious observance superfluous, but at this point Bliss himself felt 'the urgent need for some reassurance that sudden death did not automatically annihilate the human soul: perhaps Faith could prove stronger than a stubborn disbelief.'[40] To this end he went to Brompton Oratory, received instruction, and was received into the Catholic Church.

In a letter to Herbert Howells of 30 May 1918 written from the flat he is renting in Eaton Square, London, he writes a remarkably frank assessment of where he feels he is at this point: 'The guards and the Catholic Church leave a great stamp on one's personality – but I think I remain mostly unchanged – still con fuoco, as Dent says of me – I have been converted into neither an errant snob by the one, nor a narrow-minded visionary by the other. Musically, I believe I grow, I have a small and ill tuned piano up here, and at present my musical library consists of the 48 and Debussy's Preludes – my reading library of Jean Christophe, some

Keats, a little Yeats, life of St Just of 1790 French fame, Rupert Brooke, Catullus, Addison, and some Meredith. This may give a clue to my inward state'.

His postscript to this period was to note that 'early in 1919 I got my release from the army: one large part of my life was over and another, in prospect totally different, was to begin. I was twenty-eight.'[41]

## Chapter Three

# THE DIAGHILEV EFFECT

The effect of release from the army and of now being able finally to begin his career – aged twenty-eight – was galvanizing. Realizing what a late starter he had been forced to become threw Bliss into frenetic activity. But more than this, he determined that everything he wrote from now onwards would be wholly different from all his previous work. He began to forge new friends and gather experiences from every field of artistic endeavour to broaden his vision and begin the crucial task of networking which would lead to all-important collaborations in the future. But to one old friend, Herbert Howells, he wrote a very telling letter just after his twenty-seventh birthday:

Guards Camp, Tadworth, Surrey 4/8/18

My dear Herbert,

I was 27 on Friday which I spent at home – it is dreadful, Herbert, to approach 30 with all ones ambitions held back from fruition by fate. How I hoped to be a modern da Vinci stamped with the character-istics of an Englishman – instead a humble subaltern of the Brigade of Guards with a leaning towards musical expression, which no one thinks much of, least of all the author.

New beginnings had obviously been in his mind for some time before he left the army as one short work showed, marking the crossing of a musical chasm. *Madam Noy* should be considered the most important of all his compositions from this time as it was in this three-minute song that he effectively reinvented himself. Everything he had written up to this point was well-crafted and showed obvious signs of a serious aptitude for composition and some creative flair. But with *Madam Noy* he became at one single stroke the serious contemporary composer, even, in British terms, an *enfant terrible*, not that he was in any way an *enfant* and what he wrote was not remotely earth shaking. But there were several aspects of this song which marked him out from almost all his British contemporaries. First, the text: although he didn't know who E.H.W.M. was when he decided to set the poem, only later discovering that it was Edward Meyerstein (1889–1952) and from a volume called *Black and White Magic* published in 1917, he saw something in this imagery which fitted his desire to upset the status quo, to create a stir, to be, in short, *avant-garde*. The poem itself is what Bliss described as a 'witchery' poem of the 'Old Mother Hubbard' type. Essentially, a nonsense poem about an old witch who goes to the beach to find a bone which she will add to other ingredients to make a magic spell. Later, she is disturbed by a knocking at the door and a whispered demand for the return of the bone. She throws it outside and it falls to the ground just as the conditions for the realization of the spell are revealed. She curses in despair over her bad luck. The critic of the *Westminster Gazette* of 25 June 1920, writing of the song's premiere at the Wigmore Hall (Anne Thursfield was the soprano and dedicatee) noted 'what there was in such childish lines to induce anyone to expend so much energy in the setting of them it was hard to discover.'[1] This probably delighted Bliss.

The second unusual aspect to this song is the instrumentation: soprano, flute, clarinet, bassoon, harp, viola and double bass – an unusually colourful and original ensemble as far away from the mainstream in Britain as can be imagined at this time. It was subversive, and mirrored the Bloomsbury Group's literary upsetting of the status quo of which Walton's *Façade* was the outstanding musical expression. But that was four years after *Madam Noy*'s conception. Where did all this come from? We have already noted that Bliss enjoyed visiting the ballet with friends and especially Diaghilev's ballet company in his London seasons where they first heard Stravinsky's ground-breaking ballets. In a country where Debussy and Ravel were *the* moderns and were a huge influence on many British composers it is salutary to remember that the earthquake which was *The Rite of Spring* had happened back in 1913 (in a season which also featured Debussy's *Jeux*) in Paris.

Diaghilev's ballet company had begun a London season in 1911, had to stop during the war years, but reappeared in 1918 but only as a single item in a variety bill at the Coliseum presumably to get their collective toes in the door again, restarting properly the following year at the Alhambra. If we really are to take Bliss at his word and get to know him through his music then *Madam Noy* is *the* breakthrough in our detective story. For it is here, for the first time, that we see a hint of drama, a love for a stage, and a decidedly exotic sound world which was to re-launch his paused career and become such a hallmark of his musical output at least in the short term. He said that this and the works which followed were 'essays in the exploration of sound right up to the *Colour Symphony* in 1922.'[2]

In making these claims for Bliss's originality – in British terms – through his 'exploration of sound' it must also be made clear that the other significant British composers finding their post-war feet were doing so in their own very different but original way. Holst's *The Planets*, Delius's unique sound world, and Vaughan Williams's gentle, but ultimately seismic revolution are but three examples of Britain developing its unique musical voice at this time. Elgar was still the 'grand master' of English music whose Cello Concerto was premiered in 1919, the ultimate elegy for those war years and not only a lost generation but a lost era. No line in the sand could be clearer, however, than that 1919 concerto and Bliss's 1918 *Madam Noy*.

The joyful irreverence of Bliss's music in this song, the wonderfully sinister knocking on the door given by a bassoon's plaintive (and humorous) falling thirds, the characterful florid music given to the upper winds, and the harp providing the harmonic textural 'glue' all show his finger held up in the wind testing the new direction of travel. A bewildered newspaper review was all the encouragement Bliss needed to follow the signpost. Quite why a very miniature score of the song (about postage stamp size according to Bliss) was put into the library of Queen Mary's doll's house is not known, but this was a decidedly early brush with royalty.

The 'new music' being produced around the world especially in Russia and France had wider implications than the necessity of educating journalists. Conductors, in particular, had to learn how to direct complex scores with intricate rhythms. Ernest Ansermet, for instance, interviewed by John Drummond about new works for the stage commissioned by Diaghilev and others made the point that 'whereas at the beginning of the century even very difficult works, like *Heldenleben* of Strauss, or *Also sprach Zarathustra,* or *Elektra* or Debussy, were always written in 4/4 time, 3/ 4 or 2/4, I mean full numbers, but just after the First World

War, or even a little before, Stravinsky began writing music changing the bar all the time, making an irregular cadence: 5/8, 2/8 and so on. It was necessary to invent, for this new kind of rhythm, a new conducting technique. That is why, before my time and until my time, conductors never had lessons in conducting. They had models... since this time [they] have begun conducting classes, which were not existing before my time.'[3] Ansermet also made the point that he had known Stravinsky well and that whilst he 'was an attractive man, always very lively, full of spirit, temperament, and working very hard'[4] he was also 'very authoritarian' and he felt his tempos very exactly (unlike Debussy).

His comments on the years following the Great War are fascinating and relevant here: 'The days after the First World War were a turning point. We had passed through a period in which music was always conceived in a determined tonality... to a music which coordinated several tonalities together in a simultaneity, something we call polytonality. It was never a question of polytonality in the school of Schoenberg. With Schoenberg the music had to be tonal or atonal. But polytonal, he wouldn't have known what that was. Polytonality was started by Debussy in our time, though we find, if we want, polytonal passages by Bach, and it was always in the music also of Beethoven. In the finale of the Ninth Symphony, there's a moment when we have a major third in one voice and a minor third in another. So, it is polytonal. Of course, this polytonal music was very difficult to understand for the public, and that made for the difficulty we had to impose this music after the First World War, when came the atonal music... When you hear polytonal music several times, you finish by understanding it. If you hear atonal music, you will never understand it, not better after twenty times than at the first hearing. So, it is very different. But for the public it is rather embarrassing, because they see no difference between a music that is difficult to understand and a music that is difficult to understand because there is nothing there to understand.'[5]

In fact, Bliss was far more interested in his 'experiments in sound' than in complex barring and rhythms, nowhere resorting to the head-spinning rhythmic complexities of some of his continental contemporaries. Yet he achieves similar lightness of touch, dancing effects, theatrical gestures and shows a very keen ear for colour – far in advance of anything his earlier music might lead the listener to expect. Psychologically, this is an interesting turn in our attempt to tease out who Arthur Bliss was through his music. His student friend, Herbert Howells, reinvented himself by completely changing his handwriting at about the same time in his life to a beautiful Italianate script presenting himself, at a stroke, in a wholly different way to the world. Bliss's stylistic shift was of a similar order of magnitude and every bit as fundamental. But what does this say about this new style? Is it skin deep? Is it the painting of a picture of what he feels he *should* be rather than what he actually is? It is notable that later on, he reverted to a more romantic style, and his grand opera *The Olympians* (1949) was even compared with Puccini. But let's give Bliss an opportunity to convince us that in this immediately post-war period this was the way he wanted to express himself and not pre-judge the outcome until there is considerably more evidence to assess. He said at one point: 'As a young man I was all for sound for sound (sic) sake. And then one grows up and realizes that an aural experience, however exciting it may be, is simply not enough. Your life becomes full of emotional experiences and you want to try to express them.'[6]

1919 saw a number of new compositions including a Piano Quintet for his friends, the Philharmonic String Quartet, and him to play. The score of this work has now been lost but not the story of the French premiere of the work at the Salle Gaveau in Paris. Josef Holbrooke had organized it and was due to premiere his *Symphonic Quintet*. However, he forgot his passport and was horrifically sea-sick crossing the channel with his colleagues on his way to give the premiere. He was refused entry to France and had to return in his 'green' condition. When he got back, he sent a telegram to say that the concert should be postponed. This was a disaster all round especially as the agent had lined up an influential audience. When the time came for the revised concert date the hall was almost empty except for a few people amongst whom was Darius Milhaud. But the friendship that ensued brought Bliss into the influential circle of *Les Six*, among them Honegger, Poulenc, Auric and Milhaud himself. An interesting reminiscence by Bliss from this time was a visit to the composer Maurice Delage's house facilitated by an introduction by Edwin Evans. Delage asked Bliss to play no more than sixteen bars of his own music in order that Delage might assess Bliss's personality. After a tap on the shoulder to halt him, Bliss's personality wasn't mentioned again though Stravinsky's was, Delage asserting that in just a few bars of *Petruchka* 'the whole man was there.'[7] Not a life-affirming experience for Bliss but perhaps one that affirmed his devotion to the Russian composer whose music (amongst others) was at the root of Bliss's own new style. This raises again the question as to whether Bliss was more of an on-stage actor when composing rather than someone who really expressed his deepest inwardness for us to hear. John Amis, a life-long friend of Bliss, who was probably more qualified to speak of his music than many, wrote in his moving introduction to the fascinating volume called *Arthur Bliss: Music and Literature* that 'I think Bliss was a private person. His music never wears its heart on its sleeve, despite its occasional tenderness; it is not impersonal (quite the opposite) but there is always a certain objectiveness. There is warmth in the harmonies...'[8] Amis then goes on to single out the opening of the first string quartet as the music he feels contains the essence of Bliss's style. We will return to this when we come to that point in our story. For now, we are still searching for clues, seeing if Bliss wants to lead us by the nose or the heart.

Bliss's second 'essay in timbre' was an eight-minute chamber work for mezzo-soprano, tenor, flute, cor anglais, string quartet and double bass called *Rhapsody*. Very different from *Madam Noy* and inhabiting a completely different world of imagination – so different indeed that the listener is left to create his own storyline as the singers have no words, singing simply 'ah' to their long lyrical lines. This is unusual for Bliss who claimed that more often than not he needed an external stimulation to his imagination. 'I have always found it easier to write "dramatic" music than "pure" music. I like the stimulus of words, or a theatrical setting, a colourful occasion or the collaboration of a great player. There is only a little of the spider about me, spinning his own web from his inner being. I am more of a magpie type. I need what Henry James termed a "trouvaille" or a "donnée".'[9]

The enthusiastic critic in the *Musical Standard* writing about the work after the premiere on 23 October 1919 described it as 'musique féerique' – which is supernatural or a fairy story. He went on to say that it was 'made up of dreams moving in the realm of emotional imagery of a curiously imaginative mind.'[10] He further underlined all this by remarking that 'Real poetry is there... of entrancing spirituality not produced by metaphysical pretensions, but by an intelligence which illuminates the rarest qualities of sensation and emotion, creating a glamour akin to a Celtic legend... Above all, he is aware of that elusive quality we term beauty. He is certainly a musician that counts.'[11] The audience demanded that the work be repeated.

*Rhapsody* was published by the Carnegie Trust under the auspices of their Musical Works Scheme. This was an initiative of the Carnegie UK Trust endowed in 1913 by Andrew Carnegie, the great American philanthropist. The first work to be published under this scheme was Howells's A minor Piano Quartet in 1917. Bliss's *Rhapsody* was published in 1921. It is interesting to speculate whether Howells was influenced by the wordless singing in Bliss's *Rhapsody*: he came to respond to Elgar's commission for the 1922 Three Choirs Festival with his *Sine Nomine*, which also has wordless singing from soloists and chorus – highly controversial at the time. This was the same year that Bliss's invitation from Elgar resulted in his *Colour Symphony*, which we will come to shortly.

Despite the enthusiasm of the *Musical Standard* critic *Rhapsody* feels something of a step backwards from the expectations raised by *Madam Noy* and it is open to question as to whether the critic found the far more easily absorbable style of *Rhapsody* more to his conventional taste. But then Bliss tells us that he was experimenting with sound and not ground breaking style. And there are thought-provoking aspects to the work which are admirably summed up by the newspaper critic. Vaughan Williams was one of the Carnegie assessors and his report shows his understanding of where Bliss was heading:

15 December 1920

This piece seems to me to have a rare and classical sense of beauty – and indicates a healthy departure from the rather heavy romanticism of much that has been sent in. It breaks fresh ground and as such it ought to be encouraged. I know it has weak points – a certain squareness and tendency to shut the music into water-tight compartments two bars long. But it has certainly great beauty of theme, harmony and colour... A in my opinion.[12]

There was general agreement from all the members of the panel (Henry Hadow and Dan Godfrey were the others) about their dislike of the use of wordless voices, but RVW was obviously persuaded and indeed used a wordless soprano in his 1922 *Pastoral* symphony.

Around this time Bliss was asked to write the incidental music for Shakespeare's *As you like it*. This arose from his friendship with the artists Claud Lovat Fraser (always known as Lovat) and his wife Grace. Lovat created wonderful, original designs for theatre sets and costumes and his friendship with Bliss led to his designs appearing on the covers of some of Bliss's works published by Curwen. *Rout* is a fine example. Through The Frasers Bliss met Nigel Playfair and Arnold Bennett who were in charge of the Lyric Theatre, Hammersmith in London. They commissioned Bliss to write the incidental music to the play which had its sets and costumes designed by Lovat Fraser. Another husband-and-wife team he had met earlier, Edward and Fanny Wadsworth, were drawn into the scheme. He was an artist Bliss admired and she a violinist with her own all-women string quartet that Bliss used for the performances. The premiere was given in the Memorial Theatre, Stratford-upon-Avon, on 22 April 1919. The score no longer exists but we know that it consisted of arrangements of Elizabethan music by Byrd, Robert Johnson, Giles Farnaby and others.

The only two other works from 1919 we know of were as a result of Bliss's initiative to form the Hammersmith Musical Society at the Lyric Theatre. Two arrangements of other composers' music were made for this: *La Serva Padrona* by Pergolesi (score missing) was performed on 29 January, and a set of *Act Tunes and Dances* by Purcell arranged for string orchestra (and published in 1923) was first heard on 5 October.

Another 'experiment in sound', a *Concerto for Piano, Tenor Voice, Strings and Percussion* was one of the next works Bliss worked on. The manuscript no longer exists, possibly destroyed by enemy action in World War II. The percussion instruments Bliss wrote for were side drum, bass drum and xylophone. The first performance was given by Myra Hess (piano) and Steuart Wilson (tenor) with an unnamed orchestra conducted by Bliss in the Wigmore Hall on 11 June 1921. We have little way of knowing at this distance exactly what that original scoring would have sounded like, but this was a work which Bliss revised four times through his life and so we know at least the sound world it inhabits. We also know from H.E. Wortham's wide-ranging article in *The Sackbut* of April 1927 that 'The voice, as in those two works (*Rout* and *Rhapsody*) was not given any words to sing as these would inevitably suggest some picture or evoke some emotion that was not purely musical – so at least I take it the composer argued. Since Arthur Bliss subsequently withdrew the work in its original form and rewrote it for piano and orchestra, one may assume that he regarded his experiment as unsatisfactory.'[13] It is more likely the case that he felt it would have a longer shelf-life in a form which would be more readily programmable.

H.E. Wortham's article is interesting on several levels, not least because he was writing contemporaneously with this period in Bliss's development. He also tries to tease out from the evidence to date what Bliss's true character or personality is. In his first paragraph he writes: 'There is so much to write about Arthur Bliss and it is so difficult to know where to begin to unravel the strands. If I say "of course you know Mr Arthur Bliss," you murmur "of course," and then you wait for me to explain before you are led up to shake his hand, that Arthur Bliss was once a very clever young man, that he has sown many wild notes in his time, but that now he is grown a serious person.'[14] He then gives a brief biography of what Bliss has done up to this point and a clear account of his military service. He notes that 'Few young men of any generation have been to a harder school than that in which Bliss and his contemporaries graduated, and it would be surprising if those who came through it alive did not show its scarifying influence in their work. In Arthur Bliss's case this is evident, I think, in two ways, in his desire to find novel combinations of instruments that would mark off the new from the old and in a certain hectic gaiety which is the predominating quality of his music in those years immediately following the war.'[15] Tellingly, he also, like John Amis, notes that Bliss 'never wore his heart on his sleeve', and further, 'But the war did, for the moment, have the reaction on those endowed with the creative genius that might be expected from such a terrific experience. One could only look upon it and continue to live by refusing to be serious. Or rather seriousness could only find genuine expression through a jesting and light-hearted irony.'[16]

Remembering the underplayed emotion in the clarinet *Pastoral* which was an initial essay, and extremely close in time in commemorating his dead brother, Wortham's analysis is strikingly to the point. One therefore wonders if the habit of emotional reclusiveness once practised became so deeply ingrained, emphasizing the British reserve of that generation, that it became his natural means of expression. Where his later music became more romantic in style this could still be thought of as 'style' rather than a loosening of the emotional tongue.

Just before we leave Wortham's thoughts it is worth pointing out that he, opposing the general view of other critics, thought *Madam Noy* to be 'a little masterpiece of its kind... It is clear from "Madam Noy" that Bliss was not, even at this critical time, disposed to any reckless experiments. His temperament was too characteristically English for that. The treatment of the voice is vocal, in spite of its unmistakably modern idiom, and the harmonic atmosphere is diatonic.'[17]

And now here's a contradiction. In the spring of 1920 (26 March to 4 April) Bliss was one of a group of musicians selected by Adrian Boult to travel to Amsterdam to see Nikisch conduct, arriving in time also to hear a performance of Bach's *St Matthew Passion* conducted by Willem Mengelberg at the Concertgebouw. Bliss was joined by Armstrong Gibbs, Scott Goddard, Leslie Heward and Boris Ord. He later wrote about the experience for the Royal College of Music magazine in a way which is interesting in relation to his own means of expression. Having talked about the various characteristics of concert halls he knows well, the Salle Gaveau ('brilliant snobbery'), the Queen's Hall ('happy holiday humour') he comes to the Concertgebouw ('a serious mien') and Mengleberg's silent entry to conduct. He goes on to compare the celebrated conductor with the drill sergeant he remembers so well from his military training. Tellingly, he comments that 'I smiled to myself as I thought that the eminent flautist could no more phrase a passage as he felt it, than I could have marked time in triplets against my neighbour's twos, that no fiddler could use a down bow in defiance of the rest... The result achieved was magnificent. And yet, in spite of one's admiration for a well-nigh perfect rendering, there would intrude this thought – if only our Drapers, our Brains, and our Jameses were here, just to show this orchestra the effect of several unique musicians infusing the general interpretation with their own individualities. Mengelberg may be a superb musician, he may be a superb conductor, but he has not the same gift of awakening enthusiasm in an orchestra that one gentleman has, who came several days later – Arthur Nikisch.'[18] So the act of true outward musical expression is essential to Bliss's view of performance but maybe not (yet, at least) as a true expression of his own deepest feelings as represented by the music coming from his pen.

Adrian Boult was a passionate follower of Nikisch having been in his conducting class in 1912 and coming out from it almost as a clone of his hero, having developed a style based on Nikisch's economy of gesture showing absolute clarity but allowing the musicians to express their own personalities. Bliss's summing up was that 'he goes for the broad interpretation of the whole, rather than for the perfection of any detail, that he appeals to the imaginative faculty rather than to one's faith in historic tradition, and that he has a way of purposely over-emphasizing points of dynamic interest and changes of tempo at his early rehearsals, which fall naturally into their proper proportion to each other and to the whole by the time the concert performance is reached.'[19] Bearing in mind how important conducting was to become in Bliss's own life – especially of his own music – these observations are key. All this had arisen as, following Parry's death in 1918, Hugh Allen, the new Director of the RCM, had asked Boult to start a conducting class. His first cohort of students included Gibbs, Heward and Ord from the group above. Interestingly, the class was taken by Bliss when Boult was away. Bliss was a student at the RCM at this time having returned in February 1919 after being demobilized to resume his interrupted studies, staying until July the following year. His experiences with Stanford as a composition teacher during his first sojourn at college were not happy as has already been described in Chapter One. It is assumed that he returned to the College to brush up on his technique and to expand his portfolio of musical expertise – hence the development of his conducting work. Certainly, the compositions he was producing would have been anathema to Stanford ('modern stinks') in this second period of study, but nevertheless, Stanford will have been intensely relieved that he had survived as he had 'fretted as the war went on and was distressed to hear of Bliss being wounded at the Somme'.[20]

If Bliss actually showed Stanford his next sound experiment, *Rout*, that notoriously irascible Irishman's famous gold pencil will not have known where to start in its critical demolition of this comedic romp which is almost a postscript to Stravinsky's *Petrouchka*. Echoing the Shrovetide fair at St Petersburg that opens Stravinsky's ballet, Bliss wrote a foreword in his score of *Rout* in which he says that 'the title "rout" is used in its old sense meaning of "revelry", and the voice part is given a string of syllables corresponding to the scraps of song that would reach a listener watching a carnival from an open window.' In fact, the opening of *Rout* is so similar to the opening of *Petrouchka* that they are almost interchangeable. But Bliss's music, whilst obviously besotted by that of the Russian and picking up its scraps from the master's table, sets out to do something very different. For one thing it is not a ballet (though its ideas are theatrical and it could be danced to) and it is a mere seven minutes long. Within that short duration lies the essence of all good musical composition – contrast, contrast of musical ideas and mood. The idea of a casual listener experiencing different 'scraps of song' is a convenient way of introducing apparently unrelated material in different styles, moods and speeds all of which add up to a lively experience to which we can all relate.

The styles Bliss uses in this piece are interesting and he is still to some degree struggling to shed some of his old skin whilst wishing to present himself as the fashionable new Turk. The section from around letter K in the score shows some of that classical lyricism, and even a modal folksong-like cadence, just before N. But it is all clothed anew and everything about this piece feels fresh and untainted. Perhaps most of all it feels *optimistic* and forward-looking, especially in these young British hands which were so recently wrapped around a rifle. The music also has a great air of confidence and of wanting to be noticed. And noticed it certainly was: the *Times* noted its cleverness and that the audience were so captivated that they insisted on its repetition. But the sting in the tail came at the end of the criticism: 'One has some misgivings about it however. Having heard several of these whimsical excursions one begins to wonder where they are leading. Are they forming an individual style with which Mr Bliss will be able to say something when he has really got something to say, or is he becoming a fashionable joker? His abilities are much too good for the latter.'[21]

But a key point is made by Stephen Banfield when he writes that 'What all this amounts to is that Bliss, certainly in his earlier inter-war works, aligned himself more with the visual arts than with literary sensibilities... True, he was friendly with men of letters, including Robert Nichols and J.B. Priestley, but there were more friendships from the art world, those with Claude Lovat Fraser and Edward Wadsworth being the most significant in the period after the First World War.'[22] It is notable that Wadsworth created the cover image for *Rout* which Banfield described as showing 'the legacy of vorticism toned down to a benign and easily acceptable form of cubism'.[23] Continuing this theme, Bliss himself made this key point:

'The idea of the instrumental groups in the classical orchestra is done away with, and the composer uses instruments that are widely incongruous in sound and dynamic value, just as Wyndham Lewis, Wadsworth, or the Nash Brothers create a picture with tones that are varying in density.'[24]

In July 1921 Bliss gave a lecture to the Society of Women Musicians in which he talked about 'What modern composition is aiming at'. While in his autobiography he confessed to 'blushing on re-reading what I then said forty-seven years ago,'[25] reading the lecture it is a comparatively mild exposition of the struggle of the new to gain acceptance. He paces through musical history describing the progress of new movements and how they in their turn became outworn. Particularly amusing is his own use of the description applied to him and quoted above when talking about *Les Six* and in particular Honegger and Milhaud who 'are too far removed temperamentally from the enervating Parisian salon to deteriorate into *fashionable jokers*'[26] [my italics]. That earlier barb from the *Times* critic must have gone in deep. In speaking of his own time, he describes Stravinsky as 'the most remarkable musician of the time'[27] and goes on to describe all the German composers whose balloons have been punctured by this force of musical nature, as described in Chapter One. He reserves a good hiding for Sir Charles Stanford whose detestation of consecutive fifths seem to blind him to whether or not a piece of music which contains them is worthy or not. This and the whole tone scale used so effectively and expressively by Debussy 'threatened the actual existence of composition'.[28]

What is perhaps most interesting from this youthful tirade is his description of the growth of the chamber orchestra of ten or twelve players 'all soloists, in the texture of whose ensemble the particular timbres stand out like coloured threads in a variegated carpet. Great sonorities of tone can be obtained by the judicious use of a few instruments, and the concerted effort produces a richness and diversity impossible to obtain with the old method of mass treatment.'[29] He describes Mahler's *Symphony of a Thousand* as 'a confused mezzo-forte' to make his point. Bliss's own philosophy at this juncture in his life he neatly summed up by saying 'we have reached an age of simplicity and vitality in expression, and that the very sincerity of our emotion has driven out all the tendencies culled from other arts, which serve only to obscure the issue of music – an issue wrapped in the word 'sound', and sound only... It always remains a mystery to me why they (musical conservatives) will entrust themselves wholeheartedly to the taxi, the aeroplane, the tube, and the telephone – all products of our time – and yet in music shrink back dismayed into the well-marked era of the stagecoach and the Puffing Billy.'[30]

Bliss was certainly the most outspoken of the young composers on the issue of contemporary music and took the German-American conductor Walter Damrosch to task in the *New York Herald* for continuing his programming of Beethoven and Brahms. Damrosch's letter to the *Daily Telegraph* ends by remarking: 'I have not yet lost my admiration for these masters (Beethoven and Brahms) and, to judge from the acclaim which your public still gives them, I fancy that there must be many in England who feel as I do. I have never heard any of the compositions of Mr Bliss, and therefore do not know whether I should class him as a disciple of that "ugliness in music" which some of the younger school seem to worship.'[31]

There is one further observation which is pertinent to our story here and that is how Bliss describes his British composer colleagues: 'Vaughan Williams, with his strong adherence to modal counterpoint, and love of national folksong, is in direct communion with Purcell, as Ravel is with Couperin. Holst, the mystic, Bax the romantic, Ireland the rugged, Goossens the exquisite, Berners the satirist....'[32] If Bliss himself were added to this list he would be the singular 'experimenter in sound' and devotee of the new Russian school. To this end, while there is no doubt at all as to Bliss's ability as a composer, his ear for sonority and his determination to sow new seed at home, what seems to be vitally missing is his *own* personality. We might get hints of character traits, especially a sense of fun, an extrovert nature, a man of action, and so on, but we never see below this surface. Maybe the new music was ideal for him in not having to expose dangerously raw emotions still livid below the surface. To this extent the new world of sound rather than emotion was the perfect vehicle for Bliss to be able to express what he wanted to say without exposing himself.

*Rout* impressed Diaghilev who asked Bliss to score it for a larger orchestra so that it could be played as interlude music in one of his Russian Ballet programmes conducted by Ernest Ansermet. There is no doubt that this close association with ballet, a lifelong admiration for Diaghilev and his devotion to Stravinsky fed the seeds of his own ballet scores, which were later to become amongst the most successful strands of his composition. By now, though, his 'experimental' works were constantly expanding and following on from *Rout*, finished in November 1920, came *Conversations*, another chamber work for flute, which also doubled bass flute, oboe (and cor anglais), violin, viola and cello. It is easy to see why the diehard members of the press would brand him a 'fashionable joker' when the movement titles of this work were:

*The Committee Meeting*
*In the Wood*
*In the Ball Room*
*Soliloquy*
*In the Tube at Oxford Circus*

For Bliss, though, this was another opportunity to explore the possibilities of sound by thinking outside the conventional 'box' into a kind of stage set. A strong element of this was a very real sense of humour in the music that, as Wortham pointed out in his article, was 'a thing alone sufficiently rare to be remarkable'.[33] Bliss himself simply felt that it was 'to enliven a musical evening in a big house.'[34] The first movement, *The Committee Meeting*, portrayed 'its ineffectual but stubborn chairman vainly trying to get his motion carried amid the frequent interruptions of his colleagues.'[35] Cleverly constructed so that the violin part monotonously plays its initial theme throughout the whole movement with a kind of Yorkshire doggedness against the lively interruptions from all other players trying to make their point. In the end the meeting gets heated with everyone 'talking' at once and even the violinist raises his voice until a metaphorical gavel is banged on the table, at which point the violinist/chairman picks up the boring old point at its habitual *mezzo-forte* before the viola attempts one final protest leading to the final *pizzicato* chord.

Bliss asks the violinist to play a monotonous *mf* throughout whilst the other instruments are instructed to play with utmost force and vigour. If we are looking for further personality clues this movement surely points to Bliss's desire to cock a snook at convention and demonstrate a singular sense of humour, in this case puncturing the dignity of the little man who basks in the illusion of his importance. He is also – apparently – oblivious to the inevitable pounding the music will get in the press. The *Daily Mail* of 21 April 1921 noting that 'it is an irreverent age. Was music once a holy art? Did the masters once contrive sublime syntheses of Love, Life and Death? We are much too knowing nowadays for any such hollow romance... Mr Arthur Bliss composes *A Conversation in the Tube at Oxford Circus*. It is really the triumph of Nietzsche, with his motto, "Let instinct live", over his pretentious old enemy.'[36] But Bliss will have relished his brief moment as *enfant terrible*. This was living life on the edge, making people sit up and talk, and most importantly, talk about Arthur Bliss. No press is bad press here.

The second movement of *Conversations* called *In the Wood* in other hands might well have been a pastoral idyll but not in Bliss's. Gentle, certainly, but more of an idle stroll observing and listening to bird song. The unresolved seventh in the final chord is beautifully inconclusive as the cellist trills away into the distance. Another gently subversive movement, *In the Ball Room*, sweeps away the ball gowns and stuffy rituals of the older generation and hums its way through a light-hearted, on-your-tip-toes triple metre dance. The bass flute seems to suggest a slightly husky, deep voiced, lady companion who is very modern.

The fourth movement *Soliloquy* is a solo meditation for cor anglais. Again, the choice of instrument marks out a keen ear for the unusual. It is even possible that this is the first time the instrument was used in a solo capacity in chamber music.[37] The haunting, plaintive sound of the instrument sets the mood for this beautiful interlude that has a perfect formal balance and an instinctive feel for the character of the instrument.

The final movement, *In the Tube at Oxford Circus*, is the most substantial of the work and seems to be part pictorial description (à la Honegger's *Pacific 231*, which had not yet been written – and indeed, as a friend, one wonders if the Swiss composer had heard Bliss's work that inspired *him*) and part people observation. The movement begins with a train-like rhythmic ostinato but moves into sections of more reflective music of varying types and combinations of instruments. It is this extremely keen ear for *sound* which seems to be a reflection of Bliss himself here. No instrument is used for the sake of it, everything has to do with timbre, transparency and clarity of expression. There is still a strong reflection of Stravinsky in this music, but the music is no less strong, or personal, for it. The first public performance was given at the Aeolian Hall in London on 20 April 1921 having been performed privately the previous January.

Also performed on 18 January that year at the Aeolian Hall were his *Two Nursery Rhymes* for soprano, clarinet (later arranged for viola by Lionel Tertis) and piano. Bliss sets two short poems by his old Cambridge friend Frances Cornford. The first is *The Ragwort* (originally called *The Thistle*) and the second is *The Dandelion*. The brevity, the nonsense-poem feel, the almost comedic observation, all these things appealed to Bliss in his gestural, stagey, clear-textured mode. These are epigrammatic miniatures staged for effect. No emotion, no life-enhancing melodic lines, but a beautifully crafted reflection of Cornford's delicious enhancement of a few wayside flowers. Only the first song has the full ensemble. *The Dandelion* is accompanied only by clarinet (or viola). Bliss was the pianist in the first performance with soprano Gladys Moger and clarinetist Frederick Thurston.

The sheer amount of music pouring from Bliss at this time is testimony to his prodigious work ethic together with his passionate desire to make up for lost time and determination to make his mark. Tantalizingly, his music for a production of *The Tempest* produced by Viola Tree and Louis Calvert at the Aldwych Theatre and first heard in February 1921 was lost in a bombing raid during the Second World War. Almost incredibly, years later, however, a manuscript draft score of the overture and first scene was found. The Overture is typical of the way Bliss's mind was working at this time. It is a representation of the storm in Shakespeare's play. Again, the instrumentation is key to the whole conception: tenor and bass voices, grand piano, trumpet, trombone, four timpani, side drum, tenor drum, gong, cymbal, big drum and clapper with four players for the percussion. Bliss wrote of the production that it was 'an extraordinary amalgam of all styles – all styles of acting, all styles of scenic design and especially all styles of music. I was called upon to compose special music for Scenes 1 and 2, Scene 3, Act III, and Scene 1, Act IV… My other collaborators were Arne, Sullivan with additions by Raymond Roze, and Frederic Norton of *Chu Chin Chow* fame.'[38] Fascinatingly, and showing his keen feel for the dramatic, Bliss wanted to place timpanists amongst the audience to give them the visceral feeling of immersion in the storm but the management felt this to be a step too far. A compromise was reached where the timpani were put on stage and the rest of the orchestra in the pit. Of the various reviews which followed none was more keenly read than that of Ernest Newman whose only words of unequivocal praise of the production were for Bliss's own music, writing: 'The only music that matters is that of Mr Arthur Bliss, who, with a fearsome array of kettle drums, has given us a storm in the opening scene that is not only terrifying in an imaginative way, instead of the merely noisy way of the old stage thunder, but has the additional and great merit of reducing the scenery and the actors to their native insignificance... Mr Bliss has written some music that I should like to hear again under more satisfactory conditions than those of the theatre.'[39]

Perhaps most tellingly, though, Newman goes on: 'It is the most imaginative piece of theatre music that I have ever heard. Mr Bliss is a young musician of a curiously lively, questing mind. He has experimented a good deal in unusual instrumental combinations, and always we feel that there is a reason, rooted in the thought itself, for the music being laid out just as it is... Altogether, Mr Bliss strikes one as a composer from whom something may be expected.'[40] And what a great stroke of good fortune the discovery of this overture has proved to be as it adds much to what we now know of this incredibly fertile and formative period of Bliss's career.

Bliss's first foray into the arena of orchestral music came as a result of the imaginative Patrons' Fund scheme run by the Royal College of Music which gave emerging composers an opportunity to have their compositions played and to learn from the experience. Scores had to be submitted to a panel to be judged as to their worthiness and Bliss sent in his *Two Studies* originally called *Studies for Full Orchestra* of which we have numbers two and three with no indication as to what happened to number one. What we do know, however, is that Bliss, feeling apprehensive about this big step and wanting advice from a seasoned expert, took the work to Gustav Holst for scrutiny. He wrote movingly about grabbing the opportunity to talk to great creative artists when you can as, thinking they will be around for years to consult, suddenly an early death deprives the aspiring composer of their sage advice. He felt this deeply about Holst of whom he wrote 'I was only with him a few times, but each is indelibly engraved on my memory by some short pithy statement that he made. He had the utter honesty of opinion that riveted attention.'[41]

In relation to these orchestral *Studies,* he made profound criticisms that Bliss knew instinctively were correct, including asking when the second *Study* was actually going to begin – after looking at the first couple of pages. An all-night sitting correcting endless copyist's errors preceded the rehearsal/performance which took place, as he noted, 'in the over-resonant Concert Hall at the Royal College of Music'. But it was a start and it is clear that Holst's example and his forensic observations went in deep. Bliss related the occasion when he was sitting with Holst in 1930 hearing Vaughan Williams rehearse *Job* for the first time. He recalled that 'Holst always probed like a fine surgeon to the root of the difficulty' and recounted a moment when, 'Suddenly Holst… listening with a frightening intensity, said to himself, "That doesn't come off. I must go and tell him." He stepped on to the platform, looked at the score with Vaughan Williams, discussed and suggested, and then came back to his place, while the composer spoke to the players. The section was then tried over again, but with what a difference of sound! – Clarity instead of thick obscurity.'[42]

Clarity and an acute ear for texture, as we have been examining, are two of Bliss's great strengths in writing for instruments, and it is interesting to hear that nothing is compromised when he is writing on a larger scale. Perhaps Holst was instrumental in this too, but it is doubtful that he had much to offer in terms of the overall orchestration scheme (as opposed to making individual instrumental suggestions) as Bliss knew his sound world and it is abundantly clear from all the works so far discussed that his ears were keenly attuned to harmony, texture and colour. It might be interesting to speculate as to whether his lack of experience of, or particular sympathy with the Anglican choral tradition helped him to move more quickly away from contrapuntal and textural 'norms' when he was developing as a composer as his music shows little or no influence of this medium which was so powerful in its effect on others of his and previous generations. In fact, as we shall see, his choral music does not feel a natural medium for his creativity, nor does he have such a natural feel for choral as opposed to solo vocal writing.

What is constantly apparent in all his post-war music is his love of effect, of drama, of a stage (real or imagined) and of painting pictures in music.

Of the *Two Studies* the first is deeply indebted to Vaughan Williams (with nods to Debussy) and is a beautifully judged pastoral idyll. What impresses is the spare use of the orchestra. Every instrument tells in the texture. The build up to the hugely impressive climax is masterly and when that moment arrives one cannot but feel that Bliss had this music in his mind when he reached the climactic section of the *Meditations on a Theme by John Blow* some thirty years later where the theme (which also has remarkable similarities in outline with Blow's) is heard in relief in a similar way. Only an occasional strident dissonance reminds one of

the composer who reveres Stravinsky. The second *Study*, however, is very much the Bliss we know of this period with energy, panache and lots of Stravinsky-like gestures and sounds permeating the score. Dissonance, whilst certainly not gratuitous, is far more telling and the effects are real and effective, especially horn trills, trombone *glissandi*, side-drum solo and colourful bass clarinet moments. We also have the first appearance of a very particular Blissian dissonance which recurs often where the root of a chord is raised by a semitone. A good example occurs in bar 37 where the chord of E major on beat one has an F natural at its base, and the chord of A major on beat two is given a B flat for its lowest note. Similarly in the previous bar, the two chords of E major have the second trumpet subversively playing that raised semitone, an F natural. We will hear this often as time goes on. What is clear here is that Bliss had a vivid scene in his mind, and despite the bland title it is obvious that he was enacting a scenario in his mind.

The Bliss scholar, Giles Easterbrook, in his booklet notes for the recording of these pieces, made the interesting observation that he felt that there had been a first *Study* and that it had been withdrawn after visiting Holst. As he writes: 'It would have had to be an *Allegro moderato*, more dramatic than the existing first study, less flippant than the second and longer than either, and it probably ended by being recycled into something else. Strangely enough there is exactly such a work, also dating from 1921, it is called *Mêlée Fantasque*.'[43] This cannot be proved of course, but it is a very interesting speculation.

The reader of this biography who is not a specialist musician and is wondering when something personal may happen to enliven this story will be asked to be patient for a little while longer, because this hurricane of creativity *was* Bliss's personal life. It cannot be stressed sufficiently just how much Bliss felt the hand of time on his shoulder, having to catch up to make his mark as a seriously ambitious composer while ploughing a highly personal furrow, and needing to persuade a baying crowd of critics of the seriousness of his credentials. He wanted to show how his small-scale offerings to date – his 'fashionable joker' pieces – were like a sketch book of ideas that would soon lead to his first really major work, *A Colour Symphony*.

Bliss's friend, the influential artist and designer Claud Lovat Fraser died in June 1921 and Bliss commemorated him in his dedication to his first publicly and professionally performed orchestral work *Mêlée Fantasque*, referred to above. Bliss himself put it like this: 'I tried to depict in it the brilliant colour and movement of the theatre that he loved and to weave into the texture an elegiac lament for his loss.'[44] The critic Edwin Evans made the point that 'In his own sphere Lovat Fraser had a pronounced hatred for all that was turgid, and particularly for uncertain colour... In his own stage work he planned that colour should stand out from colour with an incisiveness that eliminated all compromise or subterfuge, and no effect of his was ever blurred at the edges... Arthur Bliss pursues the same ideals in sound and design as Lovat Fraser in colour and design.'[45] Bliss was also fortunate to have the backing of Henry Wood who gave young composers he rated a chance to conduct a work with his New Queen's Hall Orchestra at the Promenade concerts. As Bliss remembered, 'to work in any capacity with Henry Wood was to work with a man free of conceit or megalomania, one wholly devoted to music, and generous to those younger and less secure than himself.'[46] He also had an endearing way of asking the nervous conductor to wait for a few moments while he got to his Dress Circle seat to hear the performance. Bliss noted that this gave a warm feeling of support.

*Mêlée Fantasque*, along with *Rout,* shows Bliss's deep infatuation with Stravinsky. In fact, he summed it up when he wrote that he 'tried to convey the rhythmic verve and Bakst-like colour of many of Lovat Fraser's paintings, in what is virtually my first ballet score.'⁴⁷ The *Observer* critic of 16 October 1921 felt that 'technically, my present criticism of the piece is that it is too broken, and contains passages that appear to be mere interpolations included to show us some orchestral possibility.'⁴⁸ What that writer failed to recognize was that this score is both a reflection of a dramatic Lovat Fraser painting, and the idea of someone scanning a scene – a town square perhaps – where different things are happening and Bliss's aural picture moves with the eyes as they take in points of activity or repose. It is a highly pictorial work, and the fact that he feels it could be danced to emphasizes the point. At twelve minutes duration it is a substantial paragraph of music through which Bliss maintains interest as much by his use of orchestral colour as by his *donné* or given subject matter.

From the substantial paragraph to the miniature in settings of Walter de la Mare was Bliss's next move. De la Mare was one of the truly great British poets of this period. He had a naturally musical feel to his poetry, had been a chorister at St Paul's Cathedral as a child, and his vivid imagery, his wide-ranging imagination, in both nonsense and serious poetry, was magnetically attractive to composers.

Bliss was one of many composers of this period who set his words to music, and it is interesting to see him working on a domestic scale in his *Three Romantic Songs* after the vivid palette of orchestral colours in *Mêlée Fantasque*. The distinguished mezzo-soprano Anne Thursfield premiered them with Bliss at the piano in the Wigmore Hall in January 1922. As we have seen Thursfield had given the first performance of *Madam Noy* (and recorded it) and so Bliss knew her voice well and will undoubtedly have had it in mind when writing these songs.

The first, *The Hare*, is a dark poem about a witch-hare which, when challenged under the bright moon darted away 'like a ghostie o'er the field' leaving Bliss to write a warmly relaxed ending. Perhaps of most interest, though, is *Lovelocks* where de la Mare describes in the most sensual terms the Lady Caroline who, beautifying herself for the day, offers the composer with the greatest opportunity for word painting to which Bliss seems incapable of responding. Compared with Herbert Howells's white-hot setting of these words (in *A Garland for de la Mare*) this is a really lacklustre appreciation of female beauty in music and maybe offers another level of insight for our search. It is perhaps even more surprising given that at this time he was completely bewitched by a girl he had met who he described as 'a wonderful dancer, and her beauty exhaled an animal magnetism which immediately enticed the male. At all times she needed men, and knew how to get them. The attraction being almost entirely physical was all the more exciting and unsettling.[49] Bliss even chased her across Europe to Switzerland bearing songs, but found her entangled with another man when he got there! The songs were immediately ripped up. So, he was certainly not insensitive to feminine beauty and wiles, but given the opportunity to describe them in music he falls sadly short.

It is interesting that the poems come from de la Mare's *Songs of Childhood* published in 1902 when de la Mare, in a strange twist of fate, was working for the Standard Oil Company of which Bliss's father was Chairman. Of more serious interest, though, is de la Mare's judgement about observation from a child's perspective of a poem that is so obviously sensuously adult. Bliss's dark take on what is essentially a lightly observed scene begins promisingly enough with its falling left-hand triplet figure but it rarely moves from this, and images like 'candleshine', 'cherry-boughs in May', 'the window smouldered keen with frost', and 'yet still, she twisted, sleeked and tossed Her beauteous hair about' are simply missed opportunities for exciting word painting. Is this Bliss's reluctance to wear any kind of heart on his sleeve? But if so, why choose these sensuous words to set?

*The Buckle* is much more successful partly because it is full of the *Petrouchka* fair music where Bliss feels entirely at home. A light-hearted, fairy-tale poem to which Bliss responds in kind. The songs are dedicated to the children of his new family, Patric, Cynthia (step-brother and sister) and little Enid (half-sister), following his father's re-marriage.

# Chapter Four

## *A COLOUR SYMPHONY*

One of the key moves at this time in the field of contemporary music was the formation of the International Society for Contemporary Music (ISCM) in August 1922. This originated in a festival of modern chamber music which was part of the Salzburg Festival. It attracted some of the major names of the day including Webern, Hindemith, Bartok, Kodaly and members of *Les Six*. Bliss attended with a group of British composers and the musical fare was varied. There were recent songs by Richard Strauss, a chamber work for wind trio and piano by Milhaud, Bartok's first Violin Sonata, and Bliss's own *Rout* in which Hindemith was amongst the violists. There was a hostile reaction to Webern's *Five movements for string quartet* to the extent that shouting by opposing factions in the audience rendered the performance impossible to continue. Bliss, however, heard the work again a few days later under calm conditions and he retained the miniature score he obtained with an appreciative comment inscribed in its flyleaf by Webern. He remembered that 'It was the first time that I had met Schoenberg, Berg, or Webern. I greatly regretted that my ignorance of German kept me from talking to Webern, though I should have to admit to him as I did years later to James Joyce that I had not found the clue to real appreciation.'[1]

Bliss was certainly not backward in ensuring that his name was on everyone's lips as the up-and-coming avant-garde composer of the moment. In a wide-ranging article about him which Edwin Evans wrote for the *Musical Times* in January 1923 Evans began by making this point: 'Many musicians have been a little mystified – some of them, apparently, even a little irritated – by the unprecedented rapidity with which a composer, utterly unknown at the beginning of 1919, was transformed into a celebrity before the end of 1921. Some of the comment upon this extraordinary episode in recent music has not been informed by as much good nature as one would wish, and the explanation has been sought either in some personal pushfulness on the part of Arthur Bliss himself, or that mysterious entity known as 'influence.'[2] Evans goes on to remark that had this just referred to every work from *Madam Noy* it would be easy to see that it was purely public reaction to each new work in turn which created this phenomenon as they regularly asked for works to be repeated at their first hearing. *Rout* was asked for twice more at its first performance, and the two *Nursery Rhymes* always created a clamour for repetition making them very popular with singers. Evans's interesting assertion, however, is that he wonders if it is the music which the public is responding to with such enthusiasm, or the subject matter which, as he puts it: 'It is exhilaration, not differing very considerably from that which may be derived from any scene of visible animation. The connection between the music of *Rout* is a close one. Looking down upon such a carnival we would be exhilarated, and desire to take part in it. When we hear *Rout*, we have an impulse to pick up anything handy and join in. It arouses an almost primitive instinct, and primitive instincts have much to do with philosophy.'[3]

This leads on to a discussion of energy in music, where Evans gets to the heart of the matter. 'Energy is more communicative than sentiment, and the music in which energy predominates will always enjoy a certain advantage in this respect. It is to that initial advantage, in all probability, that Bliss owes the rapidity of his success. The greater part of his music expresses the energy of a buoyant personality, bursting with life. It is, like his own manner of speaking, impatient to get to the point.'[4] How well put, and what a useful piece for our personality jigsaw puzzle. The problem which Evans points to is that this insistence on energy, on effect, colour and brevity, is that he became open to the charge that he was 'playing at music'. In the previous chapter the phrase was 'fashionable joker'. But Evans points very clearly to one overriding characteristic when he writes that 'So far as these "stunts" themselves are concerned... they proceed from Bliss's preoccupation with tone-colour. Of all English composers today, he is the one most intimately concerned with sound.'[5] And in terms of being a modernist Evans also makes the important point that 'His musical speech does not consist of an unbroken string of pungent words, but he has a useful stock of these available when required.'[6]

There is much to assimilate here and especially at this turning point in his compositional path. It is something to which we will return at various points in this narrative and which will concern us when considering Bliss's legacy and his place in the current public consciousness.

Unlike Stanford, for whom, as we have noted, Bliss's music was undoubtedly unpalatable, Elgar had a real eye for those who he felt were likely to take the language of music forward as he knew it must, and Bliss had been given the seal of approval. As we have seen his early string quartet had been enjoyed and Elgar wrote to Herbert Brewer at Gloucester in response to a request for advice about up and coming composers that 'it would be a first-class thing for the festivals to get in real new blood and away from the heavy dullness of the – well, you know.'[7] He went on: 'Whatever they do has some vitality and grip... these men will do away with the remnant of the notion that everything must be a sort of Ch. of E. propaganda.'[8]

This manifested itself in an invitation to Bliss from Elgar to lunch at the Royal Societies Club, then in St James's Street, London, in December 1920. Also invited were Adrian Boult, Anthony Bernard, Eugene Goossens, John Ireland and W.H. Reed (leader of the London Symphony Orchestra and close friend of Elgar). Howells was also invited but couldn't attend. The purpose of this friendly meeting was to ask Bliss, Howells and Goossens to write a new work for the 1922 Gloucester Festival. Quite why Ireland was asked when he was not to be so favoured is something of a mystery and must have contributed to his general feeling of insecurity.

Bliss wrote that 'The luncheon went a bit awkwardly with Elgar at his most nervous; then, when the coffee came, he suddenly told us the reason of our being gathered there. He wanted Howells, who was not present, Goossens and myself each to write a new work for the Gloucester Festival of 1922: no limitations on the form of the new works were imposed.'[9]

It is interesting to see how each composer rose to the challenge of this important commission. Howells and Goossens each wrote choral works with orchestra: Goossens chose to set just two verses of Walter de la Mare's poem *Silence*, subtitling it *A Choral Fragment* for chorus and orchestra. It is a highly coloured, short work of some ten minutes duration which has completely disappeared from view. Howells wrote a fascinatingly original work for two soloists, chorus and orchestra called *Sine Nomine*, where the singers are mostly wordless. Whilst almost suffering the same fate as Goossens' work, it was revived for the Gloucester festival in 1992 and recorded more recently. Bliss, alone, took on the challenge of writing a major orchestral work, originally called *Symphony in B* but later, at Percy Scholes's suggestion, given the title *A Colour Symphony*. At last, here was a major work to counter all the chatter about 'fashionable jokers' and 'stunts'. It was as if everything he had written to this point had been a sketchbook planning for this moment.

Bliss needed what he called a *donnée* or an external idea or influence to fire his imagination and make the creative process possible. He wrote about the genesis of this symphony like this:

'I have always found it easier to write "dramatic" music than "pure" music. I like the stimulus of words, or a theatrical setting, a colourful occasion or the collaboration of a great player. There is only a little of the spider about me, spinning his own web from his inner being. I am more of a magpie type. I need what Henry James termed a "trouvaille" or a donnée. So, for weeks I sat before a blank sheet of manuscript paper trying to make up my mind what shape, what character this new big work should have. And then one day, looking over a friend's library, I picked up a book on heraldry and started reading about the symbolic meanings associated with the primary colours. At once I saw the possibility of so characterizing the four movements of a symphony, that each should express a colour as I personally perceived it. There was to be no attempt at a semi-scientific basis whatever, if there *is* such a thing. I was fully aware that colours arouse quite different emotions in different people, and that I was speaking only for myself in composing this symphony. For that reason, I did not at first give it any name except "Symphony in B". Later I was won over by the argument put forward by Percy Scholes that if I *had* found initial inspiration in the idea of colour, it was timid not to proclaim it. Hence its title *Colour Symphony* with the subtitles to the movements Purple, Red, Blue, Green.'[10]

Giving the work such a descriptive title was both a decidedly modern thing to do and, as it turned out, a serious distraction which caused more column inches of comment at the time than anything he wrote musically, though there was a general agreement that it was an impressive work. This side-tracking of thought is irritating (and must have been to Bliss) as the work is, in this writer's opinion, one of the great twentieth-century British symphonies, and there is considerable competition. Comment focused on the fact that response to colour is a highly personal thing. True. But Bliss stated in the passage above that it *was* personal, it was *his* feeling for each colour. Additionally, he gave a description of each colour which showed how he approached the mood of each movement: Purple, the colour of amethysts, pageantry, royalty, and death; Red, the colour of rubies, wine, revelry, furnaces, courage, and magic; Blue, the colour of sapphires, deep water, skies, loyalty, and melancholy; Green, the colour of emeralds, hope, joy, youth, spring and victory. The *Times* critic writing after the first performance must have felt pleased with himself when he wrote: 'I found myself referring to the programme to find out whether I ought to be seeing red, or looking blue at certain moments, and some of it certainly made many of the audience feel green.'[11] Cheap humour. But he does later say 'One feels that a razor-edge mind is at work, a young mind because it despises weakness and sentiment, and it is there, probably, that Bliss still has some growing-up to do.'[12] Well there, at least, Bliss would agree with him as three of the four movements were very substantially revised later on. Perhaps the sagest advice came from the critic in *Gramophone* magazine who wrote 'Take no notice of the colour each movement is headed with, just enjoy it as a symphony. It seems to me a finely original work, full of vitality and beauty....'[13]

Bliss himself, writing to Percy Scholes on this subject in 1923 wrote: 'I know very little about the argument on the significance of the term 'colour' in my symphony, as I do not get the press notices, but if, as I imagine, the discussion has been entirely on the NAME and not on the music, I hope it will soon end.'[14] He went on to note that at a recent BBC performance the audience had undoubtedly come to *see* something and not *hear* and were disappointed when expecting magic to be lectured on biochemistry!

The first performance in Gloucester Cathedral on 7 September 1922 was something of a nightmare (Bliss characteristically downplayed it as 'a disappointment'). Rehearsal time was very limited and, as always, much time was given to correcting copyists' errors in the orchestral parts. But to crown it all, just before the performance was due to begin it was discovered that the stage was too full, having to accommodate the large chorus needed for other works in the programme and Bliss's huge orchestra. It is difficult to imagine these days, but to remedy this, various key players seated at the edges of the stage were simply removed. Bliss remembered the Tuba player and others on whom he relied being ejected. As he noted 'it was not a happy occasion for anyone'. It is fortunate that the critics of the night saw through this mayhem to gather the essential quality of the symphony.

Herbert Howells, in a Three Choirs recollection essay, wrote colourfully about the year's commissions: 'In other levels and moods that year, strangely "comparative" verbal and other two-edged compliments were disturbing the background of events. Arthur Bliss, in the heyday of his volcanic Anglo-Americanism, was present to give the first performance of *A Colour Symphony*: Eugene Goossens, as much Belgian as English, and already a brilliant young conductor, had come, bringing his new work *Silence*; and there was a third young man, just plain Forest of Dean, with *Sine Nomine*, which a patient audience had to endure while it waited for the brilliant certainties of *Elijah*... It was at luncheon, immediately after *A Colour Symphony*, that the great trumpeter J.J. Solomon beckoned to me and offered me his new-coined, strangely "comparative", two-edged verbal compliment: "well, young man, after the Symphony this morning, even *Sine Nomine* seems tolerable." '[15] In all honesty, these comments say more about Howells who was self-denigrating to a point, but also *to* a point. Of far more interest here, though, is his description: 'volcanic Anglo-Americanism' which is the first time Bliss's hybrid ancestry has been mentioned musically. Quite what Howells meant by this observation is not clear but might seem to reflect a perception of anything coming from the United States as extrovert and perhaps light-weight. Perhaps Howells is himself indulging in a little 'two-edged' comparative comment.

Bliss's work is, by any standards, a far greater contribution to the canon of British music than *Sine Nomine*, original as that work might be in its own way. It is also difficult to assess what might in real terms be considered American in Bliss's symphony. There is no jazz influence and it was surely the search for such indigenous musical types that was characterizing the new American music of such composers as Aaron Copland and George Gershwin who, although a few years younger, were contemporary with Bliss. Also contemporary, to a degree, were the 'serious' American composers like Walter Piston, Roy Harris and William Schuman whose numerous symphonic offerings were still to come. So, again, we fall back on the general feature of rumbustious energy as the critical feature dominating comment. And yet, in this work, there is considerably less 'volcanic' energy than in some of Bliss's previous scores, and certainly in comparison with many of those yet to come.

The colours are carefully chosen to ensure maximum contrast and, contemporary as it is, strip away the hyperbole, and one is left with a classic four movement symphony in the grand tradition, not classic in the sense of using classic forms but nevertheless rather Elgarian in character with long-limbed melodies and carefully used heady moments of dissonance. This, of course, judged at a distance of a hundred years and what we at this point in time now feel to be easy listening. The first movement (Purple) is a slow movement of great beauty and what he described in a letter written in 1970 to his great friend, the artist George Dannatt, as 'funeral [sic] or ecclesiastical shade of deep purple'. The irony of all this is that he goes on in the same letter to write that 'I think I concentrated on colours of a rather primitive kind, as my own colour sense is not actually very sure – sometimes I find it difficult, for instance, to pick out red berries in green foliage!'[16] Had the commentators of the time known that little golden nugget what a field day they would have had.

The Scherzo movement which follows is Red. Suddenly the Elgarian cobwebs are blown away as we move to a Stravinskian ballet score. Here we have the Arthur Bliss of recent familiarity. But even here the great lyrical sweeps between splashes of energetic colour have a deeply ingrained English character to them, and the contrasting restful section which acts as a Trio might in a classical symphony, seems to emphasize the overall energetic outpouring which is the spirit of the movement. Bliss described this movement to Dannatt as 'a real scarlet, the hue of embers hotly glowing'. The tuba has important work to do and must have been heart-breaking to the composer when ejected from the stage for the first performance.

The third movement, a slow movement, is, in Bliss's letter to Dannatt, a 'Picasso blue – not a deep Prussian? blue, but one observes it in the sky early and late in the year.'[17] Blue is noted as being the colour of sapphires, deep water, skies, loyalty, and melancholy in Bliss's original description. Ten years after the premiere of the symphony Bliss made a major revision of the work but left this movement completely unaltered. There was obviously something in this movement which he could see as being a pointer to the future development of his music, music which might be seen as coming to maturity at around the time of the revision of this symphony in his choral symphony *Morning Heroes*. Christopher Palmer, describing this movement wrote of 'the slow movement, pastoral in character with much flute arabesque and lazy lapping rhythms as of the movement of water against a moored boat or stone pier on a drowsy July afternoon.'[18] Here is the nearest he came to writing in the English Pastoral vein with melodies redolent of folksong. Some of the more dissonant sections would not have been foreign to a Vaughan Williams orchestral score but the overall effect is still far more cosmopolitan, and in the knowledge of all that had led up to this moment in Bliss's career thus far one's ears are not naturally attuned to an English soundscape and there are constant reminders, often as much in the orchestration as in the melody or harmony, of his alignment with the Russian school. This is undoubtedly part of the reason for the freshness of this highly original symphony, especially in English terms.

The fourth movement, 'green' (the colour of emeralds, hope, youth, joy, spring and victory). The later description to George Dannatt is interesting as Bliss describes 'a spring green gradually deepening through yellow green to a fierce dark green.'[19] The movement is a double fugue the first of which has a sinuous, mysterious subject (almost Schoenbergian in character) which seems a long way from the youthful, joyful characteristics in

Bliss's description. But the roots go deep and flower into something unexpected. In fact, dissonance apart, there is a return to an Elgarian sweep just
before the second fugue subject appears making a completely new, gossamer-light soundworld. Here is really virtuoso orchestration which marries
*Petrushka*'s street scenes with the triumphant ending of *Firebird*. Through
the joining of both fugue subjects at the end, a relentless timpani part and
powerful brass chords which would seem to pre-shadow the culmination
of the *Meditations on a Theme by John Blow* many years later and even to
have inspired the ending of Britten's *Young Person's Guide to the Orchestra*,
Bliss concludes a remarkable and ground-breaking new symphony.

Much of the early work was done in Vaughan Williams's house in Cheyne
Walk, by the river in London. RVW lived and worked on the top floor,
R.O. Morris, the writer of that invaluable volume *Contrapuntal Technique
in the XVIth Century* had the middle floor and Bliss worked on the ground
floor. As he remarked, Morris was an effective sound barrier between RVW
and himself. Bliss wrote that 'I loved working there in so sympathetic and
creative an atmosphere. I got to know R.O. Morris very well, or as well as he
allowed anyone to penetrate his reserve. He loved claret, and he loved cats:
with one of the latter curled up purring in his lap, and a glass of claret at
hand, he would challenge me to chess, his elegant fingers moving the pieces
with sure logic to my final defeat. Years later I dedicated my ballet *Checkmate*
to him in memory of those happy evenings.'[20]

Elgar's reaction to the symphony was not enthusiastic and caused a
fracture in their friendship. Bliss mended this six years later by dedicating his *Pastoral* to Elgar and received an ameliatory reply but with
a degree of frankness which must have been wounding: 'Frankly, I was
greatly disappointed with the way you progressed from years ago. There
was so much "press" of a type I dislike and newspaper nonsense. I can
easily believe you were responsible for little or none of this but it rankled
a great deal because I had great hopes for you: I had affection. It will seem
vulgar to you if I add that commercially you have (I believe or was led to
believe) no concern with the success of your works – an unfortunate side
of art which we penniless people have always with us, and try to ignore.
I hoped you were going to give us something very great in quite modern
music, the progress of which is very dear to me; and then you seemed to
become a mere 'paragraphist'. I am probably wrong and trust I was.'[21]

This letter reveals a number of insecurities on Elgar's part, perhaps
most notably the dig at Bliss's financial security, but also the fact that
Bliss had accrued a considerable press interest in his work. The ultimately
insulting description of Bliss as a 'mere paragraphist' was probably best

summed up by Michael Kennedy as Elgar's 'jealousy of the artistic and financial success of a younger man.'[22] And yet Kennedy adds a conundrum here when he writes of Elgar: 'How interested he really was in their music (up and coming composers) is problematical. He did not, as Vaughan Williams did when he attained a similar pre-eminence in English music, attend almost every first performance of a new English work. The truth is that, like Delius, he was not very interested in the work of his contemporaries and juniors. He helped people he liked as men rather than as musicians.'[23] If this is really so then it would seem to show an almost personal vendetta against Bliss for this period.

Bliss dedicated the symphony to Adrian Boult who conducted the first performance of the heavily revised score at the Queen's Hall in London on 27 April 1932. Robert Miekle makes a key observation about the revision of the second movement where Bliss, in his revision, had substituted a new first Trio which makes no formal sense when the theme of the old first Trio appears in the coda. Bliss revised this symphony after the premiere of *Morning Heroes* and Miekle suggests that the re-writing of part of this work connected it thematically more overtly to *Morning Heroes* where the theme of the new first Trio is almost identical to a key theme in the fifth movement of *Morning Heroes* (Spring Offensive) and there is 'accordingly a strong link between the works: it is almost as if *Morning Heroes*, with its text, makes explicit a latent preoccupation of the original *Colour Symphony*, whereupon the revision of *A Colour Symphony* brings that preoccupation to the surface, but only in the light and experience of *Morning Heroes*.'[24] In other words the two works are connected through the death of Bliss's brother Kennard, and it is notable that Wilfred Owen's words at this point are 'Why speak they not of comrades that went under?' Well, in *A Colour Symphony* Bliss was not able to speak overtly of his brother, but there is a key connection in Bliss's words to George Dannatt relating to the first movement (Purple) being a 'funereal or ecclesiastical shade of deep purple'. Remember, too, that one of the descriptive words Bliss used for the colour was 'death'. The opening of the whole work can be seen as stately death march. 1922, when this work was commissioned, was only four years after the end of hostilities, and only six years after Kennard's death, and Bliss's psychological wounds (not to mention the actual ones) went very deep and were only to be exorcised by the writing of *Morning Heroes* only eight years later. The connections between the two works are fundamental indeed.

# Chapter Five

# LOVE VIA THE STAGE:
# THE 'VOLCANIC ANGLO-AMERICAN'

Bliss's father had remarried in June 1918, aged seventy-one, and Brian had acted as his Best Man. His new bride, Ethel, (his fourth wife, and forty-six years younger) was a war widow with two children, Cynthia (b.1909) and Patrick (b.1911) from her previous marriage, and a six-year-old daughter, Enid, who was an unexpected late arrival from her new marriage. Frank wanted to return to his own country before it was too late and to show the country to his sons as neither had visited America yet. He sold the house in Holland Park and prepared for the monumental move (sixty-seven trunks were shipped) after so many years in England. For Frank, Ethel and their children the move was a permanent one. For Arthur and Howard it was an extended but not permanent trip. Howard didn't travel with the family but joined a year later.

Apart from a genuine desire to support his father in his move, and having a keen interest in seeing the United States, it is a fair question to ask why Bliss decided to make this fundamental two-year break with England at this critical time in his career. The *Colour Symphony* was still ringing in people's ears and the column inches were essentially favourable even though, as we have seen, he was put through the wringer for his shorter works leading to it. He was certainly now a recognized name. The war had changed everything but Bliss felt that there was still a burning desire to return to the pre-war status quo by a proportion of the population and that the music being most lauded seemed to reflect those sentiments. Therefore, in going to the States so soon after the war he was wanting to observe and participate in, even for a short time, a new world which was unfettered by centuries of tradition which, however much music may have moved forward in the past fifty years in England, saw a public whose appetite was more satisfied by Vaughan Williams and his impressionist retro-style than anything which looked outwards to Europe and beyond. Constant Lambert in his forensic scrutiny of the contemporary music of his time *Music Ho!* said of Vaughan Williams's *Pastoral Symphony* (1922 – and therefore exactly where we are in our timeline) 'it is no exaggeration to say that the creation of a particular type of grey, reflective, English-landscape mood has outweighed the exigencies of symphonic form. To those who find this mood sympathetic, their intense and personal emotional reaction will more than compensate for the monotony of texture and lack of form.'[1] (Lambert knew perfectly well, of course, that the *Pastoral Symphony* actually reflected the French wartime landscape.) Sam Ellis has made the point that 'Vaughan Williams managed an achievement at this time which largely eluded Bliss: he reached out to a broad public... In making his name as a moderate British avant-gardist, Bliss's stylistic alignment was with the European modernists: Schoenberg, Bartok and Stravinsky. This may have won him a loyal following in some quarters, but not a lasting public affection.'[2]

Perhaps unsurprisingly, knowing what we do of his later work with film and the stage, not to mention the inherently balletic works already written, Bliss formed close friendships and allied himself with modernist artists, something which was to continue to be of critical importance all his life. We saw this in the previous chapter in relation to *Rout* and other works of that period. This marked him out as someone different from the crowd of current British composers for whose music the public demonstrated a greater enthusiasm. Why not, therefore, take a break and see what the New World had to offer?

Before leaving he wrote an article for a periodical called the *Musical Mirror* in which he wrote: 'Modern music is as young as the film industry, and there should be a great future for the alliance of the two. A man I certainly intend to open negotiations with at Los Angeles is Charles Chaplin. He would make an excellent subject for musical treatment.'[3] This was, of course, prophetic, for although he did not meet Chaplin, within a decade he was to be the film composer of the moment and through H.G. Wells about to transform music for that medium. In the same article he jokingly commented that he was 'running away before England, which is the most critical country in the world, finds me out.'[4] This showed a frustration with the British press who were always suspicious of new trends in music, and so there was another hope for this period: new world: new ears.

A key point made by Stephen Banfield about the contemporary music to which Bliss aligned himself was that 'we may note that the images (being represented in music) themselves are essentially those of popular culture: Picasso's minstrels and serenaders; Stravinsky's circus animals, travelling players, pierrots and puppets; Bliss's fairground and carnival evocations which give to his musical vocabulary in "Rout" and elsewhere tempered but unmistakable accents of dance music and street music – all these are attempts at aligning the contemporary arts with images of sound, colour and movement that are experienced much more immediately and vividly than was possible in the Romantic tradition with its literary bias.'[5]

The family sailed on 23 April 1923 on the *Aquitania* to New York. This beautiful, four-funnelled, ship had only recently been returned to transatlantic passenger service after being requisitioned as a troop transport and hospital ship for the war. The refitting to prepare for this included the engines being changed from coal to oil-fuelled and a general re-installation of all the luxury items which had been put in storage during the war. The voyage took four days and the ship docked on the 27th. Frank Bliss, absent from his home country for so long, wanted to spend some time revisiting old haunts and as Bliss recalled, 'Once in New York, my father tried to find the site of the office in which he had worked as a boy, but it was a hopeless task in that completely rebuilt city. But he did find his old University, Brown, in Providence, looking much the same, and was invited by the present young occupant into the rooms he had once used himself.'[6] The 1920s were an exciting time to be in New York which was still in the process of exponential growth through the extraordinary philanthropy of its richest men like Andrew Carnegie, the Vanderbilts and Astors many of whose houses on Fifth Avenue were like palaces. Here was a vibrant and cultured 'new world' which was exciting to anyone, and to Bliss in his current state of mind, an obvious land of opportunities.

On leaving New York the Blisses stopped at Lake Mohonk about eighty-five miles almost directly north. The beautiful setting for this lovely stretch of water was an obvious stopping point and it was here that Bliss wrote *The Ballads of the Four Seasons*, his first music written on American soil. He had packed a variety of books in his luggage and for this set of songs he used poems by Li Po, a Chinese poet of the Tsang Dynasty born in the year 701, recently translated by Shigeyoshi Obata. Li Po apparently left home in 725 to wander the Yangtze River valley and write poetry. A drunken lifestyle eventually led to his death as a result of falling overboard trying to catch the reflection of the moon in the water! Whether or not the references to water inspired Bliss in his present surroundings, and especially the second, *Summer*, which begins 'On the mirror lake…', there is no doubt that the final song, *Winter*, will have resonated strongly describing, as it does, a woman working her fingers to the bone in the freezing cold to finish a jacket she is making for her loved one, a soldier serving at the front. The courier will come in the morning to take it to him.

The cycle of four songs represents the seasons but Li Po doesn't describe them in natural terms but finds a *scena* for each. *Spring* is a love story, *Summer* sets the scene for an amorous adventure, *Autumn* and *Winter* are both characterized by chill winds (*Autumn*), icy cold (*Winter*) and separation through war. Bliss's settings have a real sense of progression and form his first *cycle* of songs. The first is redolent of the pastoral vein he left behind in England, the second is full of summer quickness of spirit in its compound time dancing, finishing with a rather suggestive little rising semiquaver figure anticipating Queen Hsishih's amorous encounter with the King of Yueh. *Autumn* is a fascinating setting. The text has this image: 'From ten thousand houses comes the sound of cloth-pounding'. This was part of the ironing process, which apparently created a shrill metal sound, so Bliss starts the song with a representation of this from the piano, *Vivace*. He then introduces a slow ground bass just for the left hand over which the soprano sadly sings of the cloth pounding (which might be seen as cloth being cleaned for the soldiers who were away, thus connecting it to the fourth song). *Vivace* returns, ground bass returns, and then an impassioned outburst from the singer who bewails the separation from her soldier beloved. The song ends on an anguished discord. *Winter* is characterized by a military march accompanying the singer trying desperately to finish the jacket for her absent soldier and ends, like the previous song with another impassioned outburst which dies away in desperation and exhaustion to a quiet ending. While the musical language is nothing like so advanced as some of his earlier works this cycle represents a real step forward in the creation of a group of songs intended to be performed as a set.

From Lake Mohonk the family moved to Canada, crossing the Rocky Mountains, and from there on to the Pacific Coast to San Francisco via Vancouver. Bliss felt the Pacific coast to be unbelievably beautiful. It was as if his American heritage through his father was coming into focus and something in Bliss himself was being revealed. A crucial meeting took place at the University of California at Berkeley (San Francisco) where he met the composer Albert Elkus who was to be a key figure in Bliss's life at the outbreak of the Second World War. This early connection with him and his family laid the foundations of a deep, life-long friendship.

San Francisco wasn't the Blisses final stopping point. About 350 miles down the famous coast road US101 was the beautiful city of Santa Barbara which Bliss described as the Pacific Coast's 'greatest gem' and where their 'long trek' ended. This, they knew, would be the ideal place for Frank and Ethel and their family to search for a place to live. Just east of Santa Barbara is the community called Montecito. Beautifully situated in hilly country which falls away to the sea they found the ideal property at Paradero, 15, School House Road, and it was here that Frank lived until his death in 1930. Bliss doesn't mention his father's death in his autobiography but Frank was interred in Santa Barbara cemetery where there is a plaque commemorating both his and, much later, his wife's lives. The plaque is situated in the apse of the chapel. Built in 1867, it was therefore still relatively new when Frank was interred with space left for Ethel when her time came.

Bliss's half-brother, Patrick Mahoney, wrote a colourful personal sketch of Arthur at this time for Bliss's 80th birthday in 1971, bringing him very much to life:

'With twenty-one years difference in our ages, the rapport between us was hardly one of brothers, but I remember his continuous kindness to my sister Cynthia and myself, buying us presents and taking us to our first moving-picture show. I recall his exuberant gaiety, especially. A childlike mirth leaped and danced in him; he was always bubbling with quips and jests. This laughter-loving mood... was soon to be quenched, to some extent at least, by the advance of years and marital responsibilities... All his life, Arthur has gravitated to exciting people in his own orbit and in Santa Barbara he gave of himself to every cultural project into which he was invited.'[7]

Bliss himself painted a picture of Santa Barbara as the playground of the wealthy before the Wall Street Crash of 1929. But like all such communities in the States philanthropy was almost always close at hand which helped to sustain a thriving Community Arts Association. Inevitably Bliss was involved in this straight away composing the incidental music for a play on King Solomon and, as he said, 'I placed my modest little band in the wings, and contrived to simulate the sounds of the building of the Temple by rhythmic tapping on steel bars of different pitches.'[8] This brings recollections of the approach to his music for *The Tempest* so enjoyed by Ernest Newman two years earlier.

Bliss decided to return to New York for the winter of 1923, taking a small apartment off Times Square. The New York 'electric vitality' was exactly what he was looking for, feeling that 'there is something about the cold champagne air of New York in the autumn and winter that marks the place out from all other great cities. Whenever I pass through it during those months of the year, I experience the same exhilaration: "Life will now start anew!" New York seems to scream, "nothing is unattainable". I could never do serious work there ... but for an electric shock to the imagination it is unique.'[9]

Needless to say, part of that 'electric shock' were the girls who he found endlessly distracting but essentially empty-headed. He became acquainted with a group of rich American girls for a time, the sort who seemingly needed for nothing and who could have anything at the click of their manicured fingers. 'They were clearly self-sufficient... hardly needing attendant men... Great riches emit a heady intoxicating perfume, but the aroma can quickly enfeeble, and indeed stifle artistic ambition.'[10]

In order to clear his mind and focus on some composition, he enrolled at the MacDowell colony for artists in Peterborough, New Hampshire, which had been founded by the composer Edward MacDowall in 1907. They provided a private cabin for work, with lunch being delivered to the door in order not to disturb concentration. Bliss found the resultant expectation to deliver inhibiting, soon left, and was glad to return to New York.

It may seem as if this privileged young man was simply moving from distraction to distraction and that an inability to work revealed a lazy mind. To some extent this may actually be true. He had already admitted that he had 'quickness and facility, but not the faculty of concentration... I preferred to skim like a humming-bird moth from piece to piece rather than remain a caterpillar meticulously devouring a single leaf.'[11] Although referring to an episode at school this was probably a life-long characteristic which he had to work hard to overcome when real concentration was needed – as it often was especially later on when working against the clock. The other key thing to remember, which Bliss repeated many times, was that he found writing music for its own sake extremely difficult. He needed an external idea, a stimulus, onto which he could latch and develop a compositional thread. This was undoubtedly an additional problem at the Colony.

What was soon to materialize, however, was a far more interesting initiative which gave rise to his second American work *The Women of Yueh*. Edgard Varèse and Carlos Salzedo had founded an International Composers' Guild in 1921 stating 'They have realized the necessity of banding together and fighting for the right of each individual to secure fair and free representation of his work... The International Composers' Guild disapproves of all "isms"; denies the existence of schools; and recognizes only the individual.'[12] Worthy aims, and certainly what Bliss was looking for at this moment. The initiative wasn't quite as simple as Bliss relates in his autobiography, however. Various strict rules had been drawn up by Varèse and Salzedo, which included only allowing *first* performances. When Claire Reis, the tireless chairperson of the executive committee, organized a second performance of Schoenberg's *Pierrot Lunaire* this went directly against these principles and a schism developed which led to the formation of a new organization, the League of Composers, in March 1923. Bliss was recruited as an Executive Board member and his song cycle *The Women of Yueh* was premiered at the Guild's inaugural concert in the Klaw Theatre on 11 November that year. This was the same venue that Reis had secured for the second performance of Schoenberg's *Pierrot Lunaire.* Another tacit agreement was breached in order to allow Bliss's work to be heard, that works by members of the Board should not be heard in the first season. Bliss was made an exception 'in order to capitalize on the prestige gained from his American appearance.'[13] This is an interesting observation in its own right, and would seem to suggest that Bliss's name had crossed the Atlantic to considerable effect already.

*The Women of Yueh* is connected to *The Ballads of the Four Seasons* in various ways, principally in setting further poems by Li Po (again from the translation by Shigeyoshi Obata) and in being another cycle of songs connected thematically through the poems' subject matter. Whereas the *Ballads* were simple settings for voice and piano, here Bliss evokes the sound world of his pre-*Colour Symphony* short works in using an instrumental ensemble of flute, oboe, clarinet, bassoon, glockenspiel, triangle and side drum with soprano solo. Another 'study in sound'. Each of the poems describes a different girl in flirtatious situations and varying moods. The Mirror Lake referred to in the fifth song is also referred to in *Summer,* the second of the *Ballads.* Bliss hints at neo-orientalism in the first song with characteristic flute arabesques but goes no further. The close connection he made in Santa Barbara with Henry Eichheim, an expert on Asian music, and one of the first American composers to combine the sound of indigenous Asian instruments with western orchestral colours, was in its infancy and saw no influence in these songs. It was later that Bliss would connect with Eichheim's extensive collection of instruments which he left to the University of Berkeley after his death.

Perhaps the most eye-opening experiences for Bliss during these months was hearing Monteux conduct the *Colour Symphony* in Boston.

'It was the first time I had heard a great American orchestra and I was astounded; I had never imagined such virtuosity possible. At his first rehearsal I learnt one practical lesson. Monteux had had to spend a considerable time over one particular passage in my score, and in the interval, he pointed out how much easier I could have made it for the players if I had adopted a simpler notation. Ever since then I have avoided the temptation to make my music *look* intricate... the orchestral player must be the first consideration.'[14] Other happy experiences abounded: Casals rehearsing the cello section in the orchestral break where he had seen something which could help them in Debussy's *La Mer*, Bliss joining other orchestral musicians at a later concert in running through Brahms's Horn Trio just for fun *after* a concert. As he put it: 'Chamber music *after* an orchestral concert! In London?'[15]

Perhaps most interesting, however, was putting the Monteux experience against his visit to Philadelphia to hear Stokowski conduct Tchaikovsky's fifth symphony 'that made my hair rise'. 'No two conductors could be further apart in their approach to music... both were great artists in sound. Stokowski revelled in its dramatic power... he was also a strong disciplinarian. My first impression... was of a super Rolls-Royce being driven by a man who had himself made every gadget; yes, but *driven*. Monteux did not drive. He allowed his players freedom to take part with him in the interpretation... His magic lay in his sensitive ear and wonderfully intelligent eyes, not in the dramatic gestures of hands.'[16] For a composer so concerned with sound and colour, these two experiences – so different and yet so complimentary – added greatly to his appreciation of orchestral possibilities.

Crucial, at this time, was a meeting with the great American patroness of music, Elizabeth Sprague Coolidge, with whom Bliss was to forge a close friendship and from whom he would soon receive a commission for an oboe quintet. It seems that Bliss's future mother-in-law, Gertrude Hoffman, was a good friend of Mrs Coolidge, and according to Paul Jackson, they used to go on drives together, undocumented in the Hoffman dairies but clearly remembered by Trudy Bliss and related to Jackson.[17]

Trudy, Frank Bridge and his wife Ethel had been invited to attend her music festival in Pittsfield, Massachusetts and Bliss joined the party. Eugene Goossens was commissioned to write a string work (his Sextet) for the festival and so frustrated Coolidge by his lack of communication that she threatened to pull the commission from him and offer it to Arthur Bliss. As it turned out he completed it in time and all was well.

Bliss had to wait another three years for his commission from her. As Susan Borwick wrote, reviewing Cyrilla Barr's biography of Coolidge, she 'was thoroughly American. Responding to criticism that the Coolidge competitions neglected American composers, she wrote to the Library of Congress music librarian Carl Engel: "I have almost at the point of the bayonet insisted upon American works in Boston and Europe".'[18] But it is true that all her early commissions were given to British composers. There was, however, a significant move in the States to take pride in its native composers who were starting to speak with an American accent and to loosen ties with the classic Germanic tradition. The foundation of two of the great music schools at exactly this time, Juilliard and Curtis, followed the trailblazing example of Eastman in 1912. These were serious steps forward for American composers who, through organizations like the International Composers' Guild and League of Composers were also being given opportunities to hear their music performed. It may well be that Bliss's dual British/American ancestry smoothed his path with Coolidge, and assuaged her conscience on the thorny issue of being seen to support indigenous composers.

Not long after this Bliss wrote his *Two Interludes* for piano dedicating the first to Elizabeth Sprague Coolidge and the second to Ethel Roe Eichheim, the pianist wife who, with her husband, Henry Eichheim, already mentioned, were friends in Santa Barbara. It is notable that the only original music written during his time in the States was piano music, songs and a string quartet. It is as if he needed the time to recover from the great labour of the *Colour Symphony* and also, perhaps, to see what America might offer him in terms of new musical stimulus. It is notable that he gave the manuscript of the original version of the *Colour Symphony* to the Library of Congress in Washington probably spurred into this act of generosity by his experience of hearing it so brilliantly performed by Monteux. It was also the first of his works to be heard in the States. In February 1925 Elizabeth Sprague Coolidge gave the manuscript of the *Two Interludes* to the Library of Congress which was a demonstrable seal of approval for Bliss and the foundation of all that followed through her patronage.

The *Two Interludes* in a way show Bliss's stylistic dilemma. His reputation, as we have seen, was as a decided modernist, and so many of his more experimental works leading to the symphony were eye (or ear) catching for their outward looking, European-facing character. But lurking underneath all this modernist bravado was a romantically beating instinct which was to grow significantly in the coming years.

Small as it is, the first of the *Two Interludes* seems to encapsulate this dilemma very clearly. A highly discordant, dramatic opening which returns almost rondo-like throughout the piece is balanced by wistful, romantic theme in thirds which seems to win out in the end by transforming the opening material into slow, gently discordant reminders of the opening which fade into a concordant ending. It is very effective. The second *Interlude* is a hybrid. There seems to be some attempt to reflect Henry Eichheim's passion for Asian instruments and culture in some of the filigree figuration, but rather curiously the overall effect is an amalgam of French elements (Satie and Ravel) with hints of Stravinsky (*Petrouchka* again). It is like an improvisation where snatches of memory flow from the fingers. It is an effective piece but shows just how much Bliss was still searching for his own personal voice.

The orchestral work he did work on during 1924 was a revision of the *Concerto for piano, tenor and percussion* originally written in 1920, referred to in Chapter Three. This was a work to which he would return a number of times during his career. This first new look was a fundamental change to a *Concerto for two pianos and orchestra* and this formed the basis of the versions that followed. The Concerto was performed in December 1924 by the Boston Symphony Orchestra conducted by Serge Koussevitsky with the pianists Guy Maier and Lee Pattison. Bliss, however, wasn't happy with the result and destroyed the manuscript. A new revision was worked at over the next four years and would be performed in London with Henry Wood at the helm in 1929.

Two other compositions from this American period need to be mentioned, the first is a work which was not known about until after Bliss's death, a string quartet in three movements dating from around this time which exists only in manuscript. The existing score is a working manuscript of the whole work but missing a substantial section from the second movement which it is likely Bliss had removed in order to revise and replace but apparently never did so. Thus, a tantalizing incomplete work. It is interesting to speculate as to whether the string quartet he refers to in his autobiography which he had submitted for a prize and which he tells us 'mysteriously vanished', might be this work and that these were the preliminary workings before a fair copy was made. It seems somehow unlikely that he would have worked on two quartets in this period.

The other is a substantial piano work: *Masks*. Dedicated to the publisher Felix Goodwin, who Bliss described as 'enthusiastic and ambitious for British Music', it has four masks: *A Comedy Mask, A Romantic Mask, A Sinister Mask* and *A Military Mask*. Although only some ten minutes in duration these pieces amount to a major addition to Bliss's output to this point. There are various interesting elements. First, the title which relates to the stage which was to become so important to Bliss and which seems to reflect different aspects of his own persona. Second, the obvious 'trouvaille' or peg on which to hang his musical ideas so key to his compositional process. Third, the ever-present shadow of his wartime experience writ large in the final movement but, being a mask, not overtly. So, in many senses these pieces are autobiographical, they are *Bliss*'s masks.

The first, the *Comedy Mask*, reflects his own infectious, humorous and bubbling personality – his step-brother's description of his 'exuberant gaity'. The second, *A Romantic Mask* treads a thin line between Chopin and Rachmaninov reimagined by Stravinsky. The heady climax is a truly passionate overflowing. The *Sinister Mask* is, strangely, hardly sinister at all with its repeated melodic figure until the very final bars which are allowed to die away on a discord which seems to say, 'this is what I meant...'. The final *Military Mask* has all the martial elements you would expect but underneath it all is a dark shadow and a deeply unsettling ending. *Masks* wasn't premiered until after the newly married Blisses had returned to London when Arthur Benjamin played them at the Faculty of Arts Gallery in Golden Square, London on 2 February 1926.

Bliss returned to Santa Barbara in January 1924 to find his brother Howard had arrived the previous month, accompanied by the violinist Roderick White. The opportunity of forming a new chamber group with White, Howard (cellist), and Bliss as pianist was eagerly seized and they lost no time in giving concerts for the local Arts Association. Bliss now settled into the community with a sense of purpose and less *wanderlust* (for now). He lectured, conducted and wrote incidental music for stage performances as required. Later in the year he was appointed Director of Music for the Arts Association and as he wrote to the writer Ulrich Nisbet (another Englishman who married an American girl) 'I have a quaint appointment as Director of Music (for the Arts Association) which may keep me here for several years',[19] showing how fluid his plans were and how settled he was feeling. Another local appointment added to his list of activities when he was appointed music critic of the Santa Barbara Morning Press, in which role he was not afraid to speak his mind unequivocally about performers and performances that did not meet with his approval. This must have made for interesting relationships within the small Santa Barbara community.

He developed long-lasting friendships, especially with the Eichheims, but also with the artist Frank Morley Fletcher, who had just become

Director of the Santa Barbara School of the Arts. Just as Henry Eichheim was passionate about the East, its culture and its musical instruments, Morley Fletcher introduced Japanese coloured wood painting into Western art, having been introduced to it by Fernand Cormon during his studies in Paris. All this in Santa Barbara. Moreover, Morley Fletcher invited Donald Francis Tovey to come to give a series of lectures and recitals. Bliss found him both fascinating and seriously intimidating simply for the extent of his vast musical knowledge.

The wish to meet Chaplin in Hollywood having proved impossible, the road from Santa Barbara along the coast to Los Angeles was never-theless very well-travelled.

His experiences of the Hollywood Bowl, both as part of the audience and as a conductor, were memorable, as was what he described as 'an even more dramatic setting for music… the theatre in the Bohemian Grove, north of San Francisco …'[20] the giant redwoods forming the wings of the stage'. He remembered a Bohemian group camping there and producing an opera in this extraordinary natural arena.

Bliss conducted a performance of *Elijah* in Santa Barbara gathering amateur forces together, rehearsing hard and adding to the chorus good local string players. The wind and brass, however, came from the Los Angeles Philharmonic amongst whom were a number of old friends from the Queen's Hall Orchestra in London. At dinner with them that evening alcohol was supplied by the distinguished horn player Alfred Brain (Dennis Brain's uncle) despite prohibition (which was rather more relaxed in California). The next day, Bliss was seriously unwell and had no doubt that he had been poisoned. The doctor was called and admin-istered what Bliss thought might be strychnine, and gave a further dose just before Bliss went on stage to conduct. Despite Bliss's concerns that he might find rows of empty chairs in the orchestra which should have been occupied by fellow drinkers he was relieved to find them all present and apparently none the worse for wear.

At certain points in this story Bliss lets his guard down and we have a 'credo' moment. The American composer Roy Harris visited him to ask him to look at some of his recent work. Later, in 1939, when Harris's third symphony was heard Bliss felt that this was at last a voice 'free from European influence.'[21] His reflections on Harris's work led him to declare that 'There is a tendency to depreciate a national idiom in favour of some international style, whereby it is often difficult to tell whether the composer is a native of Manchester or Osaka, Stuttgart or Minneapolis. Personally, I get bored with this musical Esperanto. I prefer infinite variety in all aspects of life, whether in cooking, language, architecture or music. I hope the distinctive and refreshing flavour of regional genius will always have a welcome.'[22]

A new theatre had just been built in Santa Barbara, the Lobero Theatre. It was originally built as an opera house in 1873 but by the 1920s was in serious need of rebuilding. It was decided to rebuild it as a theatre, and the Spanish Colonial Revival style was chosen to blend in with the town's general architectural style.

Little did Bliss know how important this theatre was to become to him in so short a time. It was felt appropriate to cast the inaugural performance using local actors. The play chosen was *Beggar on Horseback* by Kaufman and Connelly, which had only just been premiered in New York that February. The plot was based on the principle that if you give wealth to the undeserving, they will be the worse for it: 'Set a beggar on horseback, and he will ride to the devil'. Bliss became involved in it because he could play the piano on stage as the central character, Neil McRae, is required to do. McRae, an impoverished composer, is troubled by how hard he has to work at odd jobs to make ends meet. He loves Cynthia Mason but is urged by a friend to consider marrying Gladys Cady, the daughter of a wealthy industrialist. The engagement takes place but conflict is inevitable and, in the end, he realizes that he must choose love over money. The engagement is broken off after they realize their incompatibility and Cynthia is restored to her rightful place in his affections. It is a comedy with a serious message.

Playing opposite Bliss as the poor girl, Cynthia, was a girl called Trudy Hoffman, who lived in what is now 2653 Glendessary Lane near the Old Mission in Santa Barbara. She was twenty-one and a student at Radcliffe College, a women's liberal arts college in Cambridge, Massachusetts that acted as the female college balancing the all-male (at that time) Harvard University. Bliss was immediately smitten. As he put it 'I had been in love many times in my life, and had been made unhappy and disturbed by each experience. The emotional crises always came when I had to make the final decision as to whether marriage would bring fulfillment to life, or an eventual frustration.'[23] He even consulted a fortune teller in Cambridge about his love life when a student and remembered her pronouncement that he would not marry until he was in his thirties, and then it would be for life.

The Hoffmans were a significant Santa Barbara family. One branch (Bernard and Irene) bought the land in the town centre for the new theatre and an adjacent shopping precinct, and Ralph Hoffman, Trudy's father, became a noted botanist and ornithologist (he was the author of the first comprehensive bird field guide). He was appointed to succeed William Dawson (the museum's founder) as Director of the Santa Barbara Museum of Natural History, a museum which has gone on to achieve a considerable international reputation. This love of nature was naturally passed on to Trudy, who would regularly go on botanical expeditions with her father.

The beauty of the Pacific scenery and the wealth of nature in all its forms enticed Arthur and Trudy, and as the run of rehearsals progressed, they would drive back to her house together often sharing picnics in the 'scented lemon groves bordering on the phosphorescent Pacific Ocean. The mis-en-scene could not have been more beautiful,'[24] Bliss wrote of this time. 'It was soon evident to our audience', he added, 'that where I was concerned the drama on the stage was being re-enacted in real life off the stage. After the show finished, Bliss was invited to join the Hoffmans on a camping trip in Southern California. The roads were often rough going in those days before their later metalling. They visited the Mojave Desert and the Yosemite and Bliss remembered that 'There were wonderful things for the newcomer to see – the hot colour of the desert and the sandstorms, the gigantic Joshua trees, the cool greenish skies at dawn and sunset, the delicacy of peach and apricot blossom in spring and great drifts of Californian poppies after the rains. We camped in Owen's Valley and then climbed into the Sierras on horseback. With my senses sharpened by love, I thought I had never seen such grand and dramatic landscapes.'[25]

Arthur and Trudy were engaged in September of 1924 and married on 1 June 1925 in the Old Mission Church in Santa Barbara 'amid a host of relations and friends'.

The reception was held at Trudy's aunt and uncle's house (Bernhard and Irene Hoffman) in Garden Street, very near the Mission in a recently built (1919) house. It is regarded as another fine example of the Spanish revival style designed by the architect James Osborne Craig, with a sizeable garden ideal for a large gathering like this.

After the heady excitements of the wedding, they set off to honeymoon in Carmel, a beautiful town by the sea on the Monterey Peninsula about two hundred miles north of Santa Barbara. From there they went on to San Francisco and New York by train, sailing from there to England on 13 June 1925 in the SS *Orbita*, a rather less grand ocean liner than the *Aquitania* on which Bliss had sailed to America two years earlier but a sleek and beautiful ship nevertheless. It was one which, when owned by the Royal Mail, doubled as the transport for mail between the two countries.

Poor Trudy! Imagine the shock of arriving in 1920s London with its grim aspect, pollution, dense fogs, overcrowding and general sense of everyone for themselves. For a young girl used to the fresh air, the sheer almost unrivalled beauty of the Pacific coast, the small Santa Barbara community, as well as her community of university friends on the east coast – all this will have made that London arrival, probably so full of expectation, a dismal disappointment albeit tempered by the white heat of new love and the happiness of her new marriage. Bliss knew all this and wrote sensitively about it in *As I Remember*. The positives were that this square is in Kensington, an affluent part of London and, despite what Bliss called 'its grim aspect' had a garden within its confines, as many of these London squares do. But the Blisses only had a studio flat and the sense of confinement after the open Californian spaces will have initially felt like an imprisonment. But, as Bliss wrote, 'Whatever nostalgia she must have frequently felt she bravely minimized, and our life was varied and happy. To feel even closer to my musical life, Trudy at this time went regularly to the Royal College of Music, where she studied theory with R.O. Morris and took singing lessons.'[26] Bliss also sympathized with her having to 'face the unknown groups with whom I had been brought up'. A foreigner in a new country, however similar the languages may be, will always feel an outsider for some time. Trudy, though, was a strong and determined girl who was not only deeply in love, which helped, but had made her bed and was determined to lie on it with purpose.

For Bliss, there was the knowledge that he now had to make a new start, that having been away from England for two years – a long time – he was going to have to work hard to re-establish himself in the eyes and ears of a sceptical press and fickle public. He wrote about American audiences that 'They have not yet had the time to acquire deep prejudices, judging rather by a simply criterion as to whether a work interests or moves them.'[27] It is easy to read into this the wish that English audiences might also vote with such instincts and open their ears with interest and enthusiasm to the new.

Bliss felt it important to show his new wife something of her new country, and to show her that London is only one side of what England has to offer. Therefore, they set out to drive to the West Country and, on the way, visited Thomas Hardy, introduced by Bliss's brother, Howard, who was both a friend and an avid collector of Hardy letters and manuscripts: he even owned Hardy's cello at one time. Bliss recalled that he had set a poem of Hardy's as a student at the RCM, which Stanford had refused to look at, describing the poem as 'unpleasant' – a slightly 'loose' country girl encountering love that she regretted but which led to finding love with the man she truly loved. Stanford will have read 'and he came and he tied up my garter for me' and that was enough for his prudish sensibilities. Hardy introduced them to the Granville-Barkers, with whom they had lunch the next day. Harley Granville-Barker was a hugely influential figure of the day in the theatre world as actor, director and playwright. Success brought with it wealth and the Blisses found the formal atmosphere stifling and the occasion dominated by his wife (complete with cockatoo) where Bliss would have preferred to have a probing conversation with her husband. The large house reminded Bliss of his inability to compose in grand surroundings, which amounted almost to a phobia. Rather like his youthful dream about Beethoven, there was another dream he described following a visit to the Vatican, where 'I imagined how glorious it would be to work in one of the splendid long galleries… with a piano at either end. I would strike out a theme on Piano A and then slowly pace the 260 feet to distant piano B. By the time I reached there, my theme would have sprouted… In this way, treading many a mile, the musical conception would flower into finality. The dream was from every angle nightmarish, for I can only work in a small remote room, where every object and even muddle is friendly, and the cozy environment invites concentration and effort.'[28]

Two more piano works from this 're-start' time are key to our story. The first is apparently inconsequential *Toccata* written in London in 1925 and dedicated to his new wife. It's a four-minute stand-alone celebration work of considerable challenge to a pianist. It also marks a stylistic step forward in his piano writing from earlier works and leads straight to the *Suite*, which is the major piano work of the period. The *Toccata* reminds us vividly of Bliss's outward-facing stance. Here is a work that Prokofiev might have owned. Truly pianistic, light on its feet, celebratory in its evocation of pealing bells, lyrical in its contrasting central section, and humorous in detailing, and always having colourful sound worlds in his mind such as the section marked *quasi fagotti*. It's a tour-de-force.

But this short piece was just a warm-up for the *Suite for Piano*, which Bliss noted could be performed complete or its separate movements programmed individually. Why is this work so important? First, it is a major work for the instrument that, when played complete, is some twenty minutes duration. Second, it is deeply personal in a way that is relatively rare in Bliss's output. Going back to our initial search for hints in his music that would reveal Bliss the man, then here, especially in the third movement, an elegy for his dead brother, we have a gut-wrenchingly heartfelt piece from which it is almost difficult, even disrespectful, to move on to the dramatic final *Variations*, such is the emotional power that Bliss conveys.

One of Bliss's obvious traits discussed before is his sense of the dramatic which leads so naturally to his successful works for film and stage. Even this *Suite* begins with a short *Overture* which sets the scene and seems to demand that the listener move onto what follows despite Bliss's sanctioning of the extracting of individual movements. The movement is discursive and develops through figuration rather than theme. This kind of writing led to the pianist Mark Bebbington, who recorded all Bliss's piano music, commenting that 'his music needs the active participation of the listener; passive listening will reveal relatively little – the listener needs to engage constantly and Bliss doesn't hand over his music's riches easily.'[29] So there is a degree of enigma here, an enigma perhaps aimed at hiding what lies close beneath the surface. It is also suggested that there is anger present in the aggression of a number of his works and that this was a well-concealed personality trait.

If Bliss felt that he had to work hard on his return to England, it is also abundantly clear that he was wanting to move forward stylistically and not inhabit the audience-pleasing world of the music being written by contemporaries like Ireland, Howells or York Bowen. This is in no way to denigrate the fine piano music of these composers but to underline just how different – and *intentionally* different – Bliss's sound world was. Even the *Polonaise*, the second movement of the *Suite*, sounds deliberately subversive and when recognizable snatches of dance-like melody happen, they sound like faint echoes of a bygone age. Of course, the movement *is* a Polonaise with all its recognizable traits, but presented through a distorting mirror. Lively, effective, there is no hint of what is around the corner.

The *Elegy* dedicated to 'F.K.B. Thiepval 1916' is the most heartfelt tribute to his brother and also the only piece Bliss had written to date that shows the gaping wound left by his brother's death. Quietly crushing chords almost in the manner of a funeral march serve as an introduction without barlines. There is an extraordinary air of desolation. A downwards moving weeping figure supports a highly ornamented melody in a quadruple meter that moves the music forwards. A more forward moving version of the opening chords leads to a *quasi-chorale*, again with no barlines, just pause moments between phrases as Bach would have written. The passionately discordant climax of this section is breathtaking. Moving forward again, a massive and forcefully triumphant passage seems to say that what Kennard was and what he achieved in his short life will never be forgotten. The final bar is another quiet echo of the opening. The *Variations* that end the work are individual and based on a lively, slightly unevenly metered theme; a wide-ranging and stagey series of character sketches that could easily be choreographed.

Settling into a reconfigured life – marriage, re-establishing himself on the British musical scene, maintaining and developing his international presence and composing hard – made these early months in England a maelstrom of activity. But having already lost four years to the war and now three years to America, Bliss was really having to make up for lost time. However, America was by no means a fallow period as his experiences with Monteux and Stokowski were still ringing in his ears and this was about to bear serious compositional fruit.

The fact that he was very much in the minds of international bodies and musicians was borne out by an invitation to serve on the jury selecting new works for the 1926 International Society for Contemporary Music (ISCM) Festival. Bliss had attended the very first meeting of this new organisation in 1922 as we saw in the previous chapter. Now, given the responsibility with Edward Dent, his old tutor from Cambridge, Honegger, Scherchen and Szymanowski of selecting works, he experienced doubts about his ability to make the best selection. He, and his colleagues had the difficult task of estimating the worth of experimental scores, the effectiveness of which it was almost impossible to gauge, against those with more traditional presentation. The key thing for Bliss, however, was that he was there on the panel for this organisation that demonstrated the estimation in which he was now held by his continental peers.

The arrival of their first child in July 1926, only thirteen months into their marriage, showed how keen they were to start raising a family. Trudy gave birth to their first daughter who they called Barbara after the town where they met. As Bliss recalled 'Trudy's mother came from California for the event, and I certainly needed her affectionate companionship and support, my mood being one of anxiety and fear, then mounting to thankfulness, relief and pride... [Barbara] was soon to show evidence of her Bliss ancestry, just as our second daughter, Karen, was to be, in appearance and character, an obvious Hoffman.'[30] With all this creativity in the air, two works that Bliss had been hard at work completing appeared in close succession. Both reflected his admiration for his two conducting heroes of the moment, Monteux and Stokowski.

First came the *Introduction and Allegro* for Stokowski and the Philadelphia Orchestra. In a BBC broadcast he stated it 'startled me into a new conception of what orchestral tone could be.'[31] But that aural stimulus actually drew from him what was possibly his first recognisably personal work – a work in which the stylistic elements we are coming to know as Bliss's own coalesce here for the first time and, with some very notable exceptions, overlay the obvious homage to Stravinsky that has dominated his horizon thus far. Also key to this development is that what clearly emerges from this recipe whose ingredients we thought we knew so well, an emerging groundswell of romanticism that threatens the hitherto cherished modernity and overtakes it at key points. It is almost as if Elgar is throwing darts at a picture of Stravinsky and just missing the bullseye.

Something else that emerges from this score and which will occupy us as this story unfolds is Bliss's seeming inability to write a memorable melody. The simple melodic minor scale of D (leading up from the dominant) which, either in this version or its plain major equivalent dominates the work from start to finish, is a serviceable idea but no more. Oddly, the cellos' counter-melody that runs alongside it at the opening is far more interesting. But the two ideas together create a *mood* that is undoubtedly memorable. It is interesting that Frank Howes in his comprehensive study of *The English Musical Renaissance* writes that 'it remains true that Bliss is less successful with lyrical than with rhythmic utterance and he has never developed a personal idiom… he has remained an eclectic, and though his music is by no means derivative it does not bear an unmistakeable sign manual.'[32]

What is impressive here, however, is the mood of serious darkness, an elegiac atmosphere that is like a leitmotif nagging at Bliss's mind since Kennard's death. There is no doubt that he was compartmentalising the two distinct strands of his life – his domestic happiness, and his ever-present wartime experiences and losses that would not be exorcised until the writing of *Morning Heroes* in a few years' time.

The title of this work might indicate a clear-cut two-section form but Bliss's approach is more subtle. The *allegro* gathers pace out of the introduction but even when firmly established Bliss introduces two slower sections. The first of these *a tempo ma piu tranquillo* (figure 24) is decidedly Elgarian – lyrical and almost *nobilmente*. The pick-up at figure 27 transitions to Rimsky-Korsakov, and the *allegro* which follows at figure 29 takes us straight back to *Petrouchka* and the world of Stravinsky's fairy-tale. A hybrid, certainly, and as Bliss himself said, 'The final section in syncopated rhythm could not have been devised without my enthusiasm for Stravinsky. It was my sincerest form of flattery.'[33] But, as already noted, however much these major influences might raise their heads

99

above the parapet the final result is undoubtedly the Bliss we are learning to recognize. Given earlier comments about unmemorable themes, it is Bliss's approach to dissonance, which immediately identifies its composer and that can be as powerful an identifier as any melody or melodic shape. One of his most characteristic dissonances, noted in Chapter Three, is his subversive raising of either the root or fifth of a chord by a semitone, or using it as a minor ninth or minor sixth in a chord. This produces a very particular harmonic colour and in this work a prime example is at figure 24 (the first of the slower sections that has the feel of Elgar's shadow over it) where for the first two bars a B flat in the cellos and basses subverts the expected A, which should be providing the foundation for what is otherwise a plain second inversion chord of D major. It is little touches like this that, when they become a trademark, instantly say to us: Bliss.

The *Times* critic writing about the work's premiere at the Promenade concert in the Queen's Hall on 8 September 1926 reported that 'the new work shows a considerable development in Mr Bliss's style. There is less attempt to dazzle, and a more serious outlook than he has hitherto shown... The mere fact that one wants to hear it again is in itself a proof of merit. There were one or two flashes of the old *gaminerie* and a few unconscionably harsh moments, but on the whole Mr Bliss has turned to serious account his considerable gifts, among which his knowledge of the orchestra is conspicuous.'[34]

The other major work from this immediately post-American period is the *Hymn to Apollo* written, like the *Introduction and Allegro,* in 1926 and dedicated to Pierre Monteux and the Philadelphia Orchestra who had introduced his *Colour Symphony* to audiences in New York and Boston. The very different characters of these two works say much about Bliss's perceived differences in their approaches to conducting their orchestras. It seems more than coincidental that Stokowski should have the work with driving rhythms mirroring Bliss's comments quoted earlier about his *driving* of the Boston orchestra. The *Hymn to Apollo* is much more discursive and mirrors Monteux's highly personal and totally different approach, allowing more freedom of expression from his players.

In November 1966 Bliss was interviewed by the music critic and BBC music producer Hans Keller, which led to some fascinating reflections by Bliss, the first of which is worth recording here, despite being out of our timeline:

'I was in the Abbey at Bath. Suddenly the organ began, and I was immediately arrested by the most beautiful sound. I couldn't think what it was. I was so moved that I tiptoed up to the organ loft and there was a visiting organist… playing one of the *Méditations* of Messiaen. It was just a question of the superb registration: on getting a copy of the *Méditations*, I found that I wasn't so interested in the actual notes themselves, but I was absolutely thrilled with the sound they made; and that is one of the things that I feel essential in music.'[35]

This vividly describes Bliss's preoccupation with *sound* and his ear for colour, which he acknowledges takes precedence over everything else. He is seeming to say that the notes are subservient to the sound and therefore melody *per se* is not as important as the effect to which it is subservient. It was ultimately sound that caused him to revisit the *Hymn to Apollo* much later in his life and, as with so many of his works, make revisions. As he put it: 'It was after a second hearing at a Royal Philharmonic concert in London that I began to have some doubts, both about the proportions of the work and the actual sound of my orchestration. It didn't really fulfil what I had in mind. It was hopeless to tinker with it so soon after completing it, so I just put it by.'[36] It wasn't until forty years later that he made the revisions he felt were so essential.

'The *Hymn* is an invocation to Apollo as the god of healing, and the music moves like a procession of suppliants.'[37] So wrote Bliss of the work, and it is that quality of healing which informs the essentially gentle musical landscape. The 'healing' is undoubtedly the ever-present shadow of the war and his brother's death which, as we have seen, Bliss has tried to either express or exorcise in various compositions from these years. It is surely no coincidence that this work was completed a decade exactly (to the month) after Kennard's death.

In many ways the *Hymn* is a far more significant work than the *Introduction and Allegro* because it is not reliant on Bliss's bluster and his need to say 'sit up and take notice of me'. Interestingly, the *Times* review of the first performance on 27 January 1927 wrote that 'He has changed a good deal since the days when he entertained us with "Rout" and the like. This is a sober work, and will probably disappoint those who expect surprising exhibitions of up-to-datedness from him. True, there are some things which strike the old-fashioned ear as ugly – especially one passage of deliberate cacophony a little before the end. On the whole, however, it seemed to us interesting and finely thought, rather than felt, music, with a tone of voice of its own (a rather hard, steely tone), and a continuity of design which made it easy to follow.'[38] As often with these reviews they reflect more the prejudices of the reviewer than an objective view of a forward-looking piece of new music. There is, however, a real willingness here to see beyond the 'cacophony' to what Bliss was achieving. This demonstrates that he was now a composer whose music would be listened to with a sense of expectation. That is a moment of arrival and, for Bliss, a feeling that he had now, to a great extent, made up for his lost time.

By way of an epilogue to this moment of arrival and departure in his career there are two songs which deserve our attention from these years. The first is *Rich or Poor* setting a poem by W.H. Davies, whose poems he set several times, and the other is *A Child's Prayer* setting a gentle poem by Siegfried Sassoon. Both these are, in a sense, domestic offerings. The first, a reflection on his recent marriage, and the second a prayerful offering to his new-born daughter. Both have that gentle, slightly modally-inflected sincerity which comes from the deepest well of love, and it is interesting to reflect on the two kinds of love in Bliss's recent music: the desperation of love in loss, and the celebration, muted through the former, of love gained. Simplicity of expression packs the greater punch and although not 'simple,' the more heartfelt plea for healing in *Apollo* may hold a brighter torch in our search for the real Arthur Bliss.

# Chapter Six

# TOWARDS *MORNING HEROES*: 1927–1930

A priority for the Blisses was now to introduce Barbara to her grand-parents. Frank Bliss was now eighty and while still apparently strong and healthy was of an age where uncertainty is in the air. Living at such a distance meant that they had to take a significant time away from home to make the visit to California, travelling by sea and train. Before they left, Bliss had an invitation in a letter dated 18 February 1927 from Elizabeth Sprague Coolidge to write an oboe quintet for Leon Goossens to play at her Venice festival in September this very year. Bliss wrote warmly to her: 'I write at once to assure you I accept with great joy… It will be an inspiration to write something for Leon Goossens to play at one of your splendid concerts, and I am looking forward to doing a work worthy of that.'[1] In the same letter he says that 'little Barbara… pressed down several keys on the piano with evident enjoyment not unmixed with a frightening surprise.'[2]

On 31 July he wrote again to Mrs Coolidge from Santa Barbara to announce that 'your work for oboe and string quartet has been finished some four or five weeks',[3] indicating an intense period of work. As he remarked: 'The work is really quite an Anglo-American one, as two movements were written in London, and the third in Mohawk, among the Catskills (mountains).'[4] This was where he and the Bliss family had stayed on their way to California when Frank Bliss moved from England. It must have carried very happy memories to make him want to show Trudy the place and for it to inspire this music.

On 31 August, Bliss wrote to Mrs Coolidge to say that they would be arriving in Venice on 9 September, and how much he and Trudy 'were looking forward tremendously to being with you again, and if there is

any atmosphere more congenial for listening to music in, I have yet to find it. Affectionately yours...'[5] and he signs off with an unusually excited 'Hurrah' on a separate page.

The Oboe Quintet was the first of Bliss's works to be written with a particular soloist in mind. This would prove a seminal experience which would be repeated time and again through Bliss's career as he used the musicianship, depth of knowledge of the instrument, and virtuosity of particular soloists as a spur to his creative imagination. He remembered taking a gondola 'across the lagoons to the Lido to rehearse with the Venetian String Quartet, and the performance in the Conservatorio Benedetto Marcello was all that I could have desired.'[6]

The work itself is in three movements. The first is closely argued starting in reflective mood but moving to a scherzo-like central section before bringing back the opening mood again. The second movement is powerfully reflective and again has that quality of close thematic integration with a considerable intensity building as it proceeds. Its final bars moving into compound time act as a gentle bridge into the hijinks of the finale which has the lively *Connelly's Jig* built into it, suggested to Bliss by the critic Edwin Evans. The quintet is highly attractive work and is impressive for its skilful instrumental writing, for the total integration of the oboe part into the ensemble, and for its obvious sincerity of expression giving us a rare glimpse beneath the surface of Bliss's persona.

The quintet is dedicated to Mrs Coolidge who, in turn, presented the manuscript to the Library of Congress in Washington. The Blisses made their way home by car accompanied by Mrs Coolidge visiting Berlin, where they arranged a cinema party for her and her rather large entourage as a thank you for all she had done. Bliss was amazed by his wife's plucky dealing with the lack of sufficient seating for the group which was promptly dealt with by the manager in response to what Bliss called her 'imperious words!'

The next port of call was Amsterdam where they stayed at the impressive Amstel Hotel. Just before they left Amsterdam to continue to England Bliss wrote a touching letter to Mrs Coolidge:

*The Amstel Hotel, Amsterdam*

My very dear Mrs Coolidge,
I do not want to leave the hotel without writing you a letter of gratitude. These past few weeks from Venice until now have been one long
stimulating pleasure for me, and I feel that I go back to my studio
with renewed courage and with twice the determination to continue
writing.[7]

As for many composers, words form a deeply significant part of their creative process, and they can offer key insights into composers' minds, their psychological issues, their hopes and aspirations – in other words a kind of avatar which stands alongside and expresses in the third person what the composer then expresses in the first. It is a crucial relationship. We have seen Bliss's need for what he called a *donnée* or an external stimulus to his imagination to get his creative mind working. Words could fulfill that function. We will see how important this is later in the chapter in relation to *Morning Heroes* and shortly in relation to *Pastoral*. But it also leads us to question those works of his which are for voice with no words. How much of this approach is a genuine search for a new soundscape, and how much is it hiding from personal scrutiny – scrutiny which might come from examining a choice of text and inferring a state of mind or even a personal preference? Gerald Finzi, one of the greatest British songsmiths of the twentieth century, had no qualms about exposing his obsession with passing time and it was no surprise that he turned to Thomas Hardy to express in words what he needed to express in music. With Bliss there is a much greater reticence which contributes to our difficulty in removing the actor's mask and revealing the person beneath.

There are some poetry anthologies from the first half of the twen-
tieth century which seem to have been a source of inspiration to composers looking for texts. Robert Bridges' *The Spirit of Man* was one such published in 1915 in the midst of the ravages of wartime and

including poetry, prose and philosophical ponderings with the reader being invited in its Preface to 'bathe rather than fish in these waters' by the then Poet Laureate. A rather humbler anthology was published seven years later in 1922 simply called *Shorter Lyrics of the Twentieth Century 1900–1922*. This was compiled by the poet W.H. Davies whose Foreword is compelling in its plain-speaking honesty and its no-nonsense approach to the choices made for inclusion. 'It is not made out of friendship to certain poets, but from the pure love of poetry. That speaks for its honesty.'[8] The final paragraph of the Foreword has the most amusing quip: 'It is agreed that an anthology, to be good, must hold surprises … the worst poets have charged the highest fees for the use of their work.'[9] This plain speaking alone encourages further investigation of the collection as does his assertion that 'I am determined to run no risk of being offered a knighthood by omitting patriotic poems which, made for schools, are mostly bad.'[10] This slightly subversive approach will have appealed to Bliss who used the volume for his cycle of *Four Songs* which were premiered on 6 April 1927 at the Grotian Hall, London by Sybil Scanes (soprano), Paul Belinfonte (violin) and George Reeves (piano). This was, of course, before the Blisses left for the States. The provenance of these songs is unsure and Giles Easterbrook, in a forensically detailed prefatory note in the score, writes that 'all that can be said with accuracy is that *The Mad Woman of Punnet's Town* was certainly written after October 1922, that *Vocalise* was probably written in early 1927.'[11]

These songs are an example of the 'private' Arthur Bliss where there are glimpses of deeper things. Although written over a number of years it is likely that he conceived them as a set from the outset. They are unusual partly for their inclusion of a violinist as well as a pianist but, typical of Bliss in these earlier years, the two central songs are for voice and violin alone – again that keen ear for *sound* – and the third, *Vocalise*, is wordless with the voice and violin simply duetting in and out of each other's lines. This takes us back to earlier wordless works like *Rout* and *Rhapsody* but here put to much more reflective, personal ends. After the bleak imagery of Charlotte Mew's *Sea Love* this movement acts both as a gentle scherzo and also as a moving forward to the dark-hued, but fiercely energetic *The Mad Woman of Punnet's Town*. The choice of poems for this set tells us little, except that Bliss is able through them to find something that resonates and draws from him a surprisingly personal response.

Bliss first met the poet Robert Nichols back in 1917. He described their ensuing friendship as 'close but uneasy' and went on to say that 'His was a complex personality compounded of many warring elements. Sometimes he would be wildly exuberant and excitable, at others he would sink into black depression and self-pity. Always generous and loyal to his friends, he would then alienate them by some mad Quixotic action, embarrassing to both giver and taker…What kept our friendship alive was my respect for his creative gifts.'[12] It is notable that Nichols was invalided out of the army with shell-shock which may have had a profound effect on his subsequent life and explain some of his erratic behaviour. He died young, at the age of 51 in 1944. A mark of Bliss's respect for his work was the considerable proportion of his new choral and orchestral work, *Pastoral (Lie strewn the white flocks)*, which uses his poetry.

Bliss had been approached by Harold Brooke for a new work for his choir – the Harold Brooke Choir based in London. Brooke was also a Director of Novello's and promised that the work he wrote would be published by his firm which was quite an incentive for Bliss who at this stage had no relationship with a single publisher. Thus began what he described as a 'close alliance' which lasted for the rest of his life and included the Blisses' annual Christmas card (*see* overleaf) which was specially printed for them. Bliss wrote endearingly about Brooke after his death in 1956 in the *Musical Times,* pointing out that he 'entered my life at a time when I needed encouragement; as a wise counsellor he came to the first performances of all my music associated with his publishing house.'[13] Interestingly, Bliss remembered that Brooke disliked his early works but that at the point we have now reached at the end of the 1920s he began to 'feel an inclination towards my music.'[14] Bliss thought Brooke was a good choral conductor and observed 'I look back on the first performance of this *Pastoral* in May 1929 as being one of the most poetical it has ever received.'[15]

Perhaps the most interesting aspect of this new work is that it turns its back on the experiments in sound of recent times and moves on from where we can now see the *Four Songs* were leading. People had been made to sit up and take notice of the young firebrand but now, approaching a first stage of maturity, Bliss can begin to write the music that stirs him emotionally. In terms of his personal growth, that is a major step forward and a further step towards the cathartic moment of *Morning Heroes* which was just around the corner. Another spur to this change might be the rift with Elgar which had been sitting on the back burner ever since the *Colour Symphony*. In dedicating *Pastoral* to Elgar, Bliss was not only hoping to mend that fractured relationship but to answer the withering criticisms which Elgar had unkindly thrust at him. Thus, *Pastoral* is a key

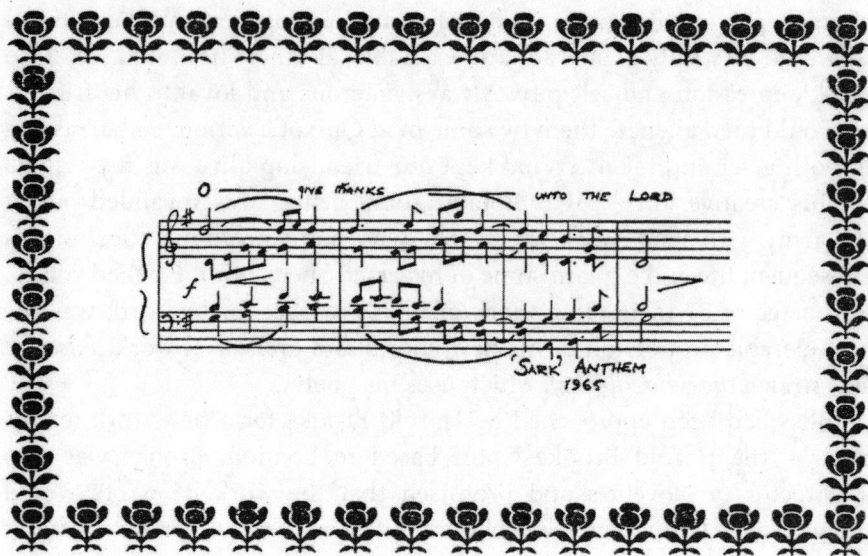

work in Bliss's development which stands aside from musical criticism and assessments of its worth.

Key, too, is Bliss's choice of texts for the work. It is the first time he used an anthology of poetry, something he was to do several times as the years progressed and which would be a key feature of *Morning Heroes*. As he put it, 'I found it very attractive to choose verse from quite different epochs, each poem having the same general subject as its theme. However widely separated the centuries, music has the mysterious power of linking them together.'[16] Thus, poems by Ben Jonson, John Fletcher, Poliziano, Theocritus and three by Robert Nichols make up the storyline depicting a Sicilian day from dawn to dusk.

The idea for the theme of *Pastoral* came to Bliss when he was holidaying in Sicily with American friends from Santa Barbara. They revelled in the beautiful scenery, Bliss singling out Palermo, Agrigento and Syracuse. 'It was in this latter place, when one morning I had set out to explore the site of the classical fountain of Arethusa, a copy of the *Idylls* of Theocritus in my pocket, that I found the theme of my choral work. The southern light, the goat herds, the sound of a pipe, all evoked the image of some classical pastoral scene.'[17] Perhaps unwittingly, Bliss is here, too, creating a dramatic *scena* as if for a ballet. This feeling is enhanced by the continuous nature of the work and perhaps especially in its orchestral interludes, most impressive of all being *Pan's Saraband* lying between *A Hymn to Pan* and *Pan and Echo*. Bliss's orchestration for strings, flute and timpani is highly economical and helps to create that state of simplicity born of the storyline. The flute part, almost naively reminiscent of panpipes, nevertheless builds on the numerous works already experimenting with arabesque-like figures which form such a feature of the writing here. The sense of sensual abandon in some of these flights of fancy reminds us that Bliss was still a hot-blooded young man who identified with the potency of youthful lust so key to these piping shepherds in this beautiful scenery. A further point is Bliss's use of the title 'Pastoral' which is an interesting about-turn given the prevalence of the English pastoral school in full swing and against which Bliss had been fighting with every fibre of his being. But *Pastoral* is no evocation of rolling Gloucestershire fields or of folksongs which might be associated with them. In fact, given the poems of Robert Nichols written in 1917 in the heart of the war, and coming from a volume called *Ardours and Endurances* the resonance of calm following the storm of war is clear to hear as is the delineation of the term 'pastoral' as a picture postcard and its other, classical illusion.

Frank Howes, always a keenly objective observer, felt that it contained 'some good ideas, "Pan's Saraband" for instance, but suffering as a whole from too much artifice and contrivance and too thick a texture.'[18] A curious conundrum, this, where it is Bliss's keen ear for sound and colour which has been such a hallmark of his style hitherto. But, thick-textured this work is despite its economical forces. Perhaps the best example of this and, *Pan's Saraband* aside, the loveliest movement in essence, is *The Pigeon Song* for soprano solo, flute and strings setting Nichols's deeply-felt love song. Bliss responds with an equally heart-felt musical response but where the flute trills to its heart's content in high register duetting with the singer, the strings, all divided except the double basses, create a heavy base for such high-flying love-making. It would seem that Bliss's intention was to create a wrap-around warmth of sound for this poem but instead the effect is, in too many places simply muddy. The sense of relief when the lower strings are silent is palpable. Oddly, there seems to be an aural hangover from Vaughan Williams's *Tallis Fantasia* but lacking that work's textural clarity. The start of the *Finale*, another orchestral interlude, is equally opaque with all strings, including double basses, now divided. It also pays unashamed homage to the English school before moving off into more familiar Blissian territory when the choir enters.

The anonymous reviewer (of the music, not the performance which he had not heard) in the *Musical Times* made this point: 'At a time when so much new music and poetry reflects something of the hardness and cynicism of a post-war and mechanized age, it is a refreshing surprise to find a composer of an extended work setting his scene in Arcadia, with fluting Pan as the central figure.'[19] But this is surely the nub of the matter for Bliss.

One of the most significant things to follow the premiere of *Pastoral* was Bliss's reconciliation with Elgar, who much admired the work. He wrote:

'Under conditions far from good I listened to the performance of the *Pastoral* you so kindly dedicated to me: the transmission or reception (I know nothing of the workings of the BBC with aerial sprites) was not good. But I could judge that your work is on a *large* and *fine* scale, and I like it *exceedingly*. The Pan sections suited me best but that is only a first hearing notion. Some of it puzzled me, but I am none the less sympathetic: thank you!'[20]

The time had come for the Blisses to move from their cramped quarters in Redcliffe Square to rent a large, spacious house overlooking Hampstead Heath. This was East Heath Lodge which Bliss described as having 'a fine position, abutting right on the heath, with a splendid view – from our roof we could look straight across to the Crystal Palace…(The) living-room on the first floor provided a beautiful studio to work in, and it was here that I started on my most extensive work since the *Colour Symphony*, a choral symphony to be called *Morning Heroes*, destined for the Norwich Festival of 1930.'[21] The very exclusive position of their new house served to underline both Bliss's own growing success and the privileged and monied background from which he came. Large, solidly-built house as it was, the piano at which, according to Bliss's wife, he always composed, could be clearly heard, giving her tantalizing snatches of a work in progress which she would eventually hear in a play-through once finished. In a delightful letter from Hubert Foss (founder and first music editor for Oxford University Press) to his wife Dora on 19 December 1928 he writes this colourful description:

'Then hurriedly to dine with Arthur Bliss. She (Trudy) is so charming – dressed in a very full and floppy pink flowered silk with a complexion like a peach – quite lovely. They have a house on East Heath Road which stands just above that triangle between E Heath Rd and Willow Rd – a lovely house indeed and quite beautifully arranged by them inside – a little attitudinising as usual from Arthur, but all very friendly and nice and comfortable. We discussed art and books and music all the evening – a very nice light dinner beautifully served and the studio afterwards, all very decorative and jolly.'[22]

It was a pleasant coincidence with far-reaching consequences that after the move to Hampstead the Blisses became acquainted with J.B. Priestley who, with his wife and young family had also recently moved to Well Walk, very close to the Blisses' house. Bliss described his high energy levels whether playing tennis or billiards, playing the piano or arguing a point, and as an excellent mimic. This key friendship was to become central to Bliss's life some years later when they collaborated on their opera, *The Olympians*.

In the summer of 1929 Bliss went to visit his father in Santa Barbara for what turned out to be the last time, soon after the premiere of *Pastoral*, sailing on the SS *Adriatic*. On his return he set to work on a completely different type of composition. It is a puzzle as to why this work, *Serenade* for orchestra and baritone (Bliss's title), seems to have been relatively overlooked in the Bliss canon. Not only is it a substantial twenty-five-minute work, but it is scored for an economically-sized orchestra and seems to place itself squarely between the modernist style of earlier works and a more lyrical, romantic approach which we have seen beginning to emerge. In fact, this work could be regarded as *the* pivotal moment when Bliss finally grows into his own skin. We recognize everything here but there is now a feeling of confidence in his voice which has been a long time coming and will reach full maturity in *Morning Heroes*.

*Serenade* is an orchestral work with a vocal element, not a song cycle with orchestra, hence Bliss's title. But it is also a 'personal' work; not because of any incident or commission, but because it is about love and is dedicated to Trudy. Bliss was sitting in an art gallery, looking at what he thought he remembered as a Fragonard depicting lovers desporting themselves in an arcadian scene, when the idea came to him of writing a 'vocal serenata' reflecting what he had been admiring: a lover courting his lady. He actually thought of reviving the tradition of the vocal serenata but there is no evidence of it leading other composers to follow his example. There are four movements which tell his story. The first is orchestral and describes the swashbuckling youth laying out his stall to gather the attention of his beloved. In the second he sings a setting of a poem *Fair is my Love* by Edmund Spenser as he settles down to his love-making. The third movement, *Idyll*, purely orchestral, is the depiction of his lady and is one of Bliss's loveliest creations. Its inspiration is obvious and very touching. The final movement is a setting of *Tune on my pipe the praises of my Love* by Sir John Wotton where the flute takes its cue from this injunction.

Christopher Palmer in typically adjectival mode puts it beautifully when he wrote: 'We know this Bliss very well – the orchestra flashes and crackles, rhythms dance and leap (tranquillity never absolute); chords, in avoiding the bland or commonplace, continually (and congenially), confound expectation.'[23] He also points out that his influences have been perfectly assimilated. This is true though they are still very much in evidence, particularly Stravinsky who is still Bliss's key reference point.

On 13 March 1930 Bliss was given the singular honour of presenting the Royal Philharmonic Society's gold medal to Ralph Vaughan Williams, and just a few days later, on the 18th, the first performance of the *Serenade* was given by the baritone Roy Henderson with the London Symphony Orchestra conducted by Sir Malcolm Sargent in the Queen's Hall, London at a Courtauld-Sargent concert. The *Times* reviewer was bemused by the whole enterprise feeling that the description of the lover in the first movement represented 'a rather unpleasant gentleman trying to show off to his lady', and that the *Idyll* showed that Elgar's influence was still very much alive. Overall 'These songs of tame vocal line and rather elaborate orchestral decoration leave one wondering what the composer has really intended to do with this Serenade of many ideas, none fully realized.'[24] But this was someone who obviously hadn't yet come to grips with Bliss's language. However, an objective observer might agree that the nature of the first movement describing the young man 'laying out his stall' is often curiously portentous and aggressive in contrast to the image portrayed by classic works of art showing the man as proud, yes, but also supplicant in the face of the beauty he hopes to win. This (like the furore over the title of the *Colour Symphony*) shows the inherent danger of the need for an external stimulus where another observer may have a wholly different feeling about what that stimulus may imply.

In relation to this, Eric Blom, writing about music in England in the twentieth century, makes this point about Bliss: 'Whether we like his music or not is a matter of indifference to him, or at any rate the artist in him. He says categorically what he has to say, and there is an end to it. Really an end, once he has finished a work, for he will make the next one an entirely different task. He likes setting new problems for himself over and over again and then solving them by finding a new style suited to them... Not all works will appeal to any one hearer. Some have been repellent, some almost enchantingly attractive; but each one has been, whether a work of art or only an *objet d'art*, shaped with unfailing skill and determination.'[25] This is a perceptive appreciation and allows

112

us to consider further personality traits: those of determination, of the ploughing of a personal furrow with single-mindedness (another aspect of determination) and being separate from current national trends which set him apart from his own contemporaries.

But is this self-imposed separation more of a realization that his musical offerings were very different from the way mainstream British composers were expressing themselves during these years, often with a lyricism which simply eluded him? It is quite possible that one of the reasons for his speedy decline in public consciousness after his death was that his music, however brilliant, descriptive, colourful or moving it might be, is simply unmemorable because of the lack of readily recalled melody, which helps to ensure longevity. Bliss's music grows from musical lines, however gestural the surroundings may be, and melodic invention is an important element of his work. It is therefore interesting to speculate whether this apparent weakness in Bliss's musical armoury may be due to his lack of formative choral background which was often a common feature of the development of many of his British contemporaries?

After all this, it is interesting that his next work would be a choral symphony, but not a choral symphony in the mould of any other of that genre. It is a good example of what Blom described above as Bliss making the next work 'an entirely different task'. Also of interest is the question Blom raised in relation to melodic invention. It is a legitimate question to ask, about whether a realization of his limitations had a bearing on the principal novelty of *Morning Heroes,* the use of a narrator rather than vocal soloists. More on this will follow later.

The Norfolk and Norwich Festival is one of the oldest in the country, tracing its roots back as far as 1772 as a fund-raising event to support the local hospital. For much of its existence it was a triennial festival that attracted major conductors as its Musical Director, with Sir Henry Wood in this role from 1908 until 1930. It was Wood, therefore, who asked Bliss for a major new work for his last festival. Bliss's response was of course a keen acceptance but then began his usual period of uncertainty as to what form the new work should take and what his *donnée* would present. Harvey Grace writing about *Morning Heroes* in the *Musical Times* before the premiere started his article with a thought-provoking pair of paragraphs in which he picked up a question put to him: 'How is it that while novelists and poets have during the past ten years produced a flood of books about the War, composers have been practically silent?'[26] He continues by suggesting that 'post-war literature has had the easy task of expressing weariness, disillusionment, disgust; it has been concerned with propaganda, and with the application of whitewash or pitch to the reputation of war-time politicians and commanders. Such things provide a fruitful field for writers, but barren ground for composers. Yet it must have occurred to many that by now, twelve years after the firing of the last shot, there must be something for music to say that has not yet been said – something that would attempt to deal with the heroisms and griefs, not of a particular war, but of war itself. At first sight it would seem that here is a task for the poet; but his medium is now print rather than the voice… An orchestral work might get near the mark… but… only the poet and composer working together, and speaking through orchestra and mixed chorus, could achieve the right blend of universality and detail.'[27]

We have no contemporary record of Bliss's habitual agonizing over his subject matter here and it may indeed be that, for once, he knew exactly what he wanted to write almost as if he needed a medical prescription. Chapter Two described in some detail Bliss's wartime experience, his lucky escapes from wounding and being gassed and the ever-present feelings of horror which, in common with all who fought, was never far from the surface of his consciousness. The loss of his brother, for whom he had both a profound love and deep respect, gave a singularly raw edge to the memories of those four terrible years. The nights were obviously worst when the subconscious really got to work and the nightmares came repeatedly. For him it was the same scenario again and again: 'I was there in the trenches with a few men; we knew the armistice had been signed, but we had been forgotten; so had a section of the Germans opposite. It was as though we were both doomed to fight on until extinction.'[28] As he went on to say, 'If sublimation, the externalizing of an obsession, can be thought of as a cure, then in my case I have proved its efficacy.'[29] This may be true insofar as curing the nightmares is concerned but one wonders if the anger, frustration and sadness ever left him as there are so many works which contain funeral processions, and the constant need to express aggression (however that is dressed up) has to have its basis in some psychological disturbance. In this connection it is interesting that the portrait of the young suitor in the recent *Serenade* which caused the critic to comment that he was a 'rather unpleasant gentleman' is a prime example of this which might, in fact, have elements of self-portrait about it where, instead of the classic image of the romantic suitor, we have a troubled young man laying his soul bare and expressing his need for solace in a soulmate. This is all conjecture but Bliss was perfectly capable of writing heart-warming music when so moved. As Christopher Palmer put it, 'The atmosphere of much of Bliss's best music is … predominantly tense and anguished; even the moments of lyrical serenity or confidence often cloud over and become troubled and apprehensive, filled with doubts and questionings.'[30]

What was, perhaps, Bliss's *donnée* for *Morning Heroes* was not the actual subject matter, though that will have been its initial impetus, but the choice of texts – another anthology – which he, again, gathered from a variety of sources from different ages and widely differing styles: Homer in the translation by George Chapman, Whitman, Li Po, Wilfred Owen and Robert Nichols. The effect of the variety of texts from such different sources is, of course, mitigated by the unity of the subject matter and also helps to make the expression of more universal relevance. All these poets resonated in some personal way with Bliss: his father had told him and his brothers Homeric tales on walks in their childhood, making a deep impression on his youthful imagination. He also remembered a boy at his first school in London who 'lives for me through his talent for drawing, and for sketches, mostly in ink, of a precise character. They were copies of warriors as commonly seen on Greek pottery.'[31] The distance in time of the Homeric tales from *The Iliad* somehow served to underscore the universality of war and its effects in whichever age it occurred. The importance of Walt Whitman to Bliss was discussed at the start of Chapter Two where he made the observation that *Drum Taps* was the only poem he had come across which had any relation to the feeling he had experienced in war. He used two of Whitman's poems from *Drum Taps* in *Morning Heroes*. Li-Po's poetry Bliss had set earlier in his *Ballads for the Four Seasons* and so was a familiar writer. This, then, brings us to the contemporary poets, Wilfred Owen and Robert Nichols. Nichols, again, we have encountered recently as one of the poets Bliss used for his *Pastoral* and who was also a personal friend (and who signed himself 'Thine tadpolean'). Owen, significantly, is new to Bliss as a composer, though he was a friend in pre-war days when they would meet up socially and go to concerts together. Surviving letters from Bliss to Owen show the ease of their friendship. That connection was obviously a driver in the choice of Owen's poetry for this new work written over thirty years before Benjamin Britten wrote his iconic *War Requiem* which was to refocus attention on Owen's war poetry (and the premiere of which was to have such a disastrous outcome for Bliss's *Beatitudes*). Added to this was the deeply personal connection Bliss felt through the death in combat of both Owen and his brother. The dedication Bliss decided upon was to his brother and also 'all other comrades killed in battle'.

The symphony is in five movements. The key slow movement acting as central focus has on either side of it a quick movement, and the first and fifth act as a prologue and epilogue; a palindromic shape. The opening orchestral prelude is quite unlike anything else in Bliss's output to date and is in style far closer to the symphonic style of Arnold Bax than anything we might have expected at this stage of Bliss's career. Additionally, the funeral procession which is underpinned by a gently treading double bass is also given an unmistakable reference to the famous funeral march from Chopin's Piano Sonata in B flat minor as if to connect it indissolubly to the theme of death.

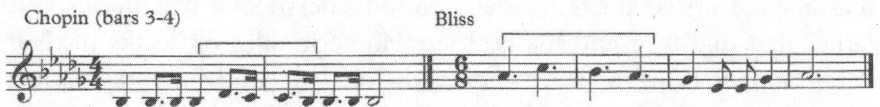

This is somehow emphasized at the moment where the narrator makes the statement: 'Come now, have pity and abide here upon the tower, lest thou make thy child an orphan, and thy wife a widow', at which point the horns announce the theme which accrues an added poignancy.

We must refer back to the issue of the oration. Bliss himself considered the pitfalls: 'The problem of mixing spoken words and music – so as to make the amalgam satisfying to a musical listener – has to be solved anew on each occasion… It can be argued that its use really begs the question, and that in any case the result is some "hybrid" or "sport", but I maintain that in *Morning Heroes* I was perfectly justified in nominating an orator to declaim the chosen texts. These depicted two intensely dramatic incidents, the first in prose, the second in verse. In both it was necessary that the words should be clearly projected, and that varying the pace at which an experienced actor might wish to speak them should be of prime consideration.'[32] He went on to acknowledge that there was an issue arising from the initial Homeric scene where there were two characters in play, Hector and Andromache, and that there was a case for making this an operatic duet. There is no doubt, however, that Bliss's decision to use a speaker was a very well-judged one. The dramatic potential is enormous, as he fully realized, and there is something incredibly powerful about the use of the spoken word especially in a situation where it is not expected and, whilst certainly not without precedent, is rare. Other composers would have found different ways of making this work musically, and there is still the issue hanging in the air of Bliss's questionable ability to make a

116

vocal duet as memorable and dramatic as he knew the simple inflections of an experienced actor could be. But let's not forget that this choice is as much a compositional one as deciding which instrument should play which line at any given moment. The key to this is what he chose to do with the orchestra throughout the narration and this is where we can now see Bliss's potential as a film composer begin to form. The whole focus of a listener's attention is on what is being declaimed by the 'orator'. We want to get involved with the story. The orchestra is therefore providing suitable background music which supports, only coming into stronger focus at key moments such as the one mentioned above where the 'funeral march' theme is played by the horns. Bliss has also thought very hard about the balance between speaker and orchestra so that there is no competition. It is all very skilfully done. What might be seen as slightly sentimental meanderings from the strings in this section is, in fact, mitigated by the power of the initial orchestral 'prelude'. The device of the flute arabesque which we have noted often in previous works comes into focus here sitting above the texture and drawing the ear, however unwillingly, back to the music which, as the oration continues and develops in emotional intensity, becomes increasingly present with brass chords accompanying Hector's prayer to Zeus for an illustrious future for his young son before everything subsides to the close of the movement.

What follows in the setting of Whitman's *Drum Taps* is an interesting amalgam of old and new for Bliss with stylistically backwards glances over the shoulder to Vaughan Williams's *Sea Symphony* (also setting Whitman) and Elgar in *Pomp and Circumstance* mode (and perhaps a hint of things to come in his role as Master the Queen's Musick). Given everything that has been said about Bliss's disconnect with the English school these are perhaps surprising until one remembers that he sang in the premiere of Vaughan Williams's symphony at Cambridge, and Elgar was an ever-present musical titan never far from the subconscious when needed. What is clear, though, is a sense of bedding down maturity in Bliss's language which is now undergoing the beginnings of a trans-formation into a more romantically conceived landscape which will develop strongly in the coming years. The language is still contemporary and there is plenty of acerbic discord which we have come to know as personal to Bliss, a key example of which occurs at the words 'At dead of night, at news from the south, Incens'd struck with clinch'd hand the pavement' (leading into figure 28 in the score). The movement is a tour de force of dramatic development, word play and choral writing which includes some highly effective work for double choir.

117

The story line of this work deals with various issues common to all conflicts. First, the poignancy of the farewell between husband and wife and in the second movement, *The City Arming*, what Bliss describes as recalling 'the spirit of devotion and self-sacrifice' in enlisting for service of thousands of ordinary people in August 1914. The third movement, *Vigil*, focuses first on a young wife who, left by herself, dreams of her distant husband to a poem by Li-Po and set for upper voices. We then return to Whitman and to the soldier who, solitary on his watch, thinks in his turn of loved ones left behind at home, set for tenors and basses. There are echoes here of Shakespeare's *Henry V* and the eve of the battle of Agincourt. The upper voices movingly rejoin at the very end with wordless, sadly falling phrases, which join husband with wife across the gulf of space and time.

The fourth movement, *Achilles goes forth to battle*, mirrors the second in being another fast, dramatic movement this time about heroism in battle. Bliss wanted to use Achilles as a pre-eminent example of manly courage who arms himself to avenge the death of his friend Patroclus. It is notable that it is Achilles who was responsible for the death of Hector who, in the first movement, was leaving his wife and son to fight Achilles, and it is Hector who takes the honours in the last section of this movement which is a roll-call of the most courageous men, Greeks and Trojans, from that time. If anywhere in this work seems to say 'this is my brother', this passionate final outburst which has a searing intensity seems to equate Kennard Bliss with this ancient, brave warrior.

What immediately follows brings this into sharp focus. The oration of *Spring offensive* by Wilfred Owen at the start of the final movement *Now, Trumpeter, for thy Close*, is seen here as putting voice to an elegy for all who died in that conflict, but perhaps most poignantly, as standing shoulder to shoulder with Kennard Bliss as two souls, personal to Arthur Bliss, lost in the midst of that mayhem. It is unbelievably touching. Where, in earlier movements, the poetry has been about other conflicts but with universal themes, we are now faced with the technicolour reality of the 1914–18 war from which there is no escape but from which, through this work, Bliss will be released from his eternal trench and find himself able at last to move forward. The work ends with a setting of a poem *Dawn on the Somme* by Robert Nichols relating specifically to the battle in which Kennard died. Starting with a dark, chorale-like music Bliss moves us to a feeling of triumph 'Oh, is it mist, or are these companies Of morning heroes, who arise, arise Toward the risen god, upon whose brow Burns the gold laurel of all victories, Hero and heroes' god, th' invincible Sun?' before winding down to a quiet a minor ending.

Critical comment following the premiere was enthusiastic and the *Times* on Friday 24 October 1930 reported: 'The significant fact is that the composer has set himself in his music to reveal thoughts out of many hearts. He has a great deal to say… and… we realize that Arthur Bliss has made his great step forward and, in saying what is old, has said something new and true.'[33] Sir Henry Wood in his autobiography remembered it as being a highlight of the '1927'[34] Festival and 'a work of great moments and one which plainly reflected the composer's wartime service.'[35]

Harvey Grace, writing in the *Musical Times*, quoted earlier, ends his article by writing: 'I do not feel that there is any risk of hailing "Morning Heroes" as an outstanding work. A study of the proof-sheets for the purposes of this article has moved and excited me to a degree that is new in my experience of mentally-heard music: and if the mere printed page can do so much, what may we not expect from actual performance?'[36] Ferrucio Bonavia writing a review of the whole festival in the *Musical Times* noted that 'It is strange to recollect that Bliss used to be the *enfant terrible* of our native composers: to-day "Morning Heroes" shows the unimaginable distance he has progressed from the days when the desire to build seemed, in him, synonymous with the itch to destroy. In the new work there is no trace of iconoclasm, of defiance of established forms courted for its own sweet sake. The key-note of the Symphony is sincerity of the profoundest kind.'[37] He goes on to say 'It is as a means and not as an end that Bliss now uses modern harmonic devices… Their existence springs from no desire to put himself "into the trick of singularity," but because he has something original to say and prefers to put new wine into new bottles. That the wine is good no one who heard the performance on October 22nd can doubt.'[38] One of the most telling comments he made later in the same review was that 'Bliss has never set patriotic bounds to his imagination: "Morning Heroes" could be sung in Germany without hurt to national pride….'[39] It is, in a very real sense, an elegy to war which is boundless and timeless. Bliss himself wrote that 'I cannot as an artist express war except in a general (timeless) sense. Achilles is THE hero, whatever humbler name he may suggest in the minds of us who live now; the parting of Andromache and Hector is the last glimpse that ANY wife catches of her husband; Manhattan epitomizes ALL "teeming and turbulent cities". Only in my reference to the Somme do I describe the particular (particular to us at any rate) and so approach more nearly the memory of him for whom this requiem was chiefly written.'[40]

Wilfred Owen's mother, Susan Owen, wrote to Bliss in appreciation of his use of her son's poem in *Morning Heroes* to which Bliss replied: 'Thank you for your most kind letter. I can tell you that the audience was profoundly moved by the recitation of your son's poem, and that at rehearsal those of the orchestra who were in the war were too affected for a few minutes to continue. It has been a quiet inspiration to me to be associated with such words, and I regret more than I can express the fact that I never had a chance to see and speak with him.'[41] Bliss had written earlier to invite Mrs Owen to the first performance and to offer her a seat next to Robert Nichols. She replied expressing her sadness in not being able to attend.

After such an enormous effort and the emotionally draining experience of completing this symphony, the next year, 1931, saw no high-water marks. *Morning Heroes* was performed at the Queen's Hall in London so marking the start of its journey to a wider audience and, in some senses, prophetic of the destruction of that very hall not many years later in the next great world conflict. But the great tasks of that year and into the following were the revision of the *Colour Symphony* and the composition of the Clarinet Quintet and the Viola Sonata. Bliss was now at the start of his forties and had reached the pivotal moment of transition into full maturity with *Morning Heroes* and was now producing some of his most valuable and enduring work. He was widely regarded as a major composer whose new work would always excite interest. But before new work was undertaken Bliss sat down to revise his *Colour Symphony* immediately after premiering *Morning Heroes*. Why was this? Was he simply in 'symphony' mode, or was there something about the earlier work he needed to bring into focus in relation to the new? Remember that the *Colour Symphony* was written in the raw aftermath of the war and it seems that Bliss wanted to revisit the earlier work almost as if he needed to connect his two symphonies, the second so overtly a requiem, to one person. Robert Meikle, writing about this revision has linked the new Trio 1 in the second movement (*Red*) of the revised *Colour Symphony* with the opening of the final movement of *Morning Heroes*. He makes a powerful case for that compound time melodic line with its rising leap followed by step-wise descent as seminal and, indeed, growing from the very opening of the whole symphony. This figure, as he writes, 'represents a goal – a kind of coming-into-focus – of their long-breathed 9/8 melodies.'[42]

The connection between these two themes in the second and third examples is plain to see. Now here are bars 6 to 8 from the opening of

*Morning Heroes*: we can see the theme forming in embryo, the quaver moving bass line and the rising and falling interval bracketed.

But why all this and, as Meikle points out, no mention in Bliss's writings of any significance attached to this obviously important figure? Here is my theory: Kennard Bliss was a fanatical Berlioz enthusiast and there are two connections which seem to coincide almost as a secret code from the third movement of Berlioz's *Symphonie Fantastique*.[43] First, its title, *Scène aux champs* ('Scene in the fields'), which carries with it that these are French fields, fields in which Kennard died. Very different, of course, from Berlioz's pastoral idyll, but that very contrast brings into sharp focus the serendipity of a moment in the world spinning on its axis. Additionally, at the movement's end, Berlioz portrays the distant rumble of thunder on the timpani that Bliss uses to accompany the recitation of Wilfred Owen's *Now, Trumpeter, for Thy Close*. This immediately precedes the next section of this movement with its compound time that equates strongly with the second point, the compound time flow of the Berlioz movement. We can see, too, the outline similarities between the principal musical ideas of both works; see the rising and falling figure at the start of Ex. 5, 6 and 7. There is thus a strong case to be made for a deliberate embedding within both these major works a personal, private connection with Kennard. Bliss noted in

his autobiography that at his last meeting with Kennard before his death he 'heard his gramophone (much Berlioz), saw his gun-emplacements and had a sumptuous meal'. The music remembered the last time he saw his brother was Berlioz; that must have gone in deeply.

It may also be that the making of this very private gesture to his brother played a significant part in the exorcism of the post-war nightmare lodged in his subconscious mind.

A huge blow fell on the Bliss family in 1931 when, so soon after Frank Bliss's death the previous year, Trudy's father died in an accident falling from a rock face whilst on one of his beloved botanical expeditions searching for rare plants. Trudy, who had been very close to her father, was deeply shocked and went out immediately to be with her family. Bliss followed soon after conducting the London premiere of *Morning Heroes* on 25 March in the Queen's Hall, taking advantage of the visit to see his recently bereaved step-mother.

In a very real sense, 1931 marked a watershed year for Bliss. He was now on the top of his game and ready to face the unexpected challenges, which would soon give him opportunities that would set him on wholly new paths.

## Chapter Seven

# THINGS TO COME: NEW PATHS

A project which straddles the cusp of the last chapter and this, grew out of a concert which Bliss attended with James Joyce, Eugene Goossens and Herbert Hughes, the Irish composer and music critic, at the Palais Royal in Paris on 28 October 1929. Hughes remembered: 'We were attending a festival of contemporary chamber music arranged by Elizabeth Sprague Coolidge, and James Joyce had accompanied us to the Palais Royal where works of Bliss and Roussel and others were being performed. The subjective association of chamber music – that is, of intimate music – with the poetry of Joyce was to us like the association of wind and wave, of light and heat; and the idea of this collaboration, urged by the emotional incidence of the festival, seemed to occur to us at the same moment.'[1] They carried on their discussion at Fouquet's restaurant and decided to make a volume of songs setting Joyce's *Pomes Penyeach* and dedicate it to Joyce. They agreed there should be a portrait (by Augustus John), and poets and other writers should join the musicians.

The original idea was to set five of Joyce's poems but then it was felt more appropriate to set the whole collection of thirteen. Bliss and Hughes approached a number of composers of whom E.J. Moeran, Bax, Roussel, Hughes, Ireland, Sessions, Bliss, Howells, Antheil, Carducci, Goossens, Orr and van Dieren eventually provided settings. Holst, Lambert, Walton and Warlock (who committed suicide in December 1930) didn't respond. Besides the frontispiece portrait, there was a prologue by James Stevens, an essay on *James Joyce as a Poet* by Padraic Colum, and an epilogue by Arthur Symons. The volume was eventually published in 1933 in a limited edition of five hundred copies. C.W. Orr wrote a rather scurrilous poem about the whole project, in the course of which he explained that the composers received no remuneration, but they were keen to be associated with it for their own profiles. In fact, the project was not a financial success and so Joyce, who was to receive the income generated by sales, ended up complaining that he didn't receive a penny. Stephen Banfield asserts that 'what is remarkable is that nearly all the English contributors were inspired to give of their best.'[2] Bliss's contribution was a setting of *Simples* and Joyce wrote to Bliss after its publication to say that he liked his setting more than all the others, but Bliss had a sneaking suspicion that, out of his natural Irish charm, he had written to all the contributors in a similar way! In fact, Bliss's song is a fine setting which Joyce described as 'rich and ample and melodious. Joyce's slightly nostalgic poem elicits a rich response from Bliss whose accompaniment is romantic to a point and further underlines his new direction of compositional travel. There was obviously something in this poem (in part coming out of his admiration for Joyce) which drew from him an unusually emotional response.

On 17 February 1932, the Blisses' second daughter was born: Eleanor Karen, known as Karen. This was a particularly happy moment in their lives following so soon after the deaths of both of their fathers. Bliss wrote that 'her gorgeous red hair was probably inherited from my mother's side of the family, some of my cousins having a similar shade.'[3] He also noted the generosity of his brother Howard in giving little Karen 'a magnificent painting by Matthew Smith' in the same way that he had done for Barbara.

Bliss was a highly sociable man who was adept at networking, so essential to the forward momentum of his career. Never one to purely take advantage of a connection or friendship, Bliss would often mark such a relationship with the dedication of a work which he felt was appropriate. Such was the case with Bernard van Dieren with whom Bliss had formed a friendship at the beginning of the 1930s and who Bliss described as 'the most enigmatic personality I have ever met' and that 'he partook of the nature of a Leonardo da Vinci, so multifarious were his inventive interests. He not only played a musical instrument, but he could make one, he not only wrote books such as his monograph on Jacob Epstein, but was a beautiful binder of books; he was a linguist, a chemist, and a composer of many songs and much chamber music.'[4] Bliss went on to say that 'continuous illness, borne with much courage, kept him mostly confined to his house, but friends went regularly to see him in St John's Wood as to some rare Delphic oracle.'[5] Van Dieren's compositional style was, like Bliss's, in a distinctly contemporary idiom, close to Schoenberg in the way Stravinsky was to Bliss, and having nothing to do with the English 'pastoral' idiom, although the dream-like qualities of his 1914 Symphony No.1 (Chinese) and the *Elegie* for orchestra and solo cello have a reflective feeling which, in other hands, could translate into an English soundworld. There is no doubt that Bliss and van Dieren, as two stylistic outsiders, would have hugely enjoyed their musical discussions and this is reflected in the dedication of Bliss's next major work, the Clarinet Quintet, to van Dieren as a mark of gratitude for the many happy hours they had spent together. It might also be said that the offering of *this* work is somehow a mark of particular affection for this quintet is at the epicentre of Bliss's high watermark of early full maturity. This was noted by the *Times* critic writing in response to the first public performance of the Quintet in which he wrote: 'In these chamber works Arthur Bliss seems definitely to have passed into a different phase of musical thought from that which dominated him when his work came conspicuously before the public ten years or so ago. He is no longer captivated by effects or tempted to follow the examples of contemporaries.'[6]

Eric Blom, writing in the *Musical Times* in May 1933, made heady claims for the work by stating that 'Only two composers having so far had an indisputable success with the combination of clarinet and string quartet, one must conclude that the medium is either extremely difficult to write for or is not worth tackling. The latter assumption is refuted by Mozart and Brahms... hence but two perfect works of the kind in a century and half or so. But now, I am very strongly inclined to say, there is a third.'[7] And so, at least in this critic's opinion, Bliss joins the pantheon of the truly great. Blom's argument centres around the problematical nature of pitting such a characterful solo instrument against a group of string players and avoiding it becoming a mini concerto. Bliss describes beautifully what he feels about the clarinet in a lecture on *Aspects of Contemporary Music* to the Royal Institution in 1934. He starts by describing the four movements of his Quintet: 'The first movement as calm and flowing, the second as energetic and spirited, the third as lyrical and romantic, and the fourth as gay and sparkling. These adjectives almost sum up the personality of the clarinet itself, one of the most lovely sounds we have in all music, and invented at the end of the seventeenth century. Just as Mozart exalted the role of the viola... so did he exploit to the full the possibilities of the new clarinet... It has a curiously varied manner of expression, being capable of sounding almost like three different instruments. In its high register it is brilliant and piercing, with an almost pinched trumpet sound; in its middle octave it is beautifully pure and expressive, with a clear even tone; in its lowest register it is reedy in sound, with a dark, mournful and rather hollow quality. It is an immensely agile instrument, capable of extreme speed and dexterity, both legato and staccato. It has a great dynamic range, extending from a powerful forte to the softest pianissimo than we have on any orchestral instrument.'[8] It is therefore clear to see just how well Bliss understands the instrument and, by his obvious enthusiasm, how much he will relish writing for it and exploring these different characteristics.

So, what is it about this work which ticks all the boxes and puts it up there with Mozart and Brahms, and why does Bliss barely mention it in his autobiography except in relation to Bernard van Dieren? A picture is gradually emerging in our search for Arthur Bliss through his music of a man, perhaps not so different from many, with a public face which says 'sit up and take notice of me' and a far more private face which, as time goes on, shows us a maturing, deep-feeling and very private face. It reminds us of the twin masks of the actor discussed in Chapter Three. But there may be something deeper here which may also be a cause of Bliss's reticence. The Clarinet Quintet comes after the revision of the *Colour Symphony* and its new connection with *Morning Heroes* discussed in the previous chapter. Now we have a major work for clarinet, Kennard's instrument. The subconscious is a powerful tool and it is quite possible that Bliss, who had described his brother as 'the most gifted of us all' wanted to write something deeply personal for him which was simply to be the best that the elder brother could produce – the only suitable tribute, perhaps, carrying his younger brother's talent forward in his mind. Where *Morning Heroes* was the grand requiem – a huge statement – not just for Kennard but 'for all comrades killed in battle', this quintet is the individual in intimate interaction with a small group allowing Bliss Wordsworth's 'thoughts that do often lie too deep for tears.'[9]

Eric Blom writes of the opening of the quintet in his *Musical Times* article quoted earlier that 'the clarinet begins alone with a long melodic line that seems at once vague and arid'. This seems to wholly misrepresent the spirit and, I am sure, the intention of this sinuous opening. In fact, knowing the likely inspiration for the work, it feels like the opening of a conversation started by the clarinet (Kennard) and which, initially being set up in the manner of a fugue, has the feel of an agreeable discourse between the participants. Notable, too, is perhaps the fact that it is the viola who responds to the clarinet, and Bliss, as we have seen, played the viola. The fact that this doesn't continue as a fully worked-through fugue is part of the picture-painting here as the conversation grows and develops with regular references back to that initial musical idea. A new theme appears as a contrasting second idea, and a recapitulation forms towards the end of the movement with echoes of both subjects. There is a wonderfully amiable feel to the whole construction before the fireworks of the next movement. The whole construct of this opening movement is interestingly summed up by William McNaught in his survey of *Modern Music and Musicians* when he writes 'Bliss has elaborated a musical texture of extreme interest. It has a peculiar inner mobility, exact and refined in its detail. The harmony has its own flavour of bitter-sweetness. There is no melody in the ordinary sense, no emotional effect of the traditional order. The effect is one of pure musical thinking, passionless and luminous, and expressing a highly articulate, if remote, order of beauty. Its spirit can be likened to the Greek, and its appeal is to a correspondingly limited audience. Bliss's best and most characteristic art therefore remains in seclusion.'[10]

McNaught picks up on elements of Bliss's work which have been commented on in earlier pages such as the issue of memorability of melodic lines and an unwillingness to share deep emotion in his music. But we have seen in these recent works, from *Morning Heroes* onwards, a far greater outpouring of emotion, and if anywhere shows Bliss wearing his heart on his sleeve it is in the third movement of this quintet, the *Adagietto espressivo*. Even in the tempo marking his intention is one of *expressiveness* and *how* the turning of the knife in an emotional wound is laid bare at key points, especially between figures 58 and 59 in the score (and picked up all over the place elsewhere) where powerfully lengthy appoggiaturas provide hugely dissonant harmony which aches for release to the inevitable concord towards which they are drawn like a compass to magnetic north, and this happens three times in succession. If this is not powerfully emotional it is difficult to imagine what Bliss could have done to intensify it further. But we can easily see the deep-seated emotional core here in this third movement. It is less visceral in the first movement but, in its own way, that haunting opening clarinet theme and the gentle fugal discussion which emerges is equally pregnant with emotion because it seems to be redolent of quietly-remembered domestic discussion etched into music but no longer possible in person.

The second and fourth movements are wholly different; the second is a vigorous scherzo but still with a very strong melodic element growing out of its second subject idea. The last movement is a brilliant *tour-de-force* and is almost determinedly happy which feels like a throwing off of the emotional shackles accrued through the earlier movements. In fact, one wonders if this is the final release of steam where that wartime nightmare was exorcised for good. All this shows that at key moments Bliss proved McNaught wholly wrong in his assessment, and that this Clarinet Quintet may be a benchmark work for everything which follows. Eric Blom made this elegant summing up: 'The combination of clarinet and string quartet now has three works worthy of filling an evening with sterling music, and they might well be given in chronological order: Mozart for elegance and easy enchantment, Brahms for deep but sober feeling, and Bliss for gracious diversion and the satisfaction of finely poised sensibility. It is no mean tribute, but the most recent of the three Quintets may safely be put last in such a programme without any falling off.'[11]

The first performance of the Clarinet Quintet was given by Frederick Thurston, the doyen of clarinettists of the period, with the Kutcher Quartet in a private performance at the Blisses' house in Hampstead on 19 December 1932 with the same performers giving it in public for the first time at the Wigmore Hall on 17 February the following year. This artistic connection with great performers was a major driving force for Bliss's creative imagination and, as we have already seen, Leon Goossens and Frederick Thurston had already been key to the success of the Oboe and Clarinet chamber works, and it was now Lionel Tertis, the viola player who single-handedly rescued the instrument from its reputation as Cinderella of the string family, who was the inspiration for Bliss's next major work, the Viola Sonata. As Bliss wrote, 'Musically speaking, 1933 was marked for me by my friendship with Lionel Tertis, and the completion of a large-scale Sonata for him. Tertis...was not only a master player, but the inspirer of a whole school of playing.'[12]

The magnitude of Tertis's achievement and reputation spurred Bliss on to writing not only a very large-scale work, but one which he later described as 'becoming a concerto for the instrument'. He even considered the possibility of orchestrating the piano part. Tertis's involvement during the composition process was, as Bliss noted, 'a master class in viola playing quite free, and I am grateful.'[13] The seriousness with which Tertis approached Bliss's intentions showed first, that he considered the work an important addition to the viola repertoire and, more, that no detail was too small to escape his notice and intention of realizing the most effective performance. Bliss, for instance, remembered being telephoned and asked which of two versions he preferred of a particular moment. He could hear no difference. 'But you *must*, the first time I took two down bows, etc..'[14]

1. Frank Bliss, Bliss's father, in 1896. (Cambridge University Library (CUL))

2. Agnes Bliss, Bliss's mother, in 1896. (CUL)

3. Hawthornden, Queen's Ride, Barnes: Bliss's birthplace. (CUL)

4. Bliss in a sailor suit in 1895, aged 4. (CUL)

5. Left to right: Kennard, Arthur, 'Duddle' (Miss Whiteford), and Howard. (CUL)

6. The Bliss family in their car with chauffeur, early 1900s. (CUL)

7. Arthur, Howard and Kennard at Shanklin, Isle of Wight, in 1898. (CUL)

8. The three brothers playing their musical instruments at Cradley Rectory, Herefordshire. (CUL)

9. Kennard in uniform, 1916. (CUL)

10. Arthur in uniform, 1916. (CUL)

11. Howard in 1917. (CUL)

12. George, Bliss's half-brother.

13. Three Choirs Festival group, 1922 (premiere of *A Colour Symphony*). Left to right: Bliss; Herbert Brewer; W.H. Reed; Elgar; Eugene Goossens; and an unknown lady. (Desmond Tripp)

14. Arthur and Trudy's wedding, Santa Barbara, 1 June 1925. (CUL)

15. Elizabeth Sprague Coolidge; portrait by John Singer Sargent. (CUL)

16. Ernest Makower (with kind permission from the Makower family archive).

17. Pen Pits. a) The Music Room. b) The veranda. c) The Blisses with architect Peter Harland (on the ladder). d) Side elevation.

a) J.B. Priestley at the time of *The Olympians*. Photo by John Gay (National Portrait Gallery)

b) Christopher Hassall in 1955. Photo by Howard Coster (National Portrait Gallery)

c) Kathleen Raine in 1971. Photo: Pamela Chandler (Performing Arts Images/ArenaPAL)

d) Eric Crozier in 1965.

18. Four librettists.

19. Signed card from Stravinsky to Bliss. (CUL)

20. Bliss family at Moosehead Lake, Maine, USA, just before the start of the Second World War, 1939. (CUL)

21. Santa Barbara group with the Henry and Ethel Eichheim seated next to Arthur with Howard standing behind. (CUL)

22. Arthur and Trudy skating in 1929 on Hampstead Vale of Health Pond.

Tertis was accompanied by Solomon in the first performance which took place at the Blisses' house with William Walton turning the pages. Tertis wrote that 'This first hearing of a most valuable addition to the viola repertoire was a private one, on 9 May (1933) at the Blisses' delightful home ... to a very distinguished gathering of musicians... It was a most exciting occasion, and we subsequently played the work many times in public.'[15] Tertis also made the point about how 'our rehearsals over the years included hours of striving to grasp the fullness of the composer's intentions, and we practised interminably to try to achieve perfect balance of tone.'[16] A further point was made by Bliss in relation to performing this work but affecting all his music, the question of tempo. He felt he could live with wrong notes and disregarded dynamics as long as speeds were right. This instinct for pace goes way back but it also emphasizes his feeling for the dynamism of his music – fast or slow – and his work with film and stage which was just around the corner demonstrated just how important this instinct was. He was genuinely distressed in recollecting performances of this Sonata which could take as much as three minutes longer than it should.

The Sonata is a four-movement work, or perhaps a three-movement scheme with an extended *Coda* which follows on *attacca* from the end of the dramatic third movement and which acts as a kind of retrospect during which there is a summing up and a revisiting of the first musical idea from the opening movement. This first movement has elements of the conversational feel created at the start of the Clarinet Quintet and some of that work's finely-wrought and intricate detailing in the interaction between viola and piano and in the piano figuration. Another important element is Bliss's personal 'take' on Sonata structure which, while classical in feel, and with plenty of both contrasting material and sense of development, does not obey the classic rules. Why should he conform when a contemporary composer is more interested in bending a scheme to his will in order that he can better express what he wants to say and moving music forward in the process? The critic Hubert Foss wrote of this work that 'a new manner has been found which more nearly expresses for musical uses the thoughts of the composer.'[17] It throws up the use of the word 'Sonata' in the same way that *Morning Heroes* is described as a 'symphony'. These terms imply a seriousness of intent, and certain expectations in terms of form and content as well as, perhaps most interestingly from Bliss's perspective, an approach to absolute music (as opposed to music written to a 'programme') which we had hitherto thought he found impossible without a *donnée*. In fact, the two chamber works really give the lie to the assumption, encouraged by Bliss, that he found composition difficult without a pictorial or other image to fire his imagination. And yet, we must be careful not to take this wholly at face value for the Clarinet Quintet was very obviously inspired by Kennard and the playing of Frederick Thurston just as the Viola Sonata was the inspiration-child of Tertis. Thus, we can see that the *donnée* took various forms for Bliss and we will see this continuing in compositions soon coming down the line.

The Sonata is a romantic work. Saying that baldly sounds almost heretical after all we have been through to get to this point, and the word has raised its head here before. But there is no disguising the assimilation of style and content into this melting pot of what can only be described as personal outpouring. The second movement of this Sonata for all its contemporary-feeling harmony and chromaticism is a deeply-felt song for the instrument. The third movement Bliss calls *Furiant* which, in its purest sense, is a Bohemian folkdance with an alternating 2/4 and 3/4 metre used by Dvořák and Smetana. Bliss takes the sound-world of the word 'furiant' as a ferocious (and ferociously challenging) dance and does indeed introduce changes of metre from two to three and back again as the movement progresses. But it is the incredibly virtuoso end to the movement which shows just how far Tertis had taken the instrument's possibilities to which he referred in his autobiography: 'I reached the age of sixty-five at the end of 1941, and the BBC invited me to broadcast in celebration of my birthday. The BBC broadcast concerts in the middle of the night at Evesham in Worcestershire in 1942, and I remember playing the Bliss viola sonata... at about three in the morning when my colleague Frederick Riddle (also a violist) was broadcasting in another studio. When I finished playing the work he burst into the studio and his first words were: "How the devil do you get up to that last bar in the third movement?"... My reply was: "The Lord only knows... Somehow my left hand at the end of a violent passage reached top E in the treble clef perilously close to the bridge." '[18]

Foss sums up his *Musical Times* article by considering major works for the viola including Hindemith's two concertos but ultimately claiming that 'of the game shot down by Tertis's inimitable skill, I should be inclined to claim this Sonata as one of the first in importance. For it occupies a place of importance in the career of Bliss as a composer, and unless I am greatly mistaken, a rare one in the annals of modern English music.'[19]

Not long after the first public performance of the Viola Sonata, Tertis gave another performance but this time accompanied by Rubinstein.

Bliss remembered that 'he had the score a day or two before the concert, but despite that he gave an electrifyingly assured performance. It is a wonderful moment for a composer when he hears his music given a deeper significance than he himself thought it could bear.'[20] Tertis remembered it slightly differently: 'Rubinstein arrived from the Continent only on the morning of the recital, and he had never seen Bliss's work. The crossing from the Hook of Holland had been rough – he had twice been thrown from his bunk. He turned up smiling all the same, and the moment he arrived we had the rehearsal and the usual balance-test in which he read the difficult piano score at sight. At the recital that evening he gave an astounding performance, making light of the intricacies and technical difficulties of the piano part, and his interpretation was perfection.'[21] Whose version of events of what really happened is pure speculation but Bliss's seems rather more likely.

The BBC and Bliss were destined to be deeply entwined. His close friendship with Adrian Boult who had been Director of Music for the organization since 1930 almost guaranteed that he would be drawn in in some way or another. We have already seen his positive views about the BBC's educational possibilities and there is no doubt that he very much approved of the direction the Music Advisory Committee was steering the programme content not bowing to a lower common denom- inator but bringing the listener's discernment to a higher level. Bliss's international reputation, his connectedness, and his nose for diplomacy recommended him for a new role as a musical adviser. It was recognized that Boult's responsibilities and pressures divided between administra- tion and conducting were too great and that he needed an assistant. All parties who were consulted about approaching Bliss for the post were enthusiastic. After being invited, however, Bliss refused to entertain the possibility of a full-time post. 'No composer could preserve his integrity under these conditions.'[22] Bliss went on in the same letter to propose that he be appointed as a Musical Programme Adviser, whose function it would be to attend all weekly meetings of the Programme Committee... 'and to be responsible to you for the suggestions made and decisions taken at those meetings with regard to all musical performances.'[23] He also asked for an office in Broadcasting House and a minimum salary of £750 a year (roughly £54,000 today). He finished his letter by pointing out that these things are 'compatible with my own personal position in the musical world.'[24] Bliss knew exactly where he stood.

Bliss was something of a wild card in being a passionate advocate of contemporary music. The Music Advisory Committee was peopled with the great and the good of big musical institutions and chaired by the Professor of Music at Oxford (Sir Hugh Allen). Inevitably this led to a rather reactionary set of views around the table and once they were presented with the proposal that Bliss join their number there was some alarm. This was presented as concern over Bliss's proposal that the job should only be part-time. Lewis Foreman, in an article about Bliss and the BBC, laid out clearly one of the principal battlegrounds. In 1936 Ernest Ansermet was being assessed as a conductor. Sydney (S.P.) Waddington and Benjamin Dale 'were dismissive – presumably associating him, as the champion of Stravinsky, Honegger and Prokofiev, with modernist works – Bliss, however, championed him. Waddington and Dale repeated their opinion that Ansermet is a second-rate conductor, but Bliss strongly defended him on the grounds of a specialist who gives certain modern music in quite an individual and what may be described as an inspired style.'[25]

In order to deal with these seemingly irreconcilable issues the recommendation was made for the formation of a smaller panel to meet weekly and, as Foreman suggests, 'by his knowledgeable and forthright style (Bliss) came to exert very considerable influence, with the general support of Adrian Boult.'[26] Part of the role of this group was to act as readers for recommending new music for broadcast, or, indeed, turning it down. But in his role as a member of the larger committee he was deeply dissatisfied with the way the proposals put forward by the committee were constantly being turned down or ignored by the higher authorities. A letter he wrote to Boult about this was passed up to the higher command and Bliss received a fairly stinging, and extremely lengthy, rebuttal of his points from the Deputy Director General. Undaunted, Bliss responded immediately with the opening gambit of 'my letter was not written either in ignorance or in a carping spirit of criticism. My object was a humbler one. As I see it, the only raison d'être for the existence of the Advisory Panel is the opportunity it gives to offer constructive comment such as a new comer in any organization can often profitably do.'[27] He indicated that he would continue writing to Boult with further thoughts. It was typical of Bliss that if he took on a task he would throw himself at it and take on all comers.

The key point with which all this had started was the proposal that Bliss should assist Boult and help reduce the latter's workload. Bliss's suggestion that he might take it on as a part-time post had foundered but Boult's urgent need of help, and the long-running saga almost inevitably ended up in the press with *The Morning Post* of 25 September 1935 announcing, erroneously, that Bliss was in the frame for the post of Director of Music at the BBC, and writing that 'he should be able to puncture corporational pomposity as effectively as did Dr Adrian Boult.'[28]

In the end Bliss left the field and the post of Assistant Director of Music went to Reginald (R.S.) Thatcher who stayed on briefly before moving as Warden and then Principal of the Royal Academy of Music. Bliss remained on the Music Advisory Committee attending the weekly meetings, but his deeper involvement and a staff post were still a few years away during the war.

After all the frenetic compositional activity leading up to 1933, 1934 arrived with something of the feel of a sabbatical about it. There are no new works performed, and while there are exciting paths being explored to which we will come soon enough, there was another preoccupation of a more domestic, but no less artistically significant nature being planned which absorbed the Blisses at this moment. Despite the lovely situation of their London home next to Hampstead Heath they began to hanker after a place in the country to which they could retreat in the spring and summer giving their young family a different experience from the hothouse of London. Trudy began the round of estate agents which was frustrating and counter-productive, finding nothing which really fitted their desired specification for somewhere peaceful and secluded. Eventually, the obvious solution presented itself on finding an ideal thirty-acre wood for sale in Somerset in which they could build their own house with a separate music room for Bliss's private study. The memorable date of finding the site was 10 January 1934. Bliss described it like this: 'The land was a tangle of undergrowth and, indeed, almost impenetrable in places, but it stood high and when cleared would have a fine view right to Salisbury Plain. The village was named Pen Selwood (the 'head' of the old forest of Selwood) and the site we had bought was named Pen Pits, and rightly so, for over practically all of it stretched circular pits some 20 to 30 feet across, out of which grew oaks and beeches. In some places the rims of the craters touched, giving the ground all the appearance of having been shelled by howitzers. Archeologists differed as to the origin of these pits, but all agreed that they were very ancient, and might have been excavated by seekers after special flint stones. Later history maintains the possibility that Alfred used the site as a camp during his struggle with the Danes. It had a dramatic look, and I remember, when the house was built and Paul and Margaret Nash came to stay with us, how the painter delighted in making sketches of these moon-like craters with their attendant trees.'[29]

Bliss's colourful description shows how deeply impressed he was by the whole *feel* of the place and he obviously sensed right from the start that it was a good place for creative work. Many people, on entering a house they are considering purchasing, have a gut feeling about a particular property. Some places draw you in and feel 'meant', others discourage by odd feelings which niggle in the mind. Pen Pits *felt* right and now followed the major decision about which architect should be commissioned to design the house.

Amongst their close friends the Blisses numbered the architect, Peter Harland. He seemed the obvious choice to design the new house for this unusual site. The key element was 'light, air and space' and a wholly contemporary approach of essential simplicity and beauty of line was the ideal outcome. Originally, Harland had suggested the shape of a grand piano as seen from the air, but expense made this impractical. As it was, a drive had to be created, the site levelled, walls built to buttress a lawn, a disused cottage (becoming a gardener's cottage later) made habitable for the Blisses to live in during construction, and a separate music room built some distance from the house. It was a huge undertaking.

Harland's daughter, Julia Waddell, remembered being told of their unconventional site visits, 'with the three of them camping in a tent on the site where the house was to be built. Trudy, with her American background and love of outdoor life, was organized and loved it, Arthur and Daddy confiding to each other they longed for the house to be finished (which it was on 23 February 1935) and were missing their home comforts – it always seemed to be raining.'[30]

Harland was not a committed modernist at this point although he had designed two isolation hospitals of distinctly contemporary design. His connection with the Blisses came through Grace Lovat Fraser. She had been the soloist in Bliss's *Rout* back in the early 1920s and was the widow of the artist Claud Lovat Fraser, Harland's cousin, who had died at the age of thirty-two whilst on holiday with Paul Nash and his wife in 1921. Claud's tragic early death was a severe loss to Bliss, who found his work, especially his set designs, inspiringly creative.

Harland created a remarkable house for the Bliss family that is now the only unaltered piece of his work of stature remaining (the Finzis' house at Ashmansworth, near Newbury, having been added to in recent years). Of his other work, one of the isolation hospitals was demolished in the 1990s and the other has been largely altered. It is a sad reflection that after the war Harland's architectural practice never regained its pre-war reputation.

The house itself has something of the feeling of an ocean liner about it with its long elegant lines, its white colour and its substantial ground floor terrace and first floor sun deck (complete with outdoor shower) connected by a fixed outdoor ladder which is very much part of the design. The water tank and chimney stacks on the roof 'projected like ships' funnels outlined with blue paint'. Trudy Bliss acknowledged Harland's skill as a landscape designer when she remarked that 'with his advice on planting and the choice of trees, the whole conception of the house was tied in to the beautiful layout of the ground around it.'[31] Alan Powers' informative article about Pen Pits and Ashmansworth in *Country Life* also details the interior in which 'the colour continued with a salmon-pink telephone to match the stair-hall curtains, above a crotchet that figured in the lino floor. In the sparsely furnished living room was a large Navaho rug and another rug made by Trudy Bliss to her own design influenced by Ben Nicholson's painting of the time.'[32] Nicholson was another of their friends with whom Bliss played table tennis. Paul Nash was a regular visitor and was made to feel very welcome in the modernist surroundings. His painting of *Landscape at Pen Pits* which hangs at the Victoria and Albert Museum in London was not originally connected with the Blisses' property.

There was no electricity to the house (or the nearby village) until after the Second World War, so it was lit by oil lamps. Bliss even had to use a wind-up EMG Gramophone in his music room. The music room in the woods was a timber structure supported by brick piers and was apparently very damp according to Bliss. 'One morning as I was playing (the piano) I suddenly heard within a few yards what sounded like a gunshot. I leapt to my feet in alarm and ran to the window; nobody was to be seen, and with beating heart I went back to my piano. I then found one of the bass strings had snapped, and it was this startling sound, in my over-reverberant wooden hut, that had led me to believe I had been shot at.'[33] Edward Wadsworth's wonderful painting of Pen Pits (*see* plate section) perhaps sums up its holiday character best of all.

It is interesting how Gerald and Joy Finzi came to the same conclusion as the Blisses in deciding to build their own house, having rejected more than a hundred on offer from agents. Visiting Pen Pits and staying with the Blisses confirmed their decision, although they favoured a more traditional 'farmhouse' design for their sixteen-acre site with its extensive views over the Berkshire countryside. Each house is a fascinating reflection of the outlook and compositional styles of the two composers.

The Blisses were now admirably set up with a lovely house next to Hampstead Heath (which they rented) and a superb country house in Somerset. Coming at the moment of the creation of some of the most significant compositions of his career, it reflects a new maturity, as well as a sense of arrival and departure. And 'departure' was certainly the unexpected twist in the tale during the building of their new house. Bliss had been asked to give a series of lectures on *Aspects of Contemporary Music* at the Royal Institution on 8, 15 and 22 of March 1934. H.G. Wells attended one of them, and Bliss rather modestly claimed that he didn't know why Wells had chosen to come – citing the possibility of seeing how someone else coped with the ordeal of lecture-giving, given Wells's own severe aversion to it. But, given that Wells was already working with the producer Alexander Korda on the film of his book *The Shape of Things to Come* he was obviously searching for the composer he felt he could work with and who would articulate, musically, his utopian vision of hope, order and world peace.

We don't know which of the three lectures Wells attended, but if it was the second, he would have heard Bliss state an artistic credo which is unequivocal in its directness of purpose:

'I believe that the foundation of all music is emotion, and that without the capacity for deep and subtle emotion a composer only employs half the resources of his medium. I believe that this emotion should be called into being by the sudden awareness of actual beauty seen, or by the vision of beauty vividly apprehended. I believe that the emotion resulting from apprehended beauty should be solidified and fixed by presenting it in a form absolutely fitting to it, and to it alone. If I were to define my musical goal, it would be to try for an emotion truly and clearly felt, and caught for ever in a formal perfection.'

He also stated that 'I do not profess to know, nor do I very much care, what is the latest thing in the world of music, or what the best people, for instance, should listen to in 1934. Music is not a fashion like women's hats... nor is it the plaything of a small and possibly vanishing social order... It is, on the other hand, a great and permanent enrichment of mankind which every fifty years or so receives such an additional impetus that the centre of gravity in music has shifted.'[34] This, plus the next statement, 'Everyone at twenty... should think that the new is all-important... But at forty, one should be not so shuttle-minded'. This is a reminder to himself that he, at twenty, was doing everything he could to be noticed but now, at forty, was in a deeper groove and past the shock tactics of his youth. But there is one more paragraph in his second lecture which seems to stand out and might well have set Wells thinking and it is this:

'Now for the machine. The conception of the machine as a thing of beauty was bound to influence music some time or other. It has been for a long time apparent in plastic and pictorial art, where we find artists scattering fragments of machines plentifully through their canvasses, and sculptors especially pleased to reproduce forms that resemble engineering models. Many machines which we see on every side of us undoubtedly possess in their lines and volumes a perfection that can well be called beauty, and this is all the more striking when these machines are related to some notion like speed, precision, power. It is perfectly natural that creative artists should try to transfer the qualities of perfection that are expressed in the machine into their own work. The texture of their work can be made more functional – every line in it can fitly play its part – there should be economy of space and material – it should generate power, race with speed, be capable of unerring and effortless precision.'[35]

Bliss then went on to refer to Stephen Spender's *The Express* and Honegger's *Pacific 231* calling them 'a new Romanticism, a sentiment evoked by the power of man-made inhuman mechanical perfection, but a sentiment just as extravagantly romantic as that of the nineteenth century founded on human individualism and liberty.'[36] Perhaps it was this seemingly unlikely territory into which a composer was straying which made Wells think that here might be someone with the right kind of imagination to be able to express his futuristic vision in musical terms. In fact, Bliss recalled this: 'One section of the film was actually shot to my musical score: there was no dialogue in it; the sequence dealt exclusively with the machines of the future.'[37]

Machines of the future were key to Wells's visionary novel published in 1933 which begins in 1940 and ends in 2054. Written in a time of world unrest with the Great Depression, widespread unemployment, Russia still coming to terms with its new political system and further problems seemingly around every corner in the West, Wells sees a way through apparently endless war to a utopian vision of peace. He predicts the coming Second World War by describing the start of a global war that lasts for so long that people forget why it was ever started. The whole world is in ruins and technology seems only to exist to advance war. In 1970 a move is made towards peace where a group of surviving engineers called 'World Communications' have formed a body called 'Wings Over the World' to outlaw war, rebuild the world and promote global peace. They drop sleeping gas 'globes', a 'gas of peace' on the town central to the story called 'Everytown' killing its war-like 'boss' and a new world order is gradually established with a huge programme of reconstruction. In 2054 a little girl is shown a video history by her great-grandfather who laments the wasted and destructive years but is also wary of the speed of current progress. He is particularly concerned about a project to build a huge space gun to send a manned capsule around the moon. This concern is picked up by others and causes a protest against such advancements which threatens the moon launch. A mob sets out to destroy the 'gun' but it is launched early. There is still disagreement, but the final rhetorical question is left ringing in the ears: 'If we are no more than animals – we must live and suffer and pass and matter no more – than all the other animals do or have done. Is it that – or this? All the universe – or nothingness. Which will it be, Passworthy? Which will it be?'

In Wells's novel the space gun and the resulting vision of space travel doesn't appear but there needed to be the dramatic development towards a climactic moment so essential to the progression of such a drama. What Korda saw in the novel were the rich possibilities cinematagraphically. Wells used no characters in his book and these were, of course, essential to a film. Wells described what he had written as 'essentially an imaginative discussion of social and political possibilities, and a film is no place for argument. The conclusions of that book therefore are taken for granted in the film, and a new story had been invented to add a human dimension.'[38]

It is not surprising that Korda saw immediately the story's possibilities. But Wells insisted that he wanted to write the script himself and, once Bliss was on board, also insisted that the music should not just be tagged on at the end. In fact, Bliss *only* accepted the commission on the understanding that his music should be part of the creative thrust of the drama and conceived with the script. Korda was 'old school' Hollywood in his view of music being the servant of the film and Wells's letter to Bliss on 16 October 1934 shows this clearly: 'I am at issue with Korda and one or two others of the group on the question of where you come in. They say – it is the Hollywood tradition – "We make the film right up to the cutting then *when* we have cut, the musician comes in and *puts in the music*." I say Balls! ... I say 'a film is a composition and the musical composer is an integral part of the design. I want Bliss to be in touch throughout... I want to end on a complete sensuous and emotional synthesis [think of Bliss's comments on emotion above – author]. So far from regarding the music as trimming to be put in afterwards I am eager to get any suggestions I can from you as to the main design.'[39]

It is salutary to remember that the era of the silent movie was only a decade or so in the past and that the integration of music into the scheme of a film, especially as Wells envisaged, was still a novel idea. Bliss had written an article back in 1922 for the *Musical News and Herald* entitled *Those Damned Films* in which he made several outspoken criticisms of the state of the art as it was in the silent movie age, starting with 'the picture house is no place for those who feel the need of a mental stimulus.'[40] And this: 'They conspire together to raise the music, which had hitherto served but to drown the twittering of the operator's lantern, to the artistic level of the picture it accompanied. They took the "don't think" policy one step further. You were not only to be *told* what was happening and then *see* it happen, but, luxury of luxuries, you were to *hear* it happen'. He goes on to assert that 'suitable music for this doping of the brain is comparatively simple. There is much music that produces no thought and does not bear thinking of... There are only two alternatives before the future music director of the films. Either... choose music that is not expressly written for the picture... and spend all your spare time hunting for the right tune, or... get some composer to collaborate with the producer and write those special cinema noises... What a proud day it will be for some of us to be featured as the sound-producing experts on a real live million-dollar movie!'[41] Now that 'proud day' had arrived.

The major issues in the process of making Wells's film lay in fundamental disagreements between him and Korda. Wells's lack of experience and his determination to have things his own way later elicited an apologia which stated: 'Alexander Korda offered to make a film which was, as far as humanly possible, exactly as I dictated. The task of putting my imaginative story into screen form was, however, far more difficult than I had imagined, and took much longer than I thought. It is only now that I realize how little I knew about the cinema when I wrote the scenario. Many of the sequences which slipped quite easily from my pen were extremely difficult to screen, and some were quite impossible. But that did not matter. The film has emerged spiritually correct, despite the fact that it now embodies many alterations suggested by Alexander Korda, William Cameron Menzies, and a score of other people.'[42] In other reflections, however, he was a good deal less sanguine.

Bliss was fired up by the project, feeling that 'I shall do a big thing with this, if unhampered'[43] and went on to write a large proportion of the music to Wells's specifications before the film was even in production. Wells had produced a first 'treatment' (script) of the story but it proved to be impractical (which he acknowledged) though Korda and his colleagues loved the concept. His second treatment was the basis upon which everything proceeded and to which Bliss produced his score of some thirty-one minutes of music covering the fourteen sequences required for the film. This second treatment was based on the latter part of Wells's novel but there were additional problems, one of which was language as the Korda brothers were speaking French and Wells, English, so there had to be an interpreter. (Korda's brother Vincent was the Art Designer for the film.) There were other technical difficulties including Korda's new sound studio at Denham which hadn't been finished by this time, a reminder that sound for film was still in its infancy. It is extraordinary, also, to think that the Kordas, due to what Norman and Jeanne MacKenzie described as 'a combination of enthusiasm and inexperience,' hired a brilliant team 'who proved incapable of translating what they and Wells wanted into film.'[44] This team included the world-renowned architects Le Corbusier and Walter Gropius both of whom were rejected as was the French artist Fernand Léger who was commissioned to design costumes. Large chunks of time were thus wasted and a feeling of halting and chaotic progress was all around.

It was still Wells's vision of the music which remained fundamental to Bliss's involvement through all the uncertainties, with Wells telling Bliss that 'I don't think Korda has much of an ear, but I want the audience at the end not to sever what it sees from what it hears. I want to end on a complete sensuous and emotional synthesis.'[45]

Thirty minutes of music were recorded with the London Symphony Orchestra conducted by Bliss on 3 March 1935 and a set of test pressings were sent to Sir Henry Wood asking him to consider a 'suite' of seven movements for the Proms which Wood accepted with alacrity, Bliss conducting on 12 September. In this way the public got to know the music long before the film was actually released, creating great expectations and becoming hugely popular in its own right. When the film premiered Decca released two 78 rpm records which featured the music for *Ballet, Pestilence, Attack and Ruins* from the March recording sessions. It is likely that these were not initially intended for commercial release but so that those whose job it was to fit the film to the music as Wells demanded could hear the scale of their task. This, in all probability, accounts for the delay in releasing the recordings in February 1936, nearly a year later. There is no doubt that the commercial release was a highly astute move giving the film excellent advance publicity which, coupled with Wells's celebrity (and notoriety in some aspects of his life) guaranteed that the film would be the most talked-about release of the moment.

Six more sides of Bliss's music were recorded but lost and Decca's third disc featuring *March* and *Epilogue* were transferred from film recordings conducted by Muir Mathieson, again with the LSO. These recordings represent the first-ever commercial sound-track recordings and show just how much the music had to be adapted to fit as required. To add to this, Chappell published piano arrangements of various numbers that show further differences between music in the film and the recordings.

For Bliss all this was essentially good, and was, of course, wonderful for his already burgeoning reputation and popularity. However, what was going on in the studio was not what Wells had originally envisaged. As Giles Easterbrook has pointed out in his luminous notes for the fine Chandos recording of the music, 'Wells was out of his depth on the set, constantly being overruled by specialists. The pragmatic Korda. . . reverted to normal production and editing practices: the recorded score no longer remotely fitted the screen action. With Bliss unavailable for rewrites, or unprepared to assist in the butchery of his music, Lionel Salter was brought in to do the surgery and Muir Mathieson to re-record it.'[46] Salter remembered that 'Bliss wrote much of his *Things to Come* score – which many regard as the finest British film music yet – in advance of the shooting (let alone of the film editing). I was charged with 'tidyings-up and surgery', a job I felt privileged (and somewhat overawed) to do, as he had been one of my musical heroes.'[47]

None of the inevitable frustrations of this whole process are voiced by Bliss in his autobiography but one or two reminiscences are interesting to our modern eyes: 'Those were the days of size in film production, huge sets, huge orchestras, hundreds of supers: the bigger the ensemble, the more important the film. At Denham whole towns sprang up, to be battered down by bombs and guns, and then rebuilt in a different setting. One section of the film was actually shot to my musical score: there was no dialogue in it; the sequence dealt exclusively with the machines of the future. The scene showed the earth being mined, roads made, houses erected, apparently without the aid of manual labour.' The nearest he came to acknowledging the inevitable changes was this: 'In spite of imaginative direction, fine acting, and an expert staff of technicians, the financial necessity of having to appeal to a vast audience meant a concession here and a concession there, a watering down in one place, a deletion in another, so that, instead of having the impact of a vital parable, it became just an exciting entertainment.'[48] He went on to remark that all Wells's predictions proved correct – even sending men to the moon – but the 'parable' of the story, its almost biblical message of world peace, has not been heeded.

A great deal of detective work has been undertaken in recent years to piece together the original score which was discarded or lost in the late 1930s (Bliss stated that it was his and not the property of the film studio). There were, however, some lucky discoveries. In 1991 four of the six missing 1935 test-pressings conducted by Bliss were discovered at the Royal Academy of Music having been donated amongst his effects by Sir Henry Wood. These were of the *Epilogue, March* and *Prologue.* After Bliss's death Trudy Bliss discovered the manuscript for *Attack on the Moon Gun* which confirmed the orchestration of the score. But this was not the end of the story, and we return to the 1930s and to Bliss's authorization of a new suite for a BBC broadcast which was still not yet the final score as published by Novello. It is worth letting Giles Easterbrook take up the story:

'The film had effectively (re-)defined the music, and audiences demanded to hear what they had come to know. He was not a fool and in June 1936 authorized a new suite, dropping the *Idyll*, and reordering other items, ending with the *March*, but also accommodating a truncated *Epilogue*, now entitled *Reconstruction*. This was still not the published suite to come but approached it'.

Significantly, he goes on to point out that there was tension between the film studio and Bliss's publisher, Novello & Co., over music that Bliss intended to use in his forthcoming ballet, *Checkmate*. Easterbrook continues:

'The bargaining chip in the difficult negotiations. . . was probably the splendid music for the Rebuilding sequence, used intact in the film but in none of its spin-offs, which Bliss later earmarked for later use in *Checkmate* (as *Entry of the Red Castles*). Significantly this music does not appear in the *Checkmate* suite either. There is no other explanation for its omission than that both publishing companies agreed to exclude it, as the price to be paid for authorization to publish these suites.'[49]

Although the music for this film had achieved an almost legendary status and remarkable popularity with the music-loving public the 'here today and gone tomorrow' attitude of film makers in discarding what is often the most durable element of their creation while simply moving on to their next project is completely at odds with the normal instinct of the composer to preserve what he has written. In this way, and in common with what composers have done since time immemorial, it is not surprising that he recycled some hard-won material for other suitable situations.

The film, whilst not financially successful, was generally acclaimed with the *Times* reporting that 'Mr Arthur Bliss has not failed to make

142

good use of his opportunity, but another power has intervened to nullify his work. For the sound in this film is so grossly over-amplified that the music becomes mere noise. . . . Anything would have done, thus amplified, so that it is impossible to detect what instruments originated this uniform, brazen din'. We need reminding, again, that the experience of sound with film to amplify the experience is a new one, and one which is not translatable from the record player or the concert hall. Later in the same review the reviewer does take a somewhat more emollient stance when he writes 'We still have hopes, based upon the experience of less ambitious productions, that music may yet take its legitimate place in the cinema; it remains for the musicians to stake out a claim for their art as something more than one among many forms of sound effects.'[50]

The ultimate assessment of *Things to Come* is a mixed one but, like all moments of seismic change, the film industry was groping its way to a new order and an absorption of new technology and method of working. This film, despite its chaotic production process, was a significant step towards modernization, which helped make possible everything we know today. It was undoubtedly a formative experience for Bliss which resulted in some of his most brilliant music, not to mention a far greater awareness of him as a composer by the general population both here and abroad. Perhaps the final word should be Bliss's assessment of Wells from a BBC broadcast in November 1950 introducing the suite of movements from the film:

'To begin with it was an adventure to see Wells himself at work. He was a man of tireless curiosity. For him, as for me, it was a plunge onto a new world, and he was always interested in the new. He was constantly in the studios, suggesting, criticizing, stimulating all and sundry. Although he knew next to nothing about musical technique, he had a genius for putting his finger on a weak spot, for pointing out a slack thought. I treasure letters and postcards from him during that time, written in his small squiggly hand, and containing a mass of directions and hints, some of which, I fear, were frankly impractical.'[51]

The growth and development of the film industry was of course mirrored in the broadcast arena. In November 1932, Bliss wrote an article for the BBC's magazine *The Listener*, giving his view of what the Corporation was doing for music in the country. It is key here, especially as the Corporation was to play such a key part in Bliss's life in a few years' time, and he was to have an earlier and serious flirtation with it as we will see in the next chapter. He could also see that it was a key route to the public in far greater numbers than any concert hall could accommodate. The BBC's new headquarters, Broadcasting House, had only been open since March that year (officially opened in May, but the first broadcast taking place earlier) and the organization had only been formed ten years previously. In that time its growth had been exponential and as Bliss wrote: 'The BBC has grown in ten years to be the greatest music-making machine, by a very long chalk, that has ever existed.'[52] The eye-opening point is what Bliss describes as 'its official aloofness' followed by this statement (imagine this in the twenty-first century. . .): 'It has obviously decided rightly and with subtlety to bridge any gulf between the public and itself by enticing the said public to creep up to its own level of taste, hoping that sooner or later complete harmony will result. It calls the tune, in fact. . . .'[53] There is an important additional point: 'The listener is not only provided with a foundation of experience which would without the radio most likely take him years of study and travel; he is also initiated into the musical language of his own day – that is important, for even lesser work of talent of our own period often speaks or should speak with more force and intimacy to us than masterpieces of other generations.' This has echoes of Bliss's tirade against the classical masters in his lecture to the Society of Women Musicians back in 1921 as a young crusader, and we are reminded of his comments about the twenty-year-old versus the forty-year-old composer above. He was a determined *contemporary* composer wanting to say new things and to give people a chance to hear them. In this he saw the BBC as full of rich possibilities.

Key to all this remarkable innovation and sustenance of the public's musical appetite is the figure of Bliss's friend Adrian Boult, Director Music for the BBC and founder of the BBC Symphony Orchestra and Chorus in 1930, 'which can be relied on without nervousness for the most exacting performance.'[54] In what might be seen as a reference to the painful memory of the premiere of the *Colour Symphony* (dedicated to Boult) he also states that 'Till recently there was no money, and therefore no time to rehearse, and unfamiliar works had to be got through as best they could, generally maimed in the process, sometimes killed... Once again, the BBC has set a standard of playing high enough to cause a perceptible stiffening and liveliness in other orchestras, which is as it should be.'[55] The long and the short of it was that not only was the general public being educated but it was getting an opportunity to hear first class music brilliantly played and sung and in the comfort of their own homes. There were, of course, many who felt the BBC's inexorable progress as a threat, especially rival orchestras who did not benefit from the security of a huge organization at its back together with the benefit of almost everything the BBC Symphony Orchestra performed being broadcast.

The key thing, however, was that new music was now heard by a far larger audience and Bliss had been a beneficiary of this for some time. The general assessment of the first ten years? 'Unquestionably a high one in music. A serious listener can in a year become acquainted with the best symphonic and chamber music of all periods performed sometimes superbly, at all times adequately. It is the equivalent, in painting, of a year's tour round the most famous galleries of the world. No one can fairly ask for anything better, and no one in any other broadcasting centre of the world can hope to get as much.'[56]

# Chapter Eight

# STRINGS, TRAVEL GUIDES
# AND CHECKMATE

The learning that continues with every new experience in our lives certainly strengthened Bliss's compositional process, and what he called 'the value of the blue pencil' made him increasingly aware of the importance of economy and clarity, two attributes essential in film music. Beyond this was the building of a daily routine which became a discipline, different for every artist. For Bliss it was the morning which was most conducive to constructive, focused work after a good night's sleep. He wrote very personally about his work habit which saw the afternoons as rest periods and the space between tea and dinner a preparation for the next morning's work. Like many composers he found that what had appeared to be insuperable problems one day were often resolved by the subconscious mind in sleep. 'When composing I often find that in the early evening session my invention flags, then stops. I cannot see the path ahead; I have apparently come to a dead end. . . . The only solution for me is the deep sleep at night: next day I play through the music right up to the point of stoppage, and most times my fingers, without faltering, carry me on to a logical solution; in my sleep my alter ego has found this for me.'[1]

What is interesting here is his use of the piano, given the complexity of his music. To be able to observe his process would be instructive, to see what the piano gave him which his inner ear did not. Another point he raises (taking us back to the *donnée*, or inspirational idea that would spur him into creativity) is that he found the process of an artist or sculptor observed in their studios more of a stimulant than discussing musical

146

ideas with other musicians. He makes special mention of Ben Nicholson, Barbara Hepworth and Mark Gertler, all of whom had studios nearby in Hampstead. Gertler was a tragic figure, born in the same year as Bliss but coming from a family of Polish Jewish immigrants. He was a wonderfully talented portrait artist who visited East Heath Lodge to paint Bliss at the piano – his mother's Blüthner with its characteristically detailed music stand seems to almost draw the attention away from Bliss himself.

He developed tuberculosis. This, together with a doomed marriage, financial worries, and an obsessive and unrequited love interest in the painter Dora Carrington (who committed suicide in 1932), resulted in his own suicide, gassing himself in his flat in 1939. There is no mention of any of this in Bliss's recollection of this period, only a wistful comment regretting that he did not possess the painting as a reminder of the artist and of that time. His general feeling for the work-in-progress of artists was summed up when he wrote: 'In looking at the struggle for realized form in a sculptor's or painter's work, I find something that instructs me in my own art.'[2]

Bliss was now forty-four and had reached the stage when every work was eagerly anticipated. With serious works in almost every genre adding to his reputation at home and abroad, and with a ground breaking film score under his belt, he needed to return to the medium of 'pure' music having, as he put it, 'got weary of only writing music that illustrated other people's ideas.'[3] This was even going to hold true imminently when his first opportunity to write a ballet score arose realizing his own plot. But before that his first 'pure music' was a work for string orchestra simply called *Music for Strings*. This title was the cause of much comment and emphasizes the point that Bliss was looking for new ways to express himself. Frank Howes, writing in the *Musical Times*, spent half a page of his article rounding on Bliss for not being able to give the work a title which told the audience (or the critics) what they should expect to hear. What commentators failed to grasp was that titles were changing as much as the works themselves. Howes felt that the most appropriate title might be 'Consort for String Orchestra' harking back to the old English form from the sixteenth and seventeenth centuries. Yet Bliss's title leaves his pages blank and ready to interest us in any way he pleases. All we need to understand is that this is going to be a substantial work and we can judge for ourselves if it is a 'concerto' in the manner of the Brandenburgs or a 'consort' in the manner of the Elizabethans.

The mid-1930s was an interesting time for the United Kingdom in terms of looking with a more outward face to the world and through the formation of the British Council in 1934, encouraging educational and cultural interchange. It was somehow typical of the arrogant thinking of the time that the world should come to us and if they didn't it was their loss. In her book about the British Council Frances Donaldson notes Harold Nicholson as attributing Britain's 'failure in the nineteenth century to an arrogant reticence based on the failing to regard all forms of self-display as obnoxious'. He went on to say: 'If foreigners failed to appreciate, or even to notice, our gifts of invention or our splendid adaptability, then there was nothing that we could do to mitigate their obtuseness. The genius of England, unlike that of lesser countries, spoke for itself.'[4] Never was a case more powerfully put for such a new body than this appalling statement. One of the most important functions of the Council was the teaching of English to students with any kind of need or interest, but committees were also set up to focus on other elements so a *Books and Periodicals Committee* backed up the language drive, and a *Music Committee* was formed and chaired by Ernest Makower amongst various other areas of operation with their own committees. Makower's committee sent musical 'ambassadors' including Myra Hess, Thelma Reiss, Keith Falkner and Cyril Smith to a wide variety of countries, as well as sending gramophone records to a number of national broadcasting companies. They brought over a group of European music critics to London to hear what was going on in the city as representative of Britain as a whole and they were also taken to Oxford to hear the choir of New College under Sydney Watson. The Makowers and the Blisses were good friends and it was no surprise that Makower should bring Bliss onto the Music Advisory Board from its inception in July 1934, given his international reputation as the contemporary British composer most performed in other countries. Bliss's association with the Council would be further cemented when, in 1947, he became a member of its governing body.

Partly because of this British Council connection Makower was much on Bliss's mind at this time and, although he makes no reference to him in his autobiography in relation to *Music for Strings*, Bliss dedicated the work to him and his wife. This may be partly in acknowledgement of the first UK performance at one of the London Museum concerts which Makower organized and funded, but is more likely to be simply a gesture of their long-standing friendship and recognition of his important work in promoting British music. However, there is another possibly more colourful reason. Makower was a silk merchant, and when the Blisses visited them for dinner one evening Makower demonstrated how really good quality silk should tear cleanly in two. Trudy Bliss recounted this story to Robert Milnes later in her life and showed how Bliss had written this surprising demonstration into the first movement of the *Music for Strings*. At figure 5 in the score the violins go helter-skelter upwards and then cascade downwards through the orchestra into a moment of complete silence before the new chordal theme is heard. This, she said, was the image of the silk being rent in two!

The gift of the dedication to Makower was a rich one indeed and, in relation to the new outward-facing Britain, it is notable that the first performance took place at the Salzburg Festival given by the Vienna Philharmonic Orchestra conducted by Boult on 11 August 1935, Makower's London performance following a few months later on 5 November given by the London Philharmonic Orchestra conducted by Malcolm Sargent.

*Music for Strings* is a big-boned work in serious mood. Our task is not to analyze his works in great detail, though this work, being seminal to his development needs some greater exploration. It shows pointers to the way Bliss is moving his art forward and away from conventional forms which have so preoccupied composers since the invention of sonata form. At the heart of this form lies the essence of all art: contrast, light and shade, development of ideas and a sense of a 'frame', which gives visual artists their definition of space and composers a defining beginning, ending, and sense of scale. So, if Bliss decides to take these elements and play with them in a different way, which does not observe the standard formalities of keys or clearly defined first and second subjects, he is entirely at liberty to do so as long as there is a clear sense of where his musical argument is heading. If the old order is abandoned, a new order has to be very persuasive of its merits to win the approval of the listeners and performers every composer looks to befriend.

Bliss knows this very well. His method is to catch the ear with an arresting thematic gesture and then to use it, or strongly recognizable elements of it, as the thematic thrust of the movement. So, the hurtling theme at the outset not only sets the mood but gives us most of the aural pointers we need for the whole movement. This comes in three main ideas with a hint of a fourth (see musical examples below).

A, B and C are all clearly characterful and aurally memorable. This is also important because the tonality of the movement shifts like an elusive shadow, rarely finding a moment of repose that says 'here is an arrival'. Even the very first chord is a second inversion D major chord, which might indicate an imminent arrival in G as tonic, but far from allowing us anything so straightforward, Bliss thrusts forward with a chromatic

Ex. 1

progression. This does indeed land on a well-defined G minor moment at the start of bar 5 (above), and we are given a second beat reiteration of G (unison), but then the train leaves the station at speed and off it hurtles: we can only observe the passing landscape and enjoy its scenery, recognizing thematic landmarks as they appear.

Contrast comes in the form of a richly scored chordal idea which, in other hands might have acted as a more formal second subject. The sinuous lines and interplay of instruments in the opening bars of the movement is given a sudden moment of arrival and textural richness at 'D' and this feeling for chordal spaciousness is what Bliss gives us, much expanded, in Ex.2 which, while acting as a new idea is almost immediately amalgamated with B from Ex.1 muddying any feeling of a clear-cut new formal section. Only seven bars later and C appears, and five bars from there A is heard. So, this is really more of a development – or perhaps a discursive conversation around key points than a bending of formal rules any misguided analyst might try to fit into a recognizable scheme.

A further demonstration of this loosening of formal ties is the way the opening movement subsides into a lengthy coda which links to the second, an impassioned slow movement using a group of soloists in its course. Towards its close there is a passage of trenchant discord (leading into figure 48) which seems to act as a focus for all the intensity built up over the course of the past eleven minutes or so. It feels so personal and with such apparent grief in its expression that one wonders whether

Ex.2 (4 bars before figure 6)

this was yet another Kennard memorial. The mood of the movement is difficult for Bliss to leave and the third movement's *Allegro molto* emerges hesitantly from the opening bars. When it does, however, it dances its way forward in relaxed mood with the thematic material from its slow introduction.

The premiere at Salzburg was reviewed in the *Times* with some enthusiasm, noting 'how thoroughly he has outgrown his post-Stravinsky phase of his career.'[5] It continued: 'The whole strikes one, however, as inventive and spontaneous.' He noted that the first half of the concert was far too long, consisting of Holst's ballet music for *The Perfect Fool*, Bax's *Tintagel* symphonic poem, and Bliss's new work. After the interval, Vaughan Williams's *Job* played to a reduced house as the audience voted with their tired feet. Bliss himself wrote to his wife, noting that 'the concert took place at 11am – a good audience, including Toscanini, Weingartner and Bruno Walter. Adrian was at the top of his form, and steered the difficult music through splendidly; applause, which I acknowledged three times from the balcony.'[6]

Something in Bliss's musical style suggested to commissioners looking to celebrate specific events that he would feel the drama of an occasion. Perhaps, also, his descriptive abilities so evident in *Things to Come*, leant weight to the notion that he would write impressive fanfares. It has been noted many times that his feeling for drama, the 'look at me' energetic quality in his music was a key characteristic of his style which would seem to qualify him perfectly for the brief, epigrammatic statement which creates expectancy and which is the hallmark of a successful fanfare. Throughout his life Bliss wrote nearly fifty individual fanfares, many of which date from his time as Master of Queen's Music. His experience in the medium stretches back to 1921, when he wrote a fifteen-second *Fanfare for a Political Address*, followed in 1930 by a *Fanfare for Heroes* in aid of the Musicians' Benevolent Fund that, extraordinarily, was used in a Soviet Newsreel film *Defeat of the Germans near Moscow*. When he came to write a fanfare in 1935 for the BBC's *In Dominion*, a programme celebrating the Silver Jubilee of King George V, he had an existing track record, and with each subsequent fanfare would be further qualifying himself for that moment when his royal duties would require him to set the scene for many solemn and joyful occasions. He had a real gift for the form.

Another of Bliss's natural gifts was the way in which he easily and effectively connected with people. These ambassadorial qualities, which were to become such an important part of his life in the coming years, were already being recognized in his work for the British Council. But now a different opportunity was offered him by the BBC. We saw in the last chapter how Bliss was deeply involved with, and seriously interested in the BBC and everything it offered the country. Now, he was offered an unusual commission and a break from composition. The BBC asked him to make what Bliss described as a musical *Pilgrim's Progress* around the country and to write up his findings for the *Listener* magazine.[7] His task was an exploration of the state and health of music outside the capital but with the added motive of seeing the effects of broadcasting in far-flung places. The depression of the 1930s, leading to some three and half million unemployed, was deeply researched at the time, and Bliss's friend and collaborator J.B. Priestley made his own *English Journey* the previous year, 'being a rambling but truthful account of what one man saw and heard and felt and thought during a journey through England during the autumn of the year 1933.'[8] Bliss's commission built on this information gathering exercise but focused attention on music making and how so often it was such a psychological 'prop' for many deeply distressed people. Priestley and others gathering the nation's temperature wrote anonymously of their subjects as examples of types. Bliss, perhaps typically of his real interest in people as already noted, or because he was genuinely moved to tell an individual story, personalized his experiences so that what he writes comes more animatedly from the page.

He followed a similar route to that taken by Priestley but went further in exploring parts of Wales and Scotland as well. The circles in this map show the places he visited.

Bliss was obviously moved by his experience, and said, 'I learnt so much about the humbler activities that get no light shone on them' and he reprinted excerpts in his autobiography 'to recall experiences that I do not wish to forget.'[9] Space does not permit an extensive review of his tour but key points illuminate his own attitudes and opinions following his experience over these months between October and Christmas. First, he focuses his attention on amateur music making. Everyone, he says, knows about the famous British orchestras but 'I aim, if possible, at pene-trating the immense activity that underlies the more spectacular high points. . . . At present a lot of it is hearsay to me. I am told, for instance, that every week throughout England alone 200,000 men and women meet to rehearse together, that 2,000 choral societies, some big, some small are actively functioning. I read of 196 brass bands in competition, of amateur orchestras, chamber music clubs, operatic societies, children's concerts, guilds, leagues, associations. What are they doing, and who are

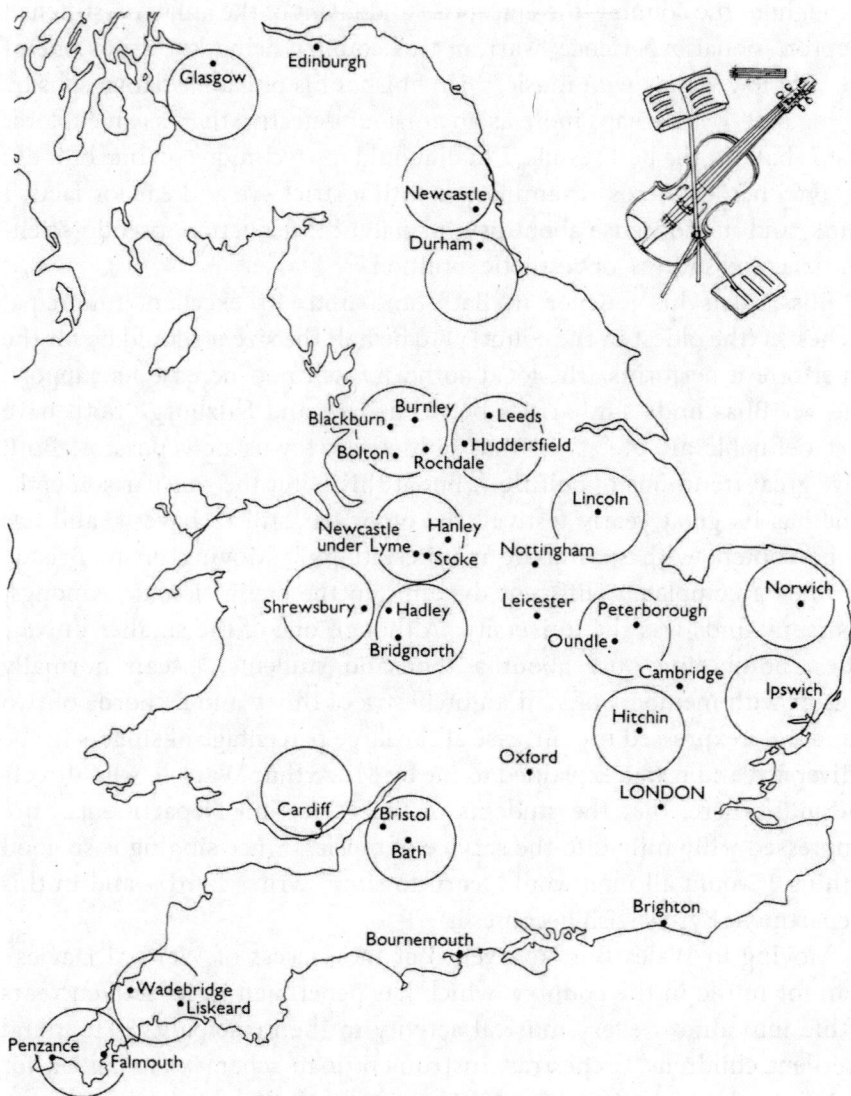

their controlling personalities? It will be very enlightening to find out.'[10] And, given his additional brief: 'Has the BBC unwittingly hindered some of these many varied societies, making it difficult for them to continue, or has it given a great stimulus to music-making generally?'[11] What he writes next shows that, in many ways, 1935 is not so different from this present day: 'On paper, at any rate, the statistics that have been given me seem to prove conclusively that however unmusically-minded *Officialdom* may be throughout the country, the enterprise and talent of the amateur, stiffened by professional experience, warrant this country being known as one of the very few 'Lands *with* music.'[12] He finishes his prefatory paragraphs by saying that 'it is perhaps more as an amateur detective than as an explorer that I shall get the best results. I shall mould my technique on one of those fictional heroes – cross-examination with a strict eye and ear for facts, I think, and no nonsense about psychoanalytical deduction, pseudo-scientific trial and success, or aesthetic intuition.'[13]

Bliss starts his journey in Bath, and finds its excellent municipal orchestra (the oldest in the country) to be half the size it should be for the repertoire it performs. The local authority will not increase its support, and yet Bliss finds similarities between Bath and Salzburg: 'both have that definable air of "style" that only a few towns now possess. Both have great traditions of culture... but at this point the comparison ends. One has its great yearly festival, the other has still to have it, and has to be content with spasmodic manifestations.'[14] Moving on to Bristol, he finds a completely different dynamic in the energetic city. Amongst his many finds was the university: 'Although one of the smaller universities, numbering only about a thousand students, it can normally muster with members of staff an orchestra of thirty and a chorus of two hundred. I expressed my surprise at the large percentage of singers in the university, and it was explained to me by Mr Arthur Warrell, who directs the music here, that the students of the Education Department... are empressed willy-nilly into the service of music. "Since singing is so good a thing I would all men would learn to sing," writes Byrd – and in this Department Byrd's wish becomes law.'[15]

Moving to Wales Bliss marvelled at the success of Walford Davies's plan for music in the country 'which has penetrated in its sixteen years of life into almost every musical activity in the Principality'. He found excellent childrens' orchestras, instrument loan schemes ('A collier, for instance, who under this scheme started to learn the oboe two years ago, won first prize at the National Eisteddfod this year'), and in villages like the tiny hamlet of Oakley Park where the children walk three miles to a school of some thirty children, a choir of ten singing in three parts. Bliss marvelled that 'South Wales is choir-mad. Singing is in their blood. The Welshman views music quite differently from the Englishman. It is not so much a relaxation as a justification.'[16]

Bliss moved to 'that loveliest of counties, Shropshire'. He expected music to form only a small part of what is essentially an agricultural and sporting county. Amongst many exciting musical activities he witnessed,

Bliss found a school that actively drew people from all around to music making. The headmaster had drawn up a pamphlet listing points to encourage musical activity, and especially singing. The third of these was 'To create such a love of singing that boys and girls will, in later life, desire to participate in the musical life of the places in which they live'. (What has happened in the 2020s?) He moved on to the Five Towns of the Potteries in north Staffordshire, noting the fine Victoria Hall at Hanley, and from there to Rochdale, Burnley, Blackburn and Bolton. At Rochdale, he made the interesting observation that a 'fairly sure test of a town's financial condition is whether their choral organizations are rehearsing new works or not. Can the members afford to pay the prices which publishers ask for large-scale new choral scores, or must they fall back on performances of *Elijah* and the *Messiah*?'[17] Bliss wrote in his autobiography of an amusing incident at Burnley. He had been made aware of a particularly talented and energetic young man who had recently married. Asking directions to his house Bliss arrived to find that the young man was late returning from a football match and his anxious wife was cooking their supper. Asking if he could wait and if there was anything he could do to help in the meantime, he was offered an apron. We will let Bliss take up the story: 'We were getting on in a very friendly way, when there was a smart rap on the door, and a fierce middle-aged man entered the kitchen. He glared at me, turned to his daughter (of course he *would* be the father) and shouted at her 'What's that man doing in your kitchen?' Saucepan in hand, apron-draped, I really felt at a loss to explain, and when I replied 'I come from the BBC', I thought he was going to hit me for my obvious lie. Luckily, at that moment, rapid steps were heard and the young husband appeared. Peace was restored.'[18]

Perhaps the most impressive moment of his whole tour was his introduction to the Wingates Temperance Band whose virtuosity simply astounded him as it had both Toscanini and Casals. Knowing now what was possible from an amateur group such as this encouraged Bliss to write *Kenilworth* as the Test Piece for the Crystal Palace Festival the following year.

Bliss's half-way point was the West Riding of Yorkshire where he enthused about the Holme Valley Male Voice Choir of sixty or seventy tenors and basses – 'probably the finest male chorus in England... They have an unforced power and resonance that are unknown in the South. The basses are like superb diapasons and their range is remarkable.'[19] Newcastle-upon-Tyne came next and thence to Glasgow where he noted some extraordinary music making and especially the amateur performance of Berlioz's *The Trojans* by the Glasgow Grand Opera Society conducted by Dr Erik Chisholm, whose mission was to promote performances of works almost never performed in Britain. He details the incredible obstacles overcome in order to realize the ambitious outcome but Bliss ends his report by simply saying 'I shall certainly be at the performance myself.'[20] If all sounds sweetness and light in print, in ink he wrote to Trudy that 'Glasgow in this weather is the dirtiest, noisiest, dourest and most depressing city I have ever been in... I begin to go south tomorrow. O Joy! This northern spot depresses; no one smiles.'[21]

'Southward' encompassed Leeds, York, Lincoln ('I had never been to Lincoln before, and my first view of it was unforgettable.') where he found the cathedral the hub of everything musical, before moving on to Peterborough and Oundle School where he marvelled at the whole school taking part in Bach's B minor Mass. From here he travelled the long distance to Cornwall where he noted that this county and Wales possess similar characteristics: 'Not only do the two languages sound alike, but the voices, especially as you travel further west, take on the same vibrant singing tone. The Cornishman, like the Welshman, has a natural love of music.'[22] His last two stopping points were in East Anglia: Ipswich and Norwich, which appeared in the December issue of *The Listener*. The last article was a conclusion in which he noted that he had travelled two-thousand-five hundred miles and 'the prevailing impression left with me is of the vast tracts of musical enterprise not yet seen. For instance, there is the world of brass bands. Except for one outstanding example, I have not been able to visit the representative leaders of this active side of music. Let the reader put the number of these bands at 6,000, the number of players at 150,000, estimate a total audience for their music running into millions, and he will realize the gigantic figures with which he must deal in judging the extent of this one musical interest.'[23] He notes the closeness between the professional and the amateur and how professionals are involved in developing these amateurs to the levels they attain. In terms of his BBC commission, everywhere he went he asked how broadcasting affected individuals and societies. The answer was almost unanimously that it had barely affected them at all. He relayed the story of a northern musical enthusiast who heard his local choral society broadcasting live and was so impressed that he ran to the concert hall to hear the second part in person. As Bliss pointed out, 'He was obeying a perfectly natural musical impulse.'

'To estimate the value of music in England one must travel. When representative foreign critics next come to England, they would do well on this second visit to avoid London. Let them start with a Hallé concert... the visiting critics can then be led quietly up to Huddersfield where they will hear the finest choral singing in England, perhaps in Europe. A visit to one or two prize-winning bands might interest them as much as it apparently has Casals. If they want danger and excitement let them act as judges at some important competition festival, and if they want to take away a lasting impression of something beautiful and characteristic, let them listen to the singing of our own music in the setting of an English cathedral.'[24]

With the sound of the Wingate Temperance Band still ringing in his ears the request to write a work as the test piece for the National Brass Band Festival held at Crystal Palace in September 1936 came as a welcome outlet for his new-found enthusiasm. *Kenilworth* was the outcome and Bliss dedicated it to Kenneth Wright who at this time was Boult's personal assistant. He had worked for the BBC Music Department since 1922 and became the first Director of the BBC in Manchester that year, eventually becoming Deputy Director of Music and Acting Director of Music in 1947 when Victor Hely-Hutchinson died. But it was in his role as Overseas Director of Music (1940–43) that he would come to have a particular influence on Bliss's life as we will see in the next chapter. Wright was an influential musician who was also a composer whose *Pride of Race* suite for band was featured in the 1935 National Brass Championships.

*Kenilworth* demonstrates well Bliss's adaptability as a composer. His growing reputation inevitably meant that he was now responding to invitations which might previously have been thought to be outside his comfort zone. But if his recent travels had taught him anything it was that the high quality of amateur music making needed high quality new music as much as the eminent professionals for whom he was used to writing. He also realized that virtuosity did not reside only with the professionals as he had so vividly discovered with the Wingates Temperance Band. *Kenilworth* was a good example of experience broadening the mind.

Kenilworth Castle is a magnificent structure in the town of Kenilworth, near Warwick in the English Midlands. Bliss chose to use the famous visit which Queen Elizabeth I made to the castle in 1575 as a storyline for the work. In the Preface to the original score the scenario was described like this: 'In 1575 Queen Elizabeth paid her celebrated visit to Kenilworth Castle, given by her some years before to Dudley, Earl of Leicester. At the Gate of the Gallery Tower, the Queen, mounted on a milk white horse, was greeted with a flourish of trumpets, and presented with the keys of the Castle. Immediately on entering the Tilt Yard, the Spirit of the Lake appeared on a floating island, blazing with torches, and welcomed her. The Queen stayed during 19 days of lively pastimes, plays, masques and pageants. The great clock stood the whole time at the hour of dining'. The music reflects the story line: a fanfare 'At the Castle Gates' gradually dissipates into the reflective 'Serenade on the Lake', and finally a large-scale 'March – Kenilworth' combines a Blissian approach with familiar astringent harmonies and an Elgarian broader melody (figure 19) from which a gradual increase of speed takes us back to the original energetic march. It is a highly effective nine-minute work.

The lengths to which contestants went to prepare themselves for the competition, and to outsmart the opposition was typified by the conductor of the Foden Motor Works Band, Fred Mortimer, who, with his son Harry, made the journey from Sandbach in Cheshire, where the band was based, to Kenilworth to soak up the atmosphere. They also went to see *Things to Come* several times in order to familiarize themselves with Bliss's style.

Around this time – and sadly Bliss omitted to put a year in his correspondence but it seems likely to be about 1937 – he hatched a plan for an opera on the subject of the Greek hero Ulysses in collaboration with Bridges Adams who was also a fellow British Council advisor working in their Drama Department, and an old friend from his days at the Shakespeare Company in Stratford. As the correspondence is from East Heath Lodge it has to be before 1939. He also mentions film music, which must refer to *Conquest of the Air*, written in 1937. There are three letters referring to *Ulysses*. The first begins 'I believe it is the exact vivid drama I want. I shall have to get to know it inside out before I can tackle any detail of libretto, but it will go, I feel. As soon as I have been through it carefully, I shall meet you and discuss the exact form of the scenes... It is a clear hit or miss opera – let us hit.'[25]

In the next letter, dated 25 November, he regrets: 'The fragments (of libretto) are carefully prized until the film music a week or so hence is finished. Don't fulminate or wish me in the nethermost brimstone yet.' The final letter on this project is again undated but takes a positive step in writing to Bridges Adams to say 'I want to work with you over the opera, both as librettist and dramatic overseer – I do not mind how original or unoriginal the verse or prose is as long as it has punch and singing qualities.' Why the opera was abandoned is a mystery, but it is possible that it was superseded by *Checkmate* and then the war prevented its resurrection after which it was simply forgotten.

In many ways what Bliss had been working towards throughout his career was about to come into focus with the composition of his first ballet score, *Checkmate*. With the death of Elgar, Holst and Delius in 1934 the baton was now comprehensively handed over to the next generation. Arnold Whittall pointed out that Bliss himself 'was very eloquent about the understandable nervousness of British composers in 1934. The lack of a dominating father-figure across the channel, like Wagner in the 1880s, provided ample justification for introversion.'[26] This would seem another pointer to the romantic turn Bliss's music had taken and we have seen the strength of his views on emotion in music. It is almost as if having been able to leave the expression of deep feelings to the older generation, now they were gone, Bliss and his contemporaries needed to take on elements of that mantle – and we have seen how successfully he made this transition in all the works since *Morning Heroes*.

Bliss had first conceived the idea of using the game of chess for a ballet around 1923 when he had been having dinner with the distinguished ballerina Tamara Karsavina. They had worked together a couple of years earlier when Bliss had orchestrated Christian Sinding's *Fire Dance* for her performance with Diaghilev's company in London. Talk around the table focused on dance and its contemporary possibilities with Bliss advocating its potential for drama. He particularly liked the idea of being able to control the medium – something not possible in film. Discussion turned to the drama of games and, as he said, 'the idea of the pitiless queen in chess leapt from someone's brain to become, as it happened, the starting point of the ballet *Checkmate*.'[27]

Thus the queen became the central character, 'the most powerful and ruthless piece on the board'. Grace Lovat Fraser suggested depicting the king as a feeble old man. Bliss himself felt that a worthy opponent to the queen would be an enemy knight. He remembered reading at school 'the story of a man who played chess for his life against some barbaric chieftain. If he could win, he would be set free, but play as he might he was outwitted time and again by one of the red knights, who seemed demoniacally alive and malevolently capable of anticipating every move against him. So, with these three chief personalities – the ferocious Queen, the helpless King and the enigmatic fighter, the Knight, we began to construct a scenario.'[28] This was as far as things got for the time being. But when the Vic-Wells Ballet was invited to perform in Paris they decided to commission a new ballet for the occasion and Bliss was approached. He immediately resurrected the chess scenario and got to work with a vengeance. He felt that knowing exactly what he had to write, the plot, the time-scale and the venue gave him the impetus he needed to settle down to concentrated work. The performance was scheduled for 15 June 1937 at Le Théâtre des Champs-Élysées in Paris. The Vic-Wells company had been asked to appear demonstrating the best of British dancing, music and stage design. A great deal thus hung on the success of Bliss's conception and his score.

The team Bliss and Ninette de Valois assembled included McKnight Kauffer who designed the costumes and the décor. He also brought in Bridges Adams, mentioned above. One of Bliss's great strengths was collaborating with strong, experienced and knowledgeable colleagues who were not afraid to speak their minds and whose advice undoubtedly strengthened the final result. In this case Bridges Adams was the (loud) voice of opinions and ideas which fed into the dramatic scenario. Thus, Bliss remembered one particular tip: 'If you are going to play about with an exact intellectual conception like Chess, woo your audience with a bit of realism first, and then they will accept your romantic departures from the expected.'[29] The result of this was the gradual appearance of the chess pieces on the board which, at a given moment, organized into their proper line up for the start of the game. Underlining that Blissian love of drama he said: 'I like my colours to be brilliant, and with the opposing sets of pieces clothed in red and gold, and black and silver, I certainly got my wish.'[30]

Part of the scene-setting was deciding what the opposing sides might represent: night and day, black and white, a circle and a square, Fascism and Communism, but as he wrote in his article in the magazine *Great Thoughts*, 'The laws of the theatre finally indicated the choice of two armoured figures, one in gold, the other in black, symbolizing Love and Death fighting for the lives of their subjects.'[31] The scenario is then described like this and it is worth letting Bliss take us through it:

'The scene is a chessboard, on which the Red pieces are seen assembling – first, the Pawns, light-hearted pages, then the two Red Knights, fierce and powerful fighters. The two Black Knights enter on a reconnoitering visit of chivalry. They are followed by the Black Queen, the most powerful of the pieces. Before her departure she wins the love of the Red Knight and flings him a rose. Captivated by her vitality and beauty, he dances a joyous mazurka. The two Red Bishops enter. Their dignified ceremony is interrupted by the two Red Castles, inhuman and menacing monsters. Finally, the Red King and Queen approach. The King, old and feeble, is the weakest piece of all. The parade of the Red pieces is complete.

The game begins. A savage onslaught is started by the spear-heads of the enemy Black pieces, the manoeuvre ending with the 'check' of the Red King. His Bishops and his Queen try to defend him, but in vain. The Red Knight, as champion, jumps into the arena. He brings the Black Queen to her knees but, torn between love for her and loyalty to his King, hesitates to kill. She stabs him, and his body is borne off in a funeral cortege. The Black Queen then threatens the powerless King but insultingly disdains to touch him. Left alone on the board, he attempts to flee, only to find his lines of escape blocked by the Black pieces, who enter and force him back to his throne. At the point of death, he remembers his past youth and power, and once more faces his assailants. They waver, but the Black Queen appears behind him with spear uplifted. She plunges it into his back, and he falls. It is Checkmate.'[32]

The ultimate outcome is that although Death wins, Love sets up another row of pieces showing that Death's win is not a final one.

Bliss worked on the composition of the short (piano) score in the autumn and winter of 1936 finishing it in the spring of '37. Remembering his hours playing chess with R.O. Morris when living in the Vaughan Williamses' house in Chelsea, he dedicated the work to him. Immersing himself in the drama of this murderous plot which he had created he became almost obsessed with the game, taking trips to the British Museum to read up further about it, seeking out illustrations of Charlemagne playing with Death, of outdoor games, of Indian and Chinese sets with fantastic pieces. With all this background he then had to impress de Valois with the drama and was relieved when he saw how quickly she grasped the scenario especially as she knew nothing about Chess. Bliss would play her the music with a chessboard nearby and she would sit 'as if turned to stone, a frozen image of concentration.'[33] McKnight Kauffer was equally creative and Bliss was relieved to understand that he '*thinks* musically'. Bliss's other key reflection was having to cut some of the music as timing was so key to the dancing where an overlong section might prove difficult or over-tiring for the dancers. But, as he had noted a number of times before, 'The weak passages necessarily disappear, and the structure becomes stronger and more firmly knit.'[34]

The cast was all-star including Frederick Ashton as Death, Robert Helpmann as the old Red King, Harold Turner as the Red Knight, Margot Fonteyn leading the Black Pawns and June Brae in the main role as the Black Queen. The opening night almost inevitably had last-minute problems due to a strike of scene shifters in all the Parisian theatres. As

Bliss colourfully recounted: 'This is where the experience and panache of Bridges Adams, acting for the British Council, shone brightly. Ordering food and wine to be brought backstage, he addressed the scene shifters in fluent Stratford-atte-Bowe French, enlarging on the glories of the French dramatic tradition, and on this unique entente between them and a famous British Company. Mellowed by wine, and astonished at his oration, the scene shifters leapt to their feet, the stage was set just in time, and the curtain went punctually up on the first ballet of the evening, *Les Patineurs* (Meyerbeer arranged by Constant Lambert), conducted by Constant Lambert.'[35]

The first performance, also conducted by Lambert, was an occasion in the grand manner attended by the French President, Albert Lebrun, and the British Ambassador with many other dignitaries in the audience. There was also a significant presence from the British Council including not only Makower, but also the Chairman, Sir John Power. Adolf Aber, writing about it in the *Musical Times* reported that 'The success was tremendous. Time after time applause broke in upon the acting.'[36] Earlier in the article he wrote 'The ballet *Checkmate* should actually be characterized as a *dramatic* work above all else, for it is not a ballet in the ordinary sense of the word. Our interest is held by the drama, and its representation by pantomime rather than ballet dancing in its usual form. Nevertheless, there are plenty of scenes which give the corps de ballet an opportunity to show their art... The combination of the two fundamental elements of the work, dramatic pantomime and pageantry, give a vivid impression of Bliss's power of design and the wealth of his musical palette.'[37] Clement Crisp writing in the same periodical in 1966 wrote that 'its musical realization is a score which still ranks among the finest of British ballet music... *Checkmate* has a power and a passionate expression that are still gripping in the theatre.'[38] And in one further *Musical Times* focus on the work written just before the premiere the anonymous author writes that 'Mr Bliss has never lacked rhythm. Here, with an inhuman dance to incite him, he has put spurs to his rhythmic invention and carries the music through one phrase after another of driving energy.'[39]

*Checkmate* is undoubtedly one of Bliss's most successful works that, as he said, 'has danced itself around the world'. It also elicited an invitation from Toscanini who had seen the ballet and wanted to meet Bliss, asking him to visit his London hotel suite. Bliss remembered attending rehearsals of a Beethoven cycle Toscanini was conducting in the Queen's Hall and how impressive he felt the maestro was, the orchestral musicians responding wholeheartedly to his magnetic musicianship. Toscanini's question to Bliss was simply 'Do you, as an English musician, think that I, as an Italian, take the slow movements of Beethoven rather fast?' With this opening gambit conversation flowed and the ensuing hour was impressive as Bliss remembered, as much for Toscanini's evident modesty, as anything musical they talked about.

There are twelve musical numbers in the full ballet score, but various suites of movements have been assembled and used over the years since the premiere that have helped to keep the work alive though it remained in the repertoire of Sadler's Wells for some time. After the Paris premiere the first London performance was given by the same company with Constant Lambert again in charge at Sadler's Wells Theatre on 5 October 1937.

The drama of *Checkmate* is set up by the Prologue during which the two principal players, Love and Death, face up to each other as combatants fighting for the lives of their subjects. The music of this movement is dark, full of foreboding, and grabs the attention from the first bars by its sheer intensity of mood. Prokofiev sets up something similar at the very start of *Cinderella* though Bliss maintains his mood throughout the movement as he looks ahead to the climax of the work and its murderous dénoument. *The Dance of the Red Pawns*, which follows the *Prologue*, is a light-hearted, dancing movement that glances over his shoulder to Bliss's early Stravinskian 'experiments in sound'. The beauty of the scoring lies in its transparency, and the whole effect is dancing on points with lively rhythmic ambiguities along the way. The *Dance of the Four Knights* sees the four powerful characters enter, squaring up to each other in testosterone-fuelled aggressive music which leads to a challenge of a display of daring by the Red Knights to the Black Knights which is won by the first Red Knight. The Knights and the Pawns, however, are mesmerized by the *Entry of the Black Queen*. They respond to her spellbinding aura, sensing her dangerous power. Bliss conjures up both her effortless superiority and her sexual allure exercised on the first Red Knight who follows her 'as if hypnotized'. The music skillfully conjures up the lyrical beauty of this woman and her wily danger. *The Red Knight's Mazurka* is a welcome release of tension as he celebrates being singled out by the Queen. The mood changes in the final stages of the movement, as if to foretell his fate at her hands. Bliss evokes a mysterious atmosphere at the *Ceremony of the Red Bishops* and instructs the Pawns to first lift and then lower their banners 'so as to give the stage the appearance of a chapel'. This is a mesmerizingly beautiful movement and a peaceful moment of repose before *The Entry of the Red Castles*, the music for which we know from

*Things to Come*. Bliss decided to re-use the music he had written for *The Building of the New World* sequence equating the inhuman machinery used in that scene with the 'inhuman and menacing monsters' – his description of the Red Castles.

Bliss positively revels in the description of the characters as they assemble on the chess board. This is his *donnée* – something to describe in musical terms, this and, of course, the whole scenario. *The Entry of the Red King and Queen* is the climax of the entry of chess pieces with regal music which has undertones of uncertainty as the feeble old Red King is borne in a palanquin by four bearers, the Queen walking alongside. The air is menacing and, with all now in place, the audience can see a full board of players for the first time. Straight away the Red pawns adopt a fighting position and *The Attack* begins. The pieces move around to frenetic music. The Black Queen sees an opportunity to threaten the Red King and the music suddenly falters as the options are considered. The Red King summons Red Bishop I, but he is dismissed by the Black Queen. Desperately Red Bishop II is summoned and is equally thrust aside. The Red Queen pleads for the life of the Red King to a plaintive oboe melody. The two Black Knights carry the Red Queen away to fearsome music. *The Duel* follows as the first Red Knight leaps in to champion his king. A lengthy and passionate fight ensues as the Red Knight tussles with the mixed emotions of love for the Black Queen and desire to destroy her pout of loyalty to his king. He overcomes the Black Queen but hesitates and drops his sword, taking the red rose she had given him and walks away only to be stabbed in the back by the Black Queen.

A long cor anglais solo marks the Knight being raised onto the shoulders of all the pieces except the Black Queen and a funeral cortege follows in Bliss's most lustrous ceremonial mode. *The Black Queen Dances* sees the Red King in terror for his life watching the unfolding proceedings. The music has a deliciously carefree feeling as if the Black Queen is licking the wounds of her dead assailant like sipping champagne while calculating her next move. For all the feeble King's terror the Black Queen delivers perhaps the ultimate coup-de-grâce and leaves without even touching him whilst giving a gesture of savage triumph. The *Finale* sees the Red King praying for escape in gentle musical interludes between the dramatic representation of the fighting all around with all the black forces united against him. In one final show of strength, he remembers the power of his youth and he draws himself up to his full height. Bliss's music at this moment quite obviously takes its inspiration from Walton's *Belshazzar's Feast* (a very rare example of Bliss imitating anything British). This causes the black pieces to hesitate but the Black Queen enters behind the king and plunges the spear into him. This is checkmate. The final music is demonic and ends leaving a feeling of breathlessness at the sheer calculating viciousness of the game and its principal proponent.

The press response to the premiere was enthusiastic and the *Times* noted that 'though it did not charm so easily as the other ballets…(it) may be pronounced an emphatic success – of another order. In the first place, it has a dramatic scenario and, where the idea might have been worked out as a smart and facile *divertissement*, Miss de Valois, serious artist that she is, has chosen a difficult way of treating the theme tragically, building a tense little drama out of the rivalry of chessmen. The idea has touched the imagination of both composer and artist. There is nothing glib or obvious in the music or *décor*. Bliss's richly written score is highly effective, and reflects just that atmosphere of medieval strife, of jousting and jealousy, which the ancient game suggests.[40] The critic goes on to praise McKnight Kauffer's costumes and, with some reservations, de Valois's choreography. He has not taken in that the scenario was not de Valois's but Bliss's, with help from Bridges Adams. When it was first seen in London on 5 October the report reinforced the success of the premiere, adding 'The music has enormous nervous energy, which makes the battle almost terrifyingly real. This is no mere contest of wits fought out in silence… This note of seriousness is, perhaps, the characteristic English contribution to the art of the ballet, which has not elsewhere been endowed with so much solemnity. In this kind *Checkmate* is a notable successor to *Job*' (Vaughan Williams).[41] As a final word on *Checkmate*, it is interesting to note that while the ballet remained in the regular repertoire of companies on the continent, the Vic-Wells Company dropped it, according to Kenneth Clark writing about ballet décor, because it 'remained slightly outside the spirit of Sadler's Wells' partly because of 'a brilliant synthesis of modernisms – Cubism, Futurism, and the Syncretism of Kandinsky, all made more immediate for impact in the theatre'[42] and this kind of modernism was not in the soul of the company. One only has to remember the modernism of Pen Pits, Bliss's new Somerset house, to understand just how much he admired, and was inspired by, McKnight Kauffer's work and how this was an additional driving force in his inspiration. In Dennis Arundell's *The Story of Sadler's Wells* he notes that 'The 1937–8 season saw the most important new ballet since *Job*: de Valois's *Checkmate* (Arthur Bliss)… was an impressive success.'[43] And that is all. Not exactly a resounding endorsement of one of their most original commissions.

Before leaving Vic-Wells ballet which, by the time of his next major work for them, *Miracle in the Gorbals*, had been renamed Sadlers Wells Ballet, it is worth reminding ourselves that although *Checkmate* was his first work for ballet conceived for that form, he had already had two previous one act ballets performed by the company a few years earlier in 1932. These were *Narcissus and Echo* and *Rout*. The latter we know as his work from 1921 but the music for *Narcissus and Echo* has been uncertain and we now know was his 1919 *Rhapsody*. There was a preview of the show in the *Times* on 28 January 1932 noting that 'Miss Alicia Markova will dance for the first time with the Vic-Wells ballet on Saturday afternoon, when two works by Mr Arthur Bliss will be the novelties in the programme. These will be *Rout* and *Rhapsody* for strings and two voices, which has been arranged as a ballet.'[44] This gives us certainty over the *Narcissus and Echo* question.

Markova had already performed in the ballet made to *Rout* (1921) on two previous occasions, privately in January 1927 at the de Valois Studio (with Bliss and Malcolm Sargent playing the score as a piano duet) and then later in the month at the Cambridge Festival Theatre. In response to a performance of *Narcissus and Echo* given two months later the critic wrote 'Mr William Chappell's asymmetrical costumes and Miss Valois's choreography of stylized restlessness gave us the queer unsubstantiality of a world of reflected images and false voices.'[45] Here, another distinguished designer picks up the contemporary feeling in Bliss's music in the same way McKnight Kauffer did with *Checkmate*.

# Chapter Nine

# AN AMERICAN INTERLUDE

Bliss was renowned for his sense of humour. What comes across so vividly from his autobiography is a youthful sense of fun and enjoyment in everything he does. He was a gifted mimic, and his daughter Karen remembers numerous occasions when the household would be doubled up with laughter at his impression of someone they all knew, such as Ninette de Valois. On a visit to the zoo one day, they saw two Chinese chickens courting and he made an impression of this inelegant process, flapping his arms and generally causing much hilarity. Even the things he didn't like often had their twist of amusement. The 'bubble' in his personality was often mirrored in his music, and the show of emotion such as was evident in the recent works covered in the previous chapter is therefore even more significant as an expression of a serious inner life which outward humour is often used to hide.

In this way, his trip to Baden-Baden where his *Music for Strings* was being performed in March 1937 was accompanied by the slightly ridiculous 'chain gang' reception on the morning of the concert. Bliss, turning the humorous spotlight on himself, remembered that he had no idea how to dress for the occasion where they sat drinking coffee and kirsch whilst self-important officials stood up and 'orated'. Bliss confided to Trudy in a letter that the 'musical comedy effect' of 'an evening collar and shirt, a blue suit, and patent leather shoes' would 'pass well enough.'[1] In this letter he also described the further comedy of being unable to avoid having tea with an elderly, refined English woman, a gambling addict, who had come to his concert and, visiting his dressing room afterwards, told him that he 'carried an aura of good fortune' and wanted Bliss to stand behind her during her next session at the tables to bring her good luck! Managing to transform tea into whisky (which she also preferred) he politely excused himself.

At this stage of his career Bliss was now in demand not only as one of the leading composers of his day, but also one of the most personable. This inevitably led to invitations to sit on competition juries. In June 1937 he had been approached to judge the third International Composers Competition in Warsaw which never materialized because of the outbreak of war. In May 1938 he was on the jury of the Ysye International Competition for Pianists. He was in the illustrious company of great pianists including Rubinstein and Gieseking. The frustration of this event was the chairman of the jury who Bliss described as 'an old pupil of Liszt...who was both vain and weak'. Bliss threatened to withdraw from the jury in protest against the man's constant criticisms uttered aloud to the consternation of the nervous young competitors. Offering to play the Schumann Concerto to demonstrate how the piano should be played drew from Bliss the opinion that this was 'the feeblest exhibition of piano playing of the week.'[2] Emil Gilels 'sailed away with the first prize'.

The fallout from this experience was that 'I am learning a lot by listening to these young players'. The downside was the early stages during which he heard twenty-two pianists playing the same piece by Bach and the same by Scarlatti 'and expect to hear them sixty-three time more. Never again!'[3] But all this information was feeding his mind and encouraging him to feel that he would like to write an extended work for the instrument. It is therefore almost uncanny that an invitation should arrive almost immediately after he returned from Brussels with a commission from the British Council for a Piano Concerto with Solomon as soloist for the British week at the World Fair in New York in June 1939.

In the meantime, the first of many honours Bliss would receive throughout his life was bestowed by the King of Belgium when he was appointed a Commander of the Order of Leopold II, the equivalent of a knighthood in that country, a mark, perhaps, of his growing reputation and that he had served on the jury of the prestigious Ysaÿe competition in its early years. As a further mark of growing interest in him and his burgeoning reputation, Anna Mahler, Gustav's daughter, made a highly characteristic sculpture of his head sometime between 1939 and 1940. She and her mother had fled Nazi Austria in March 1938 and had come to live in Hampstead and thus near the Blisses. She was a distinguished artist, winning the Grand Prix in Paris in 1937, and making a feature of sculpting heads of famous musicians including Schoenberg, Berg, Artur Schnabel, Klemperer, Bruno Walter, Rudolf Serkin and Eileen Joyce. Bliss was in good company.

Bliss's next flirtation with the film studio was at one and the same time amongst his least satisfactory musical experiences and yet inspired really fine music which, thankfully, was drawn together in a six-movement concert suite which gives an opportunity for the music to shine in a way it could not in the film. *The Conquest of the Air* is a documentary about the history of man's attempts to fly from the earliest suicidal jumping off buildings with wings attached to arms to the sophistication of the aircraft achieved by the start of the Second World War. Alexander Korda was the producer, known well to Bliss from *Things to Come*. The film had been planned in 1934/35 but wasn't shot until 1936. Further uncertainties delayed a first attempt at a complete film until 1938 and in another mark of its chequered progress saw six successive directors attempt to draw it satisfactorily together. On 5 March 1938 the *Times* announced that Korda's first documentary film would be shown soon in London. But still it was delayed. Finally, under the direction of Charles Frend (who also narrated), it was released as a seventy-one-minute film in 1939.

Bliss had written the music some two years earlier and the concert suite was first heard in a BBC broadcast on 11 February 1938 conducted by Muir Mathieson with the London Film Symphony Orchestra. Its first live concert performance was as part of a Promenade concert at the Queen's Hall in London on 3 September with the BBC Symphony Orchestra conducted by Bliss. Whilst the film was regarded as an important documentary for its time the music, as Stephen Lloyd has pointed out, 'is cut about with snippets and snatches at random. *The Conquest of the Air* must count as one of the most brutalized film-scores.'[4] As the film underwent drastic changes in the latest stages of its evolution some of Bliss's music which appears in the concert suite was excised from the film. Perhaps the most interesting reflection on the Suite came in a *Radio Times* article by Constant Lambert which he called *Music of the Machine Age*.

'Arthur Bliss, who has just written music for an important documentary entitled *Conquest of the Air*, has evidently been conscious of the difficulty imposed by the apparently easy subject. Those who expect an imposing array of percussion instruments and a series of orchestral stunts in the latest Franco-Prussian manner will be disappointed. Bliss's is 'straight' music for a 'straight' orchestra, and he has throughout paid more attention to the human element than to the mechanical element... This suite suggests that modern composers are at last taking machinery for granted, that they no longer are interested in mechanical realism but prefer to treat modern realism as a normal expression of the life that surrounds us.'[5]

The real issue in the final cut of the film is the cavalier way in which the music is treated. As Lloyd details, 'There is some unacceptably crude cutting where the music suddenly breaks mid-phrase with abrupt joins instead of subtle fading. Furthermore, a great deal of the music is obliterated by either the commentary or aircraft noise.'[6] The other side of the same coin sees a substantial section with no music at all suggesting that it was added after all the music had been written. The final cut of the film was shown on 20 May 1940 at the Phoenix Theatre in London. It makes fascinating viewing as a documentary of flight but the music is subservient to a degree that must have upset Bliss deeply, being reduced to almost inaudible background noise at times. Keeping his feelings of disappointment to himself is something of which Bliss became something of a past master. It would rear its head in spectacular fashion in relation to The Beatitudes in the 1960s and it shows, perhaps, the characteristics of his generation: understatement, stiff upper lip, and no ostentatious display. He makes no mention of this experience, or indeed of the film, in As I Remember.

One of the great events of the summer of 1939 was the great World's Fair in New York. It was planned in 1935 in response to the Great Depression as a way of lifting the spirits of the city and to start the process of lifting the country out of its economic turmoil. It was planned as the greatest world event since the Great War and each country had its own pavilion in distinctive designs. The World's Fair commissioned Vaughan Williams's Five Variants on Dives and Lazarus, while the British Council commissioned Arnold Bax's Seventh Symphony and Bliss's Piano Concerto. Bliss had also written on behalf of the British Council to commission a Violin Concerto from Walton for the Fair. Walton, however, was already working on a violin concerto for Heifitz but felt that it might work providing the Council did not demand that it be performed by a British violinist. In the end the concerto was withdrawn from the Fair 'not because it's unfinished but because Heifitz can't play on the date fixed (the B.C. only let him know about 10 days ago!).'[7] Walton could be very cruel in his references to others and back in 1934 whilst writing the first Symphony he had written to Dora Foss who was holidaying close to the Blisses, presumably in Somerset: 'I hope you enjoyed your holiday in spite of the adjacency of the Blisses. I love your description of his studio and of course he is just like a moustachioed cod-fish so he will be in the right environment. I hope it won't make his music even more watery.'[8] Given the energy of Bliss's music, a quality he shares with Walton, it is difficult to see this as anything other than professional jealousy. Given how generous Bliss was to Walton this reflects poorly on Walton. In Susana Walton's biography of her husband, she recalls this same event but expands on it by saying 'Dora Foss was quite shocked, and complained to her husband that she couldn't understand what provoked such a letter, since she had merely informed William in a letter to him of their amusing visit to see Bliss's new music room.'[9]

Before accepting the invitation to be the soloist in Bliss's concerto, Solomon wanted to be reassured that he would be in sympathy with both Bliss's style and his approach to piano technique. Thus began another of Bliss's inspiring connections with a great artist with whom he could collaborate in the writing of a major new work. As Bliss said, 'He was meticulous in making technical suggestions, and, when the whole concerto was ready for engraving, his editing was of the greatest benefit to me.'[10]

This commission was deeply personal for Bliss in acknowledging in his dedication 'To the People of the United States of America' his own half American birthright as well as his wife's nationality. America was deeply embedded in his psyche and this work was therefore something of a milestone moment for him in a different way from *Morning Heroes* but with equally strong familial connections. Little did he know how the ramifications of this commission and the family's decision to stay to holiday in the States after the premiere would change his life for the foreseeable future.

Bliss gave a radio broadcast for the Canadian Broadcasting Corporation in the early summer of 1941 in which he colourfully described the sense of anticipation he and his family felt as they began their trip to the States for the premiere of his concerto. 'I do not know which of the four of us was most excited. I have lived in the States before, but find that however many times I return I am never disappointed at this first sight of the New World. My wife, being American, felt it was like coming home, and my two young daughters, who had never crossed the Atlantic before, naturally found everything exciting – the fine boat that had been their home for a week, the voyage on which they had seen ice-bergs and whales, and then these gigantic towers in which people actually lived. We were a happy and excited quartet.'[11] According to Bliss the ship in which they made the voyage was the RMS *Carmania* but this was not possible as the ship had been scrapped in 1932. They actually sailed on the RMS *Georgic* on 27 May (the ship would be bombed two years later before being salvaged and returning to service as a troop ship). They travelled with Adrian Boult (who was to conduct the concerto), Solomon, and Leon Goossens, who was also performing in the British week. After the concert they were to travel to California, head on to Canada, sail down the St Lawrence and make their journey home. But events were to overtake them when war was declared on 3 September 1939.

In the background before Bliss and his entourage arrived there was a potential bombshell as, according to Scott Goddard, the man temporarily in charge of the World's Fair decided 'whether through stupidity, or bare boredom… the Fair having gone on for some time, that enough contemporary music had been heard. And so, the performance was cancelled. It took place eventually at the Carnegie Hall, and it is said that there were those present then, among the American listeners, who felt abashed.'[12] Not exactly an auspicious start, but all ended well with the premiere taking place on 10 June.

Apparently, the full score of the concerto had preceded the Blisses' arrival and had been sent by airship – surely a risky enterprise in those days. Nevertheless, it arrived safely allowing rehearsals to get under way once Boult was in situ. Bliss colourfully described the style of the concerto by saying that 'some piano concertos are written using the piano as *concertante*, some of them using it as a percussion instrument. This is one of the few I know which does use it in the traditional grand manner.'[13] Certainly, the opening gambit (an extended rush of double octaves in triplets starting in the second bar) is enough to make the most hardened virtuoso quake at the prospect. This was true of Solomon at the first performance. 'I do not feel I *can* go on and play', he opined to Bliss who had then gently to push him on stage. 'I have been ruthless to my soloist in this concerto, for the uprush of quick octaves at the opening is one of the hardest passages in the whole work, but as soon as I heard Solomon's clear articulation in these, I knew all was well.'[14]

Some space in this story has been devoted to Bliss's development from so-called *enfant terrible* to romantic. But this concerto was actually conceived, as Bliss described it above, as a concerto in the manner and lineage of Liszt, Tchaikovsky, Brahms and Rachmaninov. Amongst all the British twentieth-century offerings there is none other like it. We should remember that Bliss attempted a piano concerto back in 1932 for Birmingham but signally failed at that point, partly due to the pressure of other work at the time. All the stars were lined up for this new concerto, however, and the appeal of both the hugely diverse and inclusive Fair, as well as the feeling that he needed to represent his country to the best of his ability and, at the same time, present the USA with a gift which mingled respect with deep affection, drew a remarkable life-affirming work from him.

The piano was Bliss's instrument and his declared first love and he felt a deep affinity with it. He had studied it to a creditable standard and whilst at Cambridge had taken lessons with Ursula Crichton who had been a pupil of Ferrucio Busoni which, as Bryan Crimp has pointed out, made him Busoni's 'pianistic grandson.'[15] Working with Solomon on the Concerto brought both joy and huge responsibility. 'Besides being a master pianist Solomon has the temperament I admire – capable of great feeling, held steady in check. I try to do the same by casting my work into as formal a pattern as I can.'[16] Solomon played very little contemporary music and it was really because of his friendship with Bliss that he agreed to take the concerto on. Bryan Crimp's biography of 'Solo', as Solomon was known to his friends, painted this vignette: There was 'a lot of adjusting of the florid parts to make it fit better under the fingers. Solo and Arthur would meet at Steinways and work in a room with two pianos. Bliss would play a passage and then Solo would repeat it but in a more soloistic way. More often than not, Arthur would jump up and ask, "Quick, quick, what was that? What did you do there?" This was how much of the solo line evolved.'[17]

The orchestra taking on this concerto was the New York Philharmonic-Symphony Orchestra whose principal conductor at the time was Barbirolli. Rehearsals were held in private on the orders of the British Council who were afraid that if the British Press gave a critique of the new works before the first performance it would affect their reception. They need not have worried as the reaction from the Americans was loud and warm. Toscanini attended some rehearsals and was apparently astonished by Bliss's exciting orchestral tuttis. It is certainly music for an occasion and *The New York Times* reported that 'the audience rejoiced in the brilliant music and repeatedly called back to the stage the composer, conductor and soloist.'[18] In a letter to Panda Henn-Collins of the British Council Bliss wrote from the Barbizon Plaza Hotel in New York: 'Everything has gone off well – in fact, very well. The American public is a lovely one and I have hit it fairly and squarely in the solar plexus. Critics are measured and good but are apt to be faintly venal.'[19] In a further letter the next day Henn-Collins wrote:

'I feel as though a great weight has been lifted from me, and I know that I owe this feeling in a very large measure to your efforts. Since the rehearsal in London, I never had any doubt about the quality of our present to the American people, but I did doubt whether they would realize its worth. It seems clear, however, from the cables we have received that the American public, or such of it as had an opportunity of listening to the new works, realized, at once, the value of them.

It must have been a very great moment for you and Trudie [sic] when the applause broke out, and I only hope it compensated adequately for the nervous strain and hard work which you had undergone beforehand.'[20]

All this was, of course, in the heat of first-night excitement. Makower telegrammed to the British Council in London to say 'Concerts brilliant success. Boult and soloists received ovation. English works much appreciated. Reaction Bliss particularly favourable.'[21] Peter Pirie in his book on *The English Musical Renaissance* is more dismissive with an interesting point which has been raised a number of times before: 'Bliss's Piano Concerto makes a great splash, but does not come up with a single memorable tune. The theme that follows the spectacular opening flourish tries hard to emulate Tchaikovsky, but is an artificial construction of several fussy figures which are repeated too often and refuse to coalesce. The slow movement has a rich, almost Baxian texture, but the material must reluctantly be described as undistinguished. All the material has a contrived air, and in such a work the themes should sound spontaneous to the point of vulgarity; the concerto fancier is deprived of his tune, while the more serious musician is likely to be repelled by the brashness of the work.'[22] While there is much which is true in this coruscating criticism Pirie fails to recognize Bliss's approach to a romantic concerto in a contemporary guise which does not just follow weary stereotypes. Figuration for Bliss often carries the significance of the long-breathed melody of previous generations.

Perhaps more telling still is the long and detailed letter Bliss's brother Howard wrote to him having heard the broadcast of the concerto on 23 September 1943. He also picks up Pirie's appreciation of the second movement: 'The orchestration of the second movement seemed particularly happy, I thought. Doubtless the others are just as good – in their way – but one has less time to hear and judge – and more noise. I couldn't help laughing out loud, here in this room – during the first movement – I began to think of Hitler and "shock tactics" and "war of nerves" – it was rather as if you said to yourself – "Just LOOK at that audience" – Here I've given them three long crescendos ending with a huge climax (each of them), and there they sit, absolutely UN-stunned. Will nothing move them (or rather FIX them)? Now what else can I bring out? I don't at all mean by this that it was all just a racket – there were some grand

174

sounds and I enjoyed it all… The first movement was just short enough for me – by which you will see that I wouldn't want it any longer – I got slightly restless in the cadenza perhaps – some of it sounded rather like "padding" – or Arthur Bliss improvisations – I know it is all connected with the rest of the movement, but I couldn't help feeling that I had suddenly opened the door of your music room, and found you rambling about! (on the piano). The beginning of the last movement sounded VERY sinister – You've got something there – I mean it's good. Raises expectancy – AND we are not disappointed.' He finishes after more points by saying 'I think it is an achievement – and so, I expect, do you.'[23] How wonderful to have a brother who can write such criticism honestly and know that it will be taken in the right spirit. Gerald Finzi, writing to the poet Edmund Blunden in February 1956 mentioned that he had written to Howard about a grammatical 'slip-up on T.H.'s part' because he knew 'him to have a vast Hardy collection (as well as being something of a grammarian, which I'm not) in the hope that he could tell me where the original ms cd be found'. Howard replied offering him the original MS of 'We Field Women' – a gesture Finzi found moving. 'I was much touched, especially as I hardly know him – he is as remote and shut-in as his brother Arthur is buoyant and sparkling.'[24] A rare glimpse of Howard's personality.

The Concerto had its London premiere under Sir Henry Wood at the Queen's Hall Proms on 17 August 1939 and the reaction was again very favourable, with the *Times* critic pointing out that 'the vigour of it carries the hearer over certain passages where, it may be, the composer's inspiration flags',[25] which would seem to mirror Howard Bliss's earlier comments. But the *Times* critic also pointed out that 'there is a genuine individuality in the music'. The bravura nature of this big-boned work has ensured that there has been no shortage of pianists wanting to tackle its challenging demands. But of all the pianists in Bliss's lifetime after Solomon the one who touched Bliss most was Noel Mewton-Wood with whom he went on to work a great deal and to whom he dedicated his Piano Sonata (1952) only to learn of Mewton-Wood's suicide soon afterwards at the age of thirty-one in December 1953. Bliss described him 'as one of the finest exponents of the concerto… One performance he gave with me, and which I shall never forget, took place in Ankara on the occasion of the opening of the new Opera House in the spring of 1948. As Noel was starting the virtuoso cadenza at the end of the first movement, the biggest black tomcat that I ever saw stalked on to the platform and settled himself down by the pedals of the piano. Noel was too concentrated on his playing to be aware of his companion, but he must have heard the ripple of laughter among the first rows of the audience.'[26]

The *Piano Concerto* was the first of Bliss's solo concertos, the violin and cello concertos coming in 1955 and 1970 respectively. The medium of the concerto was one which suited Bliss's sense of the dramatic, and in the *Piano Concerto* he used the concept of the solo protagonist against the crowd to heighten the drama in what is still a unique concerto from a British composer. The focus of attention in this work is its dramatic outer movements with their dazzling displays of technical virtuosity from the soloist, but in the central movement there is an emotional core which might even be seen as a heart-felt tribute to his late (American) father, acknowledging the enormous legacy of a powerfully supportive upbringing. Maybe, too, the serendipity of the fact that had his father not chosen to return to the States for his final years, Bliss would never have met his wife. There is much here for Bliss to mull over in reflective mood in this powerful, elegiac movement with angular, yearning lines. In its second subject he finds one of those rare figures which has a simplicity more associated with the slow movements of Gerald Finzi, connecting deeply with an emotional core which through that very simplicity is infinitely touching.

Ex.1

In preparation for travelling to the States Bliss was in correspondence with Serge Koussevitsky about the possibility of performing his *Music for Strings* while in America. On 3 March 1939 he wrote:

'After fourteen years I am coming to New York in June to be present at the first performance of my new Piano Concerto there. I am going to remain in the east until September 1st, and wonder whether during those three summer months there would be any possibility of my being able to appear personally to conduct a work of mine either in Boston or at the

Berkshire Festival? Please forgive me for communicating with you about this, but after these many years I do not know in the least what musical conditions are in the States, or whether my appearance would be of any interest or not.

I do not think that either my *Music for Strings*, my Suite from the ballet *Checkmate*, or my later works have yet been played there.'

But things were to move swiftly, throwing the family's plans into confusion. Once the concerto premiere was done, the plan was for the Blisses to take a camping holiday after first splitting up so that Trudy and the girls, now aged thirteen and seven, went to stay with relatives in Stockbridge, and Bliss went with Boult to Ravinia Park near Chicago, where a programme of outdoor concerts was featuring some of his music. After rejoining the family, Bliss moved on to Moosehead Lake in Maine for their camping adventure, with the intention of boarding the ship for the return voyage in either Montreal or Quebec.

Rumours had been circulating for some time about a possible explosion of hostilities but in their remote rural location current news was difficult to come by. The rumours, however, were hardening into something more tangibly worrying and they felt it best to pack up and return to Stockbridge and hear the news first hand. It was there, on 3 September, they heard that war had been declared on Germany. Bliss had first met the composer Albert Elkus in 1923 when his father had moved to live near Santa Barbara. Elkus was Chairman of the Music Department at the University of San Francisco at Berkeley. He was a widely respected musician who had been in touch with Bliss about performing the March from *Things to Come*. At that stage Bliss had replied saying that he had lunched with Pierre Monteux who had asked for his 'cordial greetings' to be passed on to Elkus. Bliss also expressed the wish for a 'more important work' to be played, adding that he still toyed 'idly with the dream of coming out to the Pacific Coast next year – but it remains a dream.'[27]

Elkus travelled from the west coast to attend the premiere of Bliss's Piano Concerto and afterwards asked if Bliss might like to come as a visiting professor for a couple of terms to deliver a series of lectures on English music. At that moment Bliss had thanked him warmly and promised to consider it when he returned to England. Now, however, it seemed like a lifeline. He had cabled Adrian Boult, who was back in England, to ask if there was any role he could fulfill if he returned but Boult's advice was to wait. Their decision was made when they heard that a passenger ship had been sunk and they felt they could not put themselves in such danger. Bliss therefore gratefully accepted Elkus's offer and they moved temporarily to Belmont, a town close to Boston, where Trudy Bliss had been born. He then settled down to research the history of English music for his lecture series.

It is easy to imagine someone of Bliss's generation, with his ingrained sense of loyalty and who had fought in the First World War with distinction, harbouring feelings of guilt being isolated in a foreign country unable to help the current war effort. In the same way that soldiers whose lives were endangered often found the smallest thing of beauty accrued extraordinary value, Bliss recounted how, visiting the Boston Museum of Fine Arts one afternoon in a depressed mood, encountered Renoir's *La Danse à Bougival*. He felt that it was 'so strongly constructive, so full of rich humanity, that I felt ashamed of my cold depression and defeatism... In that one picture art showed its power to triumph over the miseries and brutalities that war brings in its train. Indeed, all art worthy of the title should add to the excitation of life.'[28]

In the meantime, along with his English music research, Bliss was still trying to interest Koussevitsky in programming his *Music for Strings*, or another of his recent works. On 22 September he wrote: 'Having been caught in America by the war with my wife and children, I am staying the winter working here close to Boston. I should so much welcome the opportunity of seeing you again and if you are sympathetic to my music of going through some recent scores of mine with you... Cut off as I am from Europe temporarily, I shall be doubly grateful for such a gesture.'[29] Bliss continued his charm offensive on Koussevitsky through October and it seems as if he had a breakthrough as he wrote on 18 November that 'Some weeks ago you kindly told me you would like to include my *Music for Strings* in your symphony programmes either at the end of November or the beginning of December as a first performance in America. Now my stay in Boston is drawing to a close, I actually leave about December 20th, and I have told both Ormandy and Goossens that the work is not yet available, so as to have the honour of a first public performance in this country with your orchestra.'[30] It seems, however, that Koussevitsky did not perform the work after all. It is clear to hear the note of frustration in Bliss's final letter to Koussevitsky on 22 December: 'Before I leave Boston, I must write a message of farewell to you. I had hoped to do so personally... I shall take with me the memory of your wonderful performances and your orchestra. If one of these days you bring to vivid life my *Music for Strings* you know what I shall feel though I be 3,000 miles away.'[31]

Christmas was spent near Chicago with more of Trudy's relatives, before they moved to the west coast and a rented house in Warring Street, Berkeley in the heart of the university. The building in which Bliss gave his lectures on the first floor was what is now called the Dwinelle Annex. The music department of the university was warmly welcoming to Bliss and his family, and some of his reservations about staying in the States were alleviated by the people who were to become lifelong friends.

There was some considerable correspondence between Bliss and Elkus about the content of Bliss's lectures and also his composition classes. Bliss researched his lectures in the Widener Library at Harvard University. His plans initially were to cover Dunstable and Tudor music; Tye, Whyte, Tallis and mid-sixteenth-century; Byrd and the Madrigalian era; Morley, Orlando Gibbons, Wilbye; Dowland and the lutenists; keyboard music; music under the Commonwealth; Purcell and Blow, etc. 'I shall try and relate the contemporary composer to his ancestors directly: e.g., Vaughan Williams and Tallis, Peter Warlock and the lutenists, Constant Lambert and Purcell, and I will try to keep it as alive as possible. To this end I think we ought to perform as much in class as possible – singing in however an amateur way.'[32] In relation to this last point, Bliss later recalled that he formed a large madrigal group and an excellent string quartet, and encouraged solo wind and brass players. 'I resorted to a real "gimmick" on occasions. For instance, when I was analyzing the Purcell Fantazias, I invited any student who could beg, borrow or steal a stringed instrument to bring it to the next lecture, whether they played one or not. Some twenty turned up with violins, violas, or cellos. With bows in their hands and their fingers firmly on the strings to sound middle C, they took part in Purcell's Five Part Fantazia on one note, my skilled quartet performing around them. After this participation I felt sure none of them would forget the experience of Purcell's music.'[33] In terms of composition classes he suggested lessons for those who wished to sign up and 'a few popular lectures for the many'. He suggested a title of 'Practical Problems in Composition' for the composers, and for the 'popular' class for anyone interested, 'The Well-Tempered Listener'. He also mentioned at the end of this letter the issue of housing and that it needed to be a 'roomy, quiet and practical easy house to run. I must work, and I can't here – too small, too noisy.'[34]

Bliss is concerned about accessing the music and recordings required and tells Elkus in the same letter that the following week he travels to New York to conduct his *Checkmate* suite with the New York Philharmonic and he will be able to check then. The list of recorded music he wants to present to the students makes interesting reading:

| | |
|---|---|
| Bax | Quintet for oboe and strings |
| Bliss | Clarinet Quintet |
| Boyce | Power of Music |
| Britten | Variations on a Theme by Frank Bridge |
| Byrd | I thought that love had been a boy |
| Dowland | Come heavy sleep |
| | Go, crystal tears |
| | Pavans, Galliards, Almands for lute |
| Elgar | Falstaff |
| Gibbons | Ah, dear heart |
| | Hosanna to the Son of David |
| | The Silver Swan |
| Morley | My bonnie Lass |
| | Now is the time of Maying (sic) |
| | Sing we and chant it |
| | Since my tears |
| Purcell | Dido and Aeneas |
| | Nine 4 pt Fantasies |
| | Golden Sonata |
| Rawsthorne | Theme and Variations for 2 violins |
| Walton | Concerto for viola and orchestra |
| Weelkes | As Vesta was |
| | Latmos Hill descending |
| Wilbye | Sweet honey sucking bees |
| Vaughan Williams | Fantasia on a Theme of Tallis |
| | Symphony in F minor (4th) |

Early in December he was still trying to hone his lecture programme requesting a one-hour composition session rather than two and reducing the popular lectures to three rather than four (Elkus had suggested it might be three or possibly five – leaving it to Bliss to decide). It had also been suggested that Bliss should conduct the university orchestra in a programme of his own works. Two-hour composition classes had to be accommodated because of student credits being based on the number of hours they attended seminars.

The Music Library at Berkeley has Bliss's lecture notes which show that he taught all the basic elements relating to the instruments of the orchestra including transposition issues (and requiring the students to do some simple exercises). He discussed orchestration relating to four points: 1: study of aesthetic possibilities of instruments. 2: tone colour of individual instruments. 3: mixture, groupings, blends of instruments. 4: dynamic values of instruments in relation to one another. Each instrument was then studied according to 1: construction, 2: range and transposition if any, 3: tone quality – timbre in varying registers, 4: technical resource, 5: characteristic roles. He talked about the construction of a scale and the compromises in equal temperament along with chord spacings and effective (and non-effective) note doublings – and so it went on. It was a comprehensive course for these students who, learning from such an experienced composer, especially a composer who has been so concerned with experimenting in sound and thus knowing the characteristics of instruments so intimately, must have been illuminating.

In relation to the study of the musical works listed earlier, owing to the larger than expected class sizes the university wasn't able to provide scores for all the students and thus Bliss had to invent a way of explaining what would happen next by the use of diagrams on a blackboard.

Bliss initially thought that the contract for his employment at Berkeley would be for six months, but the President of the University, Robert Sproul, wrote to him on 28 August 1939 saying that 'the term of your residence in Berkeley need not be as long as six months. Instruction begins on January 22 and the term ends about April 30, thus elapsed time is a little over three months.'[35] In accepting the invitation Bliss elicited heartwarming responses from Sproul and Elkus in anticipation of his arrival. It was a happy connection.

One of the additional bonuses of Bliss's stay in California was the proximity of two of his greatest musical heroes, Stravinsky and Schoenberg, temporarily living close by in Los Angeles. He visited both composers and enjoyed playing part of the Symphony in C as a piano duet with Stravinsky who was writing it at the time. Bliss's musical language may have moved on from his 'Stravinsky' days but the visceral energy of the Symphony's first movement was something to which Bliss related fundamentally. Visiting Schoenberg, table tennis came first, which Bliss described as 'haphazard and delightfully hilarious'. After lunch, the mood changed as they listened to Schoenberg's fourth quartet, and after that the first, during which Schoenberg paced the room, deeply affected by obviously painful memories associated with it. 'The sight of him with tears in his eyes touched a similar chord in me, and I also felt moved.'[36]

Inevitably, very little composition was achieved during this period. Bliss felt too agonized being separated from his home country in its hour of need. He felt that the Berkeley work was comparatively unimportant when he was reading distressing headlines in the British press and deeply worrying letters from his brother Howard. But he did write a set of *Seven American Poems* setting words by two American writers, Edna St Vincent Millay and Elinor Wylie. This cycle is a remarkable conception and was an obvious release for the pressure built up over recent months. They were written while the Blisses were staying in a house lent to them by his wife's relatives in Santa Barbara and Bliss wrote that 'it was eerily strange to be staying there once more under such different circumstances, and my mood at that time is expressed in my settings of seven American Poems.'[37] The choice of poets is interesting as both women were controversial in their day (both were born contemporaneously with Bliss). He wrote nine songs originally. The two subsequently omitted were also to poems by Millay. There are two possible reasons for their exclusion, first, they need to be sung by a woman where the other seven could be sung by a singer of either sex, and second, the question of mood. The two excluded songs (which were only published posthumously) have texts which are strangely different from the other poems, the first *Humoresque*, being darkly humorous, and the second *The Return from Town* relaxed in a way which feels foreign to the general mood. Bliss wanted to maintain the atmosphere which he described as carrying 'the burden of a vanished joy or beauty.'[38] Each song is brief – a distillation of ideas and mood into a concentrated moment which increases the intensity of expression in which there is a strongly nostalgic flavour unusual in the normally positive, forward-thinking composer. But sitting in Santa Barbara, scene of such happy memories of love, marriage, his father's final years and carefree music-making all those years earlier it is hardly surprising to see the middle-aged Bliss reflecting in this way especially when the world was in another period of turmoil, his beloved country at the heart of it, and he separated from it all however safe his family might be as a result.

The agony of indecision as to what to do for the best occupied Bliss throughout this period and he touchingly writes about Trudy's quiet acceptance of whatever might be the outcome. Hearing from Howard about the near misses of bombs falling next to his house in Collingham Road, London brought everything very close to home and the fear of losing another brother a very real possibility. Howard had written on 15 September 1940, 'I was making an effort to get some sleep...when the scream of descending bombs suddenly began... louder and louder the scream – until it seemed to get right into the house – then thud, thump, whack! The house just rocked, and I heard through the wall at my head the sound of falling masonry and crumbling brickwork. I felt sure the house was coming down on me... After half an hour our locality seemed safer and I came up to my landing again. In the morning I went on to my roof. Just at my corner and exactly (as I paced it) twenty-six yards behind this house was a crater ten feet deep and seventeen feet across where a high explosive had fallen... Keeping this up paralyses one's ability to think or concentrate on anything.'[39]

In the meantime, Bliss was still contacting key people in London to offer his services including Bridges Adams at the British Council and Adrian Boult at the BBC. Adams was adamant in his letter of 18 September in which he stated unequivocally that 'your job is to stay where you are and write music. There are few enough of us today who can do anything now but destroy. You are over age: you have "kept" one Great War with distinction: moreover, the composing of music should be as much entitled to a place in the schedule of reserved occupations as smelting or riveting. . . So before irrevocably deciding to abandon your young and come back to join the elderly gentlemen in tin hats who are guarding railway bridges, reflect that you are quite possibly more useful where you are.'[40]

'Useful' he may have been in his visiting professorship at Berkeley but the feelings of guilt in not being in England to help the war effort in any way he could, as well as the feelings of guilt in leading a comfortable, well-paid existence in California when family, friends and colleagues were suffering at home, meant that there was little appetite for composition. Eventually, however, Elizabeth Sprague Coolidge persuaded him to write a string quartet for the Pro Arte Quartet to be premiered at Berkeley in April 1941. On 15 November 1940 Bliss wrote to Coolidge saying, 'I hope to get the score of my quartet to you on or about January first. I should have loved to have joined my two friends Goossens and Milhaud at the New York performances, but I want to take my time over this my first string quartet, and it has got to grow at my own pace. I am very pleased with it so far, but perhaps that is no criterion, as one always loves one's last child best.'[41] On Thanksgiving Day in November he wrote to her again to report that 'I am making great efforts to finish the quartet in time for your New York concert on Jan 13th. The first two movements are almost ready for the copyist and I think I can get them off to the Coolidge Quartet ½ way through December. The third and final movement will have to wait a while, but I shall tend every minute to the work and do my very best for you.'[42]

Although Bliss clearly states that the quartet was written for the Pro Arte quartet and that its first performance was in April 1941, in fact the premiere of the first three movements took place in New York played by the Coolidge Quartet. There is no mention of this in *As I Remember* or the Catalogue of Bliss's works, and only the references to New York in these letters and in the Chronology Stewart Craggs's *Source Book* confirm that this took place. Bliss wrote to Coolidge, who was unable to attend the New York concert as she had suffered an accident, 'It is half the interest gone if you are not sitting there in front and hearing the music that you have yourself stimulated into being. The last movement of my quartet is nearly finished and will be sent off to Kroll (the leader of the quartet) in two weeks' time – in the meantime I am asking him to send me the other 3 back for slight revision before the next performance.'[43] In the same letter he expresses his deep sadness at the death of Frank Bridge, 'a fine musician and fine friend lost. I thought of you at once when I was told the news, as I know how much he loved you.'[44]

The Quartet was premiered on 9 April 1941 by the Pro Arte Quartet and Bliss, writing to Coolidge after the performance, wrote that 'The Pro Arte played my quartet magnificently. They like it, I like it and I know you will like it.'[45] Just before this date she had presented the manuscript of the quartet to the Library of Congress in Washington.

The Quartet is another seminal work from this highly unsettling period. It is interesting that he calls this his first quartet where, in fact, he had written two earlier ones. But he is discarding the immature works and only acknowledging works from his maturity so that he is represented by the best of his creativity at this point in his career. The opening slow section of the first movement is one of his loveliest creations. John Amis, a long-time friend and highly discerning commentator on all things musical, wrote a moving passage in his introduction to the series of essays on Bliss's music called *Arthur Bliss Music and Literature* in which he states 'His music never wears its heart on its sleeve, despite occasional tenderness; it is not impersonal (quite the opposite) but there is always a certain objectiveness. There is warmth in the harmonies and I would like to put forward twenty-two bars which contain what I think is the essence of the Bliss style. It is the slow introduction to the first movement of this String Quartet No.1; it abounds in sevenths, fourths, what I call "squashed" dominants, bluesy false relations, unusual superimpositions, "wrong" but immensely telling secondary notes, powerful, warm, ending up in the final chord with a wonderful cock-eyed dominant plus a false bass and a tonic B flat on top to tell you where the next chord will pitch.'[46]

The remarkable thing about this movement is that this opening could be regarded as full of regret and longing – describing his mood of the moment. But what follows almost snaps its fingers in impatience to move on. An ostinato figure is created and the music moves forward in steps, *energico* and then *Allegro con brio* and all the musical material is thrown into the melting pot, moving in and out of energetic music and relaxation of tension by turns whilst always returning to the music of that beautiful opening. Then we return to the question of style and form. Form is what Bliss creates. He doesn't shoehorn his music into well-worn formats as we have seen many times already. Style, too, is fluid, sometimes harshly discordant, sometimes intensely lyrical and romantic, sometimes rhythmically adventurous like the opening of the second movement in bars of 6/8 and 2/8, and others plain sailing with the interest focused on harmony and counterpoint. But Edward Bonavia, writing about the work in *Music and Letters* has it that 'If there is no style, one decides that one can quite well do without it, for two equally valuable things take its place quite satisfactorily: individuality and supreme skill. There is also, if one may say so a great deal of beauty... Arthur Bliss shows from the first, in the remarkable introduction to the opening movement, that he can also extract truly beautiful invention from discordant harshness.'[47] Another endorsement of that opening.

The third movement is strongly elegiac with the rising intervals of longing that we saw in the *Seven American Poems* writ large here. But the really interesting feature in this movement is the barely-veiled reference to American indigenous melody such as Dvorak used in his *New World* symphony and the *American* quartet.

The contours of this melody, the triplet at the end of the second bar with its chromatic rise, the repeated dotted crotchet/quaver rhythm and the final triplet are all redolent of a spiritual which, whether intentional or not on Bliss's part, signals a deep American connection – perhaps even a subconscious one which makes it even more powerfully connected to its commissioner and the country of its birth.

The fourth movement is fast and furious with moments of respite and has an extraordinarily dissonant send-off before it settles down into its bitter-sweet progress. It charts its own course with melodic material presented as it progresses providing signposts for listening. The Presto coda is typical Bliss bravura designed to get the audience to its feet.

Albert Elkus tried hard to keep Bliss employed at Berkeley on a temporary basis and had correspondence with the university hierarchy about it. But events overtook them when Bliss received a letter from Kenneth Wright, Director of Overseas Music at the BBC, asking him to return to England to help in his department. This left Bliss feeling more torn than ever as acceptance would mean leaving his wife and daughters behind for an unknown period of time as well as putting himself in immediate danger during the transatlantic crossing. Boult wrote a telegram to Bliss on 20 March 1941 outlining the situation: 'A new Overseas Music Department including our European and North American Services has been formed with Kenneth Wright as director. You could do vital wartime work either as Wright's second or as a general policy adviser to Home and Overseas Music. Salary £1,000 available former post. Would you consider either? If so, say when, and formal offer could follow immediately. Greetings.'[48] Bliss replied accepting either post and indicating that although his Berkeley contract ended on 31 May he could be released immediately. He was contacted by return, confirming the post of assisting Kenneth Wright and detailing what the BBC would pay towards his travel costs and what would be his responsibility.

Bliss travelled to New York arriving on 1 May with his family who saw him off on his journey to Canada travelling by train to Toronto, Ottawa and on to Montreal from where he would join the ship which, in convoy, would take him to England. There was a month's delay in Montreal before they set sail on 7 June for the twenty-six-day voyage to Bristol. During the delay period he had plenty of time to consider his position and what it meant in terms of separation from his family. His autobiography touchingly reprints some of the letters he wrote to Trudy and his daughters. A flavour is given by this short extract from the King Edward Hotel in Toronto written on 7 May: 'Such a fine crop of letters fell into my box this morning... You can't know what a fine glow I have inside me at the thought of the little core of love and beauty stationed in Berkeley... You can rest *fully* assured I shall take *every* precaution I *should* from now onwards. I have you 3, I have important work to do, and I have much more to create. So do not rest anything but easy on that score, darling.'[49] And in another letter from the same hotel on 10 May he wrote: 'From a feeling of desolation on leaving my darling and beautiful wife my spirits are rising with active things to do and will continue to do so – and that is the only source of final triumph – to get through this separation with as little despair as possible, and I *know* we shall both do it, bless you....'[50]

Finally, in a letter on 10 June, Bliss wrote, 'another pilot boat is ready to take mail off so I dash off a line to you at Santa Barbara. This is my fifth day on board (SS *Bayano*) at an Eastern Canadian port (Montreal), and as I know nothing beyond the fact that we must sail soon, I cannot tell you much. I write in a comfortable cabin all to myself and have spent the last five days walking round the deck... I wish I could tell you the conditions under which I am sailing, but I can't.'[51] Bliss reported the slowness of the convoy's progress as well as its exceptional size. The slow speed was due to reports of *Bismarck* prowling in search of prey necessitating a more circuitous route thus adding considerable distance. But he also described the antics of a group of volunteer air pilots who were not at all willing to subject themselves to the British officer who was trying to discipline them. Alcohol was consumed in large quantities in celebration of the news that Russia had joined the war effort, and ran out long before they reached Bristol!

On reaching Bristol Bliss immediately set off for London, stayed in a 'bleak' hotel ('I felt I had wandered into some black nightmare') and then was overjoyed to be invited to stay with close friends who had been next door neighbours in Hampstead, Maurice and Nancy Farquharson. The Blisses had given up the lease of East Heath Lodge on the outbreak of war, uncertain as to when they would be returning to England. Maurice was an old friend from army days and was now in the senior management at the BBC and could therefore give Bliss all the advice he needed – and the machinery (and machinations) of the BBC needed much unpacking to a novice. It was a lovely touch that Kenneth Wright, Bliss's new boss, immediately wrote to Trudy to thank her for sparing her husband. 'I see the great, the vital work we must do: the almost unlimited scope of the job: the great opportunities it will give to imagination, enterprise, and to youth, the future it must help to shape. Music can play such a role in this war as few people dream. I see all this: and knew that Arthur was the ideal colleague to help me – help us all – to carry it through.'[52]

# Chapter Ten

# THE DANCE RESUMES: THE BBC, *MIRACLE IN THE GORBALS* AND *ADAM ZERO*

The key to Bliss's early days at the BBC was a lady called Ursula Elliott. She was assigned as his secretary and Bliss was never more grateful to Kenneth Wright for anything than for her appointment to assist him. He noted her extraordinary memory, her filing system and her unflappable personality as key traits which made her invaluable. He worked at Bedford College in Regent's Park, London and having no idea what to do initially, he sat and waited. He didn't have to wait long before a pile of correspondence was dumped on his desk with, as he put it, 'inexplicable initials'. Ursula gradually created order out of chaos, and Bliss learned that once having stepped on the inexorable treadmill of the BBC's bureaucratic behemoth, it never stopped. He had to learn how to cope through the example of his more experienced colleagues.

In a letter to Trudy on 11 July 1941, he outlined his daily routine: '7.45, awakened and given a cup of tea, breakfast with Maurice, Nancy and Phoebe (Nancy's sister). Maurice takes the 24 bus, Nancy goes to her canteen, Phoebe to her doctor's consulting room, I walk to Hampstead tube, buy the *Daily Telegraph*, Warren St, bus to Baker St, 100 yds. walk to Regent's Park, Bedford College – arrive 9.45. "Good morning, everybody". In my room I find Rollo Myers and his secretary, and my Miss Elliott, attend staff lecture on short wave transmission (very interesting) – 11.30, see à Becket Williams about programmes he wants to give – kindly dissuaded him – letters to answer – 1.0, lunch in Bedford College – sort of cafeteria – fish salad and trifle – (quite good) – 2.30, investigate light music rehearsal – 4.30 see Benjamin Dale in RAM, and have tea – 5 till 5.30 with Miss Elliott – back to Hampstead – bath and dinner – Bridges (Adams) rings up – Farqs go out – write to you – tomorrow I have Gerald Finzi for lunch and hope to get him into the BBC somehow.'[1] He also mentioned that he had omitted 5.30–6.30 exercises with 'Hornibrook expert' (a system of abdominal exercises based on native dancing rituals!).

On 22 July Bliss was again writing to Trudy, reporting enthusiastically that he had dined with Stephen Spender who wanted to write an opera libretto for him – another opera project that was to come to nothing.

Bliss had a wonderful relationship with the Farquharsons who he called 'M'ong and N'ang' after seeing the Chinese Exhibition in London in 1935. Nancy recalled: 'Arthur had a very lively personality – he was often extremely witty and tended to be at his very best at breakfast. This was not *our* best time as we either wanted to read the papers or ponder the day ahead... however, he was equally lively sometimes at the end of the day... We had just returned one evening from the theatre – by Tube – A. decided that one was shorter than another and he would demonstrate the point, so we parted company and he went one way and we the other. There was very little in it but we arrived home to find A. standing at the top of the stairs in his pyjamas, yawning. He had obviously run the whole way....'[2]

Now his feet were firmly under the table Bliss needed to feel a sense of direction in his work. He had to react to letters and memoranda but he was really being employed to think about the bigger picture and make a difference. He did not just sit behind a desk, he put himself behind the microphone: 'I have three times broadcast to North America and Canada, making records which are later at night or early in the morning broadcast, two were introducing programmes by Myra Hess and a jazz pianist(!), and the third was a half an hour broadcast answering questions cabled by Americans and Canadians.'[3] He also acted as an announcer for a Promenade concert on 5 August and broadcast to the west coast of America.

In the meantime his domestic life remained bound up with the Farquharsons who were generous in their continuing hospitality, but rather than burden them with the need to look after him morning and evening he joined the Savile Club at which he reported to Trudy that he could 'dine there (very well and cheaply) to avoid being too much in the way at Heathside.'[4] He also took the opportunity of catching up with old friends in August, travelling to Evesham (BBC) to see Leon Goossens, then to Birmingham to see Leslie Heward (conductor of the City of Birmingham Orchestra, as it was then), and finally to Manchester to rehearse his oboe Quintet and see his artist friend Edward Wadsworth and his wife Fanny, before taking the midnight sleeper back to London, returning in time to get to his office for 9.30am.

There were many initiatives in which he was involved at the BBC one of which was of special interest to Bliss personally. This was a short programme *At Your Request* in which people from the area to which he was broadcasting submitted questions for him to answer. One of these programmes was aimed at his former students at Berkeley and he wrote to Albert Elkus asking if they would like to submit six questions, musical or otherwise, which he could address in a broadcast to the Pacific Coast on 2 October 1941. Bliss's broadcast was scripted and he addressed these questions: 'What are English composers doing?', 'Is there more or less music than in peacetime?', 'Does war seem to turn people to particular composers or kind of music?', 'What American music, and how much is played in England today?', and finally, 'How much music is available at small cost or free in the English democracy?' Answers were chatty but as informative as possible. He began by saying 'Hullo' to everyone – not the BBC-speak we associate with this period! Much weight was placed on the absence of male musicians who were on active service, the effect of the blackout and the importance of the BBC in broadcasting music. In answer to the question about wartime and types of music, Bliss had consulted widely before the broadcast and the general opinion was that there was a definite trend towards more serious music: 'Frivolity in any art cannot be endured'. He makes the point that Beethoven is the 'one composer whom the people need and demand above all others. Beethoven has supplanted Bach in general favour. Wagner has slipped well down the list of favourites, Sibelius still holds his own chosen public... In this war eternal truths and stark realities are there for all to see – and none can escape them.'[5] Bliss was pleased to be able to report that a great deal of American music was being performed and broadcast in England including an Anglo-American concert attended by the American Ambassador which included Samuel Barber's Symphony. Finally, in answer to the question about music at small cost to the public, he was able to talk about Myra Hess's National Gallery concerts at a shilling a time with queues of people wanting to attend stretching around Trafalgar Square. 'These concerts have been given every day, regardless of how bad war conditions are. Similar concerts have started weekly in Oxford, Bath, Cheltenham and Liverpool... Music for the people is in the air, but we have a lot to learn from you in this respect. We envy you your Hollywood Bowl, your New York Stadium and your Ravinia Park, and your many festivals, but we are determined to regain the ground we have lost here.'[6]

This direct engagement is echoed in an internal memo *The Case for Live Music* in the following January (22nd) where he notes in his first point that 'You can only hold your overseas audiences by the *personal* touch. "Live" must speak to "live". Commercial canned music will hold no one, because the same discs are obtainable all over the world and are constantly heard on local stations'. The personal touch was very much in evidence in that broadcast to the Pacific Coast, starting with the form of address. In this important statement of philosophy, he continues by stressing that 'We must proclaim in music, as in every other way, what this country stands for, what it has done in the past, and what it is doing now, and what its efforts will lead to.' In a moment of serious self-realization, he admits, 'We must have in mind the position music holds in other countries. It is our misfortune if by comparison we are uncouth, and we must not broadcast this fact. We must initiate a standard of culture at least equal to that advertised by Germany. Our own great music and our own great poetry must be broadcast by our *living* artists, who should be proud to do this service at any hour, day or night'. That a standard of culture needs to be initiated, according to Bliss, was an admission that the serious arts were only in the purview of a cultural elite. Bliss wanted to bring music and poetry to the masses and the BBC was the natural route, directly into everyone's homes.

His third point was: 'We must continue to use music as a friendly complimentary gesture. For example, we must broadcast the scores of Canadian composers sent to us by the CBC (Canadian Broadcasting Corporation), and those that arrive from South Africa, New Zealand, and Australia. Dominion artists in this country must be used. Other examples of complimentary concerts have been the weekly series "Music of the Allies", the proposed Latin-American concert, and the Stalin and Roosevelt birthday concerts. There is no compliment in commercial recordings.'[7] Bliss's work with the British Council and the benefit he had received from it personally undoubtedly fuelled this last point as he could see the enormous benefit of reciprocal interaction and the good will generated by small acts of generosity.

His fourth and final point was possibly his most powerful: 'Live music will always remain of potent use for: a) evoking memories in exiled audiences, and b) encouraging and stirring countries whose own music has been forbidden by the enemy'. As a postscript he notes that the BBC engineers have to make short-wave more reliable as the Germans were getting bigger overseas audiences simply because of the quality of the listening experience (not programme content). He ends by making the point that 'without live music, we shall simply become a talking shop, and any-how, what are we talking about?'[8] So, on one level it was a charm offensive, and on another a serious propaganda exercise.

In a letter to Trudy from the Savile Club on 31 August 1941 Bliss wrote: 'I have suggested to Adrian (Boult) that I become Director of Music and he confines his duties to conductorship of the orchestra. I want more power as I have a lot to give which my comparatively minor post does not allow me to use fully… but I doubt whether I rise to such eminence immediately.'[9] There is a real sense of self-confidence – no modesty here – just a wish to get his feet fully under the table and exercise his judgement to real effect.

One of the things which comes across vividly from Bliss's autobiography is a sense of the fun he was having both in his job and also personally catching up with old friends and happily making new ones. The other side of this coin, however, was the huge ache he felt at this long estrangement from his family thousands of miles away. A particularly telling letter written on 27 October described a happy weekend with Stephen Spender and his wife Natasha ('You would love them – sensitive, generous, modest…'). He told her of going to the theatre in the West End where Alan Bush was rehearsing a Labour Chorus in Russian songs, and how the Russian lady announcing the broadcast had joined Bush and Bliss afterwards for something to eat. At 10pm the chorus and the Bliss trio settled down to sleep on mattresses in the theatre (men in the orchestral pit, women in the dress circle). They were woken at 3.30am for the chorus to sing to North America and Canada: 'I was *thrilled* by this small choir of shopkeepers, carpenters, typists, etc'. He slept from 6.30am – 10 and then went to meet the Spenders to take the train to their home in Rye. 'Natasha Spender is a good pianist and I was awakened on Sunday morning by her practising a Mozart concerto. In this atmosphere with Stephen correcting his new poems and Natasha practising, and the well-known landscape I was overcome and frankly burst into my first tears. They were so understanding that I felt a friendship had been formed. If there is this kind of value in human beings let us set it against the horrors and *know* that it has infinitely *more* power.'[10] One of the strengths of Bliss's memoirs is the occasional lowering of his emotional guard so we are allowed to see behind the stiff upper lip so prevalent in his generation. It allows us much more access to the real Arthur Bliss and therefore the beating heart of much of the deeply felt music coming from him in these days of his full maturity.

On 28 September, a letter to Trudy mentions a possible change in his job where he may 'take Thatcher's place in the Home Service, BBC with a view to becoming ultimately DoM… I have been approached, and it is a compliment.'[11]

On 6 November he wrote again to Trudy while taking his turn at fire-watching to say that he had moved a little closer taking charge of music at the BBC: 'I shall almost certainly step up into Deputy Director of Music soon with Thatcher as my temporary Superior – we shall see!!' This mood of optimism was severely dented by Japan's attack on Pearl Harbor on 7 December partly because, as part of the coordinated attacks on various locations, Hong Kong was a target and Trudy's brother Walter lived there: 'I dread the news that something has happened to Walter'. But, almost like a child being presented with a new toy to distract him, Bliss regaled Trudy with a lively weekend in Cambridge with Hadley, Walton, Lambert and Alan Rawsthorne 'arguing and laughing and having a real grand set to – it did me good'. It seems Walton didn't mind being with the 'moustachioed cod-fish' when it suited him.

A weekend just after Christmas spent with Bridges Adams and his wife Nancy at Badingham Old Rectory, Woodbridge in Suffolk saw him taking the dog for a five-mile walk in the morning and describing 'a heavy white frost, lovely sun close to the horizon, and the ploughed fields a vivid lilac – just outside the window a perky robin – very red. The seasons in England are really most magical, and I look forward to a *whole year* sometime with you in Pen Pits – see how I have changed!'[12]

Bliss lining up for promotion at the BBC was becoming a rather tortured process with Sir Hugh Allen's reservations about him causing some friction. There was concern, not only from Allen, that Bliss might focus too much on contemporary music. In fact, by the very end of 1941, Bliss had got the measure of the musical output of the BBC. There was considerable discussion about music policy, and the appointment of joint Directors General in Robert Foot looking after administration, and Sir Cecil Graves overseeing programming, saw through any issues of Bliss's personality and musical leanings. Basil Nichols, Controller of Programmes, produced a paper about future music programming which elicited a lengthy and in-depth response from Bliss dated 30 December 1941.

He begins by stating a truism: 'A sense of music is a primal thing in mankind, and a tremendous force, for good or evil', then states a *Threefold Function of Broadcast Music*:

1. 'Inexorably to continue and expand the principle of great music as an ultimate value, indeed a justification of life.
2. Faithfully to enrich leisure hours with entertainment.
3. Physically and mentally to stimulate tired bodies and worn nerves. N.B. It betrays its trust if it debases spiritual value of music, acts as a narcotic or drug, or bores by sheer inanity.'

In a paragraph he calls *Coaxing Caliban*, he warns against the danger of seeking the maximum audience, which inevitably means wooing the lowest common denominator. He notes that the British are 'a timid nation, aesthetically and intellectually, and a bit shame-faced when appealing to the finer instincts of people. Just as the pace of a convoy is determined by the slowest ship, so often is the level of a programme determined by consideration for the lowest common intelligence. You cannot coax Caliban without losing the interest and respect of Ferdinand and Miranda. It is to the Brave New World that future programmes must inevitably appeal.'

He moves on to excoriate the ubiquitous cinema organ ('The Germans prohibit what they know is a depressant and not a stimulant') and to be very wary of what he calls 'Jazzing JSB'. 'After hearing the *Unfinished* Symphony magnificently swung by a prize jazz band at the top of the St Regis Hotel in New York, I cannot easily listen to the original Schubert... I have had a dose of Benzedrine, and naturally want some more. The jazz band can be used for artificial excitement and aphrodisiac purposes, but not for spreading eternal truths'.

He allows that some transcriptions can enlarge 'the scope of appreciation'. 'This is not simpering at classical music, like the cinema organ, or like the jazz band, but is an honest translation'. He next looks at 'Condensed Opera' and while he understands the case for it, and has witnessed some good examples, he remarks that a complete opera is broadcast in the USA every week and its audience is large and dedicated. He feels that a better alternative is to broadcast a whole act as 'opera is an art form that cannot stand much mutilation'.

He begs for moments of silence ('indispensible for life') rather than an extract of a Scarlatti Sonata faded out, 'one more bleeding chunk from the knacker's yard' with an apologetic back announcement.

His two final points are called *Scrappy-Mindedness* and *A Fantasy*. Addressing the first he complains that the *Radio Times*, like the *Daily Mail* looks like a jigsaw puzzle: 'Sensationalism sold a paper. To induce a love of sensationalism, a reader must be prevented from concentrating his attention on any one subject for more than a minute or so. Hence the birth of paragraph technique, and headline announcements. A word to the wise!' And his *Fantasy*? 'The ideal method of broadcasting throughout this country would be to have three separate channels. Available for all citizens that are worth fighting for would be two contrasting services, so that at any minute of the day he or she could draw on two of the three categories mentioned in my note on functions. For the Calibans, there would be a third service, "the dirt track", a continual stream of noise and nonsense put on by untouchables with the use of records.'[13] How might Bliss feel about the BBC in the present day?

In February 1942, Nicholls was trying to sift through the pros and cons and noted Allen's preference for three people to run the Music Department (perhaps an echo of the old Music Advisory Panel) as well as his reservations about Bliss, as Allen was against a composer/conductor and Bliss in particular 'as he thinks he is mercurial and possibly difficult.'[14] In fact, Thatcher was still recommended as Director of Music with Bliss as his assistant but Thatcher stepped aside feeling tired and not in the best of health and unselfishly feeling that 'a younger and more vigorous man should have the leadership'. Nicholls still shows his own reservations by feeling that Bliss would not be his choice as permanent Director of Music, but Bliss had anyway indicated that he would not be prepared to stay after the war for any longer than necessary. 'He is first and foremost a composer and wants to get back to freelance life when the war is over.'[15]

There was still further delay which was frustrating to Bliss who wrote Graves a personal letter requesting a decision be made: 'Upon your answer I must base my decision as to where my duties and responsibilities lie, to the Corporation, where I may have the justification of doing fine work in a responsible position and helping others to do the same, or to my own family seven thousand miles away.'[16] He also writes 'The directorship of music is not for me a glittering prize that I have schemed to get, but the very opposite. Opposed in the scales to the personal life I have voluntarily thrown aside, it weighs indeed more like a penance'. Further to this he announces that if he is appointed, he will renounce all broadcast performance of his works: 'There is little else indeed now that I can renounce'. Graves now moved to allay Allen's fears and wrote a detailed letter describing an interview with Bliss designed to tease out possible areas of tension such as whether he would understand that he did not have a completely free hand in programming and that there was a 'chain of responsibility'. All this was understood, as well as the temporary nature of the appointment. Thus, with Thatcher acting as his assistant, the appointment was agreed.

He cabled the news to Trudy on 29 March 1942. In a letter following he wrote, 'I have taken the whole thing over and am touched by the response to leadership. My salary is double what I got before, so you need have no qualms on the financial side'. Bliss also arranged to have a flexible notice period. 'This is the result of my making it *quite* clear that I feel my first and foremost duty is to you and my two other darlings…'.

And so, his term as Director of Music got under way. He laughingly described 'what I am at present, a combination of vitamin producer to a tired but good bunch, father confessor to individual round pegs in square holes, and manipulator of committees (you don't know how subtle, and tactful – yes, *Tactful*, my darling, I am becoming…)'. Bliss's personal staff constituted the indomitable Miss Elliott who moved with him from the Overseas Department and, from June 1942, Bliss acquired a Personal Assistant. His description of Peter Montgomery is amusing, describing him as 'the perfect screen between me and crashing prima-donnas, insistent composers and bores of all description… I am sure B [Barbara] would fall for him – tall, elegant, perfect manners, nice blue Irish eyes, and slightly mysterious – he has telephone calls with a Persian Princess! – So I can relax a little and, instead of signing a memorandum every 8 minutes, stir the huge department imaginatively.'[17]

If one of Allen's suspicions was the possibility of Bliss broadcasting far more contemporary music then these fears would not be allayed as Bliss certainly championed new music during his brief time with the Corporation, both in broadcast concerts and commissions. He created an iconic series called 'Music of Our Time' which was broadcast monthly from 1943. The slightly re-named successor *Music in our Time* aired for thirty years from 1965–95 until it was replaced by a more contemporary sounding *Hear and Now* on Radio 3. Until just before the war the BBC had been led in its involvement with new music by the visionary Edward Clark. Clark was a passionate proponent of new music who, through his influential position in broadcasting, cultivated connections with almost all the major composers of the day. Such was his influence that he was deeply involved in the International Society for Contemporary Music (ISCM) and for some years was its President. But he was a maverick who upset many by a distrust of those who he suspected of not sharing his enthusiasms. All this contributed to his being forced out of the BBC. But Bliss knew him well and valued his almost unparalleled knowledge of the scene and was keen to draw on his help to create the kind of programmes for his new music series which would show the Corporation's commitment to current composers and demonstrate that what was being written could also be pleasurable to listen to.

Bliss commissioned a large number of composers to write works for varying sized ensembles including Gordon Jacob, Armstrong Gibbs, Erik Chisholm, Montague Phillips, Chris Edmunds, Lennox Berkeley, Robin Milford and William Alwyn, all of whom wrote small-scale orchestral works. The wartime propaganda machine was very important especially for the overseas services and the *BBC Yearbook* for 1943 reported that 'naturally, it was also the BBC's aim to present non-British listeners overseas with a vivid picture of our own musical life, which has been proving itself so very wide awake during the war.'[18] There were problems for the BBC Symphony Orchestra, however, as they were in increasing demand by the Overseas Service and had to fulfill their quota of concerts and studio broadcasts for the Home Service. This really meant that they were overstretched and Bliss was worried that this was leading to falling standards and he was determined to correct this. Julian Herbage suggested structural changes (two extra violinists) to try to change the structure of the orchestra so it could be divided into smaller units for different repertoire when required. The suggestion was then made that the BBC Scottish Orchestra should become a full symphony orchestra which could share the burden with the Symphony Orchestra leaving the BBC Northern Orchestra as a light orchestra.

Bliss had a colourful interview printed in the *Radio Times* on 15 May 1942 in which he answered various questions as to his intentions as the new Director of Music. Answers were unequivocal. Would British music receive special treatment? 'Yes. No other country in the world can show a finer school of composers than this country and naturally our audiences want to hear their works.' Had he views on the fading-out of programmes? 'Yes, but they are unprintable! We are now coping with this technical difficulty'. Nicholas Kenyon points out that a broadcast in January 1942 of Walton's Violin Concerto was faded out before the end because of the time taken by the introductory announcement, and a similar situation occurred with Elgar's Violin Concerto later that same month.[19]

An interesting insight into Bliss's debunking of some BBC mythology related both to his own works being performed during his tenure as Director of Music and also to those employed to oversee specialist areas of music output who were generally required to give up their performing. A good example of this is related by Harry Mortimer in his autobiography. It was suggested that he should apply for the post of Brass and Military Bands Supervisor but 'the stumbling block was that in order to take the job I had to be prepared to give up all my connections with the bands (Foden's, Fairey's and Brighouse and Rastrick). Now there's a strange paradox: chosen because I was well acquainted with the subject, I must renounce all the practical first-hand knowledge in order to become an administrator!'[20] But it was Bliss who addressed the issue. 'Before I was recalled for a second interview, a different board this time, Arthur Bliss had told the panel of my experience in the band world, an advocacy I had neither sought nor expected, but a welcome and, indeed, gratifying one.

I later learned that in a moment of misguided rhetoric he had compared the original proposal with the idea of appointing Moiseiwitsch to the post of Head of Piano Recitals providing that he gave up playing the piano.'[21] A compromise arrangement was agreed.

Bliss established his HQ in London with Kenneth Wright (his old boss at the Overseas Music Department), Julian Herbage and W.W. Thompson representing the Home Service programme planners. Tuesdays to Thursdays were spent with the main department at Bedford. His own music making was rare but, on a visit to the BBC Music Department in Manchester in May he conducted the Hallé in the suite from *Things to Come* but the general lack of either composition or conducting was, like the separation from his family, a serious personal loss and underlined the necessity of his BBC work being time limited.

In the short time he remained as Director of Music, just two years, the hallmark of his influence was the number of premieres of new British music or first British performances which were broadcast by the BBC Symphony Orchestra. Among these were composers who presented Bliss with problems, especially those like Britten and Tippett who were conscientious objectors. In Britten's case, this arose through his commission to write the music for Edward Sackville-West's *The Rescue* which dramatized part of Homer's *Odyssey*, a highly significant collaboration which developed the dramatic potential of radio at this time through the close association of words and music. Bliss had initially been asked to write the music but refused. Lewis Foreman, writing about *The Rescue* claims that 'in his (Britten's) hands the score became some of the most remarkable incidental music ever written for any BBC feature.'[22] In Tippett's case it was his oratorio *A Child of our Time*. The Britten situation generated a great deal of heat. The issue was Britten's engagement to conduct the orchestra for his project. Bliss claimed that the Music Department knew nothing of this engagement. Boult had been approached but had responded that he 'was antagonistic to the composer and his works.'[23] Clarence Raybould, assistant conductor of the BBC Symphony Orchestra, was then persuaded to take it on against his will. Britten then threatened to withdraw from the project completely if he was not allowed to conduct. Things were eventually sorted out but not before Britten had written in unfriendly terms to Bliss and Sackville-West had blamed Bliss for the whole upset.

In terms of Tippett's work this was equally difficult and involved yet more irritation of Boult by the cancelling of one of the *Music of our Time* programmes. Boult had an aversion to the conductor Walter Goehr, and in an apologetic reply justifying his decision dated 12 January 1944 Bliss stated that he agreed with Boult's comments about Goehr but didn't feel that 'this broadcast should be vetoed on the grounds of the conductor.'[24] Bliss also noted that he was going to suffer from the cancellation of this programme as his *Introduction and Allegro* was to have been played, indicating that either he had had a change of heart about not having any of his music broadcast during his tenure as Director Music or the proposal was not deemed necessary by Cecil Graves when appointing him. Bliss's spirited reply to Boult emphasizes the point that he was a passionate advocate of new music and was very keen, especially at this time when prejudices were rife, to ensure fairness. Tippett was a keen advocate of Goehr and had appointed him to the staff at Morley College in London where he was Director of Music. It was therefore natural that he would want Goehr to conduct the premiere of his new oratorio. Add to that the basic theme of the work described by Bliss to Boult as 'a very serious work, lasting some hour and a quarter, and its subject is the oppressed peoples of Europe, and their faith in deliverance and you have a recipe for tolerance and even support for a conductor from an enemy nation but who, as a Jew, belonged to the ultimate oppressed minority.'[25]

Being a father at a distance was crucially important to Bliss and he kept up a significant correspondence with his two daughters, trying to maintain the bond between them. He loved to keep up with their news and they, in turn, wrote frequently to keep him informed of their activities as they grew up. As he wrote to Karen in one letter: 'you are a *good* daughter... for writing to me so often. When I want to feel extra happy, I just take up the large bundles of your letters and read them through.'[26] Barbara was now sixteen and was growing up fast and was, of course, interested in all the potential of life at that age. Bliss wrote in July congratulating her on essays she had sent him to read and which had earned her plaudits from her teacher.

Bliss had hoped that he might be sent on an official BBC visit to the States in 1943 and that this would be the means of bringing his family back to England. Both the BBC and the British Council had approved the proposal but a higher authority turned it down. In yet another twist to this tale Bliss recounted the amusing, though also slightly sinister, meeting held with Lady Cunard. Maud Cunard was an American society hostess who Lloyd George considered a dangerous woman as she encouraged politicians to indiscreet revelations at her dinner parties. She had a long-term relationship with Beecham and in her meeting with Bliss suggested that he urge the Director General of the BBC to let him step aside in favour of Beecham becoming Director of Music. In return she would use her influence to see that Bliss could rejoin his family in the States. Bliss's response was 'to laugh outright at the thought of Beecham sitting behind my desk, administering a large department, punctiliously answering memos, attending conferences, interviewing would-be-broadcasters etc. etc., but this soon turned to anger at the unwarranted presumption behind this absurd deal, and after advising her to write to the Director-General herself, putting forward all the reasons and facts, we parted very coldly.'[27]

The end of Bliss's tenure at the BBC was signalled by the return of Trudy and his daughters. After long negotiations a berth was secured for the three of them on the *Serpa Pinto*, a Portuguese ship which had gained a reputation for carrying huge numbers (some 100,000) of Jews and others fleeing from Nazi Germany to safety in Portugal. Trudy and the girls sailed from Philadelphia to Lisbon in late September and then flew by flying boat, landing at Poole Harbour in Dorset on 5 November from where she rang Bliss and the two spoke for the first time in two and a half years. Trudy took the train to London where Bliss 'dived into the black obscurity of Waterloo Station – and found them.'[28] What a reunion for the family, and what a reinforcement of Bliss's feeling that he should give up the BBC job as soon as practically possible, and return not only to family life but also to his full time composing.

Now that they were all together again Bliss had had to find somewhere for them to live, having been a lodger with the Farquharsons for all this time. He rented a flat in Cavendish Square in London 'buzz bombs or no', and spent about five more months at the BBC, announcing his resignation on 15 January 1944 and leaving on 31 March. In leaving early he was taking advantage of the flexible terms of his contract. Victor Hely Hutchinson, who was appointed to succeed him, couldn't start until later in the year and Adrian Boult therefore filled the interregnum of the summer period. Inevitably, leaving his job created mixed emotions for Bliss who had developed close friendships during his time and he wrote that it was 'with real regret' that he said a final farewell to his colleagues. Interestingly, Trudy was the one who maintained a connection with the BBC, contributing to a programme called *The Kitchen Front* about American recipes and soon being invited to give weekly broadcasts to various parts of the States about aspects of British life – programmes which would continue for some ten years. *Morning Heroes* was broadcast on 15 May as a tribute to Bliss for his work during the past two and a half years. A further honour was bestowed just before this in April by the Royal College of Music who made him an honorary Fellow. This was the first of a number of such marks of recognition by major academic institutions in the coming years.

Keeping his connection with the BBC, Bliss was asked to introduce the New Zealand Dominion Day concert broadcast on 26 September 1944 on behalf of British musicians in which the BBC Scottish Orchestra was conducted by Guy Warrack with the New Zealand tenor Hubert Carta. The music was all by New Zealand composers, Douglas Lilburn, Max Saunders and Alfred Hill.

Bliss's daughters were developing their interests and Barbara's determination to be an actress was furthered when she entered RADA for a short period before joining the WRNS where she met her future husband, Richard Gatehouse who, as Entertainment Officer at Portsmouth, and having heard of her time at RADA, sought her out to help with his dramatic performances for Navy personnel. Bliss found it a strange coincidence that Barbara met her future husband in the same way that he had met Trudy, through acting. Karen was developing her love of ballet dancing, attending classes at Sadler's Wells and eventually joining the company.

Bliss could now return to composition for the first time since returning to England. This, in itself, was like a homecoming and it was an obvious gesture to dedicate his next substantial work, *Miracle in the Gorbals*, 'To Trudy, Barbara, Karen: thanksgiving for November 5th, 1943'. This new ballet was suggested by Robert Helpmann who had danced the character of the Red Knight in *Checkmate*. The scenario was conceived by Michael Benthall, Helpmann's life partner, and such was the success of this first collaboration that Bliss worked with him two years later for his next ballet, *Adam Zero*.

The idea for the scenario of the ballet came to Benthall while posted to an anti-aircraft gun battery in Glasgow. The slums of the Gorbals in the city were notorious for their overcrowding, poverty, lawlessness and prostitution. Kenneth Clark's chapter in *Gala Performance* described the ballet's scenario as 'a horrifying, message-bearing work far from the spirit of Diaghilev, and Edward Burra's décor ... remote from the fantasies of the École de Paris.'[29] In an article about Helpmann for the *Dance Chronicle* in 1998, Kathrine Sorley Walker describes how the storyline deeply upset elements of Glasgow's hierarchy who were put on the defence about their city. The Lord Provost, James Welsh, claimed 'The traditional razor slashers of Glasgow are a pure fiction as applied to the city today', and the police supported him by stating that they could not recall 'a single instance of razor-slashing in the Gorbals throughout the five years of war'. The local Scottish Church minister had 'never come into contact with an act of serious violence.'[30] These and other statements were simply excellent publicity for Helpmann and as Sorley Walker states, 'Such flurries in civic teacups… could only sell tickets at the Princes'[31]… which it did in droves.

The scenario developed by Benthall (which has certain echoes of Dostoevsky's *The Idiot*) is brilliantly anticipated by Burra's stage cloth with a ship in dry dock with huge cranes behind. It rises to reveal a pub and a fish and chip shop with tenement buildings all around. As evening approaches a prostitute appears followed around by a group of young men. An Official (tactfully so called, but obviously supposed to be a minister of the church) sees her and she slinks into a doorway with one of the men. A solitary and pathetic girl comes on stage but disappears having seen some drunks. Lovers dance, and the prostitute tries to get her man but is foiled again by the Official. A crowd gathers as news spreads of the suicide of the young girl, who is brought on stage by two men. The Official crosses the girl's hands, showing the certainty of her death. At this point a stranger appears, approaches the body and stretches out his hand. She slowly revives and begins to dance.

The Official, resentful of a threat to his authority by this seeming miracle, forms a plan to trick the stranger and sends him to visit the prostitute on an apparent errand of mercy. The Official starts a whispering campaign so that when the stranger emerges from the prostitute's house, he finds a hostile crowd. The prostitute follows him out, her face shining with new-found faith, but the Official has organized a group of young men to attack the stranger and be finally rid of him. When he returns, they set upon him with razors and broken bottles, to which he puts up no defence, and murder him. The young girl and the prostitute return to the street to find his body. They cover his face and turn away, leaving only an old beggar with him. A new day dawns, and life resumes its sordid rhythm.

It was the realism of the story that surely appealed to Bliss, as had the visceral drama of the *Checkmate* scenario in his first ballet. These gripping dramas were far from the romantic fantasies normally associated with the genre. But all the elements of the production had to fit together, and the choice of Edward Burra as designer was inspired: he was well known for his depictions of the urban underworld. As Sorley Walker writes, 'Burra and Helpmann, not particular friends, were alike in balancing the grave and sensitive side of their natures with madcap wit. Both laid aside levity where *Miracle* was concerned, and collaborated with extreme taste and seriousness.'[32] An example of this was Helpmann's study of hand positions in El Greco's paintings which he used as a model for those of the Stranger. He briefed Bliss about this to show the kind of music he wanted on the Stranger's entrance.

Bliss's music for this ballet is imaginative and creatively responsive to the ever-changing scenario. A fine example of this is the start of the seventh scene, *The discovery of the suicide's body* where, following the Prostitute's sullen departure from the scene having been ordered off the street by the Official, Bliss begins the new scene with a flutter – like a rumour starting. After two halting fragments of energy, the music picks up in the manner of a frantic fugue as word gets around the street and people flock to the docks to see what has happened. It is a superb depiction of corporate energy directed to a common purpose.

It is interesting to see how Bliss deals with the two scenes devoted to the suicidal girl. Particularly notable is the fact that he quotes from Chopin's Funeral March (third movement of the second Piano Sonata) in the earlier movement *before* the girl has committed suicide, giving the audience an obvious heads-up as to what is about to happen. In the scene where *The suicide's body is brought in* (scene eight) he writes a mournful dance in triple time coloured by horns and an expressive oboe solo. The appearance of The Stranger continues in the same meter but Bliss chooses a set of variations on the scene's initial theme, each of which builds in intensity and volume as it leads to the miraculous recovery which changes into quadruple meter and an expressive clarinet melody.

What follows, the *Dance of Deliverance*, is a remarkable scene with an undoubted hidden agenda. Although this is an unbridled celebration of the restoration to life of this young girl with the whole cast brought into a frenzy of dance, the overt Americanisms of Bliss's music here tells us that this is his personal 'dance of deliverance' from the years of separation from his family left in America for all that time and which the dedication of the work reminds us was so recently ended. The free-wheeling jazz idiom of the music is enhanced by Bliss's instruction to the drummer that he or she should 'play in an ad-lib style' using various rhythms (four variations) as detailed in the score. It is a real tour-de-force, however alien the American jazz idiom may be to the slums of Glasgow in reality. The wind-down at the end of the scene is masterly as the Stranger talks to the crowd who then disperse leaving the Official so angry at such a powerful undermining of his position that he resorts to the Prostitute.

The same technique Bliss used for the start of the suicide rumour is used at the start of *The Slander Campaign* scene (No.13). A halting but quickly repetitive figure becomes a frenzied ostinato as the rumour of the Stranger being with the Prostitute spreads. Hostility towards him increases just as the Official hoped it would. But even when the Prostitute appears, transformed and her eyes alight with new-found faith in a scene of serenely beautiful music, we know that this is only a stay of execution. The young men whose minds have been poisoned by the Official lie in wait for the Stranger in darkly agitated music, which then becomes a dance of death as the men attack and murder him. The climax is electrifying at the moment when the Stranger dies. The final page of the score has moving funereal music during which the Girl and the Prostitute comfort each other.

The premiere of the ballet took place at the Prince's Theatre, London on 26 October, 1944. Reaction was mixed, especially from ballet purists. In the book *Ballet in Britain* by Clive Barnes, published in 1953, he sums up one view:

'*Hamlet* (Tchaikovsky) and *Miracle in the Gorbals* both played a large part in the early Covent Garden programmes. Once extravagantly praised and rapturously received, since Helpmann's retirement they appear to have sunk without trace. Very slick, with vital theatrical value, they possessed little dance interest, being more in the nature of superlatively produced and acted mime plays. Certainly, a little of them went a long way in a ballet repertory, and they have not been greatly missed. They would probably have been seen to best advantage in a company whose sole purpose was the presentation of mimed-dramas.'[33]

Arnold Haskell, in his book *Ballet*, remarks that 'For a number of reasons this must rank as one of the outstanding creations of contemporary ballet. It dares more than other works; its success is all the greater... It is a tribute to the success of the ballet that the highest praise has come from the religious press.'[34] Haskell has gone further and produced what he describes as a 'monograph' on the ballet which he states 'would not be interesting... unless that work showed the promise of a permanent place in the repertoire or set new problems in dramatic or technical interpretations that seemed to point a possible new direction in ballet.'[35] Haskell describes the work as a 'dance drama' which he feels is different from the 'all-inclusive' term 'ballet'. In dance-drama there is a definite story which dictates the whole treatment. He states that 'there is more *recitative*-dancing than *aria*-dancing', in other words more movement that develops character and action than familiar set pieces. Haskell states that *Petrouchka* is still the greatest modern dance-drama. 'Here the story is vital... *Miracle in the Gorbals*, for all its contemporary realism, is of the

*Petrouchka* school. Only if it is misunderstood, as it easily may be, will it be used to force ballet in a new direction.'[36] Further, 'Helpmann has produced what is an undoubted balletic masterpiece on a religious-sociological subject, but he has not diverted ballet to religious-sociological studies. To do so would be to deny his whole training and background and ultimately, if it were followed, to destroy ballet as we know it.'[37]

A final word from Haskell about Bliss's approach to the collaboration: 'Arthur Bliss has also had considerable experience in ballet, for which he has true sympathy and real understanding. Rare among composers, he has a great knowledge of the plastic arts and is a collector of pictures, a very relevant factor in his work for the theatre. He does not impose his score on the choreographer but is ready to sacrifice music that pleases him to fall in with the scheme as a whole. He collaborates as Stravinsky did before him, and in very much the same manner... Bliss worked with Benthall's full scenario, with Robert Helpmann and with Burra's designs spread out before him. This is important, for they gave him the clue at the most difficult moment of all, the miracle. Until that moment, he found the composition plain sailing. The composer's role in ballet is made very clear by the fact that it was Bliss who saw El Greco in the Gorbals and suggested a study of his hands and gestures'.

In 1944, not only was *Miracle* completed and performed and he left the BBC, but in March he was invited by Henry Wood to write a work for the Jubilee of the Proms that year, just months before Wood was taken ill and died on 10 August. In March Bliss had written a fanfare to honour Wood's seventy-fifth birthday and at this point Wood was keeping up his punishing schedule and dealing with the removal of the Proms to Bedford because of the constant bombing raids over London with the deadly new flying bombs. Sadly, he was too ill to conduct the 50th anniversary concert and his doctors forbade him from even listening to the broadcast. The Prom on the day Wood died began with Bliss's *Birthday Fanfare for Sir Henry Wood* and also included Walton's Viola Concerto and Sibelius's first Symphony. The season closed two days later.

While occupied with *Miracle* another engaging project was mooted in the Spring of 1944 and a contract signed on 6 June. This was the music for the film of George Bernard Shaw's version of *Caesar and Cleopatra*. Bliss didn't seem to have an easy time with his involvement in the film business and after getting his fingers burned on Wells's *Things to Come* this new venture was a great deal worse. The producer was the celebrated Hungarian Gabriel Pascal, who achieved an enviable reputation in bringing Shaw's other plays to the big screen. The most successful of these was *Pygmalion* (for which Honegger provided the music), followed by *Major Barbara* in 1940 with Walton as composer. *Caesar and Cleopatra* was the next project. Like *Things to Come*, this film was the most expensive made in Britain at its time. Bliss was Pascal's third choice composer as he had tried Prokofiev and Walton who had both refused. Shaw, however, wanted Bliss all along which caused bad feeling with Pascal which rubbed off on Bliss.

Shaw wrote illuminating letters to Bliss about the music. The first (30 April 1944) was a passionate plea for him to write a suite of movements and then license the film producers to use it so Bliss kept the rights. The second letter (7 May) was equally passionate in requesting Bliss not to write music in a quasi-Egyptian style. 'It must all be Blissful and British'. He was also adamant that he did not want his play 'Aida-ized'. The film was dogged with problems, part of which were wartime shortages but also included the star actor, Vivien Leigh, having a miscarriage following a particularly energetic retake, and the general mood was downbeat. Bliss wrote a substantial amount of music in 'skeleton score' (over eighty pages some of which were fully scored) which Shaw had suggested and which was later, and very happily, put together by Giles Easterbrook and Malcolm Binney to make a fine orchestral suite with some remarkable original music including a shimmering evocation of the sea in its second movement, a beautifully reflective *Memphis at Night* and the final movement *Supply Sequence* which Bliss used the following year for a Ministry of Information film which he called *France Arises* on the manuscript but whose official title was *Présence au Combat* – an Anglo-French production. He also used parts of it for a later government film, *Faster than Sound,* about the development of a rocket and its subsequent flight, produced in 1949.

Things were not going well, however, on the set for *Caesar and Cleopatra* and Bliss remembered that in taking Shaw's advice he started on a skeleton score but then ran into the director of the film. One look at him made it self-evident that he would never be a sympathetic collaborator and he withdrew from the assignment. In fact, he had been a good deal stronger in his opinion of Pascal saying, 'I have had unforgettable experiences with one director who, where music was concerned, was a certified lunatic, and I had to discontinue collaboration.'[38] Britten was the next composer to be approached but he also turned the offer down having consulted Bliss and noting that he had a far more equable temperament! Georges Auric was eventually hired to see the project through to its completion.

Bliss was spending much of his composing time in his 'den' at Pen Pits after his lengthy absence in America and his full-time work in London for the BBC. When they did return, a regular visitor who often stayed with them was Julia Harland, daughter of the architect of the house. She was sent to a boarding school near Wincanton to avoid the London bombings. Bliss would go to collect her from school but was so often accosted by the headmistress that he asked the girl to meet him at the bottom of the drive. Julia used to stealthily watch Bliss composing and remembered 'I would stand on tip-toe and be spellbound watching the notes he was writing just fly across the manuscript pages. The clefs and notes were executed so beautifully and quickly, I had never seen anyone write so fast before, let alone compose a music score. He would then get up and try a passage on the piano but he wrote for long stretches... I would long for a game of croquet which happened the moment he got stuck.' She also reflected 'how disciplined and organized they both were. Trudy, being American, brought the new world with her which made their life-style seem very modern and exciting. They were a remarkable couple; he with his boundless energy and vitality, she with her love of nature and outdoor life.'[39]

Bliss signed the contract for his next film on 27 March 1945. This was *Men of Two Worlds* directed by Thorold Dickinson who, unlike Gabriel Pascal (*Caesar and Cleopatra*) he described as 'a man of imagination, sensitive to music, and serious in aim.'[40] The film originated in a request from the Colonial Office to the Ministry of Information for propaganda encouraging the colonies to move towards self-government within the framework of the British Empire. A film was the outcome and Dickinson was proposed as director and moved from his work in the Army Film Unit. Joyce Cary, who had spent a lot of time working in Africa in the Civil Service, was employed as scriptwriter.

The storyline as summarized by Stephen Lloyd centres on Kisenga, an African composer-pianist who after some years of study in England returns to Tanganyika as a teacher. After his arrival an epidemic of sleeping sickness breaks out. He now has to persuade his tribe, the Litu, to move from their present land to a new area that will be free from the sickness. There is a major conflict of cultural and religious beliefs brought to a head in his confrontation with the local witch-doctor and a few years of indoctrination in European values comes head-to-head with thousands of years of African tradition. Kisenga has truly become a 'man of two worlds'. The British Film Institute sums up the plot by saying that 'the film is a creditable effort to tell an African story from the point of view of an African. The story only makes sense if we identify with

Kisenga's dilemmas. Only he can resolve a situation in which African and the European world views are at loggerheads, and he is prepared to give up his life in the struggle.[41]

Bliss was sent recordings of East African music by Dickinson, who had brought them back with him from Africa, and he found a way of skilfully weaving elements of this into a score which was still very much his own. This included using a male voice chorus and the use of indigenous folk-song. Much of the music for the film has disappeared but five sections survive. These include the most substantial movement, a concert piece for piano, male voices and orchestra called *Baraza* (meaning a 'council meeting' in native Swahili) which was published by Novello in 1946 as a separate concert work. In the film it was used at the opening as Kisenga's own Piano Concerto. There seemed to be something of a fashion for these works at the time with Richard Addinsell's *Warsaw Concerto* being the most famous example. But Bliss's avoids the clichéd Rachmaninovian excesses and relates his music closely to the African sources he had assimilated from the recordings he had been sent.

8 May 1945 brought national rejoicing as the end of the war was heralded by Germany's unconditional surrender to the Allies. Bliss's *Three Jubilant and Three Solemn Fanfares* were recorded by the London Symphony Orchestra and the trumpeters of Kneller Hall conducted by Muir Matheson and broadcast on 13 April 1945. Originally written for brass and originating in 1935 they were first used for King George V's Silver Jubilee. Bliss then expanded them for full orchestra for the 1945 broadcast. On 8 May, Victory in Europe Day, Clarence Raybould conducted Bliss's *Peace Fanfare for Children* with the BBC Symphony Orchestra on the BBC Home Service in the programme for which it had been written the previous year, *Children's Hour*. In a similar but slightly more extended vein Bliss's *March: The Phoenix-Homage to France, August 1944* was premiered in Paris on 11 March 1945 and had its UK premiere in the Royal Albert Hall on 23 May conducted (as was the Paris performance) by Charles Munch with the LPO. Bliss was now recognized as the go-to composer for these ceremonial musical gestures.

Following the Fellowship of the Royal College of Music the previous year it was now the turn of Edinburgh University to honour Bliss with an honorary doctorate which he received on 22 June. Shortly after this the BBC asked him to join their Music Advisory Panel which kept him closely in touch with developments in the organization as well as keeping his finger on the pulse of music nationally and affording him the ability to maintain influence in the organization whose music department he had so recently headed.

The first new ballet to be performed after the re-opening of the Royal Opera House (and following *The Sleeping Beauty*) was another collaboration with Robert Helpmann and Michael Benthall, *Adam Zero*. This work reignited some of the criticism levelled at *Miracle* but took them to new heights ultimately leading to its demise. Helpmann recounted that the scenario reflected the various stages of life from birth to death (A-Z) and Adam's world was represented by the creation of a ballet on stage with various key figures in the stage operation representing key figures in his life. Thus 'Omnipotence' was the Stage Director, 'Adam's Fates', the Designer, Wardrobe Mistress and Dresser, the 'Choreographer' was the woman in Adam's life who was both his lifeblood and ultimately his destroyer, eventually becoming the figure of benevolent death.

Helpmann remarked that 'The actual staging of *Adam Zero* was influenced by Thornton Wilder's play *The Skin of our Teeth* and even more by some Japanese Noh plays I was reading at the time. In one of these, written many years before Christ, the stage represents the world.'[42] From the Noh plays he created the expression of the theme of birth to death 'through the ancient theatre technique of shifting scenery, making up etc., in view of the audience and the idea of a showing a man's life through the medium of a ballet rehearsal came later.'[43] Also key to the representation of the various stages of Adam's life was the different styles of dance – 'primitive for the man's youth, classical for his prime, jazz and jive for his degenerate middle age, etc.'[44] From Helpmann's perspective it was all planned as much to show the development of different forms of dancing as to providing an acting role.

For Bliss this was an exciting project and he felt it to be his most varied and exciting ballet score. The actual staging must have been impressive as Adam's birth was represented by a totally bare Covent Garden stage which was then gradually filled as Adam's life developed only to empty again as he moved towards his lonely death. Helpmann had literally to leap into life at the start of the ballet into the supportive arms of his friends. It was in the act of this leap that his fall was miscalculated early on in the cycle of performances and forced the injured Helpmann to leave the production. It was probably this, as much as the mixed reaction to the show, which led to its early demise. In Kathrine Sorley Walker's illuminating article about Helpmann in the *Dance Chronicle* she makes a key point about reaction to the ballet, saying 'There is a curious anomaly between the immediate press (and, of course, the audience reaction) and the buildup of denigration on which, in the long run, this ballet was to founder.'[45] She notes that Helpmann's success upset some people including Frederick Ashton who grew increasingly jealous of his popularity. Also, de Valois's 'anti-dramatic ballet lobby… was to prove increasingly influential as time went on', her approach being almost diametrically opposed to Helpmann's love of drama and his use of mime which many felt to be anti-balletic.

William McNaught, writing in the *Musical Times* in May 1946 soon after the premiere, made the point of the new direction ballet was taking and noted that 'it has played chess, toyed with the zodiac, turned a lady into a fox, followed Hamlet beyond the grave, armed up with Milton, Dante and Spenser, acted a parable from St Matthew, and staged a miracle in a back street.'[46] Two of these were Bliss ballets and *Adam Zero* was now added to this list. McNaught concluded that 'there is plenty to beguile the eye and amuse or impress the mind.'[47]

Bliss very skillfully followed the 'seven ages of man' in Adam's life as reflected in the seasonal theme with its 'Dance of Spring', 'Dance of Summer', 'Approach of Autumn' and 'Approach of Winter'. These act as bookmarks through the sixteen numbers of the ballet. The score begins with a highly charged 'Fanfare Overture' which is nothing like the Blissian fanfares which are already becoming a common feature of his output. In fact, this movement seems to herald an original score which is exactly why Bliss felt so strongly about it and was so disappointed that it fell from grace so quickly. The score isn't universally even and *Dance of Spring*, while being a riot of life and energy, feels rather like a slightly overweight *American in Paris* as echoes of Ravel's evocation of dawn in *Daphnis and Chloe* are clothed in a rather heavy-handed jazz band garb. *Awakening of Love*, however, is a lovely emotion-driven movement which leads very naturally to the powerful *Bridal Ceremony* in which Bliss writes little touches of dissonance which foreshadow the pain to come later in the story. The cor anglais melody that haunts the *Approach to Autumn* sets a vivid atmosphere of regret, and out of this bursts one of Bliss's most vivid creations, *Night Club Scene*, which has the middle-aged Adam trying to keep up with the younger set in a seemingly endless orgy of boogie-woogie. Even the considerable length of the movement (for a ballet scene) suggests Adam's reluctance to admit his age and move on. But it is a vivid score replete with saxophones to give that authentic dance band sound. Perhaps the most impressive movement in the last part of this work is the *Dance with Death* which starts with hammer blows from timpani (directed to be played with two sticks) and bass drum which soon turns to consolation as Bliss quotes Walt Whitman in the score 'Lovely and Soothing Death, serenely arriving'[48] writing what feels like a folksong to the rhythm of the text. At the end it is made plain that the *Zero* is not just an A-Z of a life but that Adam's life has added up to nothing, a point made plain in the choreography as the Stage Director displays a zero on a blackboard.

The scenario is bleak, depressing even, briefly summed up in the programme where it says 'man is born, makes a success in his own particular sphere, loses his position to a younger generation, sees his world crumble before his eyes and only finds peace in death'. This is a bleak view of life indeed but Bliss's music colours Adam's passing years in a way which negates the central message of the futility of existence by the very memorability of the music which Adam's life has inspired.

Constant Lambert once again conducted the Sadler's Wells Ballet and the Royal Opera House Orchestra in the premiere which took place on 8 April 1946 at the Royal Opera House. Bliss dedicated the work to him.

The press was ambivalent about the whole enterprise and most spent their column inches on Robert Helpmann's spectacular approach and whether or not they felt the scenario was worth the effort made by all. The review in *The Sketch* seemed to sum this up as well as any when the anonymous reviewer wrote that 'the sheer volume of the action, and the splendid exuberance and theatrical validity of Mr Bliss's music, distract attention from what is often a wearisome and infantile scenario.'[49] Philip Hope-Wallace in *Time and Tide* was even ambivalent about the music when he wrote: 'Much in the presentation of this bold and poetic idea is effective, much also moving, and it is sustained by Arthur Bliss's score which, like life, is unexpected, full of good and bad patches and a medley of styles… something in the theme itself, also makes one think of *Petrouchka*'[50] – the ghost of those early works from the 1920s is still a benign presence.

Although revived in Bremerhaven in 2015 the ballet has all but fallen into oblivion but lives on in a number of guises including a pair of concert suites, one with reduced orchestration, the whole score as a piano work, and the *Night Club Scene* arranged much later in 1970 for Cyril Smith and Phyllis Sellick for three hands at two pianos.

# Chapter Eleven

# TOWARDS GRAND OPERA AND BEYOND

The period following *Adam Zero* was an increasingly busy one for Bliss. His close connection with the British Council was now cemented by his appointment as Chairman of the Music Committee followed, fourteen months later, by his appointment to the Executive Committee in July 1947. Several potential commissions were offered including an interesting proposal by the BBC asking him to contribute to a programme discussing the difficulties and opportunities in writing opera. Given that he had not yet written one, and the considerable challenges which were about to be faced when he did, it is perhaps not surprising that he turned this down. He also refused the request to write a 'Brilliant Festival Overture' to celebrate twenty-five years of the BBC's existence because, as he stated, 'I have to write music for a 'Young Person's Guide to Ballet' film'[1] – a project which sadly didn't materialize. In August the same year he again rejected an approach by the Third Programme for a new work. On the positive side, however, he was again honoured with another honorary doctorate, this time from the University of London.

Trudy Bliss was a remarkable woman in her own right, a skilled broadcaster and a fine cook who wrote a book about cooking for children called *Come into the Kitchen* in 1946. She was widely read, with a specialism in Thomas Carlyle, the nineteenth-century historian and essayist, and his wife Jane. Her book of Carlyle's letters to his wife was highly acclaimed, the New York Times writing that 'the greater part of this treasure has lain untouched until the publication of this important book.'[2] Later she published *A New Selection of her Letters* – letters from Jane Welsh Carlyle. Together with Robert Meyer and Alexie Gordon, with whom she had collaborated for the children's cookery book, she devised games for unruly children. She was nothing if not wide-ranging. Whatever she achieved – and the support of her husband throughout their marriage made it one of the great partnerships – she never felt herself to be of any significance except in relation to him. She told her good friend Robert Milnes that when she died, she just wanted to be forgotten. Milnes also remembered that Phyllis Sellick felt just the same in relation to her husband, Cyril Smith. Trudy and Phyllis used to have a nickname for each other, Trudy being 'The President', and Phyllis being 'The Director'. Milnes remembers them calling each other by these names when he joined them for supper. From being rather overwhelmed by the London cultural scene when she first arrived, as well as coping with the ordeal of meeting all Bliss's famous friends and acquaintances, she became the confident and ideal partner. She was greatly helped by Harriet Cohen who Milnes said 'rescued her' at this time and helped to build her confidence. It must therefore have been awkward for Bliss, when Director of Music at the BBC, to have to write to Cohen, as Arnold Bax remembered in his autobiography, that 'her "neglect" has been the growing conviction that her pianistic performances since her return from America do not qualify her to be included in the very limited number of first-class British pianists accommodated in the Overseas Service.'[3] Cohen rebutted this by sending a diary of her punishing schedule. But the die was cast.

A rare moment of actual collaboration between Trudy and her husband came when she wrote a radio play for the BBC called *Memorial Concert* in 1946. In a discussion between radio presenter Ronald Fletcher and the Blisses prior to the broadcast of the extract from the incidental music for the play which Bliss wrote called *Theme and Cadenza* in which the violin soloist was Alfredo Campoli, Trudy Bliss described the plot of the play as follows:

'The story was of two music students, the girl a violinist and the young man a composer. They married and shared the early disappointments and small triumphs of their careers together. Then, just as success was coming to them both, the husband was beguiled away by another woman – someone rich and mysterious. He went on composing but the quality of his music changed and his later work was never so well thought of by discriminating musicians. Now, at the point in the play when this Theme and Cadenza is heard, and this piece of course is one of his fine early works, the composer is now dead and a concert has now been arranged in his memory with his former wife, now a brilliant artist, as the soloist. In the audience sits the second wife and as she listens to this music, she becomes aware, painfully aware, that the core of the composer has never really belonged to her, that it was his first love who had had the best of him.'[4]

The music for this play is rather in the manner of Richard Addinsell's *Warsaw Concerto*, like the concert piece for piano and orchestra *Baraza* in *Men of Two Worlds* – a pastiche concerto. It demonstrates just how easily and successfully Bliss slipped into whichever style of music was needed for a given situation, one of the reasons that his film and ballet music was so effective. The broadcast of the radio play was aired on 11 March 1946 with the violinist Max Rostal and the BBC Symphony Orchestra, conducted by Lionel Salter. The premiere of the *Theme and Cadenza* extract was given at the BBC Light Music Festival by Campoli with the London Light Orchestra, conducted by Michael Krein on 31 March 1949. It makes a very attractive six-minute *bon bouche* in a programme of light music. It is sad – and typical of Trudy's opinion of herself and her role – that according to Robert Milnes she destroyed all her radio scripts.

Soon after Bliss had written the film music for *Men of Two Worlds* he contributed to a symposium on the subject of composing music for film. He said, 'I have to be brutally frank and say that the chief incentive to write for screen is £.s.d., because a composer is likely to make far more money in a little time by this sort of work than he is from the casual and not-too-frequent performances of his works in the concert hall or over the radio. But even while working against all the mechanical restrictions on inspiration it may still be possible for a musician to preserve his artistic integrity... My argument is that in the last resort film music should be judged solely as music – that is to say, by the ears alone, and the question of its value depends on whether it can stand up to this test.'[5] This is, of course, easily demonstrated by the concert suites he (and others) created and which guaranteed not only a longer life for these normally ephemeral scores but also gave people precisely what he demanded – an opportunity to judge the music as music, and not just a buried sound track to visuals.

Now came the project which was to occupy Bliss for most of the next three years. The idea for an opera was first discussed with J.B. Priestley at the Cheltenham Festival in 1945. That was the year of the first Cheltenham Festival which took place over three nights in the Town Hall between 12–15 June in which Bliss conducted extracts from *Miracle in the Gorbals* with the LPO. Richard Witts's article in *The Musical Times* tracing the origins of the Festival noted wryly that 'at the final concert Bliss over-conducted (as Boult would have it) extracts from his ballet....'[6] Bliss's conducting style was not subtle and looked rather militaristic with large gestures which were almost the antithesis of Boult's mini-malistic style. Nevertheless, he got results and was absolutely clear in his musical intentions. He was also extremely enthusiastic about the idea of a continuing festival in the town. Frank Howes, then writing for the *Gloucestershire Echo,* wrote up the possibilities for the event as a 'musical Malvern, even as an English Salzburg with the emphasis rightly on British composers.'[7] He went on to report that 'at the Festival's end the *Echo* buttonholed Mr Bliss, as he then was, and was delighted to hear him declare 'Your festival has been a great success and as an annual event it should have a great future...You have all the natural advantages. And you could attract people from the big centres... Go all out... the audi-ences you have had contained a high proportion of young people. That is a most encouraging sign.'[8] Twenty years later Bliss would become the Festival's President.

Conducting apart, it was the serendipity of time and place bringing Bliss and Priestley together which had such far-reaching consequences. The two men had become friends in the early 1930s (the late 1920s as remembered by Priestley) meeting at a musical party given by the critic Herbert Hughes at his house in Chelsea. They discovered that they were close neighbours in Hampstead, living only a few hundred yards apart, and so they shared a taxi home at the end of the evening. Their friend-ship burgeoned and they became regular tennis and billiards partners as well as enjoying the company of each other's families and many lively dinner parties. 'Gusto' was Bliss's description of Priestley's sense of fun, and Priestley, in his turn, remarked using the same adjective when he commented that 'there has always been a life-enhancing *gusto* about Bliss.'[9] Another common interest which bound these two friends was detective fiction. Priestley and Bliss would race to see who could read the latest Raymond Chandler novel. They also collected the green Penguin editions of Georges Simenon's Maigret novels. A meeting with Agatha Christie in Ankara in 1948 was a big occasion for him as he remembered her 'Queen-mother charm'. Trudy had to dispose of stacks of these books when she left her house to move to a flat in Chartwell House, a retirement home in Kensington, towards the end of her life.

With all this in common, the idea of collaborating on an operatic project seemed a natural development. Priestley had written a great deal for the stage, and Bliss, of course, a number of highly successful ballets. It wasn't surprising, therefore, that he wanted next to undertake the chal-lenge of an opera. Bliss asked Priestley to think of a subject which might work and Priestley said he would consult his notebook ('a little black shiny notebook' as he described it). Priestley found what he felt might be a good subject for operatic treatment in a note he had made about the gods of Greece and Rome turning into strolling players. As he said, 'It's an old legend. Heine mentions it.'[10] He outlined it to Bliss who liked the idea, so a scenario was sketched out.

Bliss remarked that 'As in the case of Elgar, Priestley's public image and the private man, as I know him, have little in common. In working with him on our opera I found him both generous and sensitive, and though it would make more of a story to pretend that we had plenty of rows, the truth is that we got along remarkably smoothly, he deferring to my opinion as the musician, as I did to him where stage matters were concerned.'[11] In fact, Priestley said that "unlike so may distinguished librettists and even more distinguished composers, we didn't quarrel. We never had one serious quarrel. We may have been a little at cross purposes now and again but … we were as good friends at the end as we were at the beginning.'[12]

Given Bliss's interest in Homer, instilled in him by his father in childhood, the subject matter for the opera suggested by Priestley was bound to arouse his interest as it featured a mythical scenario where, once Christianity had taken hold, the gods of antiquity were made redundant and reduced to living as a group of travelling players. On Midsummer Eve once a century, however, their powers returned for one night.

The action takes place in the south of France near a village called Berasson in Provence in the summer of 1836. Priestley's hugely successful novel *The Good Companions,* finished in 1929, also featured a group of travelling players and maybe the idea which had been in his notebooks for some years was ready to resurface for this libretto in the form of a colourful 'romantic comedy'.

The correspondence between composer and librettist tracks the course of the creation of the opera and shows both men giving and taking ideas as the final shape of the work was gradually assumed. A good example of composer v librettist is seen in a letter from Bliss to Priestley on 18 August 1945 where Bliss feels strongly about how the protagonists are introduced.

Dear Jack,

Here are some thoughts about the sequence of events. Acts 1 – I feel the players must be more important in this than they appear in your first synopsis (two of our principals are among them!). Instead of their being discovered on stage, I should much prefer a good entrance a little later on, and a scene (short) to themselves where they feel excited about the coming anniversary and, in their rags, show a slightly mysterious side to the audience, as if the coming transformation were casting a shadow before.

This Act might commence with Lavatte telling the landlady of 'The Golden Duck' (and, incidentally, the audience!) his troubles about money, Madeleine etc. What do *you* think? I believe that final laughing chorus excellent, if well led up to, and the curtain might come down on them unconsciously grouping themselves as a classical frieze, the scene mysteriously lit.

Act II – This is a grand opportunity for *me* – balletic, as you say! Why cannot Venus enter with her train, and Bacchus with his rout, rather like a Rubens picture?

Act III – I feel this is too complicated for Opera... (the letter continues)[13]

Priestley's reply on the 20th was measured and not in agreement:

Dear Arthur,

Many thanks for your letter of the 18th. I am keeping it and considering carefully the points you make.

We must be careful, however, with so many characters, not to disperse the interest. In my view, which I am certain is dramatically sound, the emphasis must be on the ordinary human beings first, and the actor-gods, no matter how tremendous they are in Act II, must be subsidiary. We must get this straight. Either the piece is about what happens to gods when they find themselves actors amongst human beings, or it must be about what happens to human beings when actor-gods come amongst them. One or the other. Any hesitation here, I swear, will be fatal to the dramatic interest. And I plump outright at once for the second – what happens to human beings when actor-gods arrive. Therefore – if you accept this view, as I'm sure you will, then the four chief characters, the real principals are Lavatte, Florac, Madeleine, Curé with Acts I and III concentrating on their affairs, and even Act II shown as affecting them... (the letter continues)

This shows a very robust exchange of views and, from Priestley, a feeling that Bliss should leave the dramatic side to him and trust his judgement.

217

There are plenty of points which Priestley is prepared to concede in terms of the music but not the overall dramatic shape of the work. A line is drawn quite firmly. The part of the letter that says 'if you accept this view, as I'm sure you will' seems to brook no argument. And indeed, Bliss responds directly a few days later by writing 'Yes, you are quite right! – let us put the *main* emphasis on the humans, and make them creatures of flesh and blood (not opera singers) – and let the Olympians play *dei ex machina*.'[14] Thus the scenario was set and so the dialogue began to arrive from Priestley. In the radio interview Priestley is at pains to point out that, despite firm opinions on the dramatic thrust of the scenario, Bliss is the senior partner. 'He has to dig deeper than the librettist... I'm not a man who easily subordinates himself but in this case I really had to.'[15]

There was much discussion about the title of the work which included 'something with *Midsummer* in it? Or *Magic?' Jupiter Tonans, The Gods Grow Old, Gods in Exile, The Gods Go By, Passing Gods, Banished Gods*, and so on. It was Harold Brooke from Novello, to whom Bliss dedicated the opera, who suggested *The Olympians* which was warmly welcomed as the ideal compromise.

The plot is a simple 'human interest' one in which Joseph Lavette, the richest but most scrooge-like man in the town is about to marry off his daughter, Madeleine, to a rich old nobleman, Armand de Craval. The celebration of this liaison is to take place at The Golden Duck tavern where a troupe of itinerant players is staying. The landlady, Mme. Bardeau, owes Lavatte money and he is seeking repayment. The players then try to leave the inn without paying and the Curé offers to intercede with Lavatte if she is more generous to the players. Lavatte then agrees to hire them at a bargain price in return for cancelling Mme Bardeau's debt. At the tavern Madeleine meets a young poet called Hector de Florac who is on his way to Paris to rehearse his own play and a romantic connection between them is formed. The players perform their play, *The Comedy of Olympus,* and, fortified by wine bought for everyone by Hector, the first Act ends in a riot of noise.

In Act Two, the players, the once-powerful Olympian gods, are reduced to singing for their suppers. On this one night when they regain their ancient powers their masque-like show features Mercury (a dancer – Robert Helpmann in the premiere), Diana, Mars, Bacchus, Venus (who doesn't sing) and Jupiter. 'The first three, bewitching the party guests, create chaos, Bacchus brings intoxication and Jupiter berates mankind for losing its soul. There is a troupe of dancers in this Act formed of the juniors from the Sadler's Wells School of Ballet, one of whom was Bliss's younger daughter Karen. In the chaos the lovers, Madeleine and Hector, become separated and Hector falls for Venus while she, bewitched, follows Diana, while, in the meantime her father, Lavatte, incurs both Mars's and Jupiter's wrath.

In Act III the reduced gods, back in human form, prepare to leave but not before they have generously reunited Madeleine and Hector. Lavatte, totally opposed to this change in his fortunes, is made to relent and agrees to their marriage.'[16]

As already seen in the exchanges between Bliss and Priestley, the big question needing resolution was what happened to the gods when among mortals, or conversely, what happened to mortals when the gods were among them. Priestley was hoping for the latter and this, happily, was what Bliss preferred. Roderick Dunnett summarized the characters in the opera as a) 'pastiche' (Bardeau, Hector, Curé and Lavatte); b) 'cardboard' (Hector and Madeleine); c) 'masque-like' (Venus – silent with or without chorus; and the four other sung gods). He also notes that the gods pose challenges as they remain gods but assume human characteristics. Priestley summed this up in a letter to Bliss of 20 August when he wrote 'I fancy that when they are actors the gods must not be too conscious of their godhood – and the night's events oughtn't to be completely clear to them. This bit is rather tricky.'[17]

The emphasis on riotous partying in the plot along with the subversive theme of the young lovers seems to have had echoes in Priestley's own youth and into his adult life where house parties lasted for several days and he would fall in love with 'different goddesses' (he married three times). All this finds echoes in The Olympians. Hector and Madeleine's passionate feelings for each other gave Bliss wonderful musical opportunities but it also raises fundamental issues of style. The opening of Act II is a prime example of Bliss leaving behind any vestige of personal style and echoing the past masters of the nineteenth century. It is all very beautiful but highly derivative. Edward Dent summed it up when he wrote that 'I enjoyed the music thoroughly; some people found a lot of reminiscences, and I certainly was hit full in the chest by Lavatte's familiarity with The Bartered Bride, but don't worry about that. The famous operas of the past are full of reminiscences of older composers...'. This is disingenuous. William McNaught puts a different slant on it when he commented that 'Bliss has wisely cleared his idiom of modern harmonic astringency. He uses quite a lot of common chords and progressions; in fact, he has gone back to the harmony of the musical gods. The result, inevitably, is a certain air of *reminiscence*',[18] and there is that word again, used by both commentators.

But if there was veiled criticism in these comments it was nothing to the post-premiere deconstruction after the disaster of the first night. Priestley, in a radio interview with Gareth Lloyd Evans, remarked that 'to say it was under-rehearsed was the understatement of a century'. Producer Peter Brook and conductor Karl Rankl were not on speaking terms, passing notes to each other rather than speaking which inevitably reduced the rehearsals to incoherence. He said that Act I was well rehearsed, Act II was barely adequately rehearsed, and by Act III 'they were playing charades... The opera as we wrote it was not properly presented, and nobody has seen it yet as we designed them to see it.'[19] Bliss's judgement was that 'Rankl, Austrian-born but with British nationality, and the Covent Garden Opera Company's music director, simply hadn't done his homework'. Writing to his close friend, the artist George Dannatt in September 1971 when working on the shortened, semi-staged performance the following year, he remarked, 'I have spent today playing on my gramophone disks of the opera that Novellos sent me yesterday, and timing the Acts. The sound is of course <u>torture</u> to the ears, the singing often flat and in Diana's case hardly ever near her notes, while Rankl hurries along desperately, hating every minute of it.'[20] There were other issues, too, such as Bliss's first choice of principal tenor, James Johnston, not being engaged until only ten days before the show opened. Furthermore, the press was invited to the dress rehearsal which proved to be a disaster not least because when things went awry with the set, the designer was nowhere to be found. As a result of this Bliss went to the Garrick Club and sat out the first performance (Thursday 29 September 1949) only appearing in time to thank people at the end.

There was so much criticism in the air of everything and everybody that a fresh assessment need to be made. The sheer scale of a grand opera, the years of work in its creation and the huge financial investment, as well as the air of expectation in a new work from such a highly respected pair of creative artists and coming so close on the heels of the end of the war, make for a distinctly partisan approach to criticism. There is no doubt that Priestley's libretto was regarded as part of the problem, but Bliss's music was subject to the criticism with which he was so often faced – too much ebullience which, with brass and percussion causing balance issues, led the critic Peter Heyworth to comment, 'The romantic music, which stems from a debased Straussian idiom, is so busy modulating that it scarcely draws sufficient breath for a long or telling phrase. The score's air of energy is similarly spurious: there is a great deal of jocose slapping of thighs, but (paradoxically) remarkably little musical movement.'[21] Part of the issue with the work is its subject matter which was hardly the stuff of grand opera. It was more a kind of *opera buffa* fattened up for Christmas.

There isn't space in this narrative to offer a blow-by-blow account of everything which could be detailed about this work but the following observations show some of its strengths and weaknesses.

The opening of Act I has a classic energetic Blissian feel to it though the busy, bustling scene it represents is heavy-handed. Stanford would not have approved of the amount of timpani in the first section ('percussion is used inversely to the amount of it'). There is relief when the orchestra thins for the second section. Lavatte's entry is impressive and the *Con Brio* section where he is deliriously happy about the coming evening's celebrations is wonderfully portrayed. There is some typically (and relatively rare in this work) Blissian dissonance here especially at Lavatte's 'triumph' (figure 22 in the score) when he boasts of the financial 'killing' he has made. This whole section reflects the 'romantic comedy' description given by Priestley. It's full of touches of humour which Bliss maximizes in the music. It is deftly scored. The description of Armand de Craval (the old nobleman to whom Madeleine is engaged) and all his honours is dramatic and the section glows with warmth and humour. Hector's entry transforms the music into pastiche Italian romantic opera and his exchange with the Curé is amusing as Hector tries to show him his new play about to be rehearsed in Paris, which is 'a masterpiece, I assure you'. The Curé extricates himself, citing a pressing engagement and meeting Madeleine on his way out. He tells her about the young and handsome Hector. After meeting him, Hector presses her into rehearsing the part of the Persian Princess with whom he has fallen in love and then proceeds to fall in love with Madeleine. The 'play within a play' succeeds well between the two and Bliss creates real drama and excellent balance between soloists and orchestra.

But what has happened to the young firebrand of the early '20s who almost single-handedly held the torch for modernism in British music? We have accepted a certain move towards romanticism in Bliss's style and the Piano Concerto is a prime example, but that work is still fully recognizable as Bliss. In *The Olympians* Bliss's style loses its personality at so many points and is subsumed into a generic romantic operatic language based wholly on nineteenth-century precedents. The question arises as to whether this is because he cannot find a *vocal* voice equating to his ease with orchestral writing – an issue which has been raised before. The *Times* review on 30 September 1949 underlines this point, noting: 'It is only the soaring tune for the solo voice that does not always arrive when it is needed, but leaves its message to the orchestra.'[22] The purely orchestral sections are generally much more interesting and are more recognizable stylistically. To this end the opera is *too* romantic and is out of step with the times. Britten's *Peter Grimes,* premiered four years earlier, was much more in tune with a contemporary approach to the genre, making *The Olympians* feeling distinctly old fashioned. The post-war era required post-war thinking. The grittiness of the subject matter of *Peter Grimes* was also far more gripping than Priestley's comedic romp and was more in tune with the mindset of a post-war nation who, while keen to be entertained, also wanted to move on from the past and be stimulated in new ways.

There is no doubting the sense of drama in the first act and the dramatic joins between scenes are guaranteed to raise the blood pressure. One senses Bliss enjoying himself and feeling that the general level of excitement will draw an enthusiastic response from the audience. Jupiter's entry marks the difference between his character and the other gods very successfully and the introduction to it is masterly.

The representation of love (at the heart of the plot) is beautifully and sympathetically drawn by Bliss even though it elicits a pastiche-like response from him. Oddly, Britten's troubled sexuality and his psychological issues set him up to write more dramatically and in a far more contemporary way about troubled people – something seen to impressive effect in operas like *Peter Grimes*, *Billy Budd* and *Death in Venice*. Bliss's contented, comfortable life finds him wanting, creatively, when more experience in troubled areas might have better equipped him to express elements even in this story which would benefit from a greater grittiness. His closeness to the subject matter of *Morning Heroes*, its personal connection and Bliss's masterly and deeply effective and affecting score, would seem to make this point with real clarity.

Bliss writes another gripping scherzo when the gods realize what the significance of the midsummer date is. This leads to a really exciting laughing chorus at the end of Act I with Mme Bardeau trying to be heard attempting to stop all the noise. It is a terrific finale.

The *Times* critic William Mann, writing of the 1972 revival, made a perceptive comment about the plot when he wrote, 'Chiefly this performance of The Olympians put me in reminiscent mood because the piece itself is so much of its period. The tale of the old Roman gods, now reduced to penniless strolling players in nineteenth-century France; the handsome romantic young poet, the benevolent comic priest, the miserly father: they are not quite the best Priestley, but they do represent an operatic equivalent of those romantic British films, in the late 1940s, when James Mason was usually the villain and Stewart Grainger the hero, and Phyllis Calvert or Deborah Kerr the virginal heroine. The Olympians inhabits just such a make-believe world of glamorous escape, and Bliss's music – at its best in the opening of the second act, still magically lovely, but often inventively unfocused, pleasant and vaguely appropriate noises that haven't quite found the right tune to dominate them – compounds the make-believe. The Olympians ought to have delighted large austerity-age audiences in 1949 and thereafter. But nowadays it seems merely to toy with the makings of music-drama.'[23]

Diana's appearance seems to awaken something fresher in Bliss and the addition here of an upper voices chorus adds a new element that is welcome, and the end of the first part of Act II is magical with the chorus suspended high up and unaccompanied. The procession of the gods is then introduced with their various characteristics, giving Bliss opportunities for variety (including the use of a full chorus) and a series of vignettes ensues including the introduction of Venus which brings the plot back to the issue of Madeleine and Hector and the fact that Hector has inevitably fallen under her spell (Madeleine: 'Hector, have you forgotten me so soon?'). The 'father' of the gods, Jupiter, brings the group to its full complement as he makes his majestic entrance. The problem with all this is the episodic nature of the procession of gods and the inevitability of the turn of the next one. The plot loses its dramatic punch as we wait for the next piece of actual action rather than a series of introductory calling cards. It simply takes too long.

In Act III there is a similar progress of vignette-like scenes which see Bliss slipping in and out of character. Hector's sudden return to his senses after being bewitched by Venus feels like a manufactured gear change and is followed by the interjection of the Curé persuading Lavatte to let Madeleine marry Hector. Lavatte blames black magic and sorcery for turning her head and seeks the Curé's help in exorcising the spell which he is convinced has been used. The four things the Curé quotes as being needed to unbind the spell: gold, a priest, a virgin maid and a noble loving youth, is wonderfully contrived and beautifully wrought in music by Bliss. What follows, however, spoils the magical effect in another period of *longueurs* with some off-the-shelf 'rum-te-tum' music which so sadly undoes the effect of what has just been so beautifully created. But as the opera draws to its close and the gods are reduced to their human characters once again Bliss creates a heightened intensity which leads to an atmospheric, quiet ending almost as if the principal characters are waking from a dream. Here are the echoes of other midsummer make-believe stories buried deep in our common folklore.

This opera feels like a point of arrival and departure in Bliss's career. On one hand it is a huge undertaking which occupied him for a substantial time and seemed, on the face of it, a natural progression from his other stage works. On the other hand, the plot is not well managed enough in terms of stage drama to maintain interest. Neville Cardus, writing in *Opera* magazine felt that 'the first act... is, for lightness of touch and graciousness of style, as good as any written so far by Englishmen... *The Olympians*, for better or worse, lives in its own particular realm of lyric antique, and over the general sky of it come from time-to-time shadows of unusual beauty and pathos'. He underlines another point when he writes: 'The score is probably a pastiche; still, in spite of miscalculations in modulation of mood and stage-action which upset the poise of the opera established in Act I, the impressions remain of much deft music, ranging from a miniature bloom to a canvas of no inconsiderable dimensions and mastery.'[24] Harold Rosenthal, writing in the same magazine, reinforces the opinion of the second and third acts when he commented that 'some drastic revision of the second and third acts appears to be necessary', and he goes on to comment that 'the first act appears almost perfect as to music and text, but the second act hovers between reality and phantasy and is a far too long and static affair, while the last act is a typical Priestley finale, untidy, inconclusive and dramatically an anti-climax.'[25]

All the critics agree on these essentials and while the 1972 semi-staged performance conducted by Brian Fairfax attempted to address some issues with even more cuts than had already been made the essential fault lines still persist and there is little hope that the work will find the enthusiasm or the finance for a fully staged comeback.

For Bliss all this was inevitably a huge disappointment but at no time in his reflections on the work does he admit to any failings of either music or libretto focusing, as did Priestley, on the failings of the production and the conductor. As he noted '*The Olympians* was understandably greeted with very mixed criticisms'[26] which seems like a masterly understatement. Edward Dent tried to buoy him up in a long letter of support but even he found much to criticise, perhaps most tellingly when he wrote 'The real trouble about the opera is that…you have put everything you had into it, and there is too much stuff – it makes the opera feel very long and rather exhausting.'[27] And, tellingly, with regard to the issue of vocal lines: 'It has too many opportunities for the singers to show off their voices (but only their *voices*, not their phrasing and style) in successions of ecstatic pauses….'[28]

One of Bliss's great strengths was his ability to move forward after a setback – and he had several in his career. This was the first time in his maturity that he had not succeeded in fulfilling the promise expected of a major commission. But, as Sir Charles Groves said in his moving tribute to Bliss broadcast on the night of his death, 'his mind and heart were always looking forward'. An example of the British 'stiff upper lip'.

A life went on around the writing of the opera, of course, and Bliss had a particularly happy interlude at the end of 1947 visiting Budapest to conduct his Piano Concerto. Getting there was problematic as it was in Russian hands and entry required a special visa only obtainable in Vienna which Bliss obtained with the help of the British Council. They were turned back at the Austro-Hungarian border and with telephone lines down they couldn't even communicate with the people meeting them on the other side. A typically serendipitous detail saw them through on a second attempt. Bliss had been given a little red five-pointed star by a friend at the Savile Club who was an enthusiast for all things Russian. He had put it in his wallet without another thought but he remembered it now and pinned it to his lapel. The Russian guard smilingly lifted the barrier and they sailed through and arrived in time for the rehearsal and concert. Bliss recalled the great warmth of the Hungarians everywhere he went and his admiration for their courage and determination at this terrible time in their history.

In the spring of 1948, he, conductor George Weldon, and the Australian pianist Noel Mewton-Wood (who Bliss rated so highly that he later wrote his piano sonata for him) travelled to Ankara at the invitation of the British Council to give the opening concert in the new Opera House. On the same trip, quite by chance, he renewed his acquaintance with Julian Huxley who was travelling there on behalf of UNESCO. Bliss and Huxley had become friends over the years and had occasionally been invited together as guests of the Priestleys on the Isle of Wight. Bliss remembered sparring with Huxley on his only appearance in the BBC *Brains Trust* programme and being sent an anonymous postcard afterwards simply saying 'How *dare* you interrupt Professor Huxley, you insignificant little person!'[29] But Bliss admitted to feeling intimidated by

Huxley's superior intellect and reflected that this was probably what led him to be so argumentative.

While still engaged with the final stages of *The Olympians*, Bliss was commissioned by Gainsborough Pictures to write the music for his next film, *Christopher Columbus*, signing the contract on 23 February 1949. Certainly not letting the grass grow under his feet, the film was premiered in London on 16 June the same year. But once again he came up against non-musical issues which led to the film's poor reception, the *Times* reporting that it had an 'inept script, flat dialogue, and feeble humour.'[30] But Bliss seemed to enjoy his part in it for once and had, through music, again to suggest the feeling of a foreign country as he had in *Men of Two Worlds*. He made the point that 'it is difficult with American and English actors to suggest the atmosphere of Spain – that is what the music has to do – so I have tried using Spanish idioms and tunes akin to those of Spain which convey the feeling and atmosphere of the age in which Columbus set forth from Spain.'[31] He ends a detailed description of the plot by saying that 'musically I found the picture extremely interesting'.

The manuscript of this film score, consisting of 135 pages, has survived – the first of his film scores to do so. The BBC broadcast two extracts in July 1949, and thirty years later three movements were put together by Marcus Dods and recorded by the City of Birmingham Symphony Orchestra. It was the recording of virtually the whole score by the Czecho-Slovak Radio Symphony Orchestra under Adriano in 1990, though, that gave the first real opportunity to hear the music for this film arranged carefully, and with modifications incorporated from the soundtrack to the film. Muir Mathieson once again directed the Royal Philharmonic Orchestra in the soundtrack recording. Bliss may have enjoyed the project but to little avail when the film 'bible', *Halliwell's Film Guide,* remarked that the film was 'an extraordinarily tediously paced historical account of basically undramatic events; interesting without being stimulating.'[32]

With two hugely time-consuming and mentally draining projects receiving a less than enthusiastic reception, Bliss decided to return to chamber music to feed the soul and restore his battered sense of self-worth. The need to do something more private and personal was probably at the heart of his decision to turn down a commission from the Arts Council to write a large-scale choral and orchestral work for the Festival of Britain in 1951. Despite this, in November 1949 he had written to Bridges Adams indicating that he and Priestley were thinking of the possibility of a new opera project, something which, perhaps not surprisingly, did not come to fruition though it showed that they were determined to come through the experience unscathed and prepared for new challenges.

The chamber music he 'retreated into' was his Second String Quartet (actually his fourth but numbered this way as his second acknowledged work for this medium). Through the spring of 1950 he worked at producing what he felt to be his best chamber music work as he told George Dannatt. He also felt that the slow movement revealed a new side of his musical personality – something to be explored shortly. The Scherzo, true virtuoso writing, elicited the comment that 'I have never written more brilliantly for strings.'[33]

The quartet was written (not commissioned) for his old friends the Griller Quartet, celebrating their twentieth anniversary in 1950. It was premiered at that year's Edinburgh Festival on 1 September. This work marks a serious departure from the First String Quartet of ten years previously and Bliss noted that 'it grew into the most substantial chamber work that I had attempted.'[34] The quartet is in four movements with the slow movement placed second. A heady mixture of emotions course through the veins of the work and this may well reflect the mixture of stimulants in Bliss's personal and professional life. The happy progress of his daughters' lives – Barbara marrying happily two years earlier and Karen doing so well in her dancing career, together with the milestone of his own silver wedding that year, meant much to reflect on with satisfaction in his personal life. But there was also no denying the professional sadness at the outcome of what should have been the climax of his maturity to this date in his opera. On the heels of all this comes a work which seems determined not only to re-establish his personal sense of self-worth, but also to say to the musical world 'here is the genuine Arthur Bliss with something important to say which demands attention'. There is a real feeling here of a desire to add a work of considerable significance to the repertoire for the medium.

The first movement has a greater adherence to classical structures, and his own analysis of the work demonstrates how closely he had thought about form where sometimes he would go off-piste to express what he wanted to say. It is hugely energetic music with a simmering undercurrent of anger or frustration in its moodscape. The second movement, marked *sostenuto* and almost entirely for muted strings, is again closely argued moving in and out of reflective and declamatory sections. The ending is beautifully conceived and its closing chords take us back to the opening dissonances but fading into a white light of silence.

The scherzo is a serious piece of virtuoso string writing. This movement barely lets the players relax for a moment despite episodes of seemingly more peaceful music. As Bliss recalled, the Griller Quartet would use this movement 'at recitals in American universities and schools just to show the outrageous demands which contemporary composers make on their instrumentalists!'[35] The finale has a gentle opening, balancing the heady fireworks of the scherzo before it takes off in a genial *Allegro* which seems to contain something of all the previous movements within its compass. This was Bliss's last chamber music work.

So, what does Bliss mean when he writes of feeling that the slow movement shows a new side of his musical personality? Well, it is certainly not just the fact that he is writing a deeply emotional movement as he has done that very powerfully before. One need only look at the slow movement of the previous quartet to see a moving and heartfelt outpouring reflecting the difficult times he was experiencing stranded in America in the early years of the war. Perhaps, coming to his sixtieth birthday the following year, he was allowing the reflection of a growing number of past years with all that had entailed for better or worse, happiness or sadness to coalesce in musical terms. We are so used to the gestural side of Bliss's musical character that something as organically conceived as this movement almost comes as a surprise. Even the two themes used are connected through their initial dotted rhythms. The build up to the climax through the second theme (three bars after figure 54), where the opening rhythm is overlaid with the character and regained slower tempo of the first, makes the organic nature of this metamorphosis plain. Where the opera score seemed something of a hotch-potch of styles this work boldly proclaims Bliss's serious musical mind with something deeply personal to say. One senses his need to reassert his credentials in this work.

Whatever the highs and lows of this recent period Bliss's place in the pantheon of the highest echelons of the music profession was now recognized by the honour of a Knighthood in the King's Birthday Honours in June 1950. He received a letter from Downing Street on 10 May asking if the honour would be agreeable to him. The investiture took place at Buckingham Palace on 4 June. Not a word of this in his autobiography but reaction was summed up in a letter from John Ireland who wrote on 2 July, 'I expect you have been overwhelmed with letters of congratulation on the recent honour conferred on you, and through you, on our profession… How I remember the early days when we used to meet at the old Pagani's (a restaurant in Great Portland Street much frequented by musicians and artists) and you would tell me of your work and ambitions…we have not come into contact as much as I could have wished – such is Fate – but I have followed all your work with joyful interest and am glad you are now so fully recognized as one of the few really authoritative and representative voices of British Music.'[36] The honour was obviously enormously gratifying to Bliss who confided in a friend that his investiture at the Palace made him 'as excited as a small boy on a Prize-Giving Day.'[37]

Bliss's brother Howard wrote to him saying 'of those who would (write) if they could – first and foremost, of Father who, though he controlled it so well – would be overcome with emotion – then, of such as Basil Johnson (Director of Music at Rugby) who, if still alive – will take enormous pleasure in writing to you – and again – differently – of poor Rootham, absurd man, who would twirl his eyebrows in a frantic effort to appear detached and not green with envy.'[38]

That autumn Trudy went to the States to visit her family in Santa Barbara while Bliss went separately to Madrid to a conference on musical copyright, representing the Performing Right Society of which he had been elected as Vice-Chairman in September. This side of his work was of real importance to him as he wrote: 'If from my mother I inherited a creative gift, from my father I acquired the need to do some practical administrative work, to organize and plan, to see theories put into practice. In the lulls between the times when music takes hold of me, and temporarily I lie becalmed, I find it necessary to occupy myself with alternative activities. I know the rhythm of my musical life very well, and can judge the intervals during which my extrovert side must exert itself. At these times it must be the American strain in me which causes me to rage at relatively unimportant details such as telephone delays… I find myself then, to my own surprise, bursting into uncontrollable anger out of all proportion to the incident that has caused it.'[39] He then went on to recount how he had lost his temper in the Madrid trip when, arriving at the hotel into which he had been booked, he was told that there were no rooms and moreover they had no knowledge of him or his booking. More than this, he was told that there were no rooms in the whole of Madrid. Taking himself off to the Ritz (the city's best hotel) they, too, told him that they were full. Placing a letter from the Spanish Ambassador in London in front of the desk clerk, however, (a practice learned from previous experiences) he was soon furnished with a 'splendidly quiet' suite.

Bliss's views on the conference and the many other such meetings he attended in a number of major cities including Madrid, Rome,

Amsterdam, Paris, London and Bergen showed that they were essentially a waste of time as music rarely featured in the discussions and the meetings descended into tussles between personalities and factions with the real work taking place elsewhere. Needing to find alternative entertainment Bliss sought out the legendary Walter Starkie, head of the British Institute in Madrid. Starkie, an almost exact contemporary of Bliss, founded the British Institute in 1940 and went on to found other centres in Barcelona, Bilbao, Seville and Valencia. It was an initiative supported by the British Council. In her book about the Council, Frances Donaldson commented that 'his appointment was one of several which showed that, if the conditions of war made great difficulties in the recruitment of large numbers of the general staff, they also made it possible sometimes to recruit men of outstanding talent and distinction. Professor Starkie (a brother of Dr Enid Starkie, to a later generation even better known) was an Irish scholar and professor of romance languages, and he had earned fame by wandering through Europe in search of gypsies and their music, earning his bread as he went by playing the violin.'[40] She went on to comment that 'Starkie was a short, fat man with a strong Irish brogue, but he spoke perfect Spanish and had considerable charm. The strength of German influence in Spain at this time was immense and probably no one but he could have built up and maintained an Institute.'[41] The British Council's Financial Controller, R.A. Phillips said of him that he was 'the most successful man the British Council has ever had in its service.'[42] Starkie's books about his travels, including the popular *Spanish Raggle Taggle* and *Don Gypsy*, underlined his dual interest in music and the Gypsies, but it was his obvious personal skills which ensured his success with the Council. In fact, a blind eye had to be turned to some financial irregularities (described as 'some terrible financial crime' by Phillips) who gave him a dressing down in the knowledge that once Starkie left the room it would be water off a duck's back, and Phillips simply had to finish by saying 'he did a wonderful job.'[43]

It is no surprise that Bliss sought out such a man with his intimate knowledge of Madrid and of Spain. As he wrote to Trudy, 'Most of my fun here I owe to the Starkie family... I think his wife is Argentinian, and he has a daughter who most kindly went around with me, and helped me shop. Through Starkie I have heard some real Spanish singing, and seen some real Spanish dancing: most of it for the tourists is quite phoney.'[44] Through another introduction he took a young and locally popular dancer out to dinner, being driven by her to the restaurant of her choice.

At the end of the meal, she received a note that she needed to leave to rescue a friend. She insisted Bliss accompany her. This resulted in a drive through old Madrid to what looked like a lock-up garage and the rescue of said friend without any explanation to the bemused Bliss who then ended the evening (or early morning as he remembered it) at another haunt and none the wiser for his exploits. He felt, at the age of fifty-nine, he was getting rather too old 'to act d'Artagnon'!

# Chapter Twelve

# MASTER OF THE QUEEN'S MUSICK

In Bliss's writing about his own life and career it is clear to infer from the character of his descriptions what is mere reporting and what actually moved or excited him. In this way his trip to Scotland in June 1951 to receive an Honorary LL.D degree from Glasgow University stands out partly for his description of the dressing up saga associated with the ritual – including the 'brilliant red gown… I always wear if I have to dress up, peacock fashion, for any function.'[1] They stayed with Ernest Bullock who was Professor of Music at the University and Principal of the Royal Scottish Academy of Music. Part of the attraction of the Scottish trip, however, was Trudy's connection with the country through her volumes of the Carlyle letters discussed in the previous chapter. Trudy now wanted to show Bliss Craigenputtock where the Carlyles lived early in their married life. The remoteness of this place was beautifully described by Trudy who wrote that to reach it 'the road winds up from Dunscore through treeless pastures, grey stone walls flung across them like a meshed net. A line of firs on the horizon, a plantation of larches down the slope, and there, across the burn, lies Craigenputtock. Remote it certainly is, but very beautiful.'[2] Bliss felt that Trudy related so strongly to Jane Carlyle because both had been wrested from their more simple natural environments through marriage and had to face up to the challenging contrast of London.

The building of Pen Pits and the designing of the garden had given Bliss an enthusiasm for growing plants and shrubs which, being a hardened metropolitan man, had not really featured in his world before. Trudy, of course, came from a family whose principal passion was botany. But as they were within striking distance of one of Scotland's famous gardens at Inverewe they wrote to the owner, Mairi Sawyer, to ask if they could visit. The Inverewe gardens had been laid out following her father's purchase of the estate in 1862 but not finished when he died in 1922. She continued his work and when the Blisses visited was in negotiation with the National Trust for Scotland to take over ownership after her death. This arrangement was timely as she died only two years later in July 1953.

The day the Blisses visited it was raining relentlessly but Mairi Sawyer was nevertheless outside tending her borders when they arrived. She insisted on a full tour of the very extensive garden. As Bliss noted 'she was not going to let us miss a single shrub'. It was fortunate that they had a change of clothes with them which, once achieved, preceded a sumptuous tea-spread.

We have encountered a number of outstanding performers who inspired Bliss to write some of his greatest works for them: Lionel Tertis, the Viola Sonata, and Solomon, the Piano Concerto, for instance. Bliss's next major work was for Kathleen Ferrier. It was a dramatic *Scena for contralto and orchestra* called *The Enchantress*. The libretto was by Henry Reed, an old friend of the Blisses who they met some years earlier while on holiday in 'that part of Cornwall which forms the landscape of Thomas Hardy's *A Pair of Blue Eyes*'. This was around St Juliot on the north-east coast of the county near Boscastle and Tintagel. Bliss described Reed as one of the most elusive of his friends but was glad to pin him down for long enough to complete this libretto. Reed suggested a scene based on *Second Idyll* of Theocritus in which the proud Syracusan lady, Simaetha, resorts to witchcraft to win back her faithless lover, Delphis. The world of this plot and its origins in a period of history both familiar to Bliss and with such resonance, remembering his father's enthusiasm for Homer, inspired an unusual and post-*Olympians* operatic scene.

The solo voice, giving us a one-sided perspective on the situation, brings an extra dramatic edge to the plot as, rather like a suicide note, it shows the edgy, end-of-the-tether state she has been driven to by this careless man who has driven her to such distraction. Bliss's manic opening gesture shows Simaetha's state, bent on revenge, and prepares us for an uncomfortable ride towards her goal of enticing Delphis through the power of magic. Her dented pride causes her to cry out that after regaining him 'I am no longer laughed at, no longer mocked! Companion or lover, he shall leave them. He shall be mine again, shall lie in my arms again!'

One senses that had *The Olympians* had a more edgy, dramatic plot, in the main, it might well have fired Bliss in a way that the comic plot simply did not as hard as he tried. It would also seem to be the reason that he couldn't find a consistent musical response to the libretto. The irony of Bliss's compositional style is that while he had a mercurial wit, was bounding with energy and enjoyed playing games with family and friends, his attempts at being humorous in music are less memorable in the main than those plots which have a serious or emotionally intense content. *The Enchantress* makes exactly this point with vivid clarity. One might almost think that Bliss is putting himself in Simaetha's position and, having found the love of his life, imagines what it might be like if she were flighty and unfaithful. Or perhaps he remembered that girl he chased to Switzerland in the early 1920s only to find her in the arms of another man. Who knows? But there is a real dramatic intensity in this work which Bliss sustains with vivid momentum over its eighteen-minute duration.

The operatic treatment is heightened by the use of passages of recitative which, being free of metre, bring an extra degree of freedom of expression for the singer, as in her opening gambit where Simaetha demands that her slave girl bring her the ingredients for her magic potion. The score is restless, constantly fluctuating, responding to the shifting elements of the story. One of the most affecting moments is the binding of the spell (figure 15) and the way when the climax is reached with the words 'the man I love' the manic agitation of her anger and frustration returns. Another key point occurs when Delphis responds to the spell and when he returns utters Simaetha's name twice with Bliss's version of a 'Tristan' chord placed in two different textural spacings which gives a considerable poignancy to the moment. The ending is angrily triumphant with two orchestral shouts which, if sung, would be 'hurrah, hurrah!' before the throw-away cadence. Bliss scored the work without clarinets and bassoons so that the more intense, nasal sound of the double reed instruments (oboe and cor anglais) could cut through and match what he described as the 'sardonic sound of muted brass'.

Although written for Kathleen Ferrier, Bliss actually felt that the role of Simaetha was almost the opposite of Ferrier's personality which he described as having a 'joyous vitality and goodness'. He couldn't imagine her 'calling on Hecate for revenge, and burning in the fire the wax image of her lover. I told her so, but she only laughed – and went on singing gloriously.'[3] He concluded that although their encounter was brief it was nevertheless unforgettable. It was also unforgettable for Ferrier who, having been diagnosed with breast cancer, had fitted out her father's bedroom as a music room. He had had a stroke and died in January 1951 while she was on tour in Rome. Until now, she had used her old, obviously rickety Cramer piano, but Myra Hess now generously loaned her one of her Steinways. This was not before she noted that 'Sir Arthur Bliss hadn't helped (the state of her Cramer) – during rehearsals for *The Enchantress* he had pummelled the keys so hard that several of them had broken.'[4] It seems that he had an excess of energy even in his playing.

The first performance of the work was given by Ferrier with the BBC Northern Orchestra conducted by Charles Groves in a studio recording on 2 October 1951 with the first public concert performance being given by Ferrier with the London Symphony Orchestra conducted by Hugo Rignold on 6 April the following year. A critic for the *Times* was enthusiastic, writing that 'The vocal scena is not a common musical form but it has some ancestry: the splendid new example, sung with spirit and dramatic power by Miss Kathleen Ferrier, derives in the last resort from Purcell. Parry and Ethel Smyth provide intermediate examples that have not established themselves, but this one can face the future with confidence. For, in the first place, the size of it is exactly right – the words… provide a self-contained episode, highly charged with emotion, which music fits perfectly. In the second place Bliss has drawn a fine, soaring vocal line of great flexibility and expressiveness. Words and music coalesce.'[5] Sadly, the prediction that the work would establish itself in the repertoire has been proved wrong and indeed the critic of the *Belfast Telegraph* described it as 'a rather rambling monologue'[6] after a performance on 15 February 1963 which might say more, however, about the performance than the work which is a compelling drama in the hands of the right performers.

Bliss's connection with inspirational performers extended much further than those at the top of their professional game like Ferrier, as he was also deeply impressed by those, like the young Australian pianist Noël Mewton-Wood, whose talent burned with an incandescent heat drawing everyone in who witnessed it like a moth is drawn to light.

Mewton-Wood had come to London to study at the Royal Academy of Music aged only fourteen and made his debut performance playing Beethoven's C minor Concerto at the Queen's Hall with Beecham aged a precocious seventeen. Bliss got to know him well and would work with him especially in memorable performances of his own concerto. But in a radio broadcast after Mewton-Wood's untimely death by suicide aged thirty-one, in 1953, Bliss remarked that he 'was much more than an outstanding pianist. His was one of the most inquiring and far-reaching minds I have met in a young man. A study of his bookshelves would show the serious and varied range of his reading. He had a great love of poetry. He admired modern painting, and knew how to add to the collection left him by his uncle, the poet Walter Turner.'[7] Bliss remembered his performance, from memory, of Hindemith's *Ludus Tonalis* – a formidable feat played, according to Bliss, with apparent ease. John Amis also remembered him playing this work on 'the little brown Steinway in the Holst Room' at Morley College. 'When Noel played Hindemith's *Ludus Tonalis* we used to fear sometimes for its safety. Noel played with a fine technique and quite out of the ordinary sensitivity and musicianship, but now and then the physicality of this young godlike creature would run away with him and he would, as they say, "go through his tone", i.e., bang.'[8] Eventually he met the partner with whom he would live for the rest of his short life, Bill Fedricks. But it was Fedrick's hypochondria which led Mewton-Wood to overlook serious abdominal pains which led to Fedrick's death. Mewton-Wood immediately attempted suicide with an overdose of aspirin but was caught in time. However, after hinting that he was getting over Fedrick's death to Amis in a long phone call, the next day, 5 December 1953, he took prussic acid and died. Amis also felt that it wasn't only the death of his partner which precipitated this awful suicide but the fact that 'he also felt that his career wasn't advancing. The Royal Festival Hall had been opened some time and whereas his colleagues played there several times he had only been asked to play there once.'[9]

Bliss had been so impressed by Mewton-Wood's playing, particularly of his own concerto, that he wrote a piano Sonata for him in 1952 adding the dedication as well. Bliss wrote that 'when with his characteristic fire and sensitivity he played this for the first time, I little thought that within two years he was to meet a tragic death at his own hands.'[10] In fact, that first performance was on 24 April 1953, only eight months before his death.

The Sonata is in three movements with a deeply serious cast of mind. The first Bliss described as having a 'steely brilliance'. The second movement is in variation form and is marked 'slow and serene', though in reality the serenity has a rather dark and often troubled hue though there is a strongly passionate undercurrent. The ending is both serene and comfortingly poised. The final movement is an Allegro which Bliss described as 'gay and lively' though, again, the gaity is elusive. It is a technical tour-de-force which Mewton-Wood relished. The general darkness of the work is an interesting twist both on Bliss's 'celebration' of his young colleague's outstanding musicianship and his playing of his notoriously challenging Piano Concerto, as well as Bliss's own description of the Sonata which would seem to temper serenity and gaity with an undercurrent of feeling which turned out to be prescient.

After Mewton-Wood's death John Amis decided to organize a memorial concert held in the Wigmore Hall on 4 December 1954. He asked Dennis

Brain, Peter Pears, the Zorian String Quartet and Britten to take part as the performers, and Bliss, Britten, Tippett, Alan Bush and Cecil Day Lewis to write works for the event. Britten wrote his third *Canticle: Still falls the night* for tenor, horn and piano. Tippett contributed a piece he had already written but felt was perfect for the occasion, the last song of *The Heart's Assurance: Remember your lovers*. Bush wrote an elegiac piece for horn and piano (Brain was to die two years later in a car accident) and Bliss and Day Lewis collaborated, Day Lewis writing a poem called *Elegiac Sonnet* which Bliss set for tenor, string quartet and piano. The poem's opening lines capture so well the sense of loss which everybody felt so keenly:

A fountain plays no more: those pure cascades
And diamond plumes now sleep within their source.
A breath, a mist of joy, the woodsong fades –
The trill, the transport of his April force.

There is little doubt that Bliss felt a fundamental grief at this loss – almost a grief like the loss of a child before their time, perhaps for the musical son he never had. Certainly, the deeply moving opening piano introduction to this work shows a depth of feeling comparatively rare in Bliss's output and reminds us that the piano represents Mewton-Wood himself. It is odd that when the voice enters one feels it almost as an interruption of Bliss's melancholy reverie. But gradually as the string quartet adds further layers of texture the opening comes into focus and the work builds to an impassioned climax before settling on a beautifully placed final *major* chord which reflects Day Lewis's final words 'Lay on his heart A flower he never knew – the rose called Peace'.

Life moves on, however, for those strong enough to withstand its turbulent waters and maybe Bliss knew Sibelius's terse comment that 'no one erected a statue to a critic' in relation to the various buffetings he had endured in recent times. Soon after *The Enchantress* had been premiered in April 1952 another work, the *Concerto for Two Pianos and Orchestra* that originally started life as the *Concerto for Piano, Tenor, Strings and Percussion* in 1920, revised and then re-written in a new form in 1924 and revised soon after that now found its final version in 1950. As Bliss said, 'I was fond of the work and did not want to see it wholly neglected. I determined therefore to rethink it for a different combination of players, and a few years later I rewrote the whole concerto for the two American pianists Maier and Pattison, to be accompanied by full orchestra.'[11] The first performance took place in Manchester given by Ethel Bartlett and

Rae Robertson with the BBC Northern Orchestra conducted by John Hopkins. The work was to have one further incarnation as an arrangement for piano, three hands, for Phyllis Sellick and Cyril Smith in 1968.

On 6 February 1952 King George VI died and his daughter, Princess Elizabeth, succeeded to the throne as Queen Elizabeth II. The Coronation would not take place for over a year but preparations began immediately and two commissions flowed from this for Bliss. The first was a contribution to a collection of choral pieces from a number of prominent British composers called *A Garland for the Queen* which would be premiered at a concert given by the Cambridge University Madrigal Society under Boris Ord at the Royal Festival Hall on 1 June, 1953, the eve of Coronation day. The piece he wrote was *Aubade for Coronation Morning* to a text by Henry Reed. The setting takes its cue from the first line of Reed's poem 'Then the first bird at dawn, *It is her day!* he cried'. Imitating birdsong is Bliss's response with the first ninety-four bars being scored for divided upper voices with two soprano soloists. There are some remarkably effective birdsong-like phrases which weave in and out of each other's lines. The setting is often gestural and has elements of fanfare about the antiphonal writing once the tenors and basses join. It is a truly occasional piece which sets the whole collection off (it is the first) to an uplifting start.

The other commission from the Arts Council for the Coronation was for the actual service itself and was *Processional* which was written to accompany the procession of Her Majesty the Queen Mother from the West Door of Westminster Abbey to her seat. It is scored for full orchestra with a prominent part for organ. Timing was all important for this great State occasion but for Bliss who knew all about minutes and seconds from his experience as a film composer this was all grist to his mill. The piece takes some nine minutes which indicates a very slow, stately procession indeed. Whilst the style is obviously a march for a great occasion the music itself is not memorable, and, again, the lack of a good tune to carry it forward seemed simply beyond him. Compared with Walton's *Crown Imperial* and *Orb and Sceptre* marches, both of which were performed at this service, Bliss's pales into a very poor third. His genius for great occasions was the short, arresting fanfare, a form in which he had few rivals. Bliss and Trudy were both present at the Coronation service and duly received their coronation medals.

1953 was to be a highly significant year in Bliss's life. Noel Mewton-Wood's premiere of his *Piano Sonata* took place at Broadcasting House in London on 24 April and the following month he received a commission from the BBC to compose a Violin Concerto. In the meantime, however, he had been hard at work on the music for a film adaptation of John

Gay's *The Beggar's Opera* making arrangements of the original airs and making such additions as were necessary for this major film produced by Laurence Olivier and Herbert Wilcox and directed by Peter Brook. As often happened there were ructions between the producers and director and Olivier was injured while performing a stunt which created insurance issues. Bliss's music was extensive with a total of fifty-five numbers used during the film which was released on 31 May. A Suite using various numbers from the film was performed by the BBC Concert Orchestra with Leicestershire choirs conducted by Vilem Tausky in October 1958 in the de Montfort Hall, Leicester, and one or two songs were separately produced and published, but the music has not yet been recorded unlike much of his other film music, although the film is commercially available on DVD.

To add to the collection of honours and awards he was amassing Bliss was now elected an Honorary Fellow of Pembroke College, Cambridge, his old college, in June. Just before this he and Trudy had become grandparents for the first time as Barbara had given birth to a baby girl called Susan. Another personal connection which strengthened the gradually loosening ties between California and London was Bliss's half-sister Enid, who had been a child bridesmaid at their wedding, and who had now started regular visits to London sometimes with her mother. Bliss wrote of Enid that 'she resembles our father in many ways; she has the same zest for life, the same ability to deal with practical affairs, the same keenness in collecting works of art, relying solely on her own taste. I have never seen her studio in Carpentaria where she displays her finds, but I know that every year she encourages what local talent there is by organizing a competition for painting and sculpture. For her amusement I wrote a short fanfare for piano and trumpet with which she and a friend can 'open' these yearly exhibitions.'[12]

It might be thought that the fanfare Bliss wrote at this time called *A Salute to Painting* might be the piece he wrote for Enid, but in fact it was written for the dinner marking the retirement of Sir Gerald Kelly as President of the Royal Academy on 28 April 1954. It is a perfect example of Bliss's understanding of what a great ceremonial fanfare should sound like. Scored for four trumpets, three trombones and timpani and lasting just over a minute this is distinctly different from a royal announcement fanfare having a greater emphasis on linear, melodic writing whilst keeping reference to the dotted rhythm which is such a hallmark of the fanfare.

In September 1953 the Blisses faced the question of what to do about Pen Pits, their house in Somerset that had been such an exciting venture for them, such a great hide-away in the country, and in which Bliss had composed so much of his output of recent years. But they now wanted to purchase a house in London and Bliss noted that it was becoming too great a responsibility. It is also likely that the cost of the property they were to buy in St John's Wood was so great that they needed to use money from the sale of Pen Pits to help finance it. 8, The Lane, just off Marlborough Place in NW8 was estimated at £7.8 million in 2021. Increasingly, Bliss was needed in London and this large detached house in its own grounds was ideal for both the seclusion he needed to compose, for entertaining and getting about town easily.

Their interest in Pen Pits never diminished, and the Blisses were pleased to be able to visit the house on several occasions after they gave it up and were pleased to see how the new owners had nurtured the garden and even improved a wild area they had tried to develop. 'Only the secluded little music-room, in which I wrote so much, has taken on a wan, ghost-like and rather sad appearance.'[13] The move to St John's Wood took place in July 1954 and on 3 October the previous year the Master of the Queen's Musick, Sir Arnold Bax, died and Bliss was appointed to succeed him soon afterwards. It is illuminating to read what Bliss wrote about Bax in his autobiography. 'The rapidity with which one musical fashion succeeds another has for the moment relegated Bax's music to some lumber-room, where it lies awaiting a new generation that will admire its uninhibited musical flow and romantic expression. During my seventy-five years (when he wrote *As I Remember*) I have seen many reputations rise and sink, and some which before my birth seemed buried for ever now exhumed with full honours… There will always be the constant ever-shining stars, and also the constellations that in rhythmic order dip below the horizon only to return… Of what magnitude is the star of Arnold Bax only time will tell what all his innate musical sensitivity and technical facility has left, to blaze for others.'[14] Bliss could very well have been writing his own musical obituary, for his music has suffered the same fate at the hands of fashion and awaits its own rehabilitation when its remarkable strengths will be realized and appreciated by a new generation of music lovers.

The *Times* reported that Bliss 'brings to an office, to which no prescribed duties have been attached since the King's Band was abolished by Edward VII, distinction as a composer, experience as an administrator, and a fresh, original mind on all artistic matters. He is senior in the generation after Vaughan Williams'. The writer also asserts that 'his contribution to *A Garland for the Queen* was the best of that collection of modern madrigals.'[15]

John Amis tells a humorous story about Bliss and Walton who 'was rather miffed when Sir Arthur Bliss was made Master of the Queen's

Music. Many years later, Gillian Widdicombe recounts, William several times brushed with death and a few weeks before he did actually die, he stopped breathing for a time. Having recovered he was asked by Gillian one day what it was like on the 'other side'. Were they, as often reported, playing late Beethoven? 'No', said William. 'It was quiet for a bit. Then there was the sound of a fanfare. *Not* one of mine actually. (*Pause*) Bliss, I suppose.'[16]

Bliss gave a talk on the post for the BBC on 2 August 1956, his sixty-fifth birthday in which he made various assertions about the role including the interesting one that 'it is one of the duties of the Master of Musick to urge the claims of music on behalf of his fellow musicians. He must also be able to write appropriate music for special occasions. I have always found these occasional pieces an interesting problem rather than a tedious chore, especially when the occasions have colour and ceremony.'[17]

One of Bliss's first commissions as Master of the Queen's Musick (he liked to retain the archaic 'k') was to write a march, *Welcome the Queen*, as she arrived home from her first tour of the Commonwealth in 1954. It was written to accompany Pathé newsreel coverage and originally included a choral version of the central section to words by the poet John Pudney. At the Welcome Home concert on 19 June the shorter, purely orchestral version (as published) was performed. This march shows Bliss settling into his 'regal' mode with absolute confidence and with a swagger which was entirely missing from his Coronation *Processional*. There is, of course, the ghost of Elgar whispering in his ear, but this is pure Bliss, and there is something else detectable here, a real affection for the monarch he was now getting to know personally and who was obviously inspiring him to raise his official game to new heights.

The other commission marking the return of the Queen and the Duke of Edinburgh from their lengthy Commonwealth tour which had lasted from November to May was *A Song of Welcome* for full orchestra, chorus, and soprano and baritone soloists which was first heard in a BBC broadcast from its Camden Studios on 15 May conducted by Sir Malcolm Sargent. The soprano soloist in that recording, and the commercial recording conducted by Bliss which followed soon afterwards, was the young Joan Sutherland, then aged twenty-eight, and for whom this was her first venture into a recording studio. The work was given its first public performance at the Proms on 29 July in the Royal Albert Hall, conducted again by Sargent but with Elsie Morrison as soloist.

Bliss collaborated with Cecil Day Lewis (who would become Poet Laureate in 1968) on the work and produced a sixteen-minute tour-de-force in eight movements that progressed without breaks. If the text is rather sycophantic it is only what was expected in those more deferential days. No-one in Bliss's position today would write a celebratory welcome ode for a twenty-first-century monarch returning from a trip abroad, however new they were, or how important the tour might be seen to be. For one thing there is now no glamorous Royal Yacht to set the scene. But this Ode is one of Bliss's most purely joyful and uplifting choral works. Christopher Palmer made the point about Bliss's music that 'The atmosphere of much of Bliss's best music is… predominantly tense and anguished; even the moments of lyrical serenity or confidence often cloud over and become troubled and apprehensive, filled with doubts and questionings.'[18] He wonders how true Bliss's assertion was that *Morning Heroes* finally exorcised the ghost of Kennard. We'll see shortly how it is possible that there is a shadow of his brother that falls over the Violin Concerto. But here, in his new Royal post, he revels in the task he has been set in welcoming back the new, young monarch and her husband. It was therefore heartening to see the *Times* critic reporting on the premiere that 'Bliss has outgrown his youthful iconoclasm (and) he has uncovered a vein of fresh and spontaneous English lyricism – his madrigal in *A Garland for the Queen* was conspicuous for it.'[19]

Bliss was now constantly in the news; organizations and institutions were lining up to ask him to join or to receive recognition from them. Of all the duties he was asked to perform, possibly the happiest for him was being asked to present Igor Stravinsky with the gold medal of the Royal Philharmonic Society on 27 May 1954. Bliss had described him as 'the most remarkable musician of the time' in his talk to the Society of Women Musicians way back in 1921 and he would not change his opinion now that he was one of the most senior and sought-after British composers. The *Times*, reporting on this occasion, noted that Bliss had 'acclaimed him as one who opened new vistas in the art of music, as one who had pursued his ideals with tenacity, and as a disturbing personality, of whom the future historian would have to take account.'[20] Helpfully the writer went on, 'At 70, Stravinsky is still an *enfant terrible*, as we have recently learned in *Cantata* (1951). But one of the disturbances to which Sir Arthur Bliss referred is certainly a permanent contribution to musical history, his use of asymmetrical rhythm.'[21] Bliss will certainly have heartily concurred with the *Times* writer, who concluded by stating that 'It was altogether a splendid occasion, worthy to greet a composer who is one of the seminal forces of the twentieth century'.

In July, Bliss was given the Freedom of the Worshipful Company of Musicians, and in the same month stepped up from being vice-President of the Performing Right Society to become its President (the recently re-named Chairman of the Board, which was itself now re-christened as the General Council), succeeding Leslie Boosey of the famous publishing house. It was the first time a composer had headed this important organization and Bliss remained in this post until his death. Cyril Ehrich, in his history of the PRS, noted that 'In addition to his international reputation as a composer, his wide range of social and musical contacts was new to the Society, and of inestimable benefit. For a time, the Council over which he presided was possibly the most distinguished in the Society's history, including Britten and Walton, as well as Coates and William Alwyn.'[22] Important changes took place during his tenure including the move to the Berners Street offices, and the enormously important Copyright Act which passed through Parliament in 1956.

In September 1954 the Western Orchestral Society approached Bliss to become their new President. This was the body responsible for the governance of the Bournemouth Symphony Orchestra with which Bliss had had connections back in the 1920s when Sir Dan Godfrey had given him the opportunity to present his new *Colour Symphony* shortly after its difficult premiere in Gloucester Cathedral. He worked with the orchestra at various times in the ensuing years (his brother Howard was also engaged by Godfrey as soloist in Elgar's Cello Concerto in March 1937) and was regarded affectionately by the orchestra, one member of which left some colourful notes about his observations of Bliss's conducting. 'His dignity, his imperious – but never autocratic – bearing, his breezy hail-fellow-well-met personality, belong to an Age of Chivalry... The orchestra loves to sit and watch him at work, and to work for him. He is incredible in his vitality and enthusiasm... He settles well back on his rehearsal seat, both arms raised and stretched forward, baton at an angle. "Now we'll take the slow movement. Relax a bit: I don't want you to strain after the effect as long as you keep the rhythm nicely defined and neat. Mind that quaver rest on the third beat; it must be felt quite clearly. I don't want any loose ends tagging over".' Right – are we ready?'[23] As John Sugden points out, it is notable that Bliss does not mention Bournemouth and Dan Godfrey in his autobiography whereas he is effusive in his praise of Henry Wood. But both these distinguished musicians did untold amounts for the cause of contemporary British music of which Bliss was a serious beneficiary. He was certainly pleased to support the Society as its new President, however, and conducted it in the newly restored Portsmouth Guildhall. As a postscript to this moment, the writer of the observations above asked Bliss how he always managed to look so lively and fit. Bliss's reply was to ask 'Do I then? Well, you know I've always worked hard – I like work. I think it does you good. I am always working. And then, of course, I've got five (six actually) grandchildren – and I think they keep me young.'[24]

Throughout this time, when not engaged in official duties, he was composing the Violin Concerto which had been commissioned in May the previous year. Alfredo Campoli was Bliss's chosen soloist and once again he was to collaborate with one of the great exponents of the instrument. As he remarked, 'I took my time over the Concerto, and found working with Campoli a most rewarding experience. His talents are manifold. In addition to his prowess as a violinist, he is a skilled tennis player, billiards player, bridge player, and driver, both daring and safe. He is also expert with his movie camera... I learnt a lot about violin technique from him. As each section of the concerto was sketched, I would take it to his house, and we would play it through together. If a passage seemed to him ineffective, he would exaggerate its difficulty, distorting his face in anguish. He would suggest an alteration, and then play it through again, murmuring "beautiful, beautiful!" I was always amused by this play-acting, but the result of his persuasive cajoling was that, whether the concerto be liked or not, it certainly is apt for the instrument.'[25]

The concerto is in three movements, the first two of which are quick with the second a scherzo. This presented Bliss with a problem as he needed the contrast which a slow movement provides, and yet wanted to give the work a brilliant finish. The amount of time Bliss had allowed himself to compose the work thus came to his rescue. The first two movements were written comparatively quickly and he was then able to take his time to consider the thorny problem of the final movement as he rehearsed the earlier movements with Campoli. Even when he had found what he felt to be a satisfactory solution, one section still divided him and Campoli. This was the bars following the unaccompanied cadenza where Bliss wrote what he described as a 'twenty-four bar passage of mysterious half-light, which, as a composer, I find a beautiful bridge passage.'[26] Campoli, however, 'after rising to his high notes at the end of this long cadenza...wishes to plunge straight into the *animato* which carries the finale to its quick brilliant close'. Bliss allows himself doubt by saying 'Which of us is right? By now, I myself am not sure. So, in future performances, I shall adopt an aleatory attitude, and allow the soloist to decide for himself.'[27]

The issue isn't quite as straightforward as Bliss makes out in relation to the overall mood-scape of the work as the first movement, despite its well-ordered use of thematic material and its overall *Allegro ma non troppo* tempo marking, is highly discursive and has a lengthy *molto tranquillo* section from around figure 35 including a beautifully Finzi-esque/Bachian treading pizzicato bass passage which transports the whole movement to a different place, changing the mood so fundamentally that it takes on the feel of a slow movement. Nevertheless, Bliss felt he wanted to have a more sustained period of reflective music as a greater contrast. The *Scherzo* second movement is interesting as the gossamer-light opening, Bliss tells us, was inspired by Berlioz's *Queen Mab* scherzo from *A Midsummer Night's Dream* 'chiefly in order to keep Berlioz's exquisite scoring before me as a warning against overemphasis'. He also wrote on the autograph score, 'like Ariel from *The Tempest*', adding at the end that 'the notes of the violin disappear into the sky.'[28] But even here there are such changes of mood and tempo during the movement that it feels driven by stagecraft akin to Bliss's ballet scores. The climax of the movement around figure 45, a violent orchestral tutti, has a darkness which was described by Christopher Palmer as 'a tutti of extraordinary violence, unparalleled elsewhere in the work.' [29] He also likened it to the 'spectral passage' in the scherzo of Elgar's second symphony. Meikle adds his own shiver of mystery by saying that 'the fears expressed... actually grow from the scherzo – they are, as it were, its dark side – its climax a macabre version of the playful introductory figure.'[30] Playful it may be but it is playful with *edge* – a darkness pervades the whole movement, so the violent tutti, cause of so much comment, is really just a removal of the pressure cooker lid letting the heat evaporate so Berlioz's 'Queen Mab' can resume control and take the movement to its skittish close. One also wonders whether, with Queen Mab in mind, Bliss might remember Mercutio's description of her riding 'over men's noses as they lie asleep' delivering their various fancies, and whether this might have given him a subtext for the changing moods and modes in the movement.

The scoring really is effective and we may wonder if the focus on Berlioz led him to think again of his long dead brother whose obsession with the French composer will have inspired Bliss to his own deeper investigation of his music all those years earlier. To this end, is it fanciful to consider that the powerfully emotive music (theme and variation) which opens the Finale may be a fond glance over his shoulder at the ghost now long-exorcised but lovingly remembered? Does one ever really get over the death of someone so close who has died in such circumstances? The psychological impact must include feelings of guilt in being the survivor. These things are bound to surface at times, whether bidden or not, and require expression to let them sleep again.

The *Allegro deciso in modo zingaro* (in gypsy style – as Bliss commented, 'a tribute to my own soloist's temperament') comes out of this reverie almost as if a sleeper has been nudged into wakefulness and a wholly new world is presented: fun, light-hearted and lightly textured. This is indeed a hallmark of the whole work, the orchestration being carefully managed so that the violin is never overwhelmed. The extended unaccompanied cadenza is occasionally, and very effectively, broken into by timpani and harp. It is partly these additions to the violin's reverie that makes the disputed slow section which follows so magically as effective as Bliss felt it to be. The *animato* which quietly but purposefully takes hold, getting quicker as it hurls itself to its brilliant conclusion, seems perfectly placed. In fact, the combination of the slow introduction to the movement and the extended reflective cadenza with its 'passage of mysterious half-light', as described by Bliss, seems to add up to a considerable slow movement. Bliss's instinct about this passage feels absolutely right and it is odd that he did not have the self-confidence to assert himself and insist that this was how he wanted the end of the movement to work.

At the conclusion of the *Musical Times* article Bliss wrote about his concerto, he remarked that 'After completing the concerto I spent a week's holiday near Genoa. I went into the famous port to see one of its treasures, Paganini's own violin. I learnt with pleasurable surprise that Campoli himself had recently given a broadcast there on this famous instrument. May this coincidence prove of good omen for our concerto!'[31]

The work was premiered on 11 May 1955 by Campoli with the BBC Symphony Orchestra conducted by Sir Malcolm Sargent at the Royal Festival Hall. The *Times* critic was boldly enthusiastic and stated immediately that 'it was time that Sir Arthur Bliss wrote such a work, for bravura and cantilena are much in his line; and it is 16 years since he gave us a concerto.'[32] He continued that the concerto 'will be welcomed by violinists, for it abounds in brilliant passages and lyrical melody, in generous solo sonority and exhilarating leggiero effects... The ideas are purposeful and fertile; all of them are not immediately striking, but they are entirely characteristic'. There is, however, a fundamental criticism: 'It is in construction that the work as yet appears least convincing: each of the three movements begins with a cogent impulse that later flags, and in each it is the lingering attraction of quiet self-communion which induces a premature atmosphere of peroration, and allows concentration to wander.'[33] It is perhaps hardly coincidental, then, that Robert Miekle in his chapter about Bliss's orchestral music details all the themes of the first movement, notes the end of the exposition, and then remarks that 'thereafter the movement grows increasingly rhapsodic – almost improvisatory, in fact... and the result is a movement far more episodic, even fragmentary, than the composer's casual allusion to "classical precedent" might lead us to suppose.'[34] Bliss's brother Howard, who always wrote trenchant criticism of Bliss's works as they appeared, wrote a letter about the second string quartet which would seem to have a bearing on this,' saying that there 'are places (in other works) where it seems to me that the real inventiveness dries up – and there is an Arthurian meandering – which always reminds me of improvisation on the Holland Park piano! [...] There seemed to me NONE of these arid spots in this quartet.'[35]

Bliss made a detailed analysis of the concerto in the *Musical Times* as referred to by Miekle, and will surely have been aware that it only went so far in describing the progress of the music. This is where contemporary composers, reading what critics write about their music, and the efforts to which they psychoanalyze as they go, must cause either a raised eyebrow or, at the very least, a flutter of amusement. For the composer the outward trappings of shape and form give a toe-hold for the analyst. Beyond that there has to be a freedom of expression which allows the composer to ski off-piste where the spirit takes him. If this feels, for some, like 'peroration', for others it will be the stuff of Bliss's 'mysterious half-light'. Furthermore, as Eric Blom pointed out, 'Whether we like his music or not is a matter of indifference to him. He says categorically what he has to say, and there is an end to it.'[36]

At about this time Bliss was in correspondence with Cecil Day Lewis about another possible opera which came to nothing. The plot concerned two sisters who would walk to the Piazza dell'esedra (now the Piazza della Repubblica) in Rome every day as it reminded them of their youth. Not the meatiest of plots and possibly a reason why it never progressed. But the work which was under way at this time, *Meditations on a Theme by John Blow*, and heading for its premiere the following February, was the commission from the City of Birmingham Symphony Orchestra for a major orchestral work funded by the new Feeney Trust for whom this was their first commission. As always, Bliss waited for his 'lucky find or incident' to get his creative juices flowing. Almost uncannily, this came from the Professor of Music at Birmingham University, Anthony Lewis, right on cue but not associated with the new commission of which he knew nothing at this point. Thinking of Bliss's new position as Master of the Queen's Musick he sent a gift of the latest volume of the

*Musica Britannica* series – *Coronation Anthems with Strings* by John Blow (1649–1708) who had been 'Composer in Ordinary' to James II, and so a predecessor of Bliss's by a different title. Amongst the anthems was a setting of Psalm 23: *The Lord is my Shepherd*. 'Playing over these Anthems I was greatly struck by the beautiful tune in the *Sinfonia* for strings which precedes the verse anthem… At once I felt compelled to write a set of variations on it. When I read through Psalm 23, I saw that each variation could illustrate one of the verses, and that as the Psalmist does not reach the joy of 'The House of the Lord' until the end of his song, I could keep, as in the *Istar* Variations of Vincent D'Indy, the full version of Blow's tune until the finale'.

Bliss was certainly inspired, and in the programme note for the premiere performance on 13 December 1955 he went further in acknowledging the *donnée* he had been granted by Day Lewis, writing 'I felt a signal omen had been granted me'. In his own autobiography he showed his feelings for this work in a rare personal admission that 'if I were to be asked for a few works that might represent my life's music, this would certainly be one of them.'[37]

The work consists of an introduction, five meditations, interlude and finale with the central theme being 'I will fear no evil'. Where another composer might have taken each verse of the psalm (in which there are six verses) and 'meditated' on each in turn, Bliss chooses to change the order for best musical and dramatic effect. Thus, the introduction deals with verses one and four ('The Lord is my shepherd' and 'I will fear no evil'); Meditation 1 focuses on verse two ('He leadeth me beside the still waters); II, verse four ('Thy rod and staff they comfort me'); III is not based on a verse but is titled 'Lambs', as implied by the role of the Lord as 'shepherd' and is a frisky scherzo; IV, verse three ('He restoreth my soul'); V, verse two ('In green pastures'). The Interlude is based on the dark verse 4 ('Through the valley of the shadow of death'), and the finale is based on verse six ('In the House of the Lord').

The opening is a pastoral reverie for strings and solo oboe whose 'quasi cadenza' we will later discover is like a free improvisation on the opening of Blow's beautiful melody. And this is how the theme gradually evolves into its full statement at the end with nudges and winks, fragments and longer breathed phrases which the listener stores up in readiness for the revelation of the whole theme. In fact, the opening bars of Blow's melody are dealt with in such a bewildering variety of ways that the innocent listener may find him or herself being led up an aural garden path wondering which scent to follow. There seems to be something of

Bliss's old playfulness here – the practical joker with friends. But here it is a detective story hunting for clues which lead to the final reveal. As an approach to variation form it is entirely refreshing as the listener is kept aurally alert not for the treatment of an announced theme but instead what that theme actually is.

Throughout, there is an emphasis on contrasting good and evil which is sharply delineated in the *Introduction* where the strings have sumptuous, almost Delius-like harmony, especially in bars 4 to 6, from which we feel a wrap-around warmth. Even the far more discordant harmonic distortion of this after the oboe's soliloquy doesn't dispel the feeling. But out of nowhere comes the shiver of evil which is as quickly dispelled by warm strings giving us a very plain statement of the opening bars of Blow's theme. The drama of this is as clear as the black and white chess pieces of *Checkmate*. There is a constant battle between these two opposing forces throughout this opening movement and in what follows in subsequent meditations which gives the celebratory statement of the theme in the Finale the role of the ultimate triumph of good over evil, of light over darkness.

In Meditation I, *He leadeth me by still waters*, the flowing compound time counterpoint mirrors Bliss's 'feeling of a gentle, flowing stream, with a comforting guide to lead.'[38] This meditation has the *feeling* of a variation without quite knowing why – except that this treatment of a theme we don't yet know is typical of so many other sets of variations from historical precedent. The real surprise is in Meditation II, *Thy rod and staff they comfort me* which is fast, seemingly angry and heavily discordant. Not much comfort here, apparently. But Bliss wanted to focus on the strength of the rod and staff where, as in St Paul's Epistle to the Ephesians 'the pilgrim is protected by power'. Meditation III, *Lambs*, is a delicious scherzo, outstandingly scored and full of light, humorous touches. Pure film music on one hand, but without the need for visual images so strong is the musical description.

Meditation IV, *He restoreth my soul* is powerfully affirmative and joyful where Meditation V, *In Green Pastures* swirls around slightly reminiscent of the first of Britten's *Four Sea Interludes* from *Peter Grimes* and maybe there were echoes of this music in Bliss's mind as he noted that it 'recalls the still waters' and that it 'starts and ends with their peaceful rippling'. The music transitions to the Interlude with a reminiscence of the opening string chords which are soon subverted by a real shiver of the premonition of evil. It is very powerful and Bliss wanted it to 'sound really sinister and frightening'. He even had in his mind the kind of obscene creatures depicted by Brueghel or Hieronymus Bosch. 'The pilgrim slowly climbs out of this dark valley' and with a palpable sense of relief sees the *House of the Lord* (Finale). Gradually the theme emerges, fragmentary at first and then finally in glorious technicolour surrounded by busy violin decorative figurations. The music subsides into a warm glow as the pilgrim reaches his goal. There is just one glance over the shoulder at what has been endured to get to this point before the final, affirmative A major chord.

Frank Howes made a key point when he wrote, 'The correct title of the Blow Variations is *Meditations on a Theme by John Blow*, the point being that Blow's tune... is not stated in full till the end and the several meditations are concerned with ideas and images derived from Psalm 23, so that the work is a symphonic poem in variation form, comparable only and at a distance with Strauss's *Don Quixote* in structure, and trebly coherent because of its literary, thematic and structural unity. The individual meditations are richly inventive, the orchestral writing virtuosic; drama is not absent, being derived from "I will fear no evil"; and the originality consists in the composer having discovered a new way of writing variations. This is possibly the most completely successful work Bliss has written.'[39] He also makes the point that 'imagination, intellect and technique combine on equal terms to produce something in the grand manner which was a gift to English music from Elgar... [that] has been saved from disappearance as a purely Elgarian fingerprint by Bliss and Walton.'[40] In Bliss's *Testament* published in the *British Music Yearbook* in 1976 after his death, which would have appeared in a Granada documentary film that was never completed, he said: 'You remember that Elgar wrote on the score of the *Dream of Gerontius* "This is the best of me", by which I think he meant "This is the *real* me". I have therefore chosen as a portrait a characteristic work of mine written at the age of 64. It is music that I should wish to have survive me. In Elgar's sense I can write in this work, *Meditations on a Theme by John Blow*, and in my choral symphony *Morning Heroes*, "this is the best of me."'[41]

Given the way we began this journey through Bliss's life as a detective story to tease out the real Arthur Bliss through his music, this is a key piece of the jigsaw. What do we really learn from this work about the '*real* me' and why did both Blow and Psalm 23 draw such inspiration from him?

Bliss's life was reaching a point in his mid-sixties when he could look back on a highly successful, whirlwind career with certain fundamental experiences remaining deeply ingrained. The 'lost' years of the First

World War, the unimaginable memories of that conflict topped by the death of his brother and his own scrapes with death; the catching up years following this and his *'enfant terrible'* works bringing him considerable public attention; his happy marriage, the separation from his family in the Second World War years and the unexpected influence he wielded through his BBC position; the growth into the establishment figure he so successfully became. All these are milestones. But add to this his character traits: the boundless energy, the sense of humour, the practical joker, the immense generosity, the sense of duty, the utterly faithful and dedicated family man, the constant looking forward rather than back (except in the sense of glances over his shoulder at past ghosts) the ordered administrator – and so on, we get the picture of someone almost too good to be true and for whom things were essentially black or white, good or bad.

It is worth noting something very personal he wrote to the composer William Alwyn, with whom he had extensive correspondence. We remember that Bliss converted to Catholicism in his twenties but lapsed and was not a church-goer. But in this last letter he wrote to Alwyn less than two months before his own death he discussed agnosticism which he described as 'one who holds that nothing is known or likely to be known of the existence of a God or of anything beyond material presence. Surely neither you nor any sensitive fine artist subscribes to <u>that</u>. Even the practical unimaginative done-to-death American astronaut on stepping on to the moon.'[42] He goes on to write of 'a super sensory world that an artist glimpses for a few seconds at times, when the dark glass becomes less opaque. In a taped lecture that Aldous Huxley gave in California... he speaks of the unimaginable beauty of shape, colour, sound etc that can be in the reach of men. But <u>he</u> thinks it can be done by pharmaceutical methods. I don't. It can more readily be glimpsed in childhood, in love, and at moments in our own art, when listening ideally to Beethoven and finding that for an instant we are standing at the same height as he. Only unlike him we cannot abide there – but that does not prove that the heights do not exist. *Belief also should extend to the mystery beyond death. I am not convinced that this is the final shutting of the door'*[43] [my italics].

So, there are glimmers of faith here which may illuminate our understanding of the *Meditations*, and although at this time, some twenty years before his death, he will not have been as occupied with thoughts of mortality as he will in his final illness, anyone in their mid-sixties will have feelings of 'the final stretch' which may occupy their thoughts in the small hours. The concept of the pilgrim journeying through hazardous terrain to reach the safety of the 'House of the Lord' will therefore have touched a nerve as will the black and white of good and evil, darkness and light, right and wrong – the chessboard and the theme of the Psalm. So, in many ways, this work is powerful precisely because it is a testament, a 'state of the nation', and thus a rare glimpse of the *real* Bliss. No wonder he felt it to be, with *Morning Heroes*, the best of him. Add to all this a truly noble melody – not of his making – and an example, in the form of the work, of looking forwards, not back, by presenting this theme in its totality at the end, triumphantly. It could almost be a metaphor for his life and work. This is certainly Bliss at the height of his considerable powers.

# Chapter Thirteen

# MUSICAL DIPLOMACY, *THE LADY OF SHALLOT,* AND OPERA FOR TELEVISION

*Meditations on a Theme by John Blow* was premiered in Birmingham Town Hall by the City of Birmingham Symphony Orchestra conducted by Rudolph Schwarz on 13 December 1955 and was given its London premiere at the Festival Hall the following 13 February. In the meantime, new commissions were coming thick and fast, some taken on and some not, like the request from the BBC in January for a work for Brass Band. Preparations were also under way for Bliss's younger daughter, Karen, to marry her fiancé, Christopher Sellick on 31 March the next year. One smaller commission which was accepted was a comparatively rare example of a church anthem, *Seek ye the Lord,* written for the centenary service of the Mission to Seamen in Westminster Abbey on 20 February, 1956. He chose his text from Chapter Five of the Book of Amos, which, interestingly, includes the words 'and turneth the shadow of death into the morning And maketh the day dark with night'. Echoes of Psalm 23 with which he had so identified in the *Meditations.*

The real focus of these early months of 1956, however, was a British Council invitation to travel to Russia leading a party of British musicians who would give concerts in Moscow, Leningrad, Kiev and Kharkov. This was the first cultural visit to Russia since the end of the war and was thus seen as an important ambassadorial exercise. One of Bliss's tasks was to attempt to ease the flow of published music between the two countries – something he was well qualified to negotiate given his role as President of the PRS but which, because of Russian red tape, he couldn't persuade the Minister of Culture to assist with. But principally it was both a charm offensive and an opportunity to showcase British music and musicians. This was a resounding success. Bliss received a letter on his return from Lord Reading, Minister of State at the Foreign Office, expressing the Government's 'appreciation for this outstanding service in improving Anglo-Soviet cultural relations.'[1] Bliss recalled (with some wry amusement) that he had sat next to Reading every day whilst at his infant school in Bayswater. They were also at Rugby at the same time.

Bliss's real challenge was gathering a group of top musicians who would all be free for three weeks in April, extremely short notice, especially for busy artists in great demand. He managed to persuade Campoli, oboeist Leon Goossens, pianist Gerald Moore, conductor Clarence Raybould, piano duo Phyllis Sellick and her husband Cyril Smith, and singer Jennifer Vyvian. Trudy Bliss also joined the party.

Bliss kept a detailed diary of the trip which, tourist-wise, was eye-opening for the group on a number of levels. For him it was the sheer scale of Moscow which he found extraordinary. 'I felt Lilliputian in the great squares and streets, and indeed in our hotel suite, which consisted of a large bedroom, dining room, reception room and bathroom… The need for a new yardstick for judging size never left me throughout the tour.'[2] He was also deeply puzzled by what he described as 'the traditional old and the revolutionary new conspicuously side by side'. He talked of being haunted by Boris Gudounov as they visited the Novo-Dievitchy Monastary, the Cathedral of St Basil and the Kremlin. 'I kept on feeling that Boris Gudounov (1551–1605) and his times were not totally inconceivable even today, in spite of the triumphs of astronauts…We found the Russians a warm and friendly people. The young would come up to us in the street, and try their English on us… They did not seem to have much curiosity about England and our way of living: they were too anxious to find out what *we* thought of *them*. Showing an interest in *their* plans and ideals was the surest way to a quick friendship, and no musicians could wish for a warmer reception than we got from the concert audiences, consisting mostly of young Russians.'[3]

The plan for the tour was to give performances of English orchestral works and then to break up into small groups or pairs for recitals. As the *Times* noted 'There is now sufficient modern English music of merit to warrant a display of it abroad such as would have been inconceivable half a century ago.'[4] The *Times* critic went on to make some keen observations about Bliss's compositional journey: 'Sir Arthur's own music, some of which will be presented in Russia under his own baton, shows the operation of a sort of natural law in English life, the acclimatization of alien elements and an

increasing mellowness. Bliss was not a foreigner like Ferrabosco or Handel…
but as a young man with a naturally eager, curious and forward-looking
mind, which he has never lost, he fell with alacrity upon the experiments, the
neo-classicism, and the iconoclasm that were wafted to these shores from the
Continent about the period of the first European war, and his music, athletic
and sinewy then as now, suffered some diminution of its individuality
through these eclectic influences… As these foreign influences diminished
there emerged a basic romanticism which was hardly suspected.'[5] One
further comment is worth relating here where the writer asserts 'There is as
much intellect as imagination at work in Bliss's mind – herein he resembles
Hindemith – and this balance is not an unmixed blessing to the creative
impulse, though in other respects it is as valuable as it is rare.'[6] One wonders
if the similarity extended to the fact that possibly the two most successful and
memorable virtuoso orchestral works by both Hindemith (*Metamorphosis
of Themes by Carl Maria von Weber*) and Bliss's 'Blow' variations were both
written to themes by other composers. The issue of the lack of memorable
melodic lines has been a leitmotif through these pages.

One of the pleasures of the Russian tour was meeting composer
colleagues from the USSR. Bliss met Shostakovich in his hotel room in
Moscow, spending a couple of hours discussing the thorny subject of
symphonic finales. Trudy Bliss had told Robert Milnes that when they were
at home in The Lane, Bliss would gather composer friends, lay scores out on
the floor, get down with them and excitedly discuss the issue of finales. Bliss
remembered also talking with Shostakovich about atonality, the unconscious influence of the audience on composers, and the role of the critic. 'I
felt affection for this shy, modest, sensitive and highly gifted musician.'[7]

All wasn't always quite so smooth as this eulogy would suggest and
Cyril Smith remembered being invited in Moscow to what he and Bliss
thought was a literary meeting but as soon as they got there he, Phyllis
and Bliss were sent onto the platform where they had to sit and listen to
interminable (and incomprehensible) speeches lasting some two hours.
Television cameras were aimed at the platform party making yawning
and any attempt at subversive whisperings impossible. Eventually it was
announced that the concert would begin and two pianos were wheeled
onto the stage. No tests were made and of course they couldn't even
try the instruments out. He remembered that some of the notes didn't
work and the lid of Phyllis's piano was stuck down making the balance
between them hopelessly one sided. Not only this, but the stools were
the wrong height (and unadjustable) and they were, of course, wearing
completely the wrong clothes for a television recital.

In Kiev they witnessed the May Day procession which, in typical style, lasted for hours accompanied by the largest brass band Bliss had ever seen including, as he counted, sixteen cymbal players. In Leningrad, the group felt the touch of history as they visited the *Aurora*, the ship which had fired the first shot towards the Winter Palace on 25 October 1917 and signalled the start of the revolution. There was a frisson of excitement around the group when it turned out that the commander of the ship was the sailor who had fired that gun. Bliss asked if the group could meet him and, discovering that the one English word he knew was Portsmouth, Bliss told him that Walton's *Portsmouth Point* overture was being performed that evening and offered a ticket for the concert which was gladly accepted.

The final leg of the tour was to Kharkov, leaving on 3 May. During the flight, Cyril Smith suffered a stroke that was to leave one arm para-lyzed. He remembered the flight as an unremarkable journey, 'although I remember thinking to myself at one stage "where on earth is my left arm?" because suddenly I felt as though I had lost it. But this was only a fleeting sensation.'[8] In the next section of their book, *Duet for Three Hands*, Phyllis describes just how serious it really was with the doctor stating categorically that he would never play again. 'Even so', she remarks, 'I did not fully believe him. I suppose it was sheer wishful thinking, but somehow I felt that Cyril would recover.'[9]

When they reached Kharkov, it was not immediately realized how serious Cyril's situation was. When they arrived, they went straight to their hotel, Smith trying to carry his own luggage and even ordering food and drink. It was soon clear, however, that he needed urgent hospital treatment and they were bustled, very fast, by ambulance over the bumpy cobbled streets through the Kharkov traffic. Phyllis had been unaccountably worried by something for the whole tour. Cyril thought it was apprehension about audience reaction and had duly spent the day in Kiev practising rather than joining the May Day party. After Cyril was hospitalized the rest of the group had to move on without them. Trudy, having returned to Moscow with the rest of the party, decided to fly back to Kharkov to be with Phyllis and Cyril for the next two and a half weeks to support them. She played patience with Cyril, or read to him to give Phyllis a chance to get some fresh air. Eventually, seeing that there was no real improvement in his condition, she flew on to Moscow while Cyril and Phyllis had to go by train as he wasn't allowed to fly.

Cyril gradually became stronger and after about two weeks the Moscow hospital doctors agreed that Cyril could return to London. They were still

23. Bliss conducting at the Proms in 1966. Photo: Eric Auerbach (Getty Images)

31. The Seignurie, Sark, Channel Islands. (Jon Arnold Images Ltd/ Alamy Stock Photo)

32. Manoir du Stang, La Forêt-Fouesnant, France.

33. George and Ann Dannatt with Bliss.

34. George Dannatt, Tantris No. 7. (The George Dannatt Trust)

35. Checkmate: The death of the Red Knight; choreographed by de Valois, Sadler's Wells Theatre, London, September 1983. (Darryl Williams/ArenaPAL)

not allowed to fly and this meant making the long journey home by train. Phyllis was heartened to receive a cable from their agent, Emmie Tillett, saying 'Anonymous friend wishes to pay fare for a friend to accompany you.' 'It was a warm, generous gesture, and to this day we do not know who the anonymous donor was, but we remain eternally grateful to him.'[10] In fact, it was Adrian Boult who made this generous gesture, as Trudy Bliss recounted to Robert Milnes many years later. They travelled back for much of the journey on the Orient Express, the most romantic-sounding of express trains. But Phyllis described it as 'drearily painted a dark chocolate brown (and) bitterly uncomfortable'. Trudy and Leon Goossens were at Victoria Station in London to welcome them home to everyone's relief.

Returning to the final leg of the group's tour, they continued what had become a triumphant progress giving two final concerts in the Kharkov Opera House before leaving for the return to Moscow early the next morning. Despite the early hour of their flight, they were waved off by a goodly number of the Kharkov Symphony Orchestra, another mark of just how friendly the tour had been. When they arrived in Moscow, they offered to give an extra farewell concert with the Moscow State Symphony Orchestra to which, despite the fact that it was officially a day off, they enthusiastically agreed. Yet more signals of friendship greeted them when they found the hall decorated with Union Jacks and Red Flags. The concert was attended by Kruschchev and the British Ambassador, Sir William Heyter, later to become Warden of New College, Oxford. The whole tour was undoubtedly a diplomatic coup which showed just how important culture could be in the development of relations between nations.

Bliss's relationship with Russia was something he was keen to pursue. The warmth of his party's reception and his own development of friendships – as with that of Shostakovich – was something he was keen to sustain. It was thus a happy moment when, two years later, he was invited by Shostakovich to join the jury of the Tchaikovsky Competition. It was one of the most successful aspects of Bliss's appointment as Master of the Queen's Music that his personality was so well suited to the ambassadorial side of the role. His interpretation of what the post entailed made his stewardship particularly successful and in this way a difficult act to follow in due course.

With so much time away from home and the rigours of organizing the tour at short notice Bliss had little time for composition. He did however respond to a commission from the Edinburgh Festival for a short orchestral work for the 1956 Festival. In a radio broadcast on 27 July, he spoke about the overture and his pleasure in writing it as his opportunity to return the compliment he had received in the two honorary degrees he had been awarded by Edinburgh University (DMus) and Glasgow University (Doctor of Law). Bliss decided to make it a truly Scottish work with its main motif a rhythmic representation of the word 'Edinburgh' presented initially as a fanfare but then woven into the texture of the music as it proceeds. There is a feeling of power about the pounding of this rhythm which Bliss felt reflected the massiveness of Edinburgh Castle perched impenetrably on its hill, the master of all it surveys. Bliss then quotes a sixteenth-century melody from the Scottish Psalter which he felt might have been sung in St Giles church (now cathedral), and this connects to the central section which is headed, 'Pavane in memory of Mary Queen of Scots' who Dr. Johnson noted was 'such a Queen as every man of gallantry would have sacrificed his life for'. But regret is not long in the air and Bliss returns to the dance ('No music for Edinburgh can leave out a reference to dancing')[11] employing the reel and strathspey rhythms to bring the work to a joyful and tumultuous ending.

The *Times* critic noted how the festival featured a number of Bliss's works, and this concert (which he conducted) also featured his Violin Concerto with Campoli. A slightly amusing point was raised when he asked if Bliss really got the rhythm of the city's name correct. Bliss sets it as four syllables: Ed-in-bu-rgh, when we are more used to three as in 'Ed-in-br'. The name is after all spelt *Edinburgh* and not *Edinborough*. Artistic licence has to give Bliss the benefit of the doubt, and the four-note motto is certainly more effective than a three-note equivalent might be.

Also on the stocks at this time were two fanfares, *Salute to the RAF* (Central Band of the RAF) and *Service of the Order of the Bath*, first performed by trumpeters of the Royal Horse Guards on 15 November in Westminster Abbey, together with a short work for military band called *The First Guards*. This was written for the tercentenary of the Grenadier Guards premiered at the Festival Hall on 2 June. Another pair of orchestral miniatures, a signature tune and interlude music, was written for an ABC Television service.

Bliss's association with the film industry was a regular part of his career path as we have seen, but it was full of pitfalls and he was often at the mercy of directors who often didn't understand or care about music. Notably he commented that, 'I soon found out that music in the final synthesis took a very humble position. In opera its influence is paramount and all pervasive, in ballet it is, at least, of equal importance with the choreography and the décor, but in the films it is subservient, and at the first sign of opposition disappears out of hearing.'[12] He also wrote, 'Often too the director of the picture is too unmusical to imagine how greatly music could enhance and sometimes save sections of his film.'[13] He was therefore reluctant to be drawn in again when asked to write the music for a film called *Seven Waves Away*, or *Abandon Ship* as it was called in the States.

The film was a Copa production directed by Richard Sale starring Tyrone Power, Stephen Boyd and Moira Lister among others in a big cast. Muir Matheson had to work hard to persuade Bliss to take the film on and Bliss dismissed his input for the film in an interview for the magazine *Film Dope* in 1974 by saying 'I didn't do much of a music score – there was a tune for mouth organ as a sort of theme song: and there was the regular – what shall I say? – hurry-flurry of disaster.'[14] There was certainly more music written than has survived, but what there is should not be written off in the peremptory way Bliss describes as *Allegro con fuoco, Allegro, and Maestoso quasi marcia funèbre*. These are powerful, stand-alone orchestral movements.

The plot is not an original one: it was foreshadowed by Hitchcock's wartime *Lifeboat* of thirteen years earlier. In *Seven Waves Away* a luxury passenger ship hits an unexploded mine, sinking and killing most of those on board. Twenty-six survivors crowd onto a single lifeboat designed for half that number. For the safety of as many as possible tough decisions have thus to be made, enforced at gunpoint by the captain resulting in the death one of the survivors. He gains support from those remaining. A huge storm breaks which they just manage to get through, but when they are eventually rescued by a passing ship the captain knows he will now be tried for murder. Where before they supported him to help the chances of survival, the remaining passengers now turn against him to save their own backs. Bliss's *Marcia funèbre* accompanies the powerful uncertainty over his future and all the moral issues which arise in such a situation, testing human resolve to its limits.

Bearing in mind that this music comes so soon after Bliss's outstanding Blow *Meditations* at the height of his powers, it is unwise to gloss over these movements too lightly. In the course of the drama music is used very sparingly, heightening its effect enormously. In a film of ninety-five minutes there are just six minutes of orchestral music plus the mouth organ music at the opening. Not all of Bliss's music is used even then, as the *Allegro* which accompanies the storm fades out into the natural sound of wind and waves after only fifty seconds of the two minutes Bliss wrote. It is a powerful film and Bliss's contribution adds significantly to it.

Soon after Bliss's successful Russian venture, he was sharing the podium at the Royal Festival Hall with the Belgian conductor, Edouard van Remoortel, in a programme given by the London Symphony Orchestra. It included his Blow *Meditations* and Tippett's *Concerto for Double String Orchestra*, together with works by Mozart and Bartok, conducted by van Remoortel. The programme was to be repeated twice in Belgium, and just before the orchestra crossed the channel it was announced that Bliss was to be their new President. The announcement was made on 9 May 1958 and the orchestra left the next day with their conductors to repeat the concert in the Grand Auditorium of the Brussels International Exhibition (an occasion Bliss did not enjoy because of the difficult acoustics) and then in the remarkable Cloth Hall at Ypres which had been destroyed by artillery fire in the Great War and later meticulously rebuilt. In accepting the Presidency of the orchestra, Bliss made the political point, reported in the *Times*, 'that the London Symphony Orchestra and the other great orchestras of Britain should be afforded financial facilities for showing what they could do abroad. He pointed out that Britain received visiting orchestras from abroad, but was unable to return these compliments because British orchestras were not granted public money to defray the costs of travel, as were their foreign colleagues.'[15] Bliss felt strongly that he should use his position as Master of the Queen's Music to lobby for music and musicians using his influence as widely as possible.

The LSO offered their services for the Ypres concert and Bliss was deeply moved, particularly by the words of the Burgomaster of Ypres who ended his speech by saying: 'Therefore, we commemorate tonight those who have never returned but gave their lives to win peace for us, while we pray that a better peace than ours may be theirs.'[16] This mood of reflection continued as everyone then walked to the Menin Gate to pay their respects to all the thousands who lost their lives in this area and whose names are inscribed there. Bliss remembered that 'As I stood there, I could not help thinking of the last time I ever saw the trenches on the Western Front. It was shortly after the Armistice. A friend and I made a pilgrimage to the places in the frontline that we had known during the war. We set off in France on bicycles. I was not drawn to return by any morbid desire such as murderers are said to have in haunting the scene of their crime, but I wanted to satisfy the craving to know what was "beyond" – what I had never been able to reach or see all those months of trench warfare – a glimpse of the dark side of the moon as it were. *What* lay further than the stumps of those battered trees in that minefield? . . . It was an eerie sensation to step out of a familiar trench into no man's land, and meet absolute silence instead of machine gun fire… A year or so later, and all this terrain was to heal over and grow fresh and green, but at that time it still depicted utter desolation. That bugle call at the Menin Gate in 1958 saluting the dead at dusk seemed not only a poignant reminder, but a dark warning as well.'[17] In so many ways, the ghost of the Great War haunted Bliss throughout his life as it did all those who were caught up in it. His natural ebullience, bonhomie, playfulness, and all the other extrovert characteristics we have come to know so well about him acted as an emotional shield which only his deepest music occasionally penetrated. It is notable that one of the two works he said represented the 'real me' was his elegy for Kennard and all his dead comrades, *Morning Heroes*.

Around this time, and although Bliss remembered it as 1958, Vaughan Williams's reply to him being dated 6 November 1957, means that it must have been just before this, a group of chosen friends which in the past had included Bliss, Howells, Rubbra and Finzi (who died in 1956) were asked by RVW to comment on a new work which a pianist would play while they followed the full score. Vaughan Williams died the following August and this was the last of these privileged occasions. Bliss remembered it as being a run-though of the 8th Symphony. In fact, that work was premiered in 1956 and so it must have been the 9th to be premiered in April 1958 which they heard. Bliss, unhappy with the contribution he had made verbally that evening, sat down to write out his thoughts more clearly in a letter. RVW's reply was greatly appreciative and ended with these characteristic comments: 'You mustn't think that your advice has not been valuable because I have not exactly followed it. When I give advice to *my* pupils, I tell them that they can do one of three things:

a)   accept it blindly – bad!
b)   reject it blindly – bad, but not so bad!
c)   think over a third course for themselves – good!'[18]

According to George Dannatt, Bliss was proud of his conversational fluency – his ability to think quickly and not need to pause to consider what to say next. He might have been a good participant in BBC Radio 4's long running verbal contest, *Just a Minute*. He would sometimes have conversation competitions with his friend, the pianist Artur Schnabel, to see how long either of them could talk on a subject without pausing. It is possible that, given his need for an external stimulus to get his imagination flowing, this was the genesis of his work for Louisville (Kentucky, USA) called *Discourse for Orchestra* which would be premiered in 1957. He provided a detailed 'programme' for the work in which he explained that 'like a spoken discourse, the work is a musical dissertation on an announced subject, which appears in the first four bars. The discourse is divided into six clearly-defined sections.

1. A preliminary survey. *Moderato-Larghetto*
2. A more disturbing view. *Con moto e risoluto*
3. A gayer and somewhat impudent one. *Vivace*
4. A contemplative view. *Andante tranquillo*
5. An emphatic restatement of the subject and a brief return to 3.
6. A peroration, sinking to a quiet close.

As in all speeches, there are a few anecdotes and small digressions, but I hope the subject appears sufficiently throughout, in some form or other, to warrant the title I have given the work.'[19]

Bliss substantially revised the score of this work in the mid-sixties, cutting the second section and re-scoring it for larger orchestra, writing in the score that 'I have devised an entirely new score, using a large orchestra and altering the proportions, with one section completely deleted'. The work is based on the slimmest of motifs, a rising second, almost as if he was boasting in music that he could create an eighteen-minute discourse on even so small a kernel of a subject as he felt he was able to do conversationally. It is an original concept, and the variety he achieves as he addresses each new mood shows why he was such a successful composer of ballet scores with their quickly changing scenes. But the rising second, of course, can be infinitely varied so that an inversion can make it a seventh, and seconds can make strings of notes into melodic lines. Add to this the orchestral discoursing between groups and single instruments and the idea of conversation is easily justified.

Whilst the loss of the original second section was a questionable decision there is no doubt that the 1965 revision makes a much more successful work overall. The effect is that of a series of variations as original in conception as his *John Blow* variations, having the similarity of thematic hints right from the start but in this case never a full theme to announce either at the beginning or end. As Marco Shirodkar notes, 'By placing this idée fixe in different guises and within shifting contexts, Bliss not only exploits his great facility for contrasts of mood and colour, but also maintains an admirable musical cohesiveness throughout a large and relatively free structure.'[20]

What is surely missing from the genesis of this work is its staging as a ballet. Whilst the concept is an interesting one, and as a listener we can toy in our minds with a developing conversation, if there is any of Bliss's purely orchestral works which seems to demand staging it is this one. The *Times* critic felt exactly the same following the 1965 revision and reported that 'as so often with this composer, the music cries out for choreography, and definitely some romantic *pas de deux* in the central *Andante tranquillo.*[21]

Although the friendship between Bliss and Christopher Hassall had started earlier, Bliss was vague about when they actually met. Like the Priestleys, the Hassalls were neighbours in Hampstead for a while. But it was at this time that they began to enjoy a close working relationship that would result in several works for the stage. Hassall was in great demand by composers for libretti either as a translator or for an original scenario and libretto. He translated from the Czech, Russian, Hungarian and Italian and provided the libretto for Walton's opera *Troilus and Cressida.* His greatest success, however, and the relationship which gave him financial independence after a very impecunious start, was with Ivor Novello for whom he became the perfect wordsmith. But Hassall was also an actor, playwright, poet and biographer of Rupert Brooke and Edward Marsh. As Bliss recalled 'he was inevitably a man that composers would look to for libretti, and indeed, many did. He often referred to himself as "the composer's moll".'[22] Hassell's collaborations with Bliss began with the ballet *The Lady of Shalott*, the television opera *Tobias and the Angel* and ended with the 1962 cantata *Mary of Magdala.* He died suddenly from a heart attack in April the following year aged only fifty-one.

Bliss and Hassell also collaborated in different ways; Hassell, the actor, recited a poem by war victim Wilfred Owen in the concert at Ypres, and, memorably for Bliss, was narrator several times in *Morning Heroes* 'for which his training as an actor and reciter made him the perfect choice.'[23] Bliss also remembered that 'among his other gifts was a beautiful voice for reading poetry'. They were both closely involved with the Performing Right Society (PRS) – Hassall was on the Board of Directors from 1952, joining Bliss who became President the following year. Bliss told of 'inspirational evenings' they would have together 'when we would shoot ideas into the air until one hit the target that interested us both.'[24] As Bliss recalled 'Christopher Hassall's sudden death at a comparatively early age left a great gap in my musical life, and deprived me of both an inspiring mind and of a generous friend.'[25]

The first outcome of their 'inspirational evenings' was the scenario for a ballet which Bliss had been commissioned to write by the University of California at Berkeley where he had taught during those early months of the Second World War. The university had built two new halls, the May T. Morrison Hall (that houses the Music Department), and the Alfred Hertz Memorial Hall, a fine concert hall. The buildings are at right angles to each other, connected by an undercover walkway.

The opening of this major new complex of buildings was celebrated with a music festival which included commissions by Ernest Bloch (Second Piano Quintet), Darius Milhaud (Symphony no.8), Roger Sessions (String Quintet), and choral works by William Overton Smith and Randall Thompson as well as Bliss's ballet which was the headline work. It was Hassall who suggested Tennyson's poem *The Lady of Shalott*, which he wrote in 1832, about the Lady who lived her life inside her castle: 'Four grey walls, and four grey towers Overlook a space of flowers, And the silent isle imbowers The Lady of Shalott'. She was imprisoned by a curse which kept her weaving night and day as 'She knows not what the curse may be'. She sees people in the distance living their normal lives but 'She hath no loyal knight and true'. When, eventually, she can bear her isolation no more: 'A red-cross knight (echoes of *Checkmate...*) for ever kneel'd To a lady in his shield... She left the web, she left the loom... The mirror crack'd from side to side; "The curse is come upon me", cried The Lady of Shalott'. She found a boat under a willow 'and down she lay; The broad stream bore her far away'. 'They heard her chanting her deathsong, The Lady of Shalott'. As Bliss succinctly summarized, 'the figure of "The Lady", living her emotional life vicariously and unable to survive when at last compelled to face reality... appealed to me.'[26]

David Boyden, Professor of Music and Chairman of the Berkeley Music Department at this time, wrote to Bliss on 24 February 1957 to say, 'We would be honored if you would accept our invitation to compose a piece for this occasion, not only because of your position as a composer but also because of your long association with us and the personal ties of individual friendship.'[27] He was offered a fee of $1000 (roughly £25,000 today). He asked for the manuscript to be delivered by 1 January the following year to allow for the parts to be made and for rehearsal. 'We hope you will be able to accept because we are counting on you to help us make this festival an exciting and memorable event'. Boyden described the new 750 seat hall with a stage capacity of some 200 players and singers as well as an orchestral pit holding about forty. He also asks 'if the idea of a ballet would attract you... the present scheme is to have a ballet evening, hiring the SF (San Francisco) ballet to dance it'.

Bliss replied on 1 March that he would be 'honoured to do this, and I think your notion of a one-act ballet a good one. In this connection if the S.F. Ballet choreographer has any ideas that appeal strongly to them, do let them write to me. It is much easier for me, in ballet, to collaborate from the start, and write to a theme that appeals to them, if it is in my orbit.[28] He also asks that the first half of the commission fee not to be paid until he is well on with the work 'otherwise it somewhat worries me'. He then tells him the wonderful news of the birth of Barbara's son, Michael Arthur, that very morning.

Things weren't all plain sailing from here, however, as having received the costs from the San Francisco Ballet Company, David Boyden had to write to Bliss to warn him that they were too high, jeopardizing the whole commission. In his letter of 3 May Boyden wrote that 'In that event, we would ask you to do something else, and perhaps you might devote a little thought to that point.'[29] However, on 13 May Boyden wrote to say 'the prospects of engaging the San Francisco Ballet look somewhat more hopeful than they did ten days ago.' He also asks if, in light of this, 'you could complete a ballet of around twenty minutes' duration so that we could have the score by the middle of January?'[30] He also refers to the choreographer for the proposed ballet: 'Lew Christiansen, who I hear is one of the three best in the United States'.

On 19 May Bliss replied with urgency that 'I think I should certainly – or <u>ought</u> certainly – to let you have a ballet score by the middle of January – at any rate the piano score from which Lew Christiansen will be working will be available.'[31] Bliss's reaction after this is illuminating: '<u>But</u> now that you mention the engagement of the San Francisco Ballet Co., and all that that entails financially – but that is contingent on my being <u>absolutely sure</u>. I get worried, like many others, a fixed day, however far off it seems, produces anxiety, and if it also means a load of financial responsibility to your committee, it may produce panic! All that I can say is that I plan to start thinking of and working at your commission in June, and I should be surprised, if I cannot produce the finished article in time. But… perhaps we both can share the natural margin of uncertainty.'[32] This voices a concern over a project which we have rarely witnessed before in Bliss's career and which may well relate to his need for a kickstart to his imagination (his *donnée*) which, until achieved, leaves him uncertain as to how he might work to a deadline if that 'gift' is later in receipt than is practical.

At last matters were put to bed in Boyden's letter of 23 May in which he remarked that 'Yesterday, with my usual gambling instinct, I engaged the San Francisco Ballet; and, just as I expected, your letter came today saying in effect that you would make every effort. I am not worried about your ability to finish the ballet in time, and I think you should dismiss that from your mind.'[33] In the course of this letter he also made the point that the orchestra would now be a student one bolstered by professionals where necessary (presumably how the cost savings were achieved) and that it was therefore doubly necessary to have the full score in good time for the preparation of parts so that enough rehearsal time was possible.

By 23 June, Bliss was not yet decided about the subject for the ballet and wrote to Boyden to say that 'I have been turning over in my mind several subjects for the ballet, and believe the enclosed myth might make an effective one [the enclosure was not with the letter]. The style should be Poussin or Rubens, definitely not classical, Greek or Roman. I am sending it also to Christiansen, and if you on the spot have a chance of talking it over with him, it might be very helpful to me. It has the advantage of employing a good male dancer – Paris – and three ballerinas for Juno, Minerva and Venus, with of course a Corps de Ballet.'[34]

This is interesting, partly because Bliss is once again showing his interest in classical mythology, and despite the problems with *The Olympians* he still feels drawn to these characters, but perhaps *because* of *The Olympians* he does not want the characters represented in the same way. However, as Boyden reported to Bliss in his next letter of 3 July, Christiansen was not keen on this proposal as they already had *The Apple of Discord* in their repertory which was the story of the Judgement of Paris. Yet another issue arose concerning the conductor of the premiere and future performances. Earl Murray was the regular conductor of the SF Ballet but Piero Bellugi, a young Italian conductor who had been at Berkeley as an assistant professor since the previous year, was another possibility. Murray assumed he would conduct and wrote to Boyden in this vein leaving Boyden to have to write saying that the issue had not been settled and that there was the additional possibility of Bliss himself coming over to conduct some performances later on. In the end Murray did conduct the first performance, probably to the relief of all concerned.

In a letter to Hassall on 8 August he wrote, 'I must write and tell you how inspiring I found the evening's discussion with you. Early next morning I got up, and put all your suggestions down in 'scenario form' to be typed – and it looks wonderfully well. The little ballet makes me all the more anxious, before it is too late, to write a work for the operatic stage with (you).'[35] So Bliss had his *donné*, and just in time.

He wrote to Boyden on 12 August to give the good news that 'I have not answered your letter of July 3rd before, because I waited until I had a firmly conceived <u>new</u> ballet in my mind. This I now have and am hard at work on it. It is founded on Tennyson's poem *The Lady of Shalott* in which I have taken some, I think, permissible liberties – it should, I feel, be danced in XVth century French or Flemish costumes – cf illuminated MSS. I shall be sending the scenario to Lew Christiansen in a week or two, and hope he will find it as promising as I do'. Christiansen liked this new scenario and Bliss promised the piano score by mid November with the full score being sent in two halves for copying at Berkeley. The scoring of the work Bliss detailed as being suitable for an opera house (2 fl, 2 ob, 2 cl, 2 fag, 4 Cor, 2 tpt, 3 tbn (tuba?), harp, celesta, timp, percussion, strings). In his letter to Boyden of 15 October he notes 'If this is impracticable for your first two performances, it must be <u>cued down</u>.'[36] Bliss also told Boyden that he and Trudy were intending to come for the first performance, returning straight afterwards for concerts in London and Brussels. In December, however, he had to send the disappointing news that it was simply not possible to 'juggle dates, and a fly – there – and – back is too (financially) impracticable. I am really downhearted that I shall not see all my friends on that occasion.'[37]

Having told Boyden that the score would arrive in late January and had a worried response, Bliss hastened to reassure him that it would be there early in the month for copying and rehearsal. True to his word, Bliss wrote on 30 December telling Boyden that Novellos were sending the first 112 pages of the full score immediately, that the next thirty or so would come the next week with the remaining fifty pages following soon after. The original manuscript was to be held at the university in perpetuity.

The scenario for the ballet had to be 'interpreted' and enlarged into a series of scenes which would make for a dramatic show. Thus, the poem as summarized earlier was weaved into a 'libretto' with a clearly defined curse, interactive characters and a deathly dénouement which brings the ballet to its inevitable conclusion. In the programme the plot was detailed as follows:

'Is Tennyson's poem, 'The Lady of Shalott,' an allegory of the dilemma of youth trapped between its desire and its dread of experience?

The Lady of Shalott is imprisoned in her tower by the threat of a mysterious curse that denies her the privilege of looking directly toward Camelot through her window. She can observe reality only as the shadowy reflections of the world outside appear in her mirror – reapers in the fields, villagers, an abbot, tumblers, knights, lovers, stately proces-sions – all of which she weaves into her tapestry; and further, through the ministrations of the imaginary 'figures of legend', clothed in black, who are the inevitable embodiments of the curse, her fate. The Red Knight sends his page to present his compliments to her and then he comes himself to offer a proposal, but he, who does not meet her ideal, is rejected, and the page is routed by the villagers. The Lady, at first only 'half sick of shadows', grows desperate after she observes the idyll of two

young lovers, a 'couple lately wed', and when the reflection of Sir Lancelot appears in her mirror, she defies the curse and springs toward him and Camelot. The curse descends: the tapestry disintegrates, the mirror shatters, and she moves through the breach to the reality of death.'[38]
It is something of an anomaly that programmes always credit Bliss with the libretto as well as the music, with no mention of Christopher Hassall even though Bliss formalized the division into scenes of Hassell's suggestions. This seems curiously ungenerous, and (if Bliss was aware of it) very much out of character.

The final score of the ballet actually runs for over forty minutes and is divided into sixteen scenes, including a prelude and an epilogue. For his concert suite, Bliss omitted two of these scenes (*Re-entry of the Page* and *The Abbott*) and amalgamated the *Dance of the Reapers* and *Dance of the Village Belle*. The music is typical of Bliss in theatrical mode: atmospheric, dramatic, light-hearted and sad by turns, but always with an eye on the possibilities for staging, giving Christiansen as many clues for his choreographic plans through aural suggestion as much as through the actual story line. The compositional process of a ballet has to suggest all aspects of the storyline in each tableau and thus the 'programme' Bliss is working to gives him a strict framework for the dancers to enact their miming of the action.

One of the most memorable elements is the prelude to the whole work, in which it is almost possible to hear the weaving of the spell, the weaving of the tapestry and the general atmosphere of repression – even depression. A sinuous six-note motif, first heard high in the violins and flute, provides a binding 'Lady' figure which appears and reappears throughout the work in many guises as the plot develops.

The balancing Epilogue is a fitting bookend following The Lady's death. Bells toll, and the gliding movement of the boat with its prow adorned with the name 'The Lady of Shalott' gives the sequence the mournful feel of a funeral cortège as the villagers come to bid a final farewell. There are wonderful orchestrally-coloured moments throughout the score, but perhaps the most inspired, dramatic tableau is the moment when the Lady defies her curse to embrace Lancelot, which Bliss builds to an electrifying, almost shuddering climax which withers away as she

wilts under the effect of the curse which then leads to her death and the funereal epilogue.

It was recognized that the Hertz Hall, fine concert hall as it is, was far from ideal for the performance of the ballet. Christensen wrote to Bliss on 8 May that '*Lady of Shalott* made its debut last Friday night under conditions that are no credit to the art of ballet. However, in spite of the handicaps, the ballet was performed with great sincerity to your music, and I do believe you would have been cheered.'[39] Alfred Frankenstein, the critic of the *San Francisco Chronicle*, writing of a later performance in the first run, noted the difficulties of the first performance but praised the performance he saw at the War Memorial Opera House in the city under proper conditions and especially 'the distinct, decided character of its own', and he went on to conclude that the ballet made 'a highly distinguished contribution to the San Francisco Ballet Company's resources' saying that 'it resembles nothing else in anybody's repertoire.'[40] He also remarked that 'One of its strongest features is the contrast of court life and folk life, or to put it more accurately, between the deathly doings in the tower and the lively doings on the green outside. This is very shrewdly managed in action and setting as are the interweaving of pantomime and dance.'[41] The pantomime Frankenstein refers to is the troupe of tumblers for whom Bliss has written wonderfully skittish music in scene eight.

Charles Cushing, a good friend of Bliss's who was a professor on the music faculty at Berkeley, wrote enthusiastically after the premiere to say 'The bewitching beauty of The Lady of S. and its robust success almost compensated for your absence – but not entirely. The entire Cushing tribe had been looking forward to seeing you and Trudy for so long that your change of plans left us, for various reasons, bitterly disappointed... The Lady is superb and Christensen's imaginative choreography was a match for it... The work as a whole preserved the poetry and mystery of Tennyson and added, I felt, and for the better, the earthy and exuberant qualities (you mentioned Bruegel) which served both as a foil for the delicacy of the allegory and as a true Arthurian touch – in both senses. The choreographer saw all of this and he caused the dancers to convey it with a conviction which was, by turns, foreboding, tender, humorous, and exceedingly moving.'[42]

As a postscript, Suki Shorer (daughter of Mark Shorer who wrote the synopsis quoted above), one of the members of the ballet corps who danced as the Red Page, sent Bliss an affectionate postcard from Buenos Aires telling him that the ballet had been a success all over South

America with very favourable reviews, 'The company as a whole has also been well received – no tomatoes or stones…'.

The reason that Bliss could not attend the premiere of his ballet was due to Shostakovich's invitation for him to return to Russia to join the jury of the Tchaikovsky International Piano Competition scheduled for April. Bliss was really delighted to be asked back and to be able to renew the friendships made two years earlier. Asking only that he be relieved of hearing the early stages he found himself once again bound up in the exciting cultural atmosphere which seemed to permeate the different generations. He said that 'There is in Russia a huge new public, composed mostly of young people, who are eager for the stimulation of fine music, and who only within living memory have been granted the opportunity to satisfy this need.'[43] He wrote a piece for the *Moscow News* of his impressions of the competition, pointing out the pressure the nine finalists face 'as they enter hall, ablaze with television lights, they see directly facing them in the stalls the seventeen members of the jury; under the chairmanship of Emil Gilels… Behind the jury sit the public, rows and rows of them. The hall has been packed for each session; often those who cannot obtain seats overflow into the aisles on either side, and stand.'[44] Two days later he concluded his impressions by saying that 'we deliberated for two hours, and it was not till well after midnight that agreement had been reached. Even at this late hour groups of eager young students were still waiting outside the Conservatoire on the chance of getting information as to the first prize-winners.'[45]

Shostakovich was President of the competition that year and Trudy and Bliss were invited to dinner with him and his wife together with Kabalevsky and Khatchaturyan and one or two others. Bliss remembered Shostakovich 'feverishly playing an elaborate game of patience with two packs of cards – to calm his nerves'. But the party easily relaxed into the 'splendid meal' his wife had cooked, well-oiled by many toasts. At some point in the meal the Shostakoviches remembered that the party was supposed to be at the Kremlin for a reception hosted by Krushchev for all the participants of the competition. 'If there is a larger or more imposing setting for a great banquet anywhere else in the world I have yet to see it… My wife and I were summoned there to be greeted by Krushchev, and as at that very moment dancers from the Bolshoi Ballet entered to entertain the guests, and everyone quickly took a chair; Trudy found herself sitting next to Krushchev, and I found a seat next to Vladimir Davidov, the favourite nephew of Tchaikovsky, to whom the *Pathetic Symphony* is dedicated… it was enthralling to hear him talk about Tchaikovsky.'[46]

After these encounters with Shostakovich a lively friendship had grown between them and it was therefore a great pleasure for the Blisses to invite him to dinner when he was visiting London the following year. They invited a Counsellor from the Soviet Embassy to join them and then took Shostakovich to hear a concert of English madrigals in the beautiful Wren chapel of the Royal Hospital at Chelsea. Having never heard English music from the sixteenth century before Shostakovich was particularly taken with the dissonant effects produced by 'false relations'.[47]

Various official functions inevitably formed part of his day-to-day life at home which included representing the Queen at the memorial service in Westminster Abbey for Vaughan Williams on 19 September 1958. Vaughan Williams had died suddenly on 26 August and his ashes were interred in the north choir aisle of the Abbey near the memorials to Purcell and Stanford. Bliss was asked by the BBC to broadcast a tribute to Vaughan Williams which he did on 14 September just a few days before the memorial service. In a highly personal statement, he remembered that 'It's more than forty-five years since I first came across his name... My first glimpse of him was at Cambridge in 1911... and it was a great event when we heard that he was coming to a performance of his song-cycle *On Wenlock Edge* at the University Musical Club. He sat in the front row in tweeds, smoking a short pipe. As always since, he was embarrassingly modest, rather blunt in speech, acknowledging our enthusiasm with a short bow and vague gestures of both hands... Vaughan Williams had deep and strange things to say in music... [he] grew in stature as the years went by, like some magnificent tree... He was a great man, as we judge great men, and it was wholly fitting that he should be laid to rest in the Abbey beside Purcell and Handel.[48]

In April the following year (1959) Bliss was honoured by a dinner given for him at the Garrick Club, and two days later he was back in Westminster Abbey laying a wreath on Handel's grave marking the three hundredth anniversary of his death. Later in the year, in October, he was once again asked to present a Royal Philharmonic Society gold medal, this time to his friend and colleague Sir Malcolm Sargent.

Bliss was twice asked to be the castaway on Roy Plumley's *Desert Island Discs* programme on the BBC Home Service. In this imaginative series, guests are asked to choose the eight records with which they would like to be marooned on a mythical desert island, and then, at the end, to choose which one of the eight they would like saved if all the others perished. Finally, they have to choose one luxury and one book (not the Bible or the complete works of Shakespeare, which are magically already there!). Bliss's first programme was broadcast on Monday 9 November

1959. His choices were the *Credo* from Bach's B minor Mass, the aria *Ach, ich Fuhl's* from Mozart's *The Magic Flute*, Ravel's *Pavane pour une infant défunte*, Stravinsky's *Dance of the Coachmen and Grooms* from *Petrushka*, Beethoven's String Quartet No.9 in C op.59/3: *Rasumovsky*, a recording of a dawn chorus, Bliss's own *Violin Concerto* and Schoenberg's *Variations for Orchestra*. His book choice was on the subject of astronomy, and his luxury was a telescope. It is notable that his second programme in 1972 was much more enigmatic and less concerned with making a serious impression which reflected his influences and musical heroes. This featured, for instance, the call of the Laughing Kookaburra and another of the sound of wolves together with music by Tom Lehrer and Ravi Shankar. As the one disc he would preserve he allowed himself a recording of his own song *Fair is my Love* more for the depth of his relationship with Trudy than because of any particular narcissistic wish to hear his music over that of others.

In October that year Princess Margaret had set a surprised media buzzing with the announcement of her engagement to Antony Armstrong Jones who she had met the previous year. Bliss was therefore called to write music for the couple's wedding in Westminster Abbey on 6 May 1960, a landmark occasion not only for its celebrity, but because it was the first royal wedding to be broadcast on television, achieving a world-wide audience of some three hundred million viewers. Bliss wrote a series of outstanding fanfares for the occasion which were played by the trumpeters of the Royal Military School of Music, Kneller Hall, and the State Trumpeters of the Household Cavalry. His gift for such small-scale occasional pieces was born out of his love for the stage and his musical affinity with the dramatic, emphasizing the ideal fit of his royal position. There were five fanfares for different moments in the ceremony including fanfares for the Sovereign and for the Bride together with an Interlude which preceded the singing of the National Anthem. Listening to these remarkable miniatures there is a palpable sense not only of occasion and of the absolute fitness of music for the moment they were to accompany, but also a tangible sense of enjoyment in the task. Fanfares can be solemn, dignified, celebratory, funereal, but also profoundly joyful, and Bliss knew instinctively how to write music for the entrance of these key royal figures.

Several other smaller works occupied him around this time including another royal offering, a short choral work celebrating the birth of Prince Andrew, *Birthday Song for a Royal Child*. This was first heard on BBC radio after the 9pm news on the evening of the prince's birth, 20 February 1960. The text of this fine choral piece was specially commissioned

272

from Cecil Day Lewis. In general, Bliss's smaller-scale choral works are some of the least interesting and, frankly, less well-written offerings in his output. It would seem to go back to his lack of connection with the English choral tradition and a lack of obvious sympathy with it. These shorter works are often far more difficult to perform than they need be, a hallmark, perhaps, of little real immersion in choral music during his formative years and a lack of sympathy with choral singing as compared with instrumental music. There is little feeling for what galvanizes choral singers to give of their best. Whether his duty as Master of the Queen's Musick encouraged him to think more deeply, or if he was more interested in Day Lewis's poem as it was madrigalian and not religious is difficult to say, but he certainly produced an attractive and celebratory part song for this royal occasion.

In July that year, Bliss had been asked to write a short work to celebrate the tercentenary of the Royal Society. The *Salute to the Royal Society* featured in a special event at the Royal Albert Hall on 19 July and was performed by members of the London Symphony Orchestra with the organist George Thalben Ball. Scored for brass, percussion and organ, this six-minute work was far more than a ceremonial fanfare, and the tribute to this important historical society will have been enthusiastically embraced by Bliss both personally and in his royal appointment.

Back in December of 1957 Bliss had written to Christopher Hassall to tell him that the idea of an opera for television had been suggested by Kenneth Wright, then Head of Television Music. He wrote encouragingly to Hassall saying 'My acceptance of this depends a good deal on whether I can secure you as my collaborator. I find you the stimulating and sympathetic artist I need for a work of this kind.'[49] By April of the following year Hassall was well on with developing the libretto with Bliss noting that 'I think we can take the skeleton now to be firmly set'. Hassall had come up with the story of *Tobias and the Angel* from the book of Tobit in the *Apocrypha*. Bliss summarized the plot as follows: 'Starting in the slave market in Nineveh where the youth Tobias hires a manservant who turns out to be none other than the Archangel Raphael, thence to the river Tigris where the monstrous fish is caught, and so to Ecbatane and the house of Raguel, whose daughter, Sara, is possessed by the devil, the story goes from one dramatic scene to another. The ensuing battle for the soul of Sara between the Archangel and the Devil, and the subsequent miraculous healing of Tobias's blind father, Tobit, give plenty of scope for film presentation.'[50]

The issues of writing for television were of course wholly different from writing for an opera house stage. But Bliss, at least, had had plenty of experience for writing music for films. This, though, was different again with the music being centre stage with the drama, not tagged on afterwards. In June he wrote to Hassall that 'I am getting enthralled with the problems posed by this TV opera; Trudy also thinks your handling of the story finely imaginative'. But he did acknowledge that 'composing for television was a new experience for me, and I had to learn as I went along. Here my film experience came in useful, as the "duration of time" factor conditions the writing; conciseness is all. What might be lengthened to twenty minutes in the theatre (a quarrel between two people for example) would have to be shortened to (say) ten minutes in the opera house, and, when the medium is the screen, to very much less.'[51] He felt he was fortunate to have Rudolph Cartier as his producer who advised him to take his watch out 'and see the second hand do its minute circle. I did so, and the time seemed endless; much could happen on the screen during those sixty seconds; I saw his point clearly.'[52] In an illuminating article in the *Times* about the opera he makes the point that 'What's so interesting about working on *Tobias and the Angel* is that, since it's intended for television the time-scale has to be much smaller. It isn't simply that they don't want an extended opera, and only partly that they are afraid people will switch off the set unless they're held in suspense. Audiences of to-day don't want to be told everything in detail, as in Wagner's symphonic monologues, and they certainly don't need to be told it a second time, as in the old formal aria with recapitulation – a hint is enough. There's a moment of climax...where this servant is revealed as the Angel Gabriel. An earlier opera composer would have expatiated at this point on the reactions and feelings of everybody present, and even a modern composer wants to make this an impressive moment. When I asked how long this passage should last, I was astonished when the music representatives of the BBC television insisted that it must on no account take longer than one minute. Another thing I've discovered… it's generally accepted that music moves more slowly than the spoken word, but for the intimacy of television presentation I've found it advisable to set the text almost at the tempo of speech.'[53]

Things progressed smoothly and fairly speedily with another possibility thrown up in the process which could have seen them collaborating on a dramatization of Bliss's John Blow *Meditations*, another project which did not materialize. A possibility which seemed closer to being realized was a television tribute (Associated Rediffusion) to Sir Winston

Churchill (who was not to die until 1965) featuring in correspondence between Bliss and Hassall early in 1960 with Hassall even producing a possible draft. Bliss wrote to Hassall: 'I was delighted to get so quickly the Churchill piece – and very fine rhetoric it is! I shall now approach Associated Rediffusion again with the script as a firm basis for the tribute they envisage. If they like it, I think I can start to work on it next month.'[54] But this, too, came to nothing.

Bliss was close to finishing *Tobias* by the end of January. He had yet to write the quintet, in which the principals of the cast exclaim their joy over the miracle of Tobias's survival after Azarias's intervention to rid Sara of the curse of Asmoday – she had murdered seven previous husbands on their wedding nights. Bliss wrote the music for this scene before he had a text from Hassall and, as he commented in the same *Times* article, 'he [Hassall] made a text that perfectly expressed the feelings of the five characters'. As Bliss pointed out, 'Christopher Hassall... has been the perfect collaborator.'[55]

As so often with this and other works, as we have seen, the title proved elusive for some time. Lionel Salter, now Head of Opera and BBC Television Music Productions, who Bliss had known for many years stretching back to his work on *Things to Come*, suggested *The Curse of Asmodeus*. This was felt to be too close to the kind of title a Hollywood movie might adopt, and eventually *Tobias and the Angel* was felt to be the best solution. Novello published the vocal score of the opera and, separately, Hassall's libretto. The opera was aired on Thursday 19 May 1960.

Possibly the most remarkable thing about this whole project is Hassall's skill in fleshing out the bare bones of the story, as told in Tobit. This, for instance, is all that is mentioned of the incident with the fish which becomes such a dramatic part of the journey of Tobias and Azarius in the opera: 'And as they went on their journey, they came in the evening to the River Tigris, and they lodged there. And when the young man went down to wash himself, a fish leaped out of the river, and would have devoured him. Then the angel said unto him, Take the fish. And the young man laid hold of the fish, and drew it to land'. Hassall's creation of a highly dramatic scene in which Tobias is pulled underwater (the fish does not leap out of the water in the opera) and fights for his life watched over, instructed, and encouraged by Azarius (Raphael), eventually overcoming the monster-like creature, is true television drama. It is given highly dramatic treatment by Bliss who is obviously in his element. It is notable that Tobias in *Apocrypha* is a younger boy who is willing to accept the orders of his slave, Azarius. Hassall makes him a young man (a tenor) and all sorts of dramatic possibilities flow from the master/slave relationship, together with the love story which unfolds when Tobias meets Sara at Ectabane. Hassall, thus, has given himself licence to be a master of invention so the work becomes the dramatic scenario Bliss needed and which kept the audience watching.

Roderick Dunnett, in his chapter on Bliss and Hassall in Roscow's compendium of articles, makes the point that the language Hassall uses 'seems a curious mixture of modernity and archaism, and perhaps reflects something of a compromise.'[56] He cites phrases from the opening scene where the shifty market trader, Bozru, is selling slaves in the market place such as: 'Gentle folk, come buy', and 'Estimable patrons of Nineveh', 'They know Bozru for an upright man and honest', and so on. Dunnett 'feels shades of a slightly dated 1950s film script… not certainly the kind of material to set an audience alight today'. But it *is* a 1950s script, and Hassall is carefully treading a fine line between modern television-speak and a script suitable for operatic treatment. It should not be forgotten that the late 1950s and early 1960s were still quite formal for whole swathes of the population, as was the way BBC presenters and newscasters dressed and spoke. Thus, Hassall's script was a step on the ladder of modernism but not yet ready to completely loosen the shackles binding convention. A further comment that elements 'have not dated well' is also questionable especially as the plot is based on such an ancient story. If it were a more contemporary plot like *Peter Grimes,* a television audience might well feel bemused by such language but opera has always asked audiences to suspend reality and some degree of stilted script goes with the territory.

Additionally, Dunnett's contention that it was 'not certainly the kind of material to set an audience alight today' is a view with which this author wholly disagrees. While any new realisation of the opera for a twenty-first-century audience would need serious modernization, it is entirely possible to see a wholly successful production from an imaginative producer with all the panoply of modern technology and film effects enlivening the production. In fact, the plot is so full of dramatic potential, that it would seem an admirable challenge for a forward-looking television network which took its cultural output seriously.

The BBC Radiophonic Workshop produced sound effects for key moments which predate the iconic Doctor Who[57] signature tune first heard three years later in 1963, another feature which would lend itself to contemporary realisation. There are scenes in which good fights evil

(Raphael and Asmodeus) in an intergalactic battle amongst the stars which looks incredibly outdated to modern eyes now so used to the full panoply of computer wizardry but which could so easily be developed into a thrilling climax of the story if presented today. The *Times* felt that it 'was possibly too extravagant a touch of fantasy (leading) into the only downright unacceptable sequences in the production'. But this was the age when these effects were being discovered and experimented with, and to have them included in a classical opera was ground breaking.

The overriding impression from the opera is that brevity is the soul of wit and that Bliss's paring down of his material into concentrated, time-limited episodes makes it a far stronger work which carries its drama much more successfully forward than in the more sprawling acres of *The Olympians*. Also, stylistically, there is a far more consistent musical language which itself backs up the progression of the drama as the plot unfolds. This is one of Bliss's greatest successes and it is unfortunate that, partly because it would seem only performable as commissioned, on television, that it has fallen completely from public consciousness. The *Times* review in May 1960 noted that 'it is an opera for television conceived as such… and not easily to be transferred to the opera stage.'[58] The reviewer concludes that 'Operas written for the stage have not always fared well on television: *Tobias and the Angel* was written for the medium, and it is perhaps significant for the future of this medium that it has inspired as effective an operatic production and performance as we have seen on the domestic screen.'[59] In an undated 1960 letter to Bliss, Hassall responded to some adverse criticism by saying 'Downhearted? Good God, no, I didn't like the production as a <u>whole</u>; for it suffered from the effort to make opera palatable to the masses, and simpler, less ingenious method, would have more effectively achieved its aim, I think. But the <u>basic</u> work – I mean your score – is, I am quite certain – a masterpiece.'[60]

A highly satisfactory postscript to the production saw it win a special merit award at the Salzburg Festival opera prize in 1962, an award set up three years earlier. Bliss did make an adaptation of the opera for the stage, acknowledging television as 'an ephemeral form' and after all the work he had put into it he made the new version 'on the chance that one day some enterprising opera company might attempt it',[61] but this has not so far been realized. The opera was dedicated by both composer and librettist to Trudy Bliss.

# Chapter Fourteen

# UNBLESSED *BEATITUDES*

The televising of all Shakespeare's historical plays was a major event for the BBC and indeed for the cultural life of the country. In those days the viewing public had only two channels available, BBC and ITV, which had begun as a commercial competitor with the BBC in 1955 in London and then gradually rolled out around the UK between 1956 and 1962. Thus, when this series was aired in 1960 under the title *An Age of Kings*, there were almost no options available and people tended to stick with the channel to which the television was tuned rather than going to the trouble of getting out of their armchairs and physically changing the channel; no remote controls in those days. The responsibility which broadcasters therefore assumed was a heavy one but was also a world of opportunity as people would rather watch something than nothing and would find themselves drawn into a world of which they may have had little knowledge or even inclination. As a way into Shakespeare, and realizing the high drama of these historical plays, the medium of television brought an immediacy and an experience of both theatre and our greatest playwright to people, many of whom knew little or nothing about either. There were fifteen episodes covering *Richard II, Henry IV, V and VI*, and *Richard III*. Eric Crozier adapted and abbreviated the plays for between sixty- and eighty-minute broadcasts. Peter Dews directed. It was a hugely ambitious project with over six hundred speaking roles and thirty weeks of rehearsal prior to live broadcast. It was a resounding success, achieving audiences of some three million for each episode.

Bliss was asked to write the opening and closing music for the episodes and a Prelude, Chorale and Postlude, a total of some seven minutes in all. Small commission as it was, it was highly significant partly because it was another connection with television at the same time as his involvement with *Tobias*, and also because the credits brought his name to a far wider audience than might be expected to be familiar with his music. It also brought Bliss into touch again with Lionel Salter who conducted the music which was performed by the Royal Philharmonic Orchestra. The two men were thrown together a great deal during this period and they had a healthy mutual respect. Salter told John Sugden that much time was spent driving to and from studios at Denham or at the BBC's own studios. 'On one evening, with Trudy sitting in the back of the car and AB driving, they came through a town where the cinemas were closing and people who had just come out were thronging the road. Salter thought AB was driving dangerously close to them and uttered a caution but a rather tired voice from the back said "Oh, don't worry him, Lionel; Arthur's always so gregarious."'[1] On another occasion Salter and Bliss were by themselves in the car 'when they passed two youths fighting on the pavement; one had an iron bar and was starting to lay into the other with it. AB immediately stopped the car, walked over to them and calmly disarmed the youth before returning to the car in the same leisurely fashion.'[2]

In a way the anthem *Stand up and Bless the Lord your God* seems to emphasize just how much Bliss's music had settled into a comfortable, rather predictable rut when he was writing 'to order'. In this case, like the much bigger work he was about to write for the new cathedral at Coventry, his anthem was part of the celebrations for the restoration of Llandaff Cathedral, Cardiff, which suffered severe bomb damage on 2 January 1941. He chose a selection of passages from the Bible and weaved them together almost as a mini cantata (the work lasts about nine minutes) with two soloists adding variety to the texture. But the effect is workman-like and, again, suffers from the lack of any memorable melodic line. Only the final *alleluia* has a touch of the old dramatic magic about it. Bliss was rarely inspired to heights of inspiration when writing church music and where this is a perfectly serviceable anthem it will probably deservedly gather dust on its shelf. It was first performed in the restored cathedral on 6 August 1960 under the cathedral's organist, Robert Joyce. In a typically generous gesture Bliss donated his commission fee to the restoration fund.

In September 1960 the Blisses were at Worcester for the Three Choirs Festival. It was Douglas Guest's first festival as the new organist at the cathedral and the programme included Frank Martin's *In Terra Pax*, Kodaly's *Budavari Te Deum*, (Bliss had presented Kodaly with a laurel wreath at the Royal Festival Hall the previous June), Petrassi's

*Magnificat* and Janacek's *The Eternal Gospel*. A very forward-looking programme which also included Bliss's *Music for Strings,* which Bliss himself conducted. As Master of the Queen's Music, Bliss was also asked to read the first lesson at the ceremonial opening service. Having its first performance that same week from the tower of the cathedral was Bliss's arrangement for brass of three Bach Chorales from the *St John Passion* performed by members of the City of Birmingham Symphony Orchestra conducted by Meredith Davies. He was the orchestra's Assistant Director and had recently been asked to take over the conductorship of the orchestra from Andrzej Panufnik who had resigned from ill-health. Davies declined the offer feeling he wasn't ready for the post, despite glowing reports from Britten and others. In a reminiscence of the Worcester Festivals, Wulstan Atkins, who was godson of Elgar and son of Sir Ivor Atkins, organist at Worcester Cathedral, remembered Elgar's arrangements of chorales from Bach's *St Matthew Passion* being played from the top of the tower in 1902, the year of the premiere of the Elgar-Atkins edition of the Passion, so there had been a distinguished precedent for this lofty music making.

On 9 March 1960, Bliss received a letter from Sir Arthur Penn, Private Secretary to Queen Elizabeth, the Queen Mother, to say 'It would give great pleasure to Her Majesty and to Princess Margaret if you were able to compose a fanfare to form part of the Wedding of the Princess, since they are mindful of the skill you have displayed in the past on comparable occasions... The Wedding is to take place on the 6th of May.'[3] Bliss, of course, acceded to the request and produced a series of fanfares for various entrances and an *Interlude* which he noted could be played before the National Anthem. Once again Penn wrote on behalf of the Queen Mother to thank Bliss for the 'outstanding contribution which your skill made to Princess Margaret's Wedding on Friday. You have no doubt received a great number of tributes to your art, but I hope that this one may give you a particular pleasure.'[4] Bliss's music for this occasion was indeed inspired and these fanfares are amongst the finest of his many examples of that medium.

The invitation to write a major new work for the consecration festival of the new Coventry Cathedral in 1962 was already in place in early 1959 whilst Bliss and Hassall were hard at work on *Tobias and the Angel.* For Bliss the opportunity to write such a work following the old cathedral's destruction by enemy action in November 1940 was a Second World War reflection of his *Morning Heroes* symphony commemorating the fallen in the first war. Also, as Master of the Queen's Music it was entirely appropriate that he should be represented by a major work as a significant gesture both of post-war national rebuilding, and reconciliation which was to become one of the cathedral's principal mission objectives. In his autobiography Bliss devotes minimal space to the discussion of this work for all the reasons we will shortly come to, and he certainly doesn't discuss its early genesis. However, in a letter to Hassall in April 1959 he writes: 'I mentioned in vague terms one of our ideas for the work for Coventry Cathedral to John Lowe at the request of his committee... I think we should meet again soon for one of our "inspirational" talks before the Provost descends on us.'[5]

Initially, Hassall's idea for the commission was for an Epiphany Masque celebrating the giving of gifts including choric songs in praise of stone, iron, wood and glass (echoes, surely, of Walton's *Belshazzar's Feast*). It was billed as the major work of the festival. So far, so good. However, John Lowe, the Festival's Artistic Director (and Head of the BBC Midland Region Music), persuaded his committee to commission Britten to write a Requiem Mass and asked Bliss and Hassall to reconsider the subject of their work. No warning signs at this stage.

On 5 August Bliss wrote to Hassall in which the 'masque' idea was still very much alive: 'John Lowe was thrilled with your synopsis – he spent a morning with me and visualizes a series of performances with something like the "Eroica" making up the rest of the time. This means we would aim at a masque lasting in all about an hour'. He also commented on Hassall's remark that he was empty of inspiration: 'It is only natural that after all your various works and tasks you should now possess "vacuity of mind". Remain like a seed in winter for the time being. Later, what I should like to have – first – are the choric songs in praise of stone, iron, wood and glass.'[6] The following month things were still swimming along with Bliss writing that 'I am thrilled that you are biting into the Coventry work. This means a good many drinks together before it falls into shape I think.'[7] And even in December Bliss was noting that 'I long for a succession of peaceful days to sink myself in the Masque. In the meantime, chaos gapes.'[8]

On 5 March 1960 Bliss had an exchange of letters arranging to meet the Provost of Coventry Cathedral on 19 April about the new work. On the 20th he was writing to Hassall to say, 'I know that the Coventry experience yesterday was a disheartening one, especially for you – and I also know that you would be justified in withdrawing, considering that it is only now that the committee feel it would like to change an idea I submitted to them last June! But I hope you will not do so, partly because I enjoy working with you more than I have done with any other collaborators, and partly because your original idea of an Epiphany Masque is the right one. I feel we should use "The giving of gifts" as <u>the</u> theme, seen through every facet, whether we touch on the broader idea of the Provost's or not – and it is the dialectics about religion and cathedrals that will find out <u>my</u> weak spot.'

Hassall obviously wrote to Bliss feeling that having done a great deal of work already on the Masque scenario he was now finding it difficult to start again on yet another big work. Bliss replied encouragingly, 'Here is Schiller's advice to a friend in similar circumstance. "The ground for your complaint seems to me to lie in the constraint imposed by your <u>reason</u> upon your imagination. It seems a bad thing and detrimental to the creative work of the mind if Reason makes too close an examination of the ideas as they come pouring in – at the very gateway, as it were. You are worried because you reject too soon and discriminate too severely." '[9]

The obvious deepening of their friendship was marked in a letter of 3 May, when Bliss started to address Hassall as 'Dear Composer's Moll or CM'. All this was going on whilst the last stages of *Tobias and the Angel* were taking shape with Bliss, noting on 23 June that Novello had agreed to publish the vocal score of the opera.

It was Hassall who came up with the idea of the Beatitudes as a suitable new subject for Coventry. This sent Bliss off researching the subject and being surprised to find, having contacted Dennis Nineham, Professor of Biblical and Historical Theology at King's College, London, that the only author 'of classic stature who has written a commentary of the Beatitudes' was the seventeenth-century Cromwellian cleric Jeremy Taylor. 'Fancy that', was Bliss's surprised reaction. Towards the end of July, he was still uncertain how to proceed and wrote that 'I hover round "The Beatitudes" but as yet can't alight anywhere. Do I need something more dramatic to get it going?'[10]

A letter from John Lowe concentrated the mind as Bliss wrote to Hassall, 'I have had a letter from John Lowe in Birmingham, who wants to know the title for our Coventry work for a general press hand-out on Nov. 17th – can you improve on my first idea? "The Beatitudes", a sacred cantata for soloists, chorus and orchestra. Music by Arthur Bliss. Poems selected by Christopher Hassall.'[11] This was agreed. These poems were mystical meditations acting as commentaries on the Beatitudes. Bliss felt that there was an inherent danger of monotony of mood and so they searched for appropriate mystical poems which would act as contrasting commentaries on the Beatitudes. Bliss, even then, felt there was still not enough drama to keep the audience interested (and to satisfy his natural urge to write in this way) and so he put four violent movements in key places which he described as 'force opposing the beatific vision'. The poems consisted of Henry Vaughan's *The Mount of Olives*, George Herbert's *Easter* and *I got me flowers to strew thy way*, together with *The Call*. By way of contrasting material there was a passage from Isaiah *The lofty looks of man shall be humbled*, and Dylan Thomas's poem *And death shall have no dominion*. Hassall added à dramatic postscript to the ninth Beatitude giving Bliss the reviling mob to let rip in a hurling of abuse and a final command to 'Kill!'. The Epilogue uses a passage from Jeremy Taylor's reflections on the Beatitudes. Vaughan Williams had, of course, set the Herbert poems in his *Five Mystical Songs* way back between 1906 and 1911 and Bliss must surely have known these iconic settings and be determined to use them in a wholly different way.

Come January 1961 and Bliss was seriously concerned about the size of the work. Writing to Hassall he complained, 'This is the problem. I have finished – in sketch form – the music down to the end of 'the Call' on your page 3. The timing is already twenty-five minutes, without the short orchestral introduction to the whole work: and I have still <u>five</u> Beatitudes, three poems, and an Epilogue to squeeze in!!! This is going to make the work very unwieldy. What <u>musically</u> is required, after the *pp* end of the unaccompanied chorus in "The Call", is another pair of Beatitudes, <u>then</u> the Dylan Thomas – and the Epilogue. What are we going to do with the rest? I feel I shall, anyhow, have to remove "Vertue", which is too alike in feeling to both "I got me flowers" and "The Call" – mystical ecstasy – but how are we going to manage the remaining five Beatitudes? Could we get two in between Easter and "I got me flowers"? but that seems to spoil a natural flow. May we have a rethink.'[12] He added that 'it is really the number (nine) of the Beatitudes that is the difficulty'.

Hassall, compliant and creative as ever, produced a revised script at the beginning of February for which Bliss thanked him on the 7th saying 'I think we will wait until the whole work is sketched out before presenting the Provost with the fait accompli... I think I now see it, clearly, in its entirety.'[13]

The short section mentioned above which ended with the command, 'kill', was requested by Bliss; 'Just <u>after</u> the last Beatitude – 'Blessed are ye when men shall revile you' etc – and immediately <u>before</u> the Jeremy Taylor epilogue I feel the need for a short angry chorus – the roar of the crowd out for trouble.'[14] And indeed this is one of the most arresting and effective moments in the whole work.

Fearing that audience expectation might anticipate too much saccharine religiosity, Bliss decided to open the work with a dramatic orchestral prelude and asked Hassall to find a quotation that would justify this to listeners. Hassall did not find this an easy task, and wrote to Bliss early in 1961: 'About the Prelude to the Beatitudes and the Quotation. I have gone through Donne and Vaughan, also Beddoes. In the latter (in an unfinished poem called "Doomsday") comes this line: "World, wilt thou yield thy spirit up and be convulsed and die?" In "The Storm" (Donne) comes: "All things are one, and that one none can be, ... so that we, except God say, Another *Fiat*, shall have no more day." '[15] He goes on to suggest another poem of Donne's but ends by saying, 'The first Donne piece, though, written about the effects of a storm at sea when it seems as if the world itself will be destroyed, does appear to me to be worth considering seriously'. And, indeed, Bliss used 'we, except God say, Another *Fiat*, shall have no more day'. Hassall ended his letter by writing 'I wonder what Trudy's opinion is? I am inclined to offer her a casting vote', showing how much they all worked as a team.

There was a considerable amount of interest in the Festival as its plans were unfolded to the general public through the press. This was hardly surprising given the feeling of hope engendered by the building of a wholly new cathedral, the first in England since Truro's in 1880 (Guildford Cathedral was commissioned in 1935 but not completed and consecrated until 1965, three years after Coventry). There were also the powerful feelings, the wounds still felt by the whole country at Coventry's wholesale devastation only twenty years earlier. The need for spiritual and mental healing and the urgency of reconciliation, especially given the appalling British response in the retaliatory bombing of Dresden, were as nationally imperative as the exorcising of the ghost of the first war and his brother's death in the writing of *Morning Heroes* for Bliss himself. On 22 November 1961 the *Times* carried an article headed *Britten's War Requiem for Coventry Festival* which should perhaps have flashed a warning light hinting that Britten's work was being seen as the major event. But it should not be forgotten that Tippett's opera *King Priam* was also being premiered alongside Peter Racine Fricker's opera *The Golden Warrior* amongst other musical works and plays. It was a wide-ranging, exciting festival. The *Times* opened by mentioning *The Beatitudes* and its cast of soloists, soprano Jennifer Vyvyan and tenor Richard Lewis with the BBC Symphony Orchestra and a 'specially formed choir' conducted by Sir Malcolm Sargent.

This 'specially formed choir' consisted of three hundred singers from nine local choirs including the Albany Opera Group, Coventry Philharmonic Society, Coventry School of Music, Fairfax Choir, Leamington Bach Choir, Rugby Philharmonic Society and Stratford

Choral Society. Meredith Davies was chorus master. This 'Festival Chorus' took on the huge challenge of both Bliss's and Britten's works, a serious undertaking for such amateur singers perhaps more used to a standard repertoire than contemporary music, especially in such quantity and to be delivered in such a short space of time.

On 18 May 1962, the week before the Festival, the *Times* made a major feature of Bliss's work with the heading *The Beatitudes Set*. It began auspiciously by announcing that the festival 'has very properly been made the occasion for much new British music, composed to enhance the completion of a new architectural monument to mankind's loftiest ideal.'[16] Bliss, Britten and Tippett are then singled out as the major new works. In this article, however, Bliss's work is given a very thorough description which, given the bombshell announcement in the final paragraph, has the feel of a consolation prize. 'The major disappointment, even before the event, is that *The Beatitudes*, having been commissioned and designed expressly for performance in the new cathedral (with its large organ), is now to be given its first performance not in the cathedral at all, but in Coventry Theatre which, I understand, has only a small organ (actually a Hammond Organ) and, of course, completely lacks the ecclesiastical grandeur of the setting, and the acoustics, for which the work was conceived.'[17]

But this was not all. Two weeks earlier Bliss was asked by Lowe to conduct the work himself, removing Sargent, it is suggested by Justin Vickers, as a 'placatory measure towards the somewhat devastated composer'. Understatement of the decade. Sargent was even listed in the programme as the conductor. This supposition on Vickers's part may or may not be true, but it is also highly possible that Sargent simply withdrew as he did not want to be seen as associating with the work which was so obviously regarded as second in rank to Britten's, and being relegated to a dismal theatre. Knowing Sargent's vanity, this is a far more likely scenario.

Bliss's own recollection in *As I Remember* is a study in masterly understatement: 'As the day for the premiere in May drew near, I realized I was in for a major disappointment. I had been led to believe that the performance was to take place in the majestic surroundings of the new Cathedral, but alas! the cathedral was needed for services and the concert was relegated to the Coventry Theatre, a maladjustment most unfortunate to me. Instead of the ecclesiastical grandeur which I had imagined, there was the ugly theatre whose stage could not properly contain both large orchestra and chorus. The latter could not be placed where their voices would tell, and some of them acknowledged that from where they were wedged in, they could not see my beat. Also, I had written an important part for the Cathedral organ. What effect could one possibly obtain from an imported small Hammond organ? We had to do the best we could. This was not the first occasion on which conditions, unrelated to musical problems, have deprived me of a reasonably successful premiere' (a reference to the premiere of the *Colour Symphony*).[18]

The glaring understatement and extraordinary generosity of this statement is Bliss's assertion that the cathedral was needed for services. Where he could have sounded off about Britten's work needing more rehearsal time and crowding his out – the real reason for shipping *The Beatitudes* to the theatre – he did not do so. Yet this must have felt like a monumental slap in the face to the Master of the Queen's Music and by far the senior composer. This is, of course, not to make any value judgement between the two works, and no serious commentator would try to make the case for Bliss's work being the iconic masterpiece which Britten's *War Requiem* undoubtedly is. But it shows a distinct lack of foresight and planning on the part of the Cathedral and especially the Festival committee in not anticipating the demands of two major new choral and orchestral works in a wholly untried acoustic with a collection of amateur choirs who had never sung together before the joint rehearsals. It was a recipe for disaster.

The *Times* music critic, in all likelihood Frank Howes, tried hard to talk the performance up. He began by commenting: 'The consecration ceremonies ended, Coventry proceeded tonight to the festivities, giving pride of place to the new cantata, *The Beatitudes*, commissioned from the Master of the Queen's Music. Sir Arthur Bliss himself conducted this first performance... The premiere tonight confirmed the regret... that *The Beatitudes* was not able to be performed in the cathedral for which it was composed. One might even claim that the new work cannot yet be justly appraised, on the basis of this performance in the utterly secular ambience of the Coventry Theatre.'[19] He went on to enumerate various weaknesses as he saw them which he acknowledged might very well not feel this way if performed in the surroundings and acoustic (and with the organ) for which they were intended. He felt that 'the orchestral movements sounded cramped, in the wrong sense, in this theatre, and the tranquil choral movements a little stolid... In this respect one must wait until the performance at Gloucester Cathedral in September for a true impression of Bliss's achievement.'[20] And indeed the same newspaper reflected on the Gloucester performance on 4 September that 'The amplitude of the cathedral suits its large design, and though, of course, there is a loss of clarity in orchestral detail the total effect is one of splendour, since the choruses, both of good and evil, are strenuous and generously scored.'[21]

The opening choral movement, Vaughan's *The Mount of Olives* is surely Bliss's attempt to wrap an aura around Jesus, somewhat in the manner of the Christus recitatives in Bach's *St Matthew Passion*. It isn't that he speaks here, but the scene is being set for Jesus's powerful words of peace following the dramatic turbulence of the orchestral prelude – and how that organ part must have been missed. The long sustained or sometimes punctuating chords with heavy reeds which on those west-facing pipe shelves in Coventry Cathedral would have sounded enormously impressive underpinning the orchestra in that dramatic prelude. One can only imagine how silly and inaudible the Hammond Organ would have been and how incredibly frustrating to Bliss perhaps especially in those sections where the choir is accompanied by organ alone.

Having said these things there really is no getting round the fact that this work lacks an overall inspirational spark. Essentially romantic in conception, it fails on two levels: one is that it is too gestural, lacking flow and the contrapuntal textures which make interaction between vocal parts both effective and naturally progressive. The other is that the melodic lines fail to sing. The Beatitude movements have a tendency to a saccharine sweetness which is completely foreign to Bliss's nature. It is in the violent movements where the music suddenly comes alive and we feel Bliss actually relaxing and enjoying himself. The best of these movements is undoubtedly the setting of Dylan Thomas's *And death shall have no dominion*. This is brilliant. The orchestra fizzes and sparkles, grunts and growls and the chorus in all their homophonic splendour becomes part of the gestural kick about. The brief ninth Beatitude is but a short interlude before the Mob picks up the same mood as the Dylan Thomas movement with a violent 'kill' shouted to the rafters at the end. This is vintage Bliss and it is worth accepting the rather too frequent longeurs of its surroundings to see such white-hot expression taking hold of the seventy-one-year-old composer.

We see something of this in the fourth and sixth movements – very different from each other – but giving Bliss an opportunity to develop a different kind of expression which he obviously finds stimulating. George Herbert's *I got me flowers to strew thy way* is a lovely offbeat macaronic setting where Herbert's words are put alongside the Latin text of Psalm 118, verse 24, *Haec dies quam fecit Dominus* ('This is the day the Lord hath made, Let us be glad and rejoice in it'). Despite the almost unchanging three beats in a bar there is something wonderfully subversive in the offbeat patterns which seem to throw our sense of where the beat is, helping the lightness of touch in Herbert's verse. In the sixth movement, *The lofty looks of man shall be humbled,* Bliss grabs the opportunity to throw his weight around, enjoying some virtuoso orchestration and equally effective quasi-operatic choral writing.

It is probably fair to say that Bliss was let down in two ways by Coventry. The first and most keenly felt, of course, was being banished from the Cathedral where undoubtedly this work would have been infinitely more effective, especially given the organ part written especially for the splendid new cathedral instrument. But, in a way, the more serious fundamental flaw in the festival's plans was the change from the initial idea of commissioning Bliss and Hassall to write a *Coventry Masque*. There is little doubt that this would have fired Bliss's imagination in a much more exciting way and probably have avoided the issue of being crowded out by Britten's new work. *The Beatitudes* is a very uneven work which includes some of his finest music but which ultimately fails to light the touch paper connecting it to a hungrily appreciative audience which might have guaranteed it a future life.

As a postscript to this saga, it is worth quoting a letter of thanks to Bliss from Herbert Sumsion, organist at Gloucester Cathedral, following the Gloucester performance of *The Beatitudes*. All the above criticism notwithstanding, there was obviously a good deal of magic in evidence: 'Thank you very much for your splendid contribution to this year's festival which everyone seems to think was one of the best ever. Certainly, your work was one of the major contributory factors to this happy result; and after you had taken the first chorus rehearsal it was evident to me that your skill and charm had worked the necessary wonders with the chorus. They immensely enjoyed singing your work and especially singing it under your guidance. I got a real thrill with doing the organ part, and I am so glad that we were able to achieve what the Coventry Singers and players – through no fault of their own – were unable to accomplish.'[22] Coventry Cathedral eventually rectified their omission with a performance of the work in September 2012.

In following the story of *The Beatitudes* through to its conclusion we have passed over the highly significant year of 1961 in which Bliss celebrated his seventieth birthday. The occasion was marked by a performance of his *Colour Symphony* at the Proms which Bliss himself conducted. Frank Howes, writing a reflection of Bliss at 70 in the *Times,* wrote tellingly that 'An artist's progress in the mind of his audience from the point at which he is regarded as a radical disturber of the peace to that at which he is greeted with honour and affection is, in reality a sign of our progress under his influence, not of the erosion of his ideals; the creations of a spoiled idealism rarely make much of an impression'.[23]

Making the point that the composer Bernard van Dieren's music is never heard today, Bliss commented 'Are we in music bound to the wheel of fashion as firmly as dress designers?'[24] In the *Times* article quoted above Frank Howes goes on to make a similar point: 'For all the polished certainty of his music, Sir Arthur is an empirical composer. "My musical goal", he is quoted as having said, "(is) to try for an emotion truly and clearly felt, and caught forever in a formal perfection". More recently he said: "I think a lot of dullness comes from the fact that a new technique, discovered on Monday, is known everywhere on Tuesday, adopted by all on Wednesday, and becomes an instructional cliché on Thursday." '[25] This is powerfully true today.

Neville Cardus writing in the *Guardian* made an equally powerful point when he wrote, '[Bliss's] work is not mentioned in a book published only four years ago dealing with music in the present century. Young men, pale with atonalism, look down on him because he is Master of the Queen's Music, and likes to spell 'music' with a k. Yet this same Arthur Bliss was rather regarded as a rebel forty years ago, and remains forward-looking as a man and as artist... His music is always virile, masculine, and the main factor in his individual style is a definite objective way of expressing his emotional, thinking, and seeing processes. He has done much to 'slim' English music, and to free instrumental character and timbre from the thick texture prevalent during his heyday.'[26] Howes also remarked in the *Times* that 'Sir Arthur's career has, one feels, been one in musical terms unusually adventurous. Jettisoning a number of early works which had attracted favourable attention, at the end of the First World War he brought a vigorous cosmopolitanism into the English concert hall ... (marking) the arrival of a musical personality of great vitality, capable of satire, fantasy, deep introspection, and, at times, Elgarian glories of pomp.'[27]

One other writer, John Warrack, celebrating Bliss's milestone, wrote about Bliss's royal post. Writing in the *Sunday Telegraph*, he commented that 'A Rugbeian ex-Grenadier, he cuts a figure reassuring in St James's but is keenly interested in the latest composing affairs. His carefully written speeches, uttered in that rather high, military voice, are "suitable" but full of thought: he will use official occasions calling for compliments to make serious pleas on music's behalf, and be prepared to leave significant gaps in the compliments. He is the spokesman who can quietly put a spoke in the wheel, and has never lost his curiosity.'[28]

One of these 'pleas on music's behalf' was made in his capacity as President of the National Music Council of Great Britain, an umbrella organization representing many of the major musical bodies such as the National Federation of Music Societies (now called Making Music), the Association of British Orchestras, the Performing Right Society and so on. He took a deputation to the Chancellor of the Exchequer (Selwyn Lloyd in Harold Macmillan's Conservative government) to seek the abolition of purchase tax on musical instruments. This was not successful, and a further attempt four years later received the same negative response from the unsympathetic Government.

In January of 1962, the year of the Coventry performance, Bliss opened an exhibition of manuscripts of works by British composers at the Royal Festival Hall and soon afterwards received another commission from the City of Birmingham Symphony Orchestra for a choral and orchestral work for the 1963 Three Choirs Festival at Worcester Cathedral. This work, *Mary of Magdela*, would be Bliss's last collaboration with Christopher Hassall.

In the meantime, more fanfares engaged Bliss in three commissions. The first of these was *Greetings to a City* for the American Wind Symphony who specialized in playing on rivers on a specially constructed one-hundred-and-twenty-foot barge which included a revolving deck-house at each end, providing a stage for the soloists and storage room for the instruments.; the main orchestral platform was backed and roofed by adjustable sounding panels. This substantial seven-minute 'Flourish for Double Brass Choir and Percussion' was given its first performance on the Thames on American Independence Day 1961. Bliss exploited the antiphonal effects of the two separately placed brass choirs to great effect. His memory of the occasion was typically colourful: 'The orchestra and the barge duly arrived, and one morning in July I went to their moorings of Battersea Park to hear them rehearse. As luck would have it there was a brisk wind blowing, and as I went out to the players in a motor boat, I saw the barge rolling quite a lot, while the breeze was blowing the orchestral parts from the stands. In spite of the unsteadiness of this strange concert platform the young players blew their best, undismayed by the fact that the wind off-shore carried their sound away from any audience that might line the banks.'[29] They had a busy Thames itinerary, from Reading and Henley to as far north as Oxford that, as Bliss noted, 'when the weather permitted [was] warmly acclaimed'.

A smaller-scale march, *Call to Adventure,* followed written for the service in St Clement Dane's Church, London on 4 February 1962 celebrating the twenty-first anniversary of the Air Training Corps. Finally, a stirring *Gala Fanfare* celebrated the opening of the British Empire and Perth Commonwealth Games on 22 November that year, performed by the Australian Air Force Band.

On 24 March 1963 Bliss was the recipient of the Royal Philharmonic Society's Gold Medal. Having presented it to Vaughan Williams, Stravinsky, Malcolm Sargent and Shostakovich he felt a particular sense of honour in the award, writing that 'to receive it now myself, and join a long list of famous recipients, gave me great delight. The occasion was the celebration of the Society's one-hundred-and-fiftieth birthday and was solely a social function. I should have liked, as is the traditional custom, to have expressed my thanks in music, but this being impossible I had to substitute words for notes, to the best of my ability.'[30] These words included a typically modest assessment of himself: 'I don't claim to have done more than light a small taper at the shrine of music. I do not upbraid Fate for not having given me greater gifts. In the endeavour has been the joy.'[31]

This reflection shows one side of Bliss's personality (albeit a natural show of public modesty). We have noted Bliss's sense of humour numerous times but around this time his daughter Karen's husband, Christopher, sent him a 'whimsical report' from an imaginary 'Work Study Officer' who, in typical 'jobsworth' fashion, having attended a symphony orchestra concert, noted wastage of effort and time thus:

'For considerable periods the four oboes had nothing to do. The number should be reduced and the work spread more evenly over the whole of the concert, thus eliminating peaks of activity. All the twelve violins were playing identical notes. This seems unnecessary duplication... Much effort was absorbed in the playing of demisemiquavers. This seemed an unnecessary refinement. It is recommended that all notes should be rounded off to the nearest semiquaver. If this were done it would be possible to use trainees and lower-grade operators more extensively. No useful purpose is served by repeating on the horns a passage which has already been handled by the strings. It is estimated that if all redundant passages were eliminated, the whole concert time of two hours could be reduced to twenty minutes and there would have been no need for an intermission.'

Bliss's response was characteristically imaginative:

*'For considerable periods the four oboe players had nothing to do*

He should know that oboe players invariably live to a very advanced age, and by the rules of the Union *cannot* be superseded. When therefore *four* players are seen, *two* are probably past the age of being able to make any sound and simply hold the instrument from time to time in their mouth (M.U. Con. Ch. IV Para. 3). The other two, presumably younger, actually play (or should) the notes before them. They certainly should *not* have been *inactive over a considerable period*. This might have been due, on the occasional notes, to this:

a)   having lost their places
b)   becoming sleepy after 'interval' in concert (see later note)
c)   simply disliking certain passages given to them by the composer

and he continued in this vein humorously noting, for instance, that 'There is *every* reason for repeating on the strings a passage which has already been handled... A horn player, especially after the interval will 'bubble' or 'squeak' a note so that the passage comes faultily to the audience. In these cases, the strings *correct*, not repeat the passage, for the information of the hearer.'[32] And so he goes on.

Underneath this humorous quipping, however, lay a deeper feeling which was very dear to Bliss's heart. Mr 'Jobsworth' as described above was, in reality, too close to the British establishment attitude to the Arts, and in the foreword to the programme book for the Royal Philharmonic Society's 1962–3 season (the season in which he received its Gold Medal) he wrote: 'But what of the future? The curse of the lack of money hangs heavily over the musical world: orchestral players are underpaid and have to resort to wearisome drudgery to make an adequate income; proper rehearsal time is too expensive and has to be cancelled; the price of seats rises and prevents the participation of the younger generation: concerts that show adventure in their programmes lose too heavily for the experiment to be repeated. This woeful story is only too well known. Authority when hard pressed gives a bit here and a bit there, but in reality, and indeed in comparison with some of our fortunate neighbours, the amount is insignificant.'[33] He then continues to outline a 'dream' scenario based on the authority which took 'seriously the benefits that music can give, and make permanently secure that which now operates on a hand-to-mouth basis'. It is notable that around this time the Arts Council of Great Britain (as it then was) only funded some one hundred organizations in the whole of the UK and it wasn't until the year after this RPS season, in 1964, that the first Minister for the Arts was appointed. Bliss's comments were not falling on entirely deaf ears. But it wasn't until the introduction of the National Lottery in 1994 (the Parliamentary Act was passed in 1993) that more significant funds became available to support Arts activities throughout the nation.

· Bliss's close connection with the Cheltenham Festival was now enhanced by a commission from the BBC for a chamber work for the 1963 festival. It is somehow typical of Bliss's generosity of spirit that the new work would be dedicated to the BBC's Controller of Music, William Glock, thereby neatly marrying commissioner and commissionee. As so often he accepted without knowing at all what he would write. In the process of waiting for a *donnée* to present itself, it was the BBC's own weekly magazine, *The Listener*, which caught his attention. One of its editions featured translations of old English riddles from the Exeter Book made by Kevin Crossley-Holland. Hundreds of these cryptic Anglo-Saxon puzzles are held in the library at Exeter Cathedral. The first of the set is typical:

My abode's not silent, but I am not loud-mouthed.
The Lord Almighty laid down the laws
· For both of us together. I am swifter than him who harbours me
And sometimes stronger too, he must strive more potently.
At times I just relax, while he must needs run onward.
But I live in him all the days of my life:
If we're ever divided, my destiny is death.
And the answer: Fish in River.

And so *A Knot of Riddles* was born. As Bliss wrote: 'The subjects are drawn from nature, from animal and bird life, and from such objects as were in familiar use at the time: they were probably recited as part of the entertainment customary at feasts.'[34] He chose seven of the riddles to set and they all form the same pattern; the singer giving the clues and then announcing the solution.

The palpable sense of enjoyment in this work, the still youthful vigour of his imagination and the vibrant sense of humour marks this out as one of Bliss's finest small-scale works. There is a great sense of relief in both the scale and subject matter following the Coventry fiasco as well as the pleasure in having secured the Melos Ensemble as the instrumentalists, having recently witnessed their outstanding recording of his Oboe and Clarinet Quintets. The vocal solo part was written with John Shirley Quirk's voice in mind, and so the performers, he knew, would give the best possible account of the work – and indeed he described the premiere, which he directed, as 'perfect'. It is scored for string quartet, wind quintet and harp with baritone soloist. All Bliss's experience with instrumental colour stemming back decades to his early experiments in sound is here, but now tempered with the romanticism which has grown like an enveloping cloak in the intervening years. However, the style might have changed and developed the connection with his youthful impetuousness that remains as one of Bliss's most recognizable character traits.

Bliss dedicated the fifth riddle, *A Bookworm*, to Ravel, writing at the head of the song, *Hommage modeste à Maurice Ravel*. He noted, wryly, 'For imagining the grub boring its way, without benefit, through some classic masterpiece I thought of the quotation with which Ravel heads his own *Valses nobles et sentimentales* – "Le plaisir délicieux et toujours nouveau d'une occupation inutile." '[35]

The overall impression of the work is one of teasing thoughtfulness guided by the head scratching which entertained the original problem solver all those centuries earlier. There is obvious flightiness of some of the music, especially *Swallows* and *A Weather Cock* which is 'puffed up' by a fanfare before allowing the bird its natural flight. *A Cross of Wood* carries the listener down a false trail before the inevitability of relating it to the instrument of Christ's Passion. The final *Sun and Moon* is wonderfully benedictory and yet ends inconclusively on a second inversion tonic chord with a flute dangling a minor sixth in the air. A wonderfully impressionistic touch. George Dannatt observed that 'the answers are given by the same soloist, generally followed by a pertinent orchestral comment, or, in two cases, by silence almost more telling and more laughter producing.'[36] After the first performance on 11 July, the *Times* critic wrote that he felt that the translations were 'pedestrian' and that this was why Bliss's vocal lines were uninteresting, making 'a less memorable impression than (their) accompaniment.'[37] Be that as it may, and here is the issue of melodic lines once more, the overall impression is one of both delight and serenity, what Giles Easterbrook so aptly described as 'its vibrant sense of being alive'.[38]

Among the many honours heaped on Bliss during his mature years perhaps one of the most unusual was the naming after him of a new Samaritan Housing Association building in Lindfield, near Haywards Heath, West Sussex. He laid the foundation stone of the Arthur Bliss House containing twenty-one retirement apartments on 24 July 1963. Bliss had taken part in a Gala concert at the Festival Hall in London celebrating a tercentenary of Anglo-Jewish relations conducting his *Meditations on a Theme by John Blow*. The Chairman of the committee organizing this event, Daniel Schonfield, was also chairman of the housing association which provided housing for elderly people who could thus be close to their families and avoid the potential loneliness of old age. A series of these houses was planned and each was to be named after a living British musician. Bliss's was the first 'to show some small appreciation for your assistance in this particular concert and for your general contribution to the world of music'. This naming of the house caused Bliss to wonder why no past musicians had been commemorated on postage stamps. He wrote to the Postmaster General on the matter but to no avail.

Just before this, on 25 April, Bliss's close friend and happiest collaborator, Christopher Hassall, died. He had been running to catch a train from Rochester to London in order to see his daughter Imogen, who was with the Royal Ballet School, perform at Covent Garden when he suffered a heart attack and died aged only fifty-one. This sudden and unexpected death robbed the world of a remarkable wordsmith and Bliss of a 'composer's Moll' of extraordinary fertility and imagination. Their last collaboration was a sacred cantata *Mary of Magdala* commissioned by the City of Birmingham Symphony Orchestra for the Worcester Three Choirs Festival with funds from The Feeney Trust which Hassall did not live to hear. This remarkable Birmingham charity had also funded the commission of *Meditations on a Theme by John Blow* for the orchestra back in 1955. It was an instinctive gesture for Bliss to dedicate this new work to Hassall's memory.

*Mary of Magdala* is untypical of Bliss and may, again, have something in its gentleness of mood of being another antidote to *The Beatitudes*. At least at the Three Choirs Festival there was no possibility of being ousted from the cathedral at the last minute. It was Bliss who suggested the theme of Mary of Magdala to Hassall as a subject matter for the Worcester cantata. In a letter of 10 March 1962 Bliss wrote to Hassall that 'I am very much attracted to writing a choral work on Mary of Magdala – a set of vignettes describing what is known through the gospels about her, any legends or miraculous circumstances connected with her... I must start work on it in July at the latest... Various inspirational evenings at your convenience will be necessary.'[39] Hassall was in the final stages of preparing his biography of Rupert Brooke and yet managed to free himself sufficiently to attend to Bliss's new work understanding the urgency of time.

Hassall's libretto presents a view of Mary that is highly contested. He shows her to be a conflation of various female Biblical characters. James Carroll in the Smithsonian Magazine made this telling point concerning this confusion:

'This story of the woman with the bad name, the alabaster jar, the loose hair, the "many sins," the stricken conscience, the ointment, the rubbing of feet and the kissing would, over time, become the dramatic high point of the story of Mary Magdalene. The scene would be explicitly attached to her, and rendered again and again by the greatest Christian artists. But even a casual reading of this text, however charged its juxtaposition with the subsequent verses, suggests that the two women have nothing to do with each other—that the weeping anointer is no more connected to Mary of Magdala than she is to Joanna or Susanna.[40]

In Chapter Eight of Luke's Gospel, he makes this description: 'Now after this [Jesus] made his way through towns and villages preaching and proclaiming the Good News of the kingdom of God. With him went the Twelve, as well as certain women who had been cured of evil spirits and ailments: Mary surnamed the Magdalene, from whom seven demons had gone out, Joanna the wife of Herod's steward Chuza, Susanna, and several others who provided for them out of their own resources.'[41] This final statement shows that these women were respectable and had their own funds to support Jesus and the Twelve. But, because they were all cured of 'demons', this became synonymous with questionable morals and the fixing of the 'prostitute' label especially by misogynous male priests anxious to warn of the dangers of the flesh and the lure of predatory women. So, Hassall's dramatic chorus, 'Look there, look there, That woman, a stranger With an alabaster box...', presumably designed to allow Bliss to let his hair down, is predicated on very unsure theological footing and is, in all probability, not Mary of Magdala at all but Mary of Bethany. In fact, Mary of Magdala isn't identified in the Bible until after the anointing incident. Be that as it may – and one wonders if any of the cathedral clergy raised an eyebrow when they read the libretto – there is no doubt that the overall meditative sound world of the work needed a burst of energy and Hassall's quasi operatic chorus which has the onlookers to Mary's anointing of Jesus's feet with the expensive oil almost spitting in derision and hatred not only at the waste of money but at the touching of Jesus by a woman, especially one of apparent doubtful repute.

Hassall's opening poetic vision sets the scene for this remarkable cantata in such a particular way: 'Ashen the sky, uncertain, grey, The hour is neither night nor day. Darkness and dawn are midway met, And a mist hangs over Olivet.' And yet, this greyness, in Bliss's hands becomes as Neil Ferris, Chorus Master of the BBC Symphony Chorus who recorded the work under Sir Andrew Davis commented, 'like the kind of light one might get in the desert – even here in the UK when the wind blows from the Sahara and we have dust in the atmosphere there is a different light in the sky'. Bliss conjures all this up from his quiet, meditative opening which could easily be the scene setting for a film in the sparse scoring, the feel of place, and the women in their sudra habits surveying the sky before their first choral entry. It is very skilled. Equally skilled is the way he eases out of this 'local colour' mode into pure Arthur Bliss at the end of the first full choral section (figure 3) in a chordal progression familiar from smaller-scale choral pieces and which appears almost unaltered in the second movement of Bliss's last work *The Shield of Faith*.

The libretto comprises the story from Chapter 20 of John's Gospel with Hassell's own poetic adaptations of two seventeenth-century poems by Edward Sherburne (1651) reflecting Mary's feelings at the anointing event, and *The Gardener* by Rowland Watkins (1662). The orchestra is unusually compact for Bliss in choral/orchestral mode using reduced wind, only two horns and two trumpets, harp, timpani and two percussion players with strings. The contralto soloist, as Mary, takes the main solo role, with a much smaller bass part for Jesus. The overall effect is deeply personal and a sense of intimacy is palpable. Who knows how much past experience played a part in Bliss's choices for this work, the acute memory of his first Three Choirs commission, *A Colour Symphony*, being wrecked by instruments being removed from the stage at the last moment, and then the whole Coventry fiasco, he may have decided to play safe with this next cathedral work. In reality, though, it was Hassell's imaginative script which set him on fire.

Having written to Hassall to thank him for the finalized libretto on 14 July, by 30 August Bliss was writing again to tell him that '*Mary of Magdala* has nearly been finished in vocal score. I have found the words and the whole "stimmung" [mood] deeply moving.'[42] This was quick work indeed and indicated a really inspired engagement with the subject. On 6 October he reported that the vocal score was now finished, but asked 'for a finished libretto, with initial stage directions to point my "dawn music" – and words to show your essential collaboration.'[43] It is likely that Bliss went on to complete the orchestration straight away so that there was plenty of time for Novellos to prepare the material for the Worcester performance. Certainly, in mid-April, the Blisses were holidaying in Provence, probably staying at La Petite Auberge in Noves, which would suggest that everything was complete so they could relax and enjoy themselves. They returned on 1 May, a few days after hearing of Hassell's death on 25 April.

One of the undoubted reasons for Bliss's connection with this work is the quiet passion of the dramatic storyline which might easily lend itself to being choreographed. Bliss had no great religious convictions, as we have seen, and as George Dannatt reminded us in his introduction to the original catalogue of Bliss's works, 'he was in no ways a practising Catholic and his sacred music is invariably orientated towards the requirements and beliefs of the Church of England.'[44] However, this is as much a human interest story as anything – a woman deeply in love with Jesus, witnessing his death and now having to wait impatiently for the Sabbath to end before she can run to 'touch him, befriend him' – only to find the tomb empty. On the way there are intensely beautiful moments, the like of which we rarely find in Bliss's music, such as Mary's effective declaration of love for Jesus leading to the words 'Loveliest rose of all the Roses of Sharon'. This is in reality a deeply moving operatic soliloquy.

Another extraordinary moment is when Mary, distraught over the disappearance of Jesus's body from the tomb, sees someone she assumes to be the gardener tending the vine. The magical way she approaches him to ask if he has moved the body (with expectant rising chords in the orchestra slightly offset by a lilting violin solo), and the two gentle utterances of Mary's name by Jesus make this one of Bliss's truly inspirational settings. The harshly discordant chords from the orchestra which immediately follow (and which are used again as a 'recognition' motif at the end of the work) mirror, or suggest, Mary's almost frightened surprise and amazed recognition. The echo of the same chordal sequence but gently now with one of Hassall's stage directions 'as if on knees' lowers the temperature and sets a beautiful duet in motion with Mary repeating the 'loveliest rose...' to a similar melodic figure as earlier. It is masterly. Hassall's beautifully integrated script maintains the gardener analogy but now makes him a gardener of souls rather than vines. The work ends with Mary almost sobbing the words 'Rabboni! Master!'

Bliss conducted the first performance himself and Norma Proctor sang the role of Mary. Bliss felt that her voice had something of the quality (timbre was the word he used) of Kathleen Ferrier's voice which had so moved him when he had written *The Enchantress*. The *Times* critic noted that 'Bliss had captured the atmosphere and written music that has less of his characteristic astringency and more of the feeling that appeared in *The Olympians* and the *Blow Variations*. While structure of the whole is firm the incidental beauties are many. Thus, the final chorus... achieves a fragrance that is perhaps new in his music.'[45] It is strange, given the economical resources of the work and its lyrical attractiveness, that it had to wait until 2019 for its first commercial recording.

A friendly incident followed the work's second performance in Hull near where Norma Proctor lived and in which she was again the soloist. Soon afterwards she appeared on the Blisses' doorstep in London with a fish she had bought from a freshly landed catch in Grimsby. As Bliss recalled, 'Never had fish tasted so fresh and delicious; it is lucky that we have the faculty of remembering gastronomic delights years after the meal has been enjoyed and digested.'[46] There is no doubt that Bliss enjoyed the good things in life and a lively description of another 'gastronomic delight' comes early in the next chapter.

This was a very busy period for Bliss: that short break in France back in April will have been not only enjoyable but a much-needed respite from a gruelling schedule of composition and other engagements. This included being Chairman of the Jury for the first Leeds International Piano Competition soon after the premiere *Mary of Magdala* on 2 September in Worcester. A completely different commission came for a test piece for the National Brass Band Championships to be held in October. This became the *Belmont Variations* named after the town in Massachusetts where Trudy was born. It is a typically virtuoso work for such a competition with a theme, six variations and finale. All those years earlier in 1935 when he made his tour of Britain for *The Listener* magazine, he was constantly amazed by the standard of amateur music making and especially of the local brass bands. We should remember his comments about the Wingates Temperance Band that 'any musician when he first hears the virtuosity of these amateur band players will be as astounded as I was.'[47] As we have seen, this experience led him to write the test piece for that year's Crystal Palace Festival, *Kenilworth*. But Wingates was only one of many of these extraordinary, virtuosic amateur bands. Thus, armed with this knowledge, Bliss knew that he could write a seriously challenging work for the National Contest at the Royal Albert Hall on 19 October. But there was obviously something incredibly positive in the air when Bliss set to work on composing this set of variations as it is an exceptional work full of imagination and colour. It is also a work which, in its third variation, puts the lie to the notion that Bliss was incapable of writing a wonderful melody, however rare it may be. Bliss didn't orchestrate the work and his short score was brilliantly arranged by the legendary Frank Wright for brass band.

There are certain genres in the classical music world that are either taken less seriously than the mainstream (including orchestras, chamber music, solo song, choirs) or which even produce a superior snigger as if these other forms of music making are less worthwhile in some way. Brass bands suffer from this more than most and it is the reason why these variations and other outstanding works like Howells's *Pageantry* and *King's Herald* are not better known. But given how busy Bliss was completing these substantial works in such a short period of time the *Belmont Variations* feels like true relaxation. It is almost as if he has taken off his tie, loosened his shirt collar, and is wearing a sports jacket… and what a result. The National contest was won by Manchester's CWS Band, and these variations were then in constant use by bands all over the world.

After a short unison fanfare, the mood quietens and a beautifully lyrical theme is announced, a theme which it is possible to see immediately will prove fertile ground for a set of variations. After a calm, gently moving first variation set up with a triplet motion against a quietly marching bass, the second tests the players as a fleet-footed toccata which requires complete precision of ensemble and a sure technique from all the players. The third variation is the emotional hub of the work, a beautiful euphonium solo weaved about with counter melodies from higher instruments and winding its way to a truly magical ending which has been wonderfully realized in Wright's imaginative scoring. Bliss follows this by a delicate waltz in variation IV featuring a cornet solo which is interrupted by a 'trio section', a cadenza for three instruments; cornet, euphonium and trombone. Another brilliant toccata-style movement in martial style is next and that is followed by a gentle cradle song in the last variation set off by a trio of trombones and gradually opening out as more instruments join with great warmth. The Finale does what might be expected in the final movement of a contest piece, showing the band off to its best virtuoso advantage and leaving a memorable impression.

*The Belmont Variations* are an example of Bliss at his professional best, providing exactly what a band needed for a bold competition work but also writing a serious piece that would add lustre to his list of works. Bliss never wrote 'down' to anyone and he had far too much respect for the brass band sector to write anything less than his best. It is interesting to speculate what it was about the medium which brought such a feeling for melodic line from him. It might be *this* which was his 'writing down' for an ensemble of brilliant but amateur musicians. Bliss had enormous generosity of spirit and the older he grew the more he wanted to help and encourage the young, aspiring amateur musician. He gave himself freely to a large number of organisations as Patron or President. It is this generosity of spirit which comes across in a work like the *Belmont Variations* and the lyricism reflects a warmth of feeling from composer to commissioner.

To emphasize just how busy this period was, Thurston Dart (known as Bob), the Professor of Music at Cambridge University, approached Bliss for a work to celebrate the quincentenary of the award of the first degree in music at Cambridge in 1464. This was also the first music degree to be awarded anywhere in the world. Bliss was approached because he was one of Cambridge's most distinguished musical alumni. As the University Musical Society was to perform the work it was obvious that it had to be a choral and orchestral work. Bliss felt strongly that the librettist should also be a Cambridge alumnus and decided to approach Kathleen Raine whose poetry he admired. Bliss went to visit her at her home in Chelsea and found her very diffident about being able to write to order. Both Dart and Bliss worked hard to persuade her and she eventually agreed. Bliss described Dart's conversation as 'a succession of champagne corks popping, and his letter-writing has the same characteristic.'[48]

Raine composed a sequence of eight poems and summed them up by saying 'the sequence attempts to suggest the evolution of music and how this follows the evolution of the world itself, first of articulate life, then of consciousness and finally of Orphic utterance.'[49] Bliss admitted to finding her words difficult to understand and, to try to make the concept easier for the singers to comprehend he made his own interpretation which he described as follows:

'This poem cycle is An Ode on Sound starting from the sound of the wind ('Voices of empty air') and then passing to the cries of gulls ('Wind's cry takes wings') who in Poem III are seen as a symbol of the soul ('phoenix-like') trying to break free. As a contrast to the screams of the gulls, the poet takes the frail reed-warbler's song ('delicate reed notes') which leads her to human song.

There is first, in Poem V, the child's song, and then in Poem VI, the mature human being's experience of joy and sorrow. Poem VII tells how only by *Art* can life's experience be fully expressed and Poem VIII is an Ode to Music ('the golden form') and to its inspirer, Orpheus.'[50] This gave Bliss his title for the work: *The Golden Cantata*.

He had marked her out some time before as a possible writer whose poems he would like to set but found them 'as fragile as shells, and as delicate as flowers, and I had refrained.'[51] The contrast between Raine and Hassall must have been stark for Bliss as Raine was so diffident about her words where Hassall was so positive, inventive, musical in his creative writing. Nevertheless, a fresh start with a new writer was bound to elicit something musically fresh from Bliss and he determined to make a success of the partnership without necessarily wanting to perpetuate it.

One day she would write rather diffidently, 'You may not find the enclosed poem any use at all: but as I wrote it it seemed to flow through moods which might be musical'. On another she could be much more forceful: 'As to putting "The Child's Song" into the past tense, I would rather not do so unless you feel you must. The reason I am reluctant is that the poem describes precisely the state in which the world is experienced as "here and now" ... without past or future, desire or regret. I would rather leave it so.'[52] The secular nature of the text seems as important as anything to Raine who, commenting on her grandchildren's forthcoming christening described it as 'an enormous piece of irrelevance'. Bliss warmed to her modesty and felt her to be a sympathetic and understanding collaborator. Indeed, her modesty was all too apparent when she wrote to Bliss after a broadcast of the work by the Huddersfield Choral Society in October 1966 that 'I was so glad to hear it again, with no longer a sense of being more than marginally involved in it, as a work. The words were like tacking stitches in the sewing (useful while working), but the work is all yours.'[53]

The occasion of this commission was of singular significance to Bliss who, in receiving an honorary Doctorate in Music, along with Michael Tippett, reminded us that he is 'not one of those who love to retrace their steps, but I make an exception of Cambridge, and felt singularly proud on this twentieth of February 1964'. Bliss was now receiving such honours from various universities in the United Kingdom, the latest of which was Bristol the previous December.

Of all the later works this cantata is the least known, the least commented upon, and it remains unrecorded at the time of writing. It is instructive to speculate as to the reasons for this neglect. Moving on from Christopher Hassall to a wholly new world of imagery and intellectual stimulation inevitably gave Bliss pause to re-evaluate his musical approach. In some ways this cantata looks back over his shoulder to his old experiments in sound where the orchestra is his box of toys, and in other ways finds him attempting to mix this with his style of choral writing which tends to chromatic density which can feel texturally muddy and be prone to intonation issues with choirs of less than professional attainment. Add to this a fragmentary approach to the word setting even within 'scenes', of which there are eight, and unless the listener engages in an unusually concentrated way with both text and music it is unlikely that they will find the core of the work easy to comprehend and may find the constantly shifting fragments tiresome. Bliss might also have taken more notice of Stanford's often given advice to use percussion in inverse proportion to the amount of it. The *Times* critic found that 'his response to some of the earlier poems is more original and striking than to the later ones – the last is set to a relatively conventional C major celebratory music, while the first drew from him some haunting and telling harmonic sequences.'[54] Certainly, the opening promises something new with its hummed chorus and sinuously nebulous lines anticipating 'Voices of empty air' – even perhaps a glance over the shoulder to Haydn's *Representation of Chaos* at the start of *The Creation*. Short-lived but imaginatively scored, too, is the start of the fourth scene which colourfully represents bird-song but which suddenly stops and the music moves in another direction, another example of his fragmentary approach. The brass fanfares leading to the solo tenor's seventh scene feel overblown in the context of their surroundings but anticipate the 'celebratory' music of the next and final scene which winds down dramatically to a very effective quiet ending.

This work feels like the professional composer fulfilling a commission but, either from simple tiredness, or a lack of real inspiration, writing a rather non-descript work which has moments of real beauty. A case of 'damning with faint praise'. As a postscript to this saga, it is worth extracting from Stanley Sadie's highly critical review of the whole concert in the *Musical Times*. He began by regretting the university's highly conservative, almost insular approach to this major anniversary and wondering why a distinguished composer from abroad could not have been invited – Dallapiccola and Messiaen were mentioned. He also regretted that the opportunity to really showcase Cambridge composers from across the centuries had been missed, or the possibility of Thurston Dart, being such a fine exponent, playing keyboard music by John Bull. As to Bliss's commission, it seemed to Sadie that Raine's 'flowery texts... had a certain relevance (to the Cambridge celebration) but had little to inspire; Bliss's treatment, almost inevitably had to be along straightforwardly illustrative lines.'[55] Like the *Times* reviewer he singled out the 'mysterious harmonic continuum at the opening... [and] the nature effects in the fourth (though Bliss's birds seem like the tamest of pet canaries compared to Messiaen's): but the omnipresence of so conventional a celebratory atmosphere, which comes very much into its own towards the end, was dispiriting.'[56] No composer writes at an even level throughout their career and this is undoubtedly one of Bliss's less successful offerings. As can sometimes happen there may be a passionately connected conductor who finds the core of the work and makes a truly convincing argument for it, but that is for the future.

Bliss was asked to write a choral piece celebrating the birth of the Queen's youngest child, Prince Edward, on 10 March 1964. The piece he wrote was called *Cradle Song for a Newborn Child*, setting a specially written poem by Eric Crozier for choir and harp or piano. It is one of

Bliss's most touching shorter choral works and was first broadcast by the BBC Chorus under Peter Gelhorn a day later on 11 March. There is something in this music which exudes affection, and this is undoubtedly what Bliss felt, very deeply, for the Queen. In the way of things, we have no actual record of the relationship between the Crown and Bliss but from all the affectionate greetings in cards and telegrams which exist in the archive, there is little doubt that he was not only highly regarded but genuinely liked by the members of the Royal Family.

Besides this, the correspondence that exists between Bliss and Crozier shows just how seriously they both took the task of this short choral piece. It is clear that it was more challenging than was imagined. Bliss wrote to Crozier on 19 November 1963, saying 'Thank you so much for the trouble you are taking over this "berceuse". Yes, these little things are more difficult than expected. As a matter of fact, my mind is particularly vacuous at the moment, but if it starts again to fill and I have a lucky find, I suggest we meet and decide on a final form.' [57] A few days later Bliss was writing to request further changes to Crozier's text and 'I should welcome a refrain that begs Fortune and Future to award happiness in full measure (instead of any further lullaby associations) and in a different rhythm.'[58] Obviously Bliss's 'vacuity' had passed: the purposeful man rarely remains inactive for long. Then comes an amusing moment when Bliss writes with humorous exasperation, 'What a nuisance! The baby is not expected till March! – so out goes "January" from the first line. "The gentle springtime sunlight fills" would suit my music, but you may devise a more euphonious line.'[59] Crozier decided on 'The gentle golden sunlight...' having had an intermediate thought of 'February' for the vexed word. Through these months of correspondence their relationship on paper remained quite formal with 'Dear Mr Crozier' eventually giving way to 'Dear Eric Crozier' and, four years later, the Christian name alone!

# Chapter Fifteen

# AUSTRALIAN INTERLUDE
# AND A VISION OF RETROSPECT

After the maelstrom of the past two years, it was time for Bliss to take some time off, at least from composing. So he and Trudy decided to visit their younger daughter, Karen, son-in-law Christopher, and their three daughters in Perth, Australia. Inevitably, the trip was combined with concerts for Bliss to conduct in Perth, Sydney and Brisbane arranged by the Australian Broadcasting Commission. They were to enjoy two months in Australia before flying to Japan to join the London Symphony Orchestra who were touring at that time. The Blisses were particularly excited by this trip as they had never before been south of the equator.

In those far-off days before aeroplanes were able to fly non-stop between London and Perth, the Blisses left London on the afternoon of 4 September and stopped for refuelling at Cairo, Karachi, Calcutta, Bangkok and Singapore before they eventually reached Perth early on Sunday the 6th. They were met by Christopher who took them to rest in a nearby hotel until lunchtime before Karen and the girls arrived bearing posies of flowers. They then moved on to a house which had been rented for them close to the family. Bliss recounted how everything had been thought of including a hired piano, a rental car and a well-stocked kitchen complete with the surprise which became a real discovery, Australian wine, which he quickly found 'could vie with any French vintage'. Another more local feature that made Trudy feel at home was the similarity between the architecture of the houses where they were staying and those she was used to in America: 'One storey high and compactly built, with a garage alongside, it had a small garden behind, and a grass lawn in front that bordered the road. Each house down the quiet street was equipped in the same fashion, but with a different design: there were no dividing hedges, and the effect was of privacy and neighbourliness combined, very like America in fact.'[1]

Something rather unexpected now emerges from Bliss's description of their time in Perth. We know that Trudy was born into a family whose great passion was botany and ornithology but what is perhaps unexpected (despite the loyalty of husband to wife) is that Bliss had become what he called a 'holiday naturalist' himself. He described succumbing in middle age to a similar, if amateur, enthusiasm and he wrote movingly of holidays spent in Europe exploring the surrounding terrain as thoroughly as possible. His description of such a trip is mouth-watering: 'each day brought its adventure with, at noon, a picnic lunch of local cheese, local wine, newly baked bread, fresh butter and chosen salami.'[2] The strength of desire for the good things in life balancing the hard work and stress of his professional life is palpable. Another telling comment was 'To be a holiday naturalist is to be free for the time being of the introspective self that can fret an artist so continuously.'[3] It was also a sociable activity (which suited Bliss well as we have seen) as something like dog walking can be, and they made good friends with a particular couple who showed them the remarkable indigenous bird life which was completely new to them with colourful names like Willy Wagtails, Mudlarks and Laughing Kookaburras. None of this may really be such a surprise if we remember Bliss's early passion for microscopes. There was obviously something lurking in his makeup which had the naturalist's investigative instinct.

The time came for Bliss to start work on the musical element of his time in Australia. While in Perth he rehearsed chamber and vocal works for performance at the university and he then flew to Sydney where a British Fortnight had been arranged by the British Council which included four concerts, the first of which Bliss had been asked to conduct. Trudy remained in Perth enjoying the company of her family whilst Bliss flew the two thousand miles to Sydney, again, like Russia, adjusting his sense of scale to this huge country and the distance between major centres. In that first concert which took place at the Conservatorium, he conducted his own *Knot of Riddles* with John Shirley Quirk as the baritone soloist, as well as his *Music for Strings* and music by Purcell, Vaughan Williams and Britten.

Bliss's account of his time in Sydney and onwards is contained in his letters to Trudy in Perth which, as ever, are informal, factual and informative down to the last detail (the laundering of his handkerchiefs and socks at the hotel being a good example). What is more interesting is a letter on 26 September which outlines his pre-concert routine: 'Presently I shall have a bath, change, have my customary pre-concert omelette and half a bottle of white wine in my room, and proceed to the Conservatorium.'[4] Bliss's ability to conduct a concert having consumed this quantity of wine is either indicative of supreme self-confidence, the knowledge that he was so inured to alcohol that his mind wouldn't be affected, or of the need for 'Dutch courage'. It is much more likely to be either of the first suggestions. The next day he was waxing lyrical about eating a delicious John Dory fish. More evidence of his enjoyment of good things.

In Brisbane the two concerts featured the *A Colour Symphony* and *The Beatitudes*, two major works, and a considerable undertaking for those performing them, especially the latter work which Bliss felt nervous about bringing off successfully but all went well. He had to get used to the bevy of reporters, photographers and television interviews in his hotel bedroom wherever he went. But as he said of this period, 'I relished every day in Australia; I liked the vast country and I liked the people, and I left it with regret'. In saying their fond farewells to Karen and her family they were thrilled to hear that they planned to come to England in 1966 for a visit and stay with the Blisses for Christmas.

Trudy joined Bliss for the flight to Tokyo but whatever romantic notion he may have harboured about this huge, teeming city was instantly banished on arrival. He had schooled himself in Lafcadio Hearn's inimitable writings about Japan in the 1920s and was expecting to see something of traditional Japanese culture which, for the Westerner, is full of magic and mystery. He wrote that 'it soon must become the largest and most densely populated of all huge cities, a super-Chicago, with immense push and drive and ruthlessness.'[5] However, he did note that 'in this seemingly Americanized capital one could still, if one sought it, find much of the traditional Japan of one's dreams.'[6] They found a small Shinto Shrine devoted to the worship of the Fox, and were given a tour of a beautiful, characteristic Japanese garden 'designed as to give the impression of a much larger space; there were small hills, miniature rivers with stepping stones, winding paths...we found everywhere in Japan the garden treated like a work of art, and the gardeners aiming at perfection.'[7] Most perfect of all was the stone garden of Daisen-in in Kyoto which was first laid out in the sixteenth century. A monk guided them through the garden explaining how the three joined gardens conformed to the Zen philosophy, and how the forms in stone and sand reflected the journey of the soul from birth to final purification reaching its final resting place at a tree similar to that under which the Buddha died.

The London Symphony Orchestra had already arrived by the time the Blisses got there and were busy preparing for the eight concerts around Japan with Istvan Kertesz and Colin Davis. Bliss joined them to conduct his *A Colour Symphony* and the Dances from *Checkmate*. One of the great pleasures of such a tour was being tourists and Bliss was particularly lyrical in describing the train journey to Kyoto during which they passed Mount Fuji. They were told that the summit was usually shrouded in cloud but on this occasion their luck held and they saw the whole mountain with absolute clarity. 'I little thought', wrote Bliss, 'way back in 1924, when Trudy and I were engaged, and we sat one morning in the Metropolitan Museum of Art in New York looking at the Hokusai views of Fuji, that forty years later we should be seeing the mountain itself, of course through his eyes.'[8]

Another memorable sight was the Festival of the Maple Leaf on the Kamo river in Kyoto. Crowds gathered to watch the procession of flat-bottomed boats, in each of which four young maple trees were planted. Groups of players and dancers in traditional costume dating back to the eleventh century added colour and characteristic sound together with other entertainments. 'Finally, the players, dancers and actors came ashore, formed up into a long column, and made their way slowly over the bridge across the river, handing to the bystanders paper maple leaves as a souvenir of this Autumn Festival: we still have ours.'[9] Also memorable for them was their personal escort who, as they were waiting at the airport, appeared breathlessly brandishing a large bottle of Săké as a leaving gift. They became very friendly. The gift which Bliss found slightly unsettling was a bound volume of photographs taken during the concerts in which he was conducting his music. 'I looked, shuddered, and resolved to profit from what I saw' was Bliss's reaction. Similar books were given to Colin Davis and Istvan Kertesz but, sadly, we have no record of their reactions.

The Blisses made the return journey to England via Hong Kong and Ceylon, neither of which they had visited before, but in both places, they had friends. For Bliss himself it was also pure relaxation with no concerts or ambassadorial engagements to fulfil. It was a short period of rest before the build-up of three months' post would have to be addressed. They saw wonderful, memorable things and felt that it was in Ceylon where they experienced the greatest beauty, wishing they could have stayed for far longer. They were able to witness one of the local festivals and were pleased to be the only Europeans there experiencing at first hand a completely different culture and enjoying the natural beauty of it. The appreciation of beauty was expressed by their driver on their return journey, stopping to see the reflection of the full moon in the Sacred Lake. Bliss's recollection of this in his autobiography recalls that 'We halted there and waited until a cloud that obscured the moon should disperse. When it finally did our driver breathed a deep 'ah', and remained transfixed admiring the beauty.'[10] Bliss wrote that he wondered in what other country one could find a corresponding sensitivity – in Ireland perhaps?

On their return home on 25 November Bliss found one interesting item in his post – an invitation from the National Book League to present John Masefield with a literary prize on the publication of his last book of poems *Old Raiger and Other Verse*. Bliss had never met Masefield and eagerly anticipated the opportunity of telling him how, when he was a student, he had bought a copy of *Reynard the Fox* in a shop off the Charing Cross Road and was so bound up in the story that, having started reading it on the tube back to Hampstead, he stood under a street light until he had finished it, unable to wait longer to discover the denouement. Masefield afterwards sent him a signed copy of *Old Raiger* with the inscription 'The days that make us happy make us wise'.

One of the most significant events of 1965 was the BBC producer John Drummond's suggestion that Bliss be the subject of an hour-long documentary television programme called *Workshop*, about his life and work. This was aired on 16 August. Drummond was a remarkable man, outspoken in his views and not always endearing himself to those in authority, yet he had a meteoric career in the BBC in both radio and television, running the Proms for ten years and ending up as Controller of Radio 3. He was knighted in 1995. Bliss described Drummond as 'an indefatigable perfectionist' and as old photographs were sought out and his long past raked over, the experience led him to consider writing his own autobiography which has, of course, been such a source of first-hand material for this biography.

Bliss and Drummond got on very well, though Bliss found the experience an ordeal 'lightened by (Drummond's) enthusiasm and gaity'. Drummond, for his part, noted that 'Bliss was absolutely charming, and I warmed to him immediately when he said, "Do you know, in the course of my life I have been three things: I have been ahead of the times, of the times and now behind the times. But I don't in myself feel any different." '[11] Drummond's summing up in his own autobiography, *Tainted by Experience*, is interesting in itself: 'Bliss is no longer really thought an important composer, but he was an excellent conductor, Director of Music at the BBC during the war, and later on every committee of the profession – an ambassador for British music, working constantly for the British Council or the Performing Rights Society… He was in one sense grand and famous, but in other ways vulnerable and modest. Beginning to doubt whether his music would last.'[12]

The programme was filmed in two locations, Bliss's St John's Wood home where he was interviewed by Drummond, and in a studio with the London Symphony Orchestra with Bliss himself conducting extracts from various works which he talked about in the course of Drummond's interview. One of the most fascinating things about the film is of course seeing Bliss talking and conducting. In tandem with this is probably the most candid page of his autobiography in which he holds up an honest mirror to himself. Here are some key elements: 'I admit to being a bad subject for the camera, as I am too for the portrait painter and the sculptor. My temperament demands activity, not a passive role. I only see myself in action… Knowing how I automatically resist the discipline necessary for a television programme such as this, I think it a triumph for the producer to have got through it at all.'[13]

'I have many pictures of myself as a child, a boy at school, a young man, and looking at these I cannot help feeling that there has been little real change in my personality, and by that, I mean my likes and dislikes, my admirations and prejudices… I have always been well aware of my own entity, and known how to preserve it, by a not particularly likeable self-assertion as a child and by encasing myself when a boy at school in an outward personality that very rarely gave my inner ideals away. I soon learnt that preservation of my true self meant adopting for the time being the part that caused me the least expense of mental stress in the company that I was in. I am aware that this far from the heroic role of the champion who wants to dominate his circle, but it served me well in the tough years at school, and in the tougher years in the Army. It enabled me, when I had endured these, to shake off the experiences that might have greatly affected me, and emerge again for my destined life in music as I truly was.'[14]

He continues, 'I suppose no one *really* knows what impression his personality makes on others: it is possible to live in a dream world, and greatly to exaggerate the respect and liking or, conversely, the boredom and dislike which you apparently cause in others. This doubt is magnified when it comes to the consideration of what one has created oneself, be it music, poetry or painting; even the estimate of one's own work varies with mood and time'.[15]

This estimate of his work was something played out in real time for the documentary. John Drummond remembered: 'I cannot forget the hurtful experience when we came to rehearse the music for the TV recording. Here was a programme celebrating the life and music of the President of the

London Symphony Orchestra, yet hardly a single section principal turned up for the sessions. Bliss looked around and said quietly, "Good morning, gentlemen. Quite a few new faces aren't there?" It seemed to me a really insulting situation, and I told the orchestra's manager, Ernest Fleischmann, what I thought. He disclaimed all responsibility, saying the orchestra was self-governing and the players chose what they wanted to do.'[16]

Watching this film, which is of course very dated to our post-millennial eyes, there are two very striking things about the musical extracts: the first is the generally bored look on the orchestra's faces. There is very little sympathetic engagement with Bliss (or even with the cameras) which looks surprisingly cold in such a programme, bringing an air of functionality to the music making. The other is Bliss's conducting. Let's try to describe his whole demeanour: he has the ramrod straight back of an Army officer coming straight from the parade ground. He is dressed in a dark suit and tie. He does not move his feet at all. His arm gestures are more often than not 'mirror' gestures where the left hand mirrors what the right does. The gestures are heavy: strong whole arm up and down movements almost as if he were conducting a military band on a parade ground. There is little clear idea of where the beat actually is, the information being given through the speed of travel of his arms. The school is that of Sir Adrian Boult but without his subtlety. He subdivides the beats to achieve a *rallentando* where a more instinctive (skilled) conductor would slow the beat down and get the orchestra to 'feel' his intention. Interestingly, in the extract from his own *Dance of Deliverance* from the ballet *Miracle in the Gorbals* you can see him mouthing 'one, two, three, four' making sure he is on the right beat of the bar, not something a really professional conductor would want to be seen doing. But it is in this music that he allows himself to show more real enjoyment (he obviously loves this piece) where normally little emotion shows, but that is the Boult school of allowing the orchestral musicians to express themselves within the beat set by the conductor who is more facilitator than dictator. It may be any or all of these things which distressed him on receiving the gift of photographs of his conducting in Tokyo. That reaction may also of course be false posturing or modesty. At the end of the film Drummond poses the question as to whether Bliss enjoyed conducting. Bliss's reply was that he would not want to be a full-time conductor – 'that would be killing' – but that he enjoyed making music with other people. Lest all the above sounds like a demolition exercise it should be remembered that Bliss was *not* a professional conductor and that, compared to many other composer/conductors, he was perfectly proficient in guiding the orchestra through often complex scores.

To illustrate his work, he chose extracts for this documentary from *Miracle in the Gorbals* and *Checkmate*, the films *Things to Come* and *Men of Two Worlds*, the short fanfare in homage to Shakespeare, and the *Homage to a Great Man* for Winston Churchill (the music played just before his funeral service), *A Colour Symphony* and most notably *Meditations on a Theme by John Blow* which he described to Drummond as being his best orchestral work.

Ten years later, Drummond asked him to write opening and closing music for a television series called *The Spirit of the Age*. Bliss accepted and went to the studio to record on 11 January 1975, conducting the LSO one last time. He died two months later, and Drummond wrote that 'he came to the studio to record it with the brass from the London Symphony Orchestra, and looked very frail. He died shortly afterwards. I felt his death keenly. He was the first really public figure to befriend me, and he had been immensely generous and kind to me over the years.'[17]

One further personal trait worth mentioning from the documentary is Bliss's voice. We would expect a 'received' or 'upper-class' accent reflecting his background and education, despite his hybrid British/American parentage. What is perhaps a surprise is the high pitch of his voice and the relatively monotone pitching which only changes when he has something emphatic to say. One wonders whether this, too, is part of his personal armoury. We have a conducting style that rarely displays emotion, a military bearing that might be seen as intimidating and may have had the effect of warning people off, and a voice which displays little emotion. Underneath all this, however, lies a very warm-hearted, generous person who throws himself into giving, whether of time or of personal encouragement and practical help.

An example of his spirit of encouragement was to the composer William (Bill) Alwyn who lived almost opposite the beautiful church at Blythburgh in Suffolk, not far from Aldeburgh and Britten and Pears. Alwyn was a fine composer (also a writer and painter) who felt he was ignored, both by the artists who might take up his music, and by those who distributed national honours (though he did receive a CBE in 1978 but this was after Bliss's death). Bliss was generous to a fault in writing to encourage him. One exchange is typical. Bliss wrote on 4 February 1973, 'This morning, looking for a book, I found your *Winter in Copenhagen* almost covered by your Anthology of XXth century French Poets, and re-read it – and this led me to want to rehear the recording of your Third Symphony. At the end I felt more impressed even than by the first time… I think it is a splendid work, often, like the enchanting *Magic Island*, ravishing to the ear, often frightening... Do not be downhearted by delays in performance of your music. I know that one day the bell will peal out loud and clear. AB.'[18] Alwyn's response three days later was effusive: 'Your letter was as manna from heaven! Such generous words, unexpected and unsolicited, have touched my heart and given me more confidence. No! that is not quite honesty – I have never lacked confidence in myself but I have suffered much from disillusionment.'[19] The irony here is that while Bliss had honours heaped upon him and enormous success in his lifetime, he has suffered an almost complete reversal since his death. The psychology of this should be the subject of another book.

Bliss had been President of the Composers' Guild of Great Britain since 1950, another of the organizations to benefit from his generosity of time and wisdom (he was also elected President of the International Confederation of Authors' and Composers' Societies for a period of two years in June of 1964). This Guild had been formed out of the Society of Authors. In Ian Johnson's book about William Alwyn: *The Art of Film Music*, Johnson states that 'Alwyn was elected to the committee of the Composers' section of the Society of Authors. Most of its board members were elderly and pompous and, according to Alwyn, its chairman ruled out of order everything that could further the cause of British music. So, in 1947, with the help of colleagues, Alwyn initiated the Composers' Guild of Great Britain. Retaining its affiliation to the parent society.'[20] In fact, the Guild was formed in 1944 and the composer Francis Routh wrote that it was Bliss who was the prime mover along with Alwyn, Rawsthorne, Alan Bush and Walton. And he gives the formation date as 1953, long after its actual founding. The common name here is Alwyn's with the apologist for him writing that he was the prime mover and shaker. Routh, with no particular axe to grind, wrote that 'The Composers' Guild of Great Britain was founded in 1953–1955 by Sir Arthur Bliss for the purpose of supporting and representing the professional interests of living British composers.'

Rallying the troops to this cause, in 1964 Bliss gave an inspiring talk to the Guild in the Connaught Rooms in London about supporting British music – something he had always been passionate about, and had done much to promote during his time at the BBC. A key passage of his talk complained that 'British music has never had an easy time in this country. We are still obsessed by the snobbish attitudes of our grandfathers, who were convinced that the only music worth hearing came from foreign countries where, of course, they do everything so much better than we do – play better, sing better, conduct better, and have the only composers worthy listening to. British music, they said... is "parochial", whereas the music from abroad is of truly international interest. Personally, I am bored with being international with everyone else... The French music I admire is not international at all; it is redolent of France. What I like about Italian music is its national character (or, if you like, its "parochial" character) ... I wish our leading musical organizations showed greater pride in what has been written since, say, the days of Elgar, and a greater courage in performing it.'[21] When he expanded on this theme in *Composer* magazine, he added that the Guild should consider promoting concerts not only of British music but representing the Commonwealth as well as 'foreign contemporaries'. He recognized the financial implications and dreamed of a sponsor who might underwrite the whole project. He felt, too, that it would 'add dignity to the scheme if it was carried out in conjunction with the Royal Philharmonic Society, whose traditional support of British music is memorable.'[22] He ended by encouraging the Guild to 'be the spearhead of an aggressive policy'.

The composer Ruth Gipps, known to all as 'Wid', a good friend of Bliss, was deeply involved in the work of the Guild, becoming its chairman and founding the Music Information Centre which eventually became the British Music Information Centre in rather grand premises in Stratford Place in London. All this was an offshoot of the Guild and operated under its auspices. Bliss wrote to Gipps in November 1967 saying: 'I feel the establishment of this Information Centre is a great step forward in the Guild's life. May it bring in many performances of all the fine music there, that so far has never had a real chance.'[23] Also at this time Bliss wrote to her about 'the World Music Bank' which was presumably a library of examples of major composers' work stored in perpetuity. 'As you know, there is a commercial recording of this work (*A Colour Symphony*) available, and I write to say that I wish my name on this list to be replaced by another composer, if possible, by one of the suggested names I sent in.'[24] Another example of the selfless elder statesman looking to give a more needy composer an opportunity.

For Sir Winston Churchill's state funeral, Bliss had provided a *March in Honour of a Great Man*. This was aired on the BBC immediately before the service on 30 January 1965 in St Paul's Cathedral. Scored for full orchestra, including two muffled side drums tuned to different pitches, the march is a dignified scene-setter for this great occasion that gripped the country in a way normally only experienced during great royal events. It is another example of his fine work as Master of the Queen's Music.

The effect of ageing is often to give significant events, dates and remembrances greater emotional weight. Bliss's *Hymn to Apollo*, written in 1926, was a 'Kennard' work – one of those works written with his younger brother in mind. We discussed its original version in Chapter Five, and Bliss wanted to revisit it, revise and improve it. Back in September 1926, the month of the completion of the original score, Bliss took his wife and baby daughter Barbara to visit Swanage in Dorset where, Bliss remembered, 'thirty or so years ago my brother and I used to spend part of our holidays.'[25] Nearly forty years had elapsed since the completion of the original score. When he had listened to the British premiere of the work at a Royal Philharmonic concert, again with Monteux conducting, he had doubts about its proportions and orchestration. He therefore put the work away and let it rest. This retrospective air which Bliss was going through made him also look again at his *Discourse for Orchestra* from 1957 about which he also had reservations and put by after its initial performance in Louisville, Kentucky. The reconsidering of significant works had something of a disadvantage to them, Bliss acknowledging that conductors who knew the original versions of works and formed their opinion at that time often did not take the time to look at revised scores – another reason why so many of Bliss's works have languished in obscurity over so many years.

Bliss wrote in almost exactly the same way about his alterations to these works. Of the *Discourse* he said: 'Later I had second thoughts (and) devised an entirely new score for slightly larger orchestra and altered the proportions of the work, cutting out one section ('A more disturbing view' – the old second section) altogether.'[26] On the published score of the second version he noted that the work was 'recomposed' in 1965. In the case of *Apollo*, Bliss rescored the work for a slightly smaller orchestra and modified its form. 'I am sure that this is a case where second thoughts are best.'[27] The problem was that Bliss regularly revised works with which he felt uneasy. Perhaps the most extreme example being the *Concerto for Piano, Tenor, Strings and Percussion,* which became the *Concerto for Two Pianos and Orchestra* in the mid-twenties. Other 'second thoughts' affected *A Colour Symphony,* the *Introduction and Allegro* (1926/1937), as well as *Apollo* and *Discourse.* There is no doubt that these revisions produced better results, but persuading respected conductors to look again at these works was a problem that he readily recognized. The first performances of the revised version of *Apollo* and *Discourse* were conducted by Bliss himself, *Apollo* in July 1965 at the Cheltenham Festival, of which he had become President that year, and *Discourse* at the Royal Festival Hall with the London Symphony Orchestra in September.

Bliss and Trudy were invited to visit the island of Sark in April that year. He had been asked to write a short anthem commemorating the four hundredth anniversary of the granting of the Royal Charter to the island. They were invited to stay with the Dame of Sark, Sibyl Hathaway. As Bliss recalled, 'It was like returning to my childhood to find, when we landed at the quay, an open victoria drawn by a brown mare, Daisy, and driven by the Constable, awaiting to take us to La Seigneurie… Many visitors must have stayed at the sixteenth-century Seigneurie, and all must have been charmed by this remote little feudal outpost, for feudal it certainly is. Like a hereditary chief, the Dame guards the right of the four hundred inhabitants to maintain their own privileges, jealously preserved.'[28]

One imagines that the Blisses must have had fun with Sibyl Hathaway, an extraordinary character who created a successful resistance to the Nazis when the Germans occupied the island. She wrote about this in her colourful autobiography, and a film was made of her wartime experiences. Bliss's commissioned anthem, *O give thanks unto the Lord*, is a setting of verses from Psalm 106. It is a short, celebratory piece that is extremely sunny, straightforward and entirely suitable for the occasion. It is likely that the choir was an ordinary group of amateur singers who formed the parish church choir, and Bliss's piece will have been entirely within their grasp. Their enjoyment will have been enhanced by being aware of the privilege of having a piece written especially for them by so eminent a composer.

One of the six ceremonial pieces he wrote in 1965 was in some ways also the most unusual of all. The *Ceremonial Prelude* was commissioned to celebrate the 900th anniversary of the founding of Westminster Abbey. The service took place on 28 December, the actual date of the founding of the Abbey, and was written to accompany the Queen from her entry at the West Doors to the chapel of St Edward the Confessor. There she laid a tribute of red roses, and then onwards to her stall in the Quire. Everything was timed meticulously, as on all these great occasions, and Bliss's work in films prepared him well for the task. This five-minute fanfare for brass and organ (with chimes at the end) had something of a cinematic melodrama about it. The music calmed towards the end, and acted as the background music to a prayer read by the Dean of the Abbey; this carried reminiscences of *Morning Heroes* in having a narration over an orchestral accompaniment. One wonders, in that iconic national building that enshrines the tomb of the Unknown Warrior, whether Kennard's ghost was felt to haunt these final pages of music yet again. It is probably fanciful, but life is short and memories long.

No major new work came from 1965, but what he might have thought to be a year of rest from composition turned out to be every bit as busy, with revisions and shorter new pieces. However, Bliss described the major event of the year as the arrival of his daughter, Karen, with her family from Australia to spend Christmas together. The air of excitement was palpable and worth recounting here: 'They sailed in the *Oriana* from Fremantle in November, Chris following later by air. Trudy could not wait patiently until they docked at Southampton, but flew out to Naples to meet them and escort them home. The ship was due early in the morning, and Trudy, too excited to sleep, saw from her bedroom window the lights of the boat as it approached Naples before dawn, and hastened down to the dock. By ill luck it was a pouring wet day, and the problem was what to do with the three little girls during their hours on land. The question being put to *them*, they unanimously voted to go for a ride in the street cars... I only mention this family outing to point out that for three young Australians, a Neapolitan tram was as novel an excitement as had been, for instance, Trudy's and my ride on an elephant's bare back the year before in Ceylon.'[29] Karen's family stayed until the end of January, making a uniquely happy Christmas for the whole family.

The timing of their visit meant that Karen and Chris with Trudy could be in Westminster Abbey for the occasion of the premiere of the *Ceremonial Prelude*. Bliss recalled that the duration was estimated at eight minutes, though in actuality it was much shorter, being timed at five-and-a-half minutes.

1966 was Bliss's seventy-fifth year. That milestone was marked by a notable letter of congratulations from Benjamin Britten, who wrote a touchingly generous letter on 4 August:

My dear Arthur,

When one is young, tales of one's elder's youthful exploits set one's sympathy vibrating strongly... 'so they know too what it is to be young and frustrated'. In my boyhood you, Arthur, were the 'avant gardist' of 'Rout', 'Conversations' and daring, possibly apocryphal Parisian exploits. You were almost a myth.

When one is very young no one is growing older, least of all oneself: time may pass, but we stand still. For me still, the zestful avant gardist of 'Madam Noy' peeps out of the silvery halo of to-day. Happy you, who can preserve youthful exuberance without youthful immaturity!

So to-day's young may perhaps find it difficult to equate the Master of the Queen's Musick with the avant-garde of 1920. If they are not blind, they will note that 'Youth's the Season made for Joys' – not for Responsibility. At 25 or so the Plateau of Responsibility comes into sight, and once on it, we are there for good.

You, Arthur, have given us 50 years of active responsibility. Few of our juniors have not been helped directly or indirectly by your practical benevolence. British music, and music in general, has profited by your experience and wisdom – the BBC, the British Council, and the PRS, to name but a few. And we do not forget your composition, which so many choral and orchestral societies, singers and chamber groups (often starved of good, playable, new works) continue to enjoy. We, thousands of us, send you our warmest thanks for all this, and, since you are the youngest 75 imaginable, look forward confidently to many more years of tireless energy and sane guidance.

Yours ever,

Ben[30]

This seventy-five-year milestone was where Bliss decided to end his autobiography. The opening of this final chapter feels ominous when he wrote 'My story draws to a close with my seventy-fifth year', but in fact he had another nine highly fertile years to live: they began with a hesitant start towards the writing of his autobiography in May. He and Trudy went to stay in a beautiful manor house in Brittany called Le Manoir du Stang, in the village of La Forêt-Fouesnant near Beg-Meil. As Bliss recalled, it was made famous as Balbec in Proust's *À la Recherche du Temps Perdu*.

It was seeing these 'coiffes' that brought back to Bliss's mind the household at Holland Park, specifically because there was a painting hanging in their living room of a Breton Pardon,[31] perhaps one by Pascal Bouveret (*see* opposite).

It seems that even when writing a book, he received a *donnée* as he wrote that 'As soon as I saw them (worn by the staff at Le Manoir), I felt a long-distant past rise up again... A stream of memories swept into my mind...'[32] and shortly, 'My pencil began to move over the paper, and before I consciously realized it my story had started without further prompting – set going by the sight of the Breton 'coiffe'.

Bliss's own story told in his own words does indeed stop there but he leaves us with one more insight by discussing the authors to whom he has felt drawn throughout his life. As George Dannatt noted, it was a shame

that he didn't also comment on the many artists who influenced him and continued to inspire him especially as his love of art was an inherited trait from his father.

Of the books and their authors, he singled out Dostoevsky as first and foremost: not for his benign, saintly characters like Prince Myshkin in *The Idiot*, but 'the cold, ruthless, awe-inspiring personalities of a Rogozhin or Stavrogin; they must have touched hidden springs in my own nature.'[33] He continued, 'From my early years Dostoevsky gave me an intense curiosity and sympathetic liking for the Slav mind both in music and in literature; this fascination never left me'. Chekov was Bliss's next mentioned author because, he said, of his loving treatment of 'failures'. 'There is something boring in reading about the successful man... On the other hand, the lives of those who, through flaws in character or ill health, or bad luck, or just lack of push, have failed in the ambitions with which they started can be read with affectionate sympathy'.

One highly personal paragraph is particularly telling: 'I have always found difficulty in reconciling the two sides of my character: one, the wish to create, which I inherit from my mother, and two, the urge to undertake practical tasks, which I owe to my father's example. This dichotomy has never been satisfactorily resolved, and I have often wondered whether the many administrative posts that I have held have not trespassed dangerously on the private domain of the composer. I am aware that many of my musical dreams have never become realities.'[34] It is uncertain quite what Bliss meant by this cryptic comment, but it is likely to be projects cherished at their inception and never being realized such as the various operatic ideas suggested to him in earlier years. It could also refer to his hopes for a work like *The Olympians*, which were so sadly disappointed, or the fiasco of *The Beatitudes*, which he never heard in its intended location.

Goethe is highlighted for *his* ability to balance his enormous administrative duties with his creativity as a great poet. 'There was obviously much to learn from Goethe's apparently serene command of his varied duties, though beneath this I think the real man spoke when he makes Wilhelm Meister bitterly exclaim "How the man of the world longs, in his distracted life, to preserve the sensibility which the artist must never abandon, if his plans to achieve a lasting work of art are to come to anything!" '[35]

He ends his literary tour with Henry James, whose characters Bliss states he cannot identify with (unlike those of Dostoevsky). It is James's 'mastery of form' he delights in. Bliss feels that James achieves in novels like *The Ambassadors*, *The Golden Bowl* and *The Wings of a Dove* 'the architectural grandeur of great symphonies. And as in great symphonies, they have to be re-experienced again and again before that grandeur is fully realized.'[36] There is one more tiny 'credo', which states that improvisation and 'haphazard methods do not for long interest me. I prefer the creed stated in a poem by Robert Frost – a whole aesthetic in eleven words.

> Let Chaos Storm!
> Let cloud shapes swarm!
> I wait for form.'[37]

His valedictory paragraphs (for that is what they sound like) state that Bliss finds his ability to concentrate is less at the age of seventy-five and, significantly, that his 'joy in writing music is on the wane'. Yet there is still a great deal of music to flow from his pen in his last nine years. In the 'postscript' chapter written by his wife, she noted that 'in all the honorary offices he held, he contributed to the administration whenever needed. He was rarely just a name on the letterhead.'[38]

This goes back to his statement about his dual nature: the happy administrator and the richly creative artist, and the balance between the two.

Whilst in reflective mode, it is rare in these pages that there has been any suggestion other than that Bliss was one of the most genial and generous of men. But John Amis remembered one distinctly disturbing occasion, the exception to the rule, during a recording for the BBC's Transcription Service. An outburst of temper erupted from Bliss, which seems out of character but obviously lurked just below the surface. 'Bad temper?', wrote Amis, 'I can only remember Sir Arthur Bliss when, one minute after we had started recording, the producer came in – startling Arthur, I admit, while he was talking – to say that inexplicably the sound had stopped coming through. The Master of the Queen's Musick went berserk. That's the only expression I can use, because not only did he trumpet abuse, but his eyes went red, as an elephant's are said to do when enraged.'[39] For many who are wound up or on edge, there is often a trigger point that can set off a demon lurking just below the surface. It can often be worse for those who spend their lives having to present a perennially genial face to the world due to their public profile.

A beautifully opposing view is related by Trudy Bliss, as she remembered that idyllic period in Brittany when the autobiography was started: 'The memory of that fortnight in May 1966 is one of the most exquisite of all the happy recollections of my marriage: a very private "point of repose" in the extremely public life Arthur was leading at that time.'[40] She went on to detail a heavy schedule that featured Paris in March for an international composers' conference, Manchester in April awarding prizes, Prague in June for the biennial conference of CISAC – the International Confederation of Societies of Authors and Composers – of which he was President that year, and then to Cheltenham for the Festival. These festivals, she noted wryly, usually divided the attendees into two groups: the performers, critics and composers, and the ordinary music-loving listener. Often these two groups would not mix, but, characteristically, 'with Arthur as President and George Budge as Chairman of the Management Committee, there was always a notable friendliness and clever blending of the two groups. In the Queen's Hotel at teatime, the afternoon concert over, or in the Festival Club in the evening, there would always be Arthur with a splendid mixture of both sorts of people around him – the jokes flying.'[41] The genial nature of Bliss's personality always made him a welcome guest and a comment made by Gerald Finzi to the poet Edmund Blunden (with whom he collaborated on his Ode *For St Cecilia*) is typical: 'I have a message for you from Arthur Bliss, who was with us for a few days, and as usual, the best of company.'[42]

Bliss had the help of two people in the writing of *As I Remember*. They had different tasks: Eric Crozier commented on the readability, content and grammar of the text, and John F. Waterhouse acted as editor. The letter responding to Crozier's offer of help was written on 28 January 1967. It obviously also responded to something Crozier had written about his current state of mind: 'Your letter needs immediate answering on two counts.

1.  You <u>shall</u> have, before the week is out, 1500–1800 typed words from my reminiscences as a sample. Now, I am free from all pretensions about these, and if you think them uninteresting, I shall not mind one whit. On the other hand, if you would like them, you shall have them on the understanding that, as they form part of a possibly large book, I must have all rights to take them later wheresoever I will. Grammar is not my forte, and your keen eye and sensitive ear may well be able to improve them. If of use to you, you might like an accompanying photo of the period for reproduction.

2.  A black cloud of angst can and does descend on every artist. While it is enveloping him there seems to be no ray, but inevitably, thank God, it lifts, sooner or later. I have tried to rationalize this condition. It does not seem to be due to ill health, for often that surprisingly is a condition for finely conceived work, nor to some sex frustration which can presumably be overcome. I believe it is due to the feeling of creative impotence, during which time the artist's pulse beats too slow for happiness. Nothing seems worthwhile, and one seems to sit with vacant face and mind, while the minutes just tick slowly away. It is in some curious way the result of too much self-absorption: I am sure it is so in my case – and the only remedy I find for this inertia of spirit is <u>change</u> – either of place, people, or of interest. One of the most interesting historical characters I know is Goëthe, and I believe his random and intense preoccupations with the theory of light, geology, botany, even court ceremonial were really instinctive attempts to rescue himself from the long months when his real creative self seemed to have left him for good. Pills are no palliative – a holiday, and (say) learning Italian enough to read Leonardi – and then to work. Good luck, Arthur.'[43]

On 31 May he was writing to Crozier to reassure him that 'your "little quibbles" are, in reality, vibrant contributions, and the script would look poorly without your corrections to all my mistakes.'[44]

Perhaps one of the most important personal letters we have from Bliss was written to Crozier on 13 November 1967. It is worth quoting in full here:

Dear Eric,

Again, I write with warm gratitude for your professional help. I find it a great stand by.

I know what you mean by 'keeping my guard up with the reader!' Lowering it is not an easy job with one's intimates still living – and I am not sure what I should reveal, <u>if</u> I did. I have never suffered from syphilis, like Beethoven, or Baudelaire: I have no extraordinary sex perversion like Swinburne or experimented with drugs like de Quincey – I have not even committed murder like Gesualdo: so what?! Biographies and autobiographies that sell to-day have something spicy as their foundation, or clang with great names that for the time being carry interest. My simple 'My life Recalled' aims at something different – and quite specific. I just hope that when my music is played in after years, the hearer will be sufficiently interested to know the kind of man, (and the manner of his living), who signs himself Arthur Bliss.

If <u>no</u> profile emerges from these pages I have failed – but the reticence is part of the man.

I am now near the final cadence, before revision, omission, extension. I am going to thrust myself on your mercy just once more!

With manifold thanks

Yours,

Arthur[45]

This describes the perennial problem of both the biographer and autobiographer very clearly: first, the issue of living friends and relatives, and second, in Bliss's case, the lack of a scandal to titivate the story. But it is with Bliss his heart-warming generosity, his enduring love and constancy for his wife and his care as a father, his sense of fun, and his work ethic together with his engaging, dynamic personality which cries out for the reader to adjudicate that his was a life lived fully and well without the need for extra-curricular stimulus.

Whilst on the subject of the autobiography, the publication of which was still three years away in 1970, it is important to note John F. Waterhouse's major contribution to the book. He lived in Brighton following his retirement from the Birmingham Post in around 1962 and wrote all his considerable letters in longhand, correcting, and making valuable suggestions about all manner of issues as they arose. We need, also, to sort out a problem of identity between him and John T. Waterhouse (Italian music expert) who is credited with this job in Stewart Cragg's Source Book. One issue is that in signing his name fully the F could equally be a T until you look for other Fs in the text to see it match up. Additionally, John F was Music Critic for the Birmingham Post, and will have come across Bliss frequently both in Birmingham and, probably more socially, at Cheltenham. Here is one example of a letter from him, dated 4 August 1968:

Two points for possible amplification (if you feel like it) I think I mentioned briefly when we met. They both concern your works of 1928–30 (Pastoral, Serenade, Morning Heroes)

a)  It would be interesting to have something more general from you about 'anthology music' – i.e. music to texts compounded from widely various sources – for I think you were the pioneer in this matter, and many English composers have since followed your lead: most notably Britten (Our Hunting Fathers, Serenade, Spring Symphony). The largest example I can think of is Sir George Dyson's Three Choirs cantata *Quo Vadis* – probably his best work and regrettably forgotten. Could you say a little more about how the idea of the *Pastoral* came to you?

b)  Might you perhaps (Morning Heroes) 'spread yourself' just a bit about the problems of writing music to spoken words?[46]

In another letter, of 6 August 1968, he praises Bliss for 'your ruthless thinning-out of the intimate letters, which must have been a painful as well as a difficult task, seems to me most admirably done, and the results exactly right for the shape and flow of the book'.[47] One curious anomaly arises in a letter dated 23 August 1968 in which Waterhouse writes: 'Your Foreword, if I may say so, is splendid and beautiful – one of your very best pieces of writing for the book, to which it will give a most propitious send-off. The Kipling anecdote is delectable, and I'm very glad you recalled it'.[48] It is odd that in the Foreword as published this anecdote has been removed leaving one to wonder what it might have been.

The writing of his autobiography occupied much of his time during 1966 and composing took a back seat. The two exceptions were the incidental music for a joint television production between the BBC and ITV called *The Royal Palaces of Britain*, directed by Anthony de Lotbiniere with Kenneth Clark as narrator, first screened on Christmas Day. Muir Matheson conducted the Sinfonia of London for the film. Bliss created a short Suite from the music which was later arranged by Frank Erikson for concert band. An arrangement was also made for solo piano. The music is much as would be expected for a film connected with royalty, music which flowed effortlessly from Bliss's pen.

A new connection for Bliss came about through the pianist Marguerite Wolff. She had been approached by Trudy to give a charity concert for the Westminster Society for Mentally Handicapped Children. Marguerite responded positively but suggested that she might give a concert with her sister Dorothy (Dolly) – four hands on one piano. The Blisses readily agreed to this. Only a few days later, Marguerite's husband died suddenly in his sleep. The concert for the Blisses then became a highly significant event for her as she could throw herself into preparing for it and distract herself from her inevitable emotional roller-coaster. As she said: 'Derrick's sudden death was terrible, but the pattern of life is strange. Sir Arthur was marvellous. He was everything a Master of the Queen's Musick should be, and a friendship started.'[49] Her old teacher, Louis Kentner went to see Marguerite to offer condolences and so their friendship was rekindled and this connection was to have a significant impact on her performances of Bliss's *Piano Sonata* and would later lead to Bliss's final piano work, *Triptych*, being dedicated to him.

Peter Davis, who worked for the British Council, suggested that Marguerite might undertake a tour of Finland. Another connection, Sir Basil Lindsay-Fynn, chairman of the Friends of Malta Society, suggested she also play there. In both these programmes a British work was required, and as Bliss was there when Davis suggested the British Council concert, he was asked to recommend a suitable work – so her relationship with his Piano Sonata began.

Marguerite made regular visits to analyze and play the work with Bliss making suggestions. In particular he noted that because the slow movement is 'excessively slow', 'immediately you have finished the first movement, place your hands ready for the slow movement, and wait, count eight crotchets (beats), to prevent the audience applauding, then begin'. As she said 'This is stagecraft. Sir Arthur knew exactly what he wanted not only in his piano music but in each of the full range of his compositions.'[50]

Robert Clarson-Leach, in his biography of Wolff, stated that 'With enormous help from Louis Kentner, and with continued guidance from the composer himself, Marguerite studied the Bliss *Piano Sonata* in depth. When she performed it in public it became evident that she was becoming not only a skilled exponent of Bliss's piano music, but something of a disciple. She was taking his music to a new audience, especially overseas. Concert organizers were quick to request that she included the Bliss *Piano Sonata* in her programme'.

Of particular technical interest is the use of the Steinway third (middle) pedal. As she noted: 'This special pedal can sustain a note or chord while other notes are being played and the sustaining pedal (right foot) is being used in the normal fashion. Use of the middle pedal goes right through the work, but especially in the first movement. It is surprising the number of pianists who do not use the middle pedal. In this sonata its use is very important.'[51]

Another reminiscence of hers shows Bliss's sensitivity. On a subsequent visit to Malta, she was asked to give a recital as part of an international television conference. She was to play Bliss's Sonata and Clarson-Leach told the story: 'An imaginative Maltese TV producer designed a beautiful set for the performance of the Bliss *Sonata*. Marguerite arrived early, to be followed by Sir Arthur and his party. When it was time to begin, he said to Marguerite, "Now, my dear, you will have to forgive me if I leave you. I have to introduce the sonata. And then I will introduce you, but then I have to go. I will watch the performance on TV tonight." Sir Arthur made the appropriate announcements, then he smiled at Marguerite and departed. He had been sitting in a chair at the end of the studio. The cameras were wheeled to the "piano end", and Sir Arthur was nowhere in sight. The relief to Marguerite was tremendous, because television on its own is a tense enough situation for a performer and it would have been that much more so had the composer himself been there... The work takes about half an hour to perform. When she finished, the red light went off and, hurrying towards Marguerite, was Sir Arthur. He had stayed in the studio the whole time, but had kept out of sight, knowing Marguerite would feel freer if she believed he was not there. He embraced her, and congratulated her. This was an example of Arthur Bliss's great understanding of the artist.'[52] She also made the point that wherever she was, whenever she played the Sonata, 'there was always waiting a telegram of good wishes from Sir Arthur Bliss'. She made the point that 'Arthur Bliss was not a man to speak volubly of his deeper emotions. He chose to let his music speak for him... Her performance had to be such that her audience could "hear" what the music had to say... There was a close understanding between composer and performer.'[53]

Wolff was a remarkable personality whose concert dresses were almost as legendary as her playing. As a student of Louis Kentner, she made her debut at the Wigmore Hall aged only ten and played under Barbirolli's baton only five years later. Peter Macleod Miller's obituary of her in 2011 made the point that she felt 'an artist should offer not merely technical brilliance to an audience, but also the mystique of a glamorous lifestyle.'[54]

All this will have fascinated Bliss with its undertones of acting backed up by the wizardry of her technique and depth of musical understanding. She wrote to him in August 1966 to tell him that she was preparing the Sonata for a recording. Bliss responded by saying 'I should like to go through it with you, as I have found players uncertain at times (my fault!) of what I meant…When you feel sufficiently prepared do come and see me.'[55] There was then some pause and in December the following year Wolff invited Bliss to dinner to reignite the project and Bliss wrote enthusiastically to thank her both for her 'exquisite dinner and delightful company' and ending by remarking that 'It may take some time, I believe, to fix a definite date with Pye for recording, but we will hope it will not be too long.'[56] In fact, they had to wait until February 1969 for the sessions. 'Can I come along to the recording room' wrote Bliss, 'or will it embarrass you?'[57] Bliss was delighted with the way she played the work and in May the following year asked if she would play it at the Royal Academy of Music in January 1970 in a concert of his music the Music Teachers' Association was promoting and which he was to introduce. Unable to offer a fee, his invitation was couched in such a way that it was difficult for her to refuse – and she didn't.

A further step was taken when Bliss wrote to Wolff to announce that he had a stereo record player on which to play her Piano Sonata recording. 'I am so grateful to you for the performance: you have done wonders for it. It sounds fine.'[58] In this same letter he mentions the *Miniature Scherzo,* which he wrote for the 125th anniversary of *The Musical Times* that same year (1969). It was based on a phrase from Mendelssohn's Violin Concerto, which was written in 1844, the same year the magazine was founded. This brilliant miniature was dedicated to Wolff, who gave its first performance in a BBC radio series called *Music Magazine* on 1 June 1969.

One further work showed just how much Bliss admired Wolff's playing and how he relied on her in a personal way. His half-sister, Enid, was married in January 1974 and asked for a piece of music from him as a wedding present. *A Wedding Suite* for piano was actually comprised of various mostly pre-existing piano works. In four movements lasting some ten minutes, movements two and three were resurrected from the *Valses Fantastiques,* which Bliss had written all the way back in 1913, and the final movement was *Enid's Blast*, originally for trumpet and piano. Wolff pre-recorded the Suite, which also has Bliss talking about his half-sister, the music and Wolff herself. All this took place after the cutting of the cake.

At the start of 1969 in the New Year's Honours List Bliss was made a KCVO. This is one of most singular Honours of the List as it is in the personal gift of the Queen. 1969 marked Bliss's fifteenth year as Master of the Queen's Musick and there is no doubt of the warmth of feeling on both sides. At the investiture in Buckingham Palace in February the Blisses were accompanied by their ten-year-old grandson, Michael Gatehouse.

An unusual commission came in the form of a request for two hymns for the *Cambridge Hymnal* which were numbers forty-one and ninety-six in the book when published. The *Cambridge Hymnal* was a completely new approach to a hymn book and was edited by the composer Elizabeth Poston and the Literary Editor, David Holbrook, Fellow of King's College, Cambridge, and published in 1967. In Holbrook's Preface, he railed against the 'ugly and poor hymns' that children had to sing in their morning assemblies. The project was an experiment in which the editors 'winnowed' some ten thousand hymns down to around one hundred. To these were added some fifty new hymns, 'mostly settings of religious poems selected by the literary editor.'[59] He adds, 'The resulting collection seems to us to put a new face on the English devotional lyric, whether for school or church. Unobscured by the dross from the nineteenth century, a strong and vigorous tradition is revealed, with all its variety and vitality.'[60] In Elizabeth Poston's Preface she claims that 'No music has been included by any contemporary composer not interested in writing a good and singable tune compatible with the words... It is to be hoped that it will be used – as it has been made – adventurously.'[61]

If Poston's claims that the 'singable tune' was a priority then Bliss's setting of W.H. Auden's *He is the Way* from *The Flight into Egypt* is a good example of the type of esoteric new hymn commissioned for this hymnal. Bliss's tune, rather typically of this collection, is distinctly unmemorable except perhaps for the opening gesture of each verse – a four-note motif, a falling scale: C, B, A and then up to D. It is not that the hymn is not effective, but it relies far too heavily on the progress of the accompaniment, the harmony, to make its musical case. The peremptory 'Amen' is curious and would seem to have a misprint where the vocal part is A and G where the piano part has two Gs. The tune is called *Santa Barbara* and was probably given this name for two reasons: the first verse asks us to 'Follow Him through the Land of Unlikeness; You will see rare beasts and have unique adventures'. This would neatly tie up with Trudy's father's love of just such adventurous expeditions. The third verse ends 'And at your marriage all its occasions shall dance for joy'. Santa Barbara was, of course, where the Blisses were married.

The other contribution Bliss made to the volume was a setting of a poem, *Virtue*, by George Herbert 'Sweet day, so cool, so calm, so bright,

The bridal of the earth and sky, The dew shall weep thy fall to-night; For thou must die'. He called this tune *Pen Selwood* after the location of their house in Somerset. Again, this is musically interesting but melodically clumsy. The first three verses are set in C minor and the final verse is intended as a radiant change into C major. One feels (as with many of the new hymns for this volume) that they are aimed at musicians and certainly not at school assembly or even possibly the more rarified world of a public school chapel. In the case of this hymn Bliss's first two lines are very lyrical and even memorable. But he spoils this with the melody for lines three and four which suddenly become angular and chromatic. Additionally, the major version for the last verse is not the same tune simply put in the major and therefore upsets the feeling of settling into a tune as it progresses. There are some very fine contributions to this collection but it is perhaps of little surprise that it has not achieved the wide use hoped for by its editors.

In June of 1966, Bliss was asked to write a short choral work for the opening of the Queen Elizabeth Hall in the South Bank complex in London. This was an unaccompanied piece called *River Music 1967* to a commissioned text by Cecil Day Lewis, who was to become the Poet Laureate in 1968. There is an interesting sequence of events leading to this commission. On 5 January 1966 John Denison, who had recently moved from the post of Music Director for the Arts Council of Great Britain to being General Manager of the Royal Festival Hall), wrote to Benjamin Britten asking him to be closely involved in the opening ceremonies of the new hall. On the 27 January Denison noted in an internal memorandum that Britten asked him to approach Bliss to write a short introductory piece: 'He was particularly anxious that Bliss should be given this opportunity and that I was to mention his (Britten's) name.'[62] The next day he wrote to Britten to say that Bliss 'was obviously thrilled and delighted, and in particular asked me to let you know how honoured he felt that the suggestion should have come from you....'[63] On the 29 June, Bliss wrote to Denison to tell him that 'Cecil Day Lewis had consented to write a suitable poem for me to set for the Purcell Singers at the Opening of the New Hall....'[64] On 2 July Cecil Day Lewis noted to Denison that the new poem 'is based on the Thames and on music...'. On 7 December, Bliss wrote to Jonathan Elkus in San Francisco to tell him that 'The Queen is opening the new Elizabeth Hall... and I am conducting a new piece for that occasion'.

As Day Lewis noted above, the text connects the new hall with its location on the river Thames and much of its fairly substantial thrust (some seven minutes long – not the 'very short introductory piece' originally conceived by Denison and Britten[65]) is concerned with flow – flow of the river itself, and the flowing of time. Indeed, there are points in this attractive work in which we can see Bliss holding up a mirror to his own life and the passing of time which, like the river, moves inexorably onwards to its final destination. This is poignantly expressed at the text 'the water music ebbs and flows' which Bliss allows to flow freely but brings to a full stop in longer notes and a pause. This feels so personally ruminative that one is almost brought up short.

Interest is maintained in what is a very sectional work by constantly shifting keys between the D major bookends. But perhaps the most beautiful part of the piece is the end. Bliss finds real inspiration in Day Lewis's imagery: 'From here and now, to all time let our proud music flow!' What is unusual from a composer more used to mirroring the fanfare potential in texts is that he sets this to be sung slower with a hint of ground bass, and where it rises to a *forte* on the word 'flow' it falls back as quickly as if someone is standing on the bank shielding their eyes and watching the river flow into the distance. And where the final gesture is a *crescendo* to *forte* the *coup de théâtre* is the sopranos and altos taking flight upwards to be left hanging in the air in triumph but also with a feeling that, as with the flowing river, the final destination is unknown. The first performance was given by the Ambrosian Singers (not the Purcell Singers as originally intended) conducted by Bliss on 1 March 1967. Reviews were far more concerned with reflecting on the new hall and its acoustic to spare much space for either the performance or the music.

More small-scale commissions kept him busy during this time including an anthem for the dedication of the shrine of the Knights Bachelor at the fine church of St Bartholomew the Great, Smithfield in London on 10 July 1968. *Lord, who shall abide in thy Tabernacle?* He sets sections of Psalms 15 and 122 and includes optional trumpeters in the final verse, but even this slightly glitzy effect cannot save this piece from feeling rather careworn and frankly unmemorable. One senses with some of the music from this time his admission that he finds the 'joy of writing music on the wane'. But, in reality, there *are* still some remarkable works yet to come and therefore one has to come to the conclusion that some commissions simply failed to interest him or fire his creative mind and, as we have seen, church anthems were close to the top of this list.

On 7 June 1968 Bliss received a command from Her Majesty the Queen via the Duke of Norfolk as Earl Marshal to compose music for the Investiture of the Prince of Wales at Caernarvon Castle on 1 July the following year. This ceremony had all the dignity and splendour of a coronation at Westminster Abbey. In fact, the setting in the spectacular surroundings of one of Wales's great historic castles, and especially Caernarvon, with its huge internal space ideal for accommodating thousands of onlookers on specially constructed stands, could not have been more impressive. As always, Bliss rose to the occasion with flair and imagination. There were three fanfares for three choirs of three trumpets and trombones placed on three different towers of the castle. The effect must have been extraordinary as one brass choir hurled its congratulatory message across space to be answered by the next and so back to the first.

As well as this he wrote a more extended *Interlude* for military band which was used twice during the ceremony. The fanfares were played by the trumpeters of the Royal Military School of Music, Kneller Hall, and the *Interlude* by the Band of the Royal Welsh Fusiliers. Bliss loved the drama of these occasions and understood instinctively what would work to best effect. Caernarvon Castle was, to him, a stage surrounded by its remarkably preserved walls and towers. He received a letter from Michael Adeane, Private Secretary to The Queen to say 'how much [she] admired your fanfares at Caernarvon. It was a wonderful and impressive ceremony and Her Majesty wishes you to know how greatly your compositions contributed to its beauty.'[66]

Drama of a different kind was required of Bliss for his next small commission. On 22 February he had a letter from Robert J Markarian representing the University of Lehigh's concert band to write a short fanfare which would be played at the football game against Lafayette College on 23 November. The Professor of Music at Lehigh University (Bethlehem, Pennsylvania, USA) was Jonathan Elkus, son of Bliss's great friend, Albert Elkus of the University of Berkeley where Bliss had taught briefly at the start of the Second World War.

Bliss will have wanted to write this piece for his friend's son, and also for such an unusual occasion. He was keen to wear humour on his sleeve when he replied to Markarian on 1 March that 'if, of course, when you receive it, you feel it may lose you the game, you must on no account play it.'[67] Jonathan Elkus replied to this on 22 April, remarking that he 'should not worry that the fanfare might bring us bad luck. We have had such bad football luck for the last few years that the fanfare could not possibly herald anything but a turn to better fortune!'[68] The piece obviously brought them good luck as they won their match that day.

Bliss sent a piano score of the piece to Elkus asking him to 'get it brilliantly set out for your Band.'[69] Elkus replied: 'The Fanfare is marvellous – I have just played it for our Drum Major, and he is also delighted. There will be no problem arranging it for our Band.'[70]

On 24 September Bliss wrote to Elkus to say, 'Trudy and I are now beginning to make our arrangements for our jaunt to New York... We shall fly to New York on Sunday November 10th, and my concert is on Tuesday November 19th. We should like to motor to Lehigh on Thursday (morning or afternoon) the 21st, for the Band-Do on that evening. We should like to see the football game on Saturday (I have never seen one!) – then motor to Philadelphia on Sunday the 24th, and catch the 19.00 Pan American plane back to London.'[71] The concert Bliss refers to was a performance he conducted of *The Beatitudes* to which members of the Hoffman family travelled long distances to attend. Trudy, in particular, was thrilled to have the opportunity of seeing family and friends. She also wrote a colourful description of the football match, which was the last of the season – 'and Arthur's presence in the stands was of as much importance as was his presence at the seminar for composition students. The opposing team, the arch-enemy – Lafayette College, had, I think won every match with Lehigh in the last five years. At half-time the score was even, two goals each; then out came the famous Lehigh band marching up and down the field playing *Salute to Lehigh* superbly, forming and wheeling with the precision of the Guards in Trooping the Colour. And lo! Lehigh scored the only goal in the second half! We travelled back to base in the bus with the band, the boys singing all the way, some of the verses omitted out of deference to their elderly guests. That night we all celebrated, and the next day six of the bandsmen and their girls cooked a traditional Thanksgiving dinner for us before we flew back to London.'[72]

As a postscript to this light-hearted interlude, Bliss was sent a copy by Elkus of the Beatles' record *Sergeant Pepper's Lonely Hearts Club Band*. His response was typical: 'I have not yet had time to play the record, but it will be an exciting moment, as it will – believe it or not – be the first time I have heard any Beatle music! I am expecting to be shattered, and completely change my idiom from now on. I see among the faces on the cover my old friend H.G. Wells, and, in the signatures inside, yours (presumably an inscription) and Vaughan Williams!'[73]

# Chapter Sixteen

# THE CURTAINS CLOSE

The choir taking part in the New York performance of *The Beatitudes* referred to in the last chapter came from the Westminster Choir College at Princeton, and following the performance the President of the College asked Bliss if he would give the Commencement (graduation) address the following June, on which occasion he would also be awarded an honorary Doctorate in Fine Arts. The ceremony was on 30 May 1969, and the Blisses decided to sail to New York rather than fly. The prospect of a relaxing week at sea out of reach of needy people and organisations was a richly pleasurable prospect. Feeling that they would need amusement during the voyage they went to London's Aladdin's Cave toyshop, Hamley's, and purchased what Trudy described as 'an enormous jigsaw puzzle; it was a detailed map of the world, which, with the consent of the steward, we spread out on a table in the bar. Passengers, stewards and even the ship's officers worked at it day after day, but it was a puzzle of such difficulty that only on the last evening of the trip was it nearing completion; we planned a celebration with drinks all round as the final piece should be put in place on sight of land. But this was not to be: during the night a fearsome storm blew up, and as we sailed past the Statue of Liberty, we were still picking up the 2,500 pieces from the floor.'[1]

Bliss's address to the Westminster Choir College students was on the subject of happiness. It is a beautifully crafted speech littered with literary references and sensitively addressing the perennial issue of what the old can tell or advise the young. 'The counsels of old age – said a French thinker – are like the winter sun which gives light but not warmth. But it is precisely *warmth* that is needed in the cold insensitive world of today.'[2]

He stated that 'we have the choice of creating some kind of heaven or some kind of hell *within* ourselves. Remember the two-winged horse that Plato depicted as yoked together in our souls, one violent and brutish, the other spirited but obedient to the will of the charioteer. We are all charioteers on the road of life. Which turning shall we take? Which horse will gain the ascendance.'[3] And in quoting Plato Trudy wrote of how she recognised the man she met back in 1924: 'the high-spirited and gifted young composer of *The Colour Symphony* (sic) who, on the first page of the manuscript of *Hymn to Apollo*, wrote in Greek the following quotation from *Phaedrus*: 'But he who, having no touch of the Muses' madness in his soul, comes to the door and thinks he will get into the temple by the help of art – he, I say, and his poetry are not admitted; the sane man disappears and is nowhere when he enters into rivalry with the inspired madman.'[4]

On this same trip, Bliss was elected an honorary life member of the American Bible Society. Lord Caradon of the United Kingdom Mission to the United Nations invited Dr. Laton Holgren, General Secretary of the American Bible Society to the performance of *The Beatitudes* who in turn invited the American artist, Carl Wuermer who wrote to say 'It was wonderfully impressive to hear Sir Arthur's "Beatitudes"; for one thing – while it was thoroughly 20th century in style, it was happily without the self-conscious, presumptive intellectual double-talk that makes most of the work of contemporary composers of today unhearable; it was obviously written to be "enjoyed" – the breadth and vigor of it brought tears to my eyes.'[5]

Just before this American adventure, the Blisses were thrilled that their daughter Karen and her family moved back to the UK permanently. They moved to Dorset, while Barbara and her family were living in London. So, as Trudy pointed out, the Sellicks visited less frequently but stayed for longer, and it was now lovely that the cousins could get to know each other. A lovely memory of her grandfather from that time came from Barbara's daughter Caroline, a highly successful actress, who remembered that Bliss was 'a very proud, strong, impressive figure in public, then at home he would be a sweet, warm man with us.'[6]

Musically, the song cycle *Angels of the Mind* would seem to clearly express these opposing sides of Bliss's life so beautifully expressed by Caroline: the public and the private Arthur Bliss. More than this, these seven songs were not written to commission or with any particular singer in mind. They simply needed to be written. Bliss's retreats into a more private world are often more interesting than the noisy outpourings of official music or the bigger-scale works which will have attention lavished upon them. To this end, if, in this final chapter, we return to our detective from Chapter One sniffing out clues which would illuminate Bliss's character and personality from listening to his music as he enjoined us to do, then this song cycle is a key piece in that search in the large jigsaw puzzle of Bliss's output.

He turned once again to the poetry of Kathleen Raine with whom he had collaborated for the *Golden Cantata*. Bliss wrote to her telling her of his wish to set more of her poetry to music but in a very different context from the last time. Raine's response was characteristically disbelieving: 'I am overwhelmed that you should have been looking into my poems for an essence worthy of music which they so seldom have captured, I fear. "Worry about money" is still with me, now I wonder how it will go set to music!' And then, in response to a question he posed about her angels:

'Yes, "Angels of the Mind" also remains with me – these are the essence, the lively companions with whom we walk, and without whose presence God helps us down on this ground. The Daimon or guardian angel as the Christians say (though I'm not sure that my daimon was ever a Christian one, he is too free) has always been a lively presence. "The Collective Unconscious" does not seem the right name for so ariel-like a presence....'[7]

At the start of his Westminster Choir College address Bliss made this point: 'What can the old say to the young that will be of much benefit? Even though they themselves were once young, and by turns were rebellious, aspiring, confident and eager, and then depressed, anxious, unsure and sad.'[8] This arch-shape is a surprising admission. If indeed it refers to Bliss himself, and is not merely an illustration generally conceived – but the imminent composition of this unsought song-cycle, the choice of Raine, whose poems seem to have been reference points for him for years, and the tacit admission of his own 'angels of the mind' contained in that word 'Yes' at the start of the previous paragraph (we don't have his letter to her asking the question) show that at this end of his life he is using these enigmatic poems as a sounding board to his inner self, remembering perhaps that none of his works would have existed without the help of a *donné*, which was *his* 'guardian angel'. George Dannatt relates the tale told by Joseph Holbrooke in his 1925 introduction to Bliss's music:

'There is the incident of the demoralized Arthur Bliss who rushed up to me one day in a music house with the dire news that he had run dry, just when his works were required, he said, in every possible direction. I told him he always had all the good fortune, and advised he used this terrible misfortune of running dry to [tell] all the journalists he knew. It was the best copy they could ever hope for. They, and all of us, were bored with the musicians who write too much, who cannot afford to run dry in this dramatic fashion; but no one had ever heard of a musician who *had* run dry. But Bliss would not be comforted: he fled from me, as from a scoffer.'[9]

This is assuredly Bliss before he had either fully accepted that inspiration would not just set his pencil working, and that he *had* a 'guardian angel' which was entirely reliable as long as he waited for it to materialize and show him his direction – and we have seen the myriad different directions from which his *donnés* came.

The poems for *Angels of the Mind* were taken from Reine's collections *Stone and Flower* and *The Pythoness and other poems*, and a curious selection they appear to be, especially when set in motion with *Worry about Money*. And yet it is the very ordinariness of this poem which makes it *extra*ordinary and introduces Raine's first 'angel'. She wrote to Bliss saying 'I wondered what you would do with that first poem and was agreeably surprised'. Me too. Reading it makes one wonder how such a poem could suggest music to a composer when such a line as 'My bank-manager could not sanction my continuance for another day' presents itself, until one remembers that such sentiments could easily form part of an operatic libretto with which Bliss would feel entirely at home.

In fact, what is impressive about this setting, and which Dannatt fails to see in his otherwise insightful introductory comments, is that Bliss is *being* the Daimon to Raine's poems. Here, in this first poem, he sets up an ostinato rhythm in the opening bars' bass line. This is a kind of scotch-snap quaver/dotted crotchet incessant rhythm which the soprano takes up on her entry, reflecting the night-time pulsing of the brain when all our worries are larger than life. It is very skilful, and instead of being surprised by the ordinariness of the imagery (how often has a composer set a poem with a bank manager in a leading role?) we are drawn into her world and realize that through the gentle nudging of her 'angel' or 'daimon' (although she says she has 'no one to advise me') she is drawn to blindly putting a finger on a text in the Bible – imaginatively set as recitative – to realizing that whatever little there is should still be shared. Perhaps, in this case, her sharing is through her words with a sympathetic composer.

336

The darkness of Raine's imagery is particularly bleak in *Lenten Flowers*, in which she describes how each flower has the potential to be instrumental in someone's murderous intent, as in the crucifixion. She ends with the warning; 'Garden by the water clear All must die who enter here'. Dark, with slow-moving chords, the feeling of the funeral march is close to the surface. This song is the closest Bliss comes to Finzi's spare settings with false relations littering the score and a feeling of hopelessness in that final injunction.

In the third poem, *Harvest*, the mere mention of Achilles made the choice of this poem a simple one for Bliss. But the poem itself is another, like the first, where day is to be celebrated as it shields the doubts of night. Day is, here, the angel who fights the battles of the mind and Bliss's setting has a sweeping, forceful energy which carries all before it.

It is interesting that Bliss should write these songs at this moment and should choose these poems. Through all these pages of his life we have seen him reticent in selecting his own choice of words for commissions, using other wordsmiths as his 'angels of the mind' choosing texts for him. But here, with no commission and just an urge to write, we see him quite purposefully choosing difficult poems with colourful imagery but all concerned with life and death. It is as if he is taking pause to consider, as he approaches the end of his seventies, both the new life of his grandchildren and perhaps, more personally, the end of his own life, which is only some five years away.

The sixth of the seven songs, *Storm*, is Bliss at his most forceful and furious: 'God in me the four elements of storm Raging in the shelterless landscape of the mind Outside the barred doors of my Goneril heart'. This final image is the most intriguing, implying obsession with power as in Shakespeare's *King Lear* character and which brings the most dramatic music of the whole cycle. The final *Nocturne* is a beautiful but dark farewell. Earlier songs have seen the night as a threatening force to be overcome by day. Here, the final angel stands guard, but Raine writes that 'It would be peace to lie still in the still hours at the angel's feet... but hearts another measure beat'. This tussle between night and day seems to obsess Raine and to find a common thread with Bliss whose reactions are amongst his most personal, thoughtful and enigmatic. This is reflected in the open fifth final chord of the cycle, which mirrors the uncertainty of the final throw: 'where float somewhere the islands of the blest.'

Bliss wrote of the work that 'For a long time I wanted to set some of Kathleen Raine's poems, but they seemed to me as delicate as flowers or shells, and I hesitated to spoil their fragile beauty…They are charged with human emotion, as if the poet had undergone a deeply affecting experience. She allowed me to call this song cycle *Angels of the Mind*, because she writes of angels, both terrible and comforting, in the same spirit as Rilke did.'[10] Raine wrote to Bliss after the BBC broadcast of the cycle on 16 December 1969 to say 'I listened to *Angels of the Mind* last night with strange, overwhelming emotion. That voice was so pure – what a lovely singer she is (Rae Woodland accompanied by Lamar Crowson) – and you had so understood the <u>pure voice</u> that sings from somewhere beyond ourselves. I have <u>heard</u> that voice when I have written poems, tho' I had not hoped I had uttered it. But your music did, and gave wings to that angel. … I wondered what you would do with that first poem but was agreeably surprised. The last was beautiful. And the charming fish – No, it is an exquisite work, and you must be happy, as I was, in your soprano.'[11]

1969 brought with it one of the most potentially disastrous acts of cultural vandalism of his time. The BBC's finances were 'a mess', to quote a parliamentary debate on the issue, and amongst the suggested savings was the disbanding of most of the Corporation's orchestras, its chorus and even closing down the Third Programme[12] as its budget was huge and its audience small.[13] The publication of a BBC paper on the future direction of the Corporation clarified their intentions. *Broadcasting in the Seventies* suggested that the BBC needed only five of its eleven ensembles (BBC Symphony Orchestra, Scottish Symphony Orchestra, The Northern Dance Orchestra, The London Studio Players and the BBC Chorus) which inevitably resulted in serious protests from the unions, musicians and politicians. Bliss weighed in heavily as the country's senior composer who had also been a past Director of Music at the Corporation. But in the end Harold Wilson's government intervened to ensure that the BBC maintained more or less the status quo in exchange for allowing the Corporation to raise the licence fee in 1971.

During this serious period of uncertainty, with hundreds of jobs threatened, arguments raged on both sides with Patrick Gordon Walker, MP for Leyton, stating that 'On the matter of orchestras, I agree with my Right Honourable Friend the Postmaster-General that anything that checks the training and employment of musicians is deplorable… if a considerable patronage element is to continue in the BBC's expenditure on music, we must give it enough money to discharge this function. Patronage is not a possible function for a corporation that we are keeping very short of money.'[14] H.P.G. Channon, MP for Southend West, made the following points in the same debate: 'The BBC wants to cut out three orchestras, the BBC Chorus and the training orchestra, and discussions are going on with the Arts Council about a number of other orchestras. I have no idea what the Arts Council can do. It does not possess a bottomless purse. The BBC might as well have discussions with the Government about providing extra cash. Lord Goodman does not produce cash out of the air, magician though he is in many ways. The Government will have to provide the cash, and if it is to be provided, that is a decision for Parliament. Musical standards have risen enormously in this country over the past few years, and opportunities have also greatly increased, but there is still much to be done. There is a great deal to be done in musical education. The BBC has played an important role in this, but the musical education system in this country is not yet satisfactory.'[15] And so the arguments developed on both sides. We see similar points being made today with regard to musical education in schools. Fortunately, the Wilson government could see the value of what the BBC could offer when properly funded and, to a great extent, this status quo has been maintained to this day.

The national anthem has been subject to remarkably few serious arrangements until recent times, but Bliss was asked to provide a substantial new arrangement by the Royal Choral Society for their American tour, and first performed in Burlington, Vermont, USA in October 1969. Given his position as Master of the Queen's Musick, making an arrangement of this tune was significant and he certainly went to town on it, including setting the controversial second verse which is almost always omitted when the whole anthem is sung. It enjoins us to scatter our enemies, confound their politics and frustrate their knavish tricks. The verse begins, 'O Lord our God arise, Scatter her enemies And make them fall'. On the word 'fall' Bliss writes an accented, *fortissimo* minor seventh for a horn player. One can almost feel his glee at this comedic touch. One of the most significant effects is where, at the start of verse three, the choir is left unaccompanied and *piano* with the tune given to the altos and the sopranos given a gentle descant on top. The orchestra rejoins for the second half and grows towards a resplendent ending. This is a fine arrangement which deserves to be more often used on occasions where space is given in a programme.

Bliss's friend, the inimitable John Amis, wrote a list of Bliss's works which he would take to a desert island (as in the BBC's long-running series *Desert Island Discs*). Top of his list was one of the Fanfares written for Princess Margaret's wedding in 1960. He wrote of it that 'it is a brilliant tiny piece, marvellously scored as always, and in one minute manages to be a complete piece, with a beginning, middle, recapitulation and end. It bangs the drum, clashes the cymbals and contains a damn good tune.'[16] Amongst his other choices was Bliss's next work: *The World is Charged with the Grandeur of God*. Amis appropriately described it as 'a work, not of a *grand papa*, but of a *vieillard terrible*', which is, of course, a reference to Bliss's early reputation as an *enfant terrible*.

The Cantata, *The World is Charged with the Grandeur of God*, came into being as a result of a request from Peter Pears for a work for a concert he planned called *Musica Senectutis* – music by composers who were still busy well into their seventies. The other composers included were Schütz, Verdi, Fauré, Haydn and Stravinsky. It was Pears who chose the texts for Bliss (as the dedication acknowledges) and he opted for the visionary, mystical word-world of the Jesuit priest-poet Gerard Manley Hopkins, a unique voice in English poetry. This work is unlike any other in Bliss's output and there really is nothing against which to measure it except on its own exceptional merits. Bliss was completely taken with the soundscape of Hopkins's poems; he opted for a brass ensemble of three trumpets and four trombones for the outer movements, and two flutes with upper voices from the choir for the second.

Whether the theme of the concert had any bearing on the almost electrically charged settings in the outer movements it is impossible to say. However, being asked for a work that demonstrates your youthful vigour two years from your eightieth birthday would seem to some a spur to show a good degree of *vigoroso*. Certainly, Pears's choice of poems helped Bliss's sense of *joie de vivre*, picking up on Hopkins's characteristically alliterative style. Just the opening lines of the first poem, *God's Grandeur*, serve as a good example: 'The World is charged with the grandeur of God. It will flame out, like shining from shook foil; It gathers to a greatness, like the ooze of oil, Crushed…'. Hopkins simply loves the sheer *sound* of words. There is inherent in these settings much of Bliss's long experience of writing for brass, and some of his naturally evolved fanfare style. To this extent the word painting relating to individual images like, for instance, 'the ooze of oil,' is limited as Bliss is more concerned with a scene rather than the minutiae within it. This is very different from, for instance, Kenneth Leighton's approach in his fine setting of the same words.

There are truly magical things which contrast with the posturing of Hopkins's 'grandeur', and especially lines which clearly touched Bliss deeply: 'And for all this, nature is never spent; There lives the dearest freshness deep down things…'. The melifluous *piano* brass writing here, mirrored by the typically angular, but nevertheless lyrical vocal lines, feels deeply personal, and Bliss must have read it that way. 'Nature is never spent' is Trudy's passion for botany, and 'There lives the dearest freshness deep down things' surely refers to their long, happy and supportive marriage. It is a moment of reflection almost like a perennially closed door which, for once, is seen ajar and promises insights from the other side, only to close once more when we get up close.

The second movement, *I have Desired to Go*, is one of Bliss's most inspired three and a half minutes of music. In an odd way this music feels tired, and while it has a beautifully pastoral atmosphere, the text takes us to another life which, one cannot help feeling, sounds attractive to Bliss: 'Where the green swell is in the heavens dumb, And out of the swing of the sea' – and it is 'out of the swing' of the heavily pressurized, publicly demanding life he has created for himself that he might harbour thoughts of 'what if?' at times and aged seventy-eight. This beautiful music feels like a dreamscape, and a happy one, too.

The third movement, *Look at the Stars*, returns to the big-scale, brass world of the first movement but responds in more detail to textual variations. Bliss's skill here is to make this movement grow from the gentle scena of the previous movement and to incorporate lyrical elements from it almost if he is reluctant to relinquish the dreamscape of Hopkins's imagery. His final five bars where the word 'look' is insistently repeated seems to say 'look deeper'. Hopkins has asked us to 'look' earlier as he makes powerful points about nature ('The world is charged with the grandeur of God) and how the power of nature deepens belief in God the Creator: 'Christ and his mother and all his hallows'. Bliss may have been agnostic in his faith but these words will have spoken powerfully to him. The extraordinary thing is how Peter Pears was unwittingly Bliss's guardian angel on this occasion, providing his *donnée* and giving him the opportunity not only of demonstrating just how fertile he still was – the theme of the concert – but, in his choice of poems, how personal this work turned out to be.

Stanley Sadie, writing in the *Times*, described Bliss as 'that happily vigorous septuagenarian' and that on the evidence of this new work 'is as inventive, as brimful of ideas as ever.'[17] This was the year of the great fire at Snape when the all-too-recently built Maltings (1967) burnt down and alternative venues had to be found quickly for the festival concerts. Bliss's work was therefore heard in the serene surroundings of Blythborough church in which 'angels of the mind' were much more present hovering above in one of Suffolk's beautiful angel roofs.

Bliss's connection with Aldeburgh was further cemented by a request from Mstislav Rostropovich for a Cello Concerto for the 1970 Aldeburgh Festival. In fact, in an interview Bliss gave to BBC Radio Solent in 1973 he said that 'For a good many years the famous Russian cellist, Rostropovich, had been badgering me for a work, as he had been badgering most of the living composers, and I had other things to do, but finally I got down to it and I wrote it for first performance at the Aldeburgh Festival with of course Rostropovich playing and Benjamin Britten conducting.'[18] This would be Bliss's fourth and last concerto and his response to the commission, as he stated in the Festival programme, was illuminating: 'I have always wanted to write some music for solo cello and orchestra; ever since as a young man I played through the classic repertoire for the instrument with my cellist brother, Howard. But it is only now that the decisive impulse has come, as a result of a suggestion of Mstislav Rostropovich. I sketched out the music in the spring of 1969, and on his acceptance of the dedication, "To Mstislav Rostropovich, with admiration and gratitude", made the final full score this March. It is a light-hearted work, at any rate in the first and third movements, and is scored for a Mozartian orchestra, with the addition of harp and celesta. There are no problems for the listener – only for the soloist!'[19]

Bliss originally called it *Concertino*, but Britten persuaded him to change the title to *Concerto* as he felt it to be a major work that deserved the title.

Bliss did himself no favours in either remark; that the concerto was 'light-hearted' or that it posed no problems for the listener. The first diminished expectations, and the second caused the writer Robert Miekle to comment that 'Yet when it is all over, we are left pondering that apparently encouraging remark from the composer, that "there are no problems for the listener", and to propose that the finest and most enduring works do in fact challenge the listener, pose problems, lay before us issues....'[20] But why does a piece of music *have* to be difficult to bear the approbation of the ages? Miekle, himself, argues the cunning and ingenuity of the construction while seemingly being frustrated by more obvious aural links between movements. Stanley Sadie, again, in the *Times* wrote that 'The piece is artfully scored. The orchestra is small and the textures are kept lucid and transparent; there are ingenuities, too, like the association of flute with muted trumpet or of horn with harp harmonics. The cello Cantilena of the Larghetto is firmly placed in the centre of the stage. Rostropovich made it speak eloquently, and its language did not seem in the least foreign to him.'[21] Sadie also noted that the Concerto 'does not merit the diminutive. It is 26 minutes long, and though not pretending to be deep or searching it emerges as a pretty substantial piece, with even a touch of the heroic about it.'[22]

So much for 'official' criticism. This work comes in direct line from a very late flowering following *Angels of the Mind* and *The World is Charged*. To this writer's mind it represents a substantial development, not in terms of style, but of content and, perhaps, a glimpse through an open door. It may be finally offering us a view of Bliss's internal world, and thus an opportunity to learn just a little more about him through his music. Miekle also suggests that Bliss's outmoded idiom compared with contemporary works by Nicholas Maw, Tippett, Berio, Morton Feldman, Elisabeth Lutyens and Stockhausen have made these other composers more enduring, and the fact that Rostropovich gave another premiere – by Lutoslawski – later in the year somehow proved the point. From a distance of some twenty years since those comments were made it is highly question-able as to whether *any* of these composers are really at the top of the music-loving public's listening list. Or maybe he is asserting that music can only have lasting value if it teases the musical literati, never mind that the public might find it both attractive as well as intellectu-ally teasing. At this late stage I find myself becoming an apologist for a composer about whom I have been solidly agnostic; surely a good example of a cutting from an attractive distant shrub taking root and flowering in one's own garden.

One of the things this work shows most clearly is just how, at this stage of his life, Bliss does not have to make a point any more. He does not have to make people sit up, saying 'This is Arthur Bliss, listen to me.' Thus, we have increasingly inward music, a far greater reliance on lyricism, conso-lation (did he write anything more beautifully consoling than the end of the slow movement of the Cello Concerto?) and a willingness, finally, to share himself a little more openly with us. Two further things here: this concerto connects strongly with a long distant past through his brother Howard, a fine cellist in his day who made recordings in the days of the 78rpm disc. This is another example of long shadows cast, as indeed is the second point: Bliss had a delayed start to his career because of his war service, which then connects with his brother, Kennard, whose life was lost so young. But this delay, as we saw earlier in this story, was what made the young Bliss do something completely different from his British contemporaries. So, it would seem that this concerto is actually a deeply personal work given motivation, as ever, by the inspirational playing of one of the great performers of the day.

Some emphasis has been placed in the preceding chapters on Bliss's seeming inability to write a memorable melodic line. In this final stage there is more serene lyricism than has been evident before. These are still not really memorable or easily singable lines, but they are *Bliss's* melodic lines – his way of expressing himself through melody. It is often angular, but now we can recognize some of those stretching intervals as yearning, straining upwards to find a goal and falling to a resolution. Ruth Gipps described it well in her seventy-fifth birthday tribute to him, when she wrote: 'His melodic line is often (though not always) widely spaced, with upward leaps of a 9th; what matters is that it is a melodic line.'[23] Bliss is endlessly compared with Elgar by commentators, and the comparison is not entirely fruitless, but Bliss's method is wholly different and his *is* a language of his day. The change from his early 'experiments in sound' came about partly through the need to write larger scale works and in the process of extending his reach he realized that he wanted to express himself emotionally, not simply intellectually. This led naturally to what some felt was a regression from being an experimenter (for which he was also criticised) to a romantic. But these 'boxes' do not allow for gradations, or for comparison to be made with his national contemporaries whose language, taking the Vaughan Williams 'school' as a leading example, is steeped in heart-on-the-sleeve expression however many exceptions there may be of a Fourth Symphony type. All Bliss's music relates to the here and now and he was never one to dig deep into our national past, whether of the Tudor period or folksong, and base a movement around it. As we have seen, once the Russian school of Stravinsky was in his bloodstream from those early Diaghilev performances witnessed as a young man, they never left him, and Stravinsky remained a hero for life.

Even in this late Cello Concerto, the climax of the second movement suddenly moves from lyrical Bliss into classic Stravinsky of *Petrouchka* or *Firebird*. There are only a few bars (even the orchestration pays homage) but it is like pulling a favourite book from a library shelf, glancing fondly, and returning it, allowing the Blissian resumption of its path to the movement's magical conclusion.

In 1969, an unusual relationship developed between Bliss and the remarkable Leicestershire Schools Symphony Orchestra, under its inspirational conductor Eric Pinkett. This was a true swansong, which would lead on beyond Bliss's death. Pinkett was a unique force, arriving in the county in 1948 to create the County School of Music. Out of this grew the Leicestershire Schools Symphony Orchestra, which he trained to achieve an unusual standard of professionalism. Not only this, but he pioneered recordings that included the first ever disc devoted to the music of Havergal Brian in 1972, then aged ninety-six. In line with this focus on introducing the schoolchildren to contemporary composers (Tippett was their President and a regular conductor), they gave a performance of Bliss's Piano Concerto with Frank Wibaut as soloist. This relationship developed further in 1970 as the orchestra recorded his *Introduction and Allegro*, with Bliss himself conducting. Then came a commission from the Isle of Man Arts Council for the schoolchildren of the island (some six hundred of them) together with the Leicestershire Schools Symphony Orchestra for a short work for upper voices and orchestra to be performed in the Arts Festival at Douglas on 16 April 1971. For texts he turned to a volume of *The Folk Lore of the Isle of Man* by A.W.Moore for *The Mountain Plover*, and to *The Atlantic Book of British and American Poetry* edited by Edith Sitwell for *Flowers in the Valley*.

Trudy remembered that they went to hear the performance 'and were enchanted by the performance under the LSSO's inspired conductor, Eric Pinkett. This, like the visit to Lehigh, left me with the magical memory of someone very old in harmonious accord with the very young.' She went on to recall how seemingly half the population of the island went down to the pier to see the orchestra off very early the following morning. 'Such sight and sound! There were the Leicestershire school-children grouped on the stern of the steamer, making music for us as it got underway.'[24]

The final, and most remarkable venture with this organisation, was when Bliss was approached for a new ballet in October 1974 as the County Music Department was expanding to open a new ballet school. At this stage he was not prepared to write a new score but suggested that the ballet, *The Lady of Shalott*, would make an ideal substitute. In November, a group of seven dancers who would take part in the perfor-mance travelled to London to visit Bliss in his home. Thames Television filmed the occasion for a documentary about its preparation and performance. Early in the film we see the girls listening avidly to Bliss describing and playing some of his music for the ballet on the piano. Perhaps most moving of all is seeing Pinkett sitting on the sofa with the girls, and watching their impressions as Bliss talks in a 'mother hen' type of way. How privileged they were to be exposed to so much in the way of cultural riches, especially coming from diverse backgrounds, as they did. Part of the film has the leading girl walking through the estate on which she lives and describing how functional it is ('I suppose it's alright in the summer when the sun shines'), but the magical world being offered to balance this is beyond anyone's expectations of the time, and was unique in the country.

Bliss was not able to see this exciting project come to fruition. The footage of the Thames documentary is fascinating, as much as anything for the opportunity to see him still talking with energy and enthusiasm, as well as playing the piano accurately and with sensitivity, so close to his own death.

In July 1970, Bliss was awarded another honorary Doctorate, in Letters this time from the University of Lancaster, and in a nice gesture so close to the premiere of his Cello Concerto, he was able to present the Gold Medal of the Royal Philharmonic Society to Rostropovich in October. This was the year, too, of the publication of *As I Remember*, his autobiography. There were many letters of congratulations amongst which was this generous tribute from his old friend, Herbert Howells:

> Nothing else cd give me greater joy than that your autobiography is a <u>fact</u>, for you and Trudy and for all who, over the years, have taken enormous pride in what you have done, and been, and accomplished. And your sending me a copy has touched me very much...It's a wonderful record of a life that seems to have maintained an almost perpetual energy and interest: with an extraordinary freedom from the useless 'ivory tower' state that might so easily have put you out of reach of your fellow-composers and the large common interests that matter so much to the whole profession of music. You and Trudy ought to be, and surely <u>must</u> be so happy in looking back and still enjoying everything 'As I Remember' has confirmed and made so clear. My affection for you goes on and on to my joy.
>
> Bless you both! Yrs Herbert

It is touching to read Trudy's deeply personal memories, written after Bliss's death, of aspects of their relaxation time together and how much the natural world features, especially birds. For instance, she wrote of their visits to East Anglia and of how they had often 'gone in May or

June to Dunwich, very handy for the bearded tits in the bird reserve at Minsmere. There, our room looked out on a lawn across which a pair of fly-catchers swooped morning and afternoon. Arthur's pleasure in the flight and song of birds sparkles through all my memories. For instance, the white front of the dipper gleaming at us from a stone at the edge of a Scottish loch; and another dipper a few years later (swimming under water this time) in a rushing river near Annecy; the flock of scarlet ibis going to roost one twilight when we were in Florida with the London Symphony Orchestra; while the return of the swifts each spring to the sky above our London garden was always a cause for celebration.'[25] She goes on to single out the *Golden Cantata* as being a favourite work because of its celebration of birds, and especially the introduction to the sixth movement.

Bliss's extraordinary Indian summer of composition continued with one of his most remarkable piano works, which was also the last he wrote for the instrument, *Triptych*. In the programme note for its first performance he rather touchingly noted, 'With this *Triptych* written last year (1970) I return to my first love, the piano. My very first published works were a jejune *Intermezzo*, a *Suite*, and a set of *Valses Fantastiques* written when I was at Cambridge, and now luckily unobtainable.'[26] The connection with Louis Kentner, warmly kindled through Marguerite Wolff and the recording of his *Piano Sonata*, blossomed into a friendship which resulted in this work and the dedication, 'with admiration and gratitude' and noting his help. Kentner gave the first performance of the work at the Queen Elizabeth Hall on 21 March 1971. Bliss had written to Kentner on 23 April 1970, offering him 'two concert pieces', *Romance* and *Capriccio*, but he decided to expand this to the three-movement work as it now stands and name it *Triptych*. The first movement was changed from a subjective *Romance* to a more objective *Meditation*.

In July, Kentner wrote to ask if Bliss would become a Patron of the Liszt Society, which he accepted 'with pride'. By 9 September Bliss was referring to the *Triptych* in a letter to Kentner suggesting that he would 'very much like one more go with you through *Triptych* before it goes to my copyist.'[27] Early February saw him still making small amendments to the *Capriccio* (third movement) and sending them to Kentner, and finally on 22 March writing to Kentner to thank him for 'that splendid performance'.

What is especially noteworthy in the *Triptych* is its apparent inwardness, its self-reflection and its foot in the door which we have noted was left just sufficiently ajar to allow us to see an Arthur Bliss rarely granted to us perhaps especially in the headier 'romantic' works. In fact, it is those more heart-on-the-sleeve works which lead us further down a blind alley in our search.

Throughout this story it is mainly the chamber works, some songs, and piano works that allow Bliss to express those 'thoughts that do often lie too deep for tears' as Wordsworth beautifully concludes his *Intimations of Immortality*. In fact, it is telling that Bliss connects this final piano work with his very first. His mind will have been partly dwelling on a long distant past and meditating (the title of the first movement of the *Triptych*) on eighty years of musical development and its forms of expression. The opening of *Meditation* seems to suggest those ticking clocks that preoccupied the youthful Bliss and which his father had to cover up as he felt the danger of fascination turning into obsession.

The opening may be based on a syncopated figure, but the start on a single note and the figure then taking life, growing into an ostinato which sits somewhere in the tenor register has the regularity of clockwork and the mood seems one of regret. If this long distant memory was in his mind, then the ghost of his brother also hovers close to this old domestic surface. Music critics and biographers are sometimes, perhaps often, guilty of reading too much into a perfectly innocent piece of music with the aim of enlivening a storyline. This writer could well be guilty as charged, but impressions can be valid whether or not their composer had such thoughts. In old age there is a tendency to reflect on the past and a movement called *Meditation* invites speculation as to what it is which is being meditated upon. Of course, we do not know, but such a small thing as those repeated notes, setting this whole powerful movement going, are highly suggestive. Bliss wrote of this movement that 'The Meditation is naturally reflective, but not unduly introspective.'[28] Stylistically, the language is fairly uncompromising with its undoubted lyricism having to fight its corner against a highly dissonant landscape. These pieces are uncompromising and not necessarily easy for an audience who will need concentration to appreciate the musical riches of this eighteen minutes of music. Only the *Capriccio*, third movement, displays an underlying sense of fun – but fun with a dark edge (the actor's black and white mask comes to mind again).

The second movement, *Dramatic Recitative*, Bliss described by saying that 'the drama in the "Recitative" rests on the contrast between rhetorical statements and bravura passages.'[29] This movement is incredibly dark and acts as a development from the first movement. There are hints of anger there, but this movement seems to be letting rip at some demon, its ending simply inconclusive – unfinished business. Quite how the *Times* critic, Joan Chissell, could sum the work up by limply stating: 'In sum a tellingly contrasted concert suite for those who like their contemporary music without tears' is inexplicable unless Kentner's performance was lacking in the obvious emotional undercurrent which, having been schooled by Bliss, is unlikely.[30] We know from John Amis that Bliss was capable of extremes of emotion and we have to accept that his music was a way of channelling such feelings. Rather like his father covering up the clocks, deep emotions were kept hidden.

This work is a very good example of why Bliss liked to work with pianists who were going to play his works. Recordings of this *Triptych* show just how different interpretations affect the whole feeling of structure and therefore its strength even in an apparently reflective movement – but reflective of what? There is intense lyricism in the *Meditation* which needs to lead the structure, and short phrase marks should not imply constant pulling and pushing of the tempo. We have seen how much care he took over Marguerite Wolff's performance and recording of the *Piano Sonata*. Here he will have taken equal care with Kentner. Composers who have a very definite concept of how their music should progress in performance need therefore either to mark their scores with clear directions or provide prefatory material which performers can read in order to better understand what is required of them. The enigmatic sound world of this work leaves too many questions unanswered and therefore too much licence to the performer not fortunate enough to have the benefit of the composer's personal advice.

The composer, conductor, pianist and oboist Ruth Gipps was a passionate devotee of Bliss's music. She was a child prodigy who grew into the profession with enormous energy not only as a concert pianist but also playing the oboe and cor anglais in professional orchestras. She founded the London Repertoire and London Chanticleer Orchestras. She was fortunate in developing a close relationship with the City of Birmingham Orchestra and their conductor George Weldon who performed a significant number of her works. To mark her admiration and respect for Bliss she dedicated her Fourth Symphony of 1972 to him, and this firmly cemented their friendship. They began corresponding back in 1952 when she asked if she could go through his Piano Concerto with him. There is a certain coolness on Bliss's part at this point ending by saying 'I think it really would be better if you wrote one yourself and played that.'[31] But they met at Steinways' studio to go through it and Bliss took her to lunch afterwards. Her devotion to his music and the number of works she conducted was remarkable and included *Checkmate*, *Knot of Riddles*, the *Introduction and Allegro*, *Meditations of a Theme by John Blow* and *A Colour Symphony* in June 1971 after which Bliss wrote 'I <u>must</u> write to thank you for your exciting performance of my Colour Symphony. That you conducted it with unfailing accuracy without a score added to the great compliment you paid me.'[32]

Just before dedicating her Fourth Symphony to Bliss, she had written a deeply searching article on Bliss's *Meditations on a Theme by John Blow* in *Composer* – the magazine issued by the Composers' Guild of Great Britain. In it she claimed in particular that Bliss's orchestration 'has achieved a mastery almost unique among contemporary composers… with every individual part as gratefully written and as shapely as a piece of chamber music.'[33] She went on to say: 'Speaking as a performing musician, I place him unhesitatingly among the giants, and believe that a number of his works…will receive the highest accolade of all, that of being standard works in later centuries'. Her reservation about the *Meditations* and the reason she felt for its comparative neglect is due to its 'curiously inept' title which 'somehow implies the dullest kind of pastiche'.

Bliss wrote to her on reading this article, and in recognition of all her championship of his music:

'Dear Wid, What a debt, past, present and future, I am piling up, to repay to you for all your generous words and deeds! Trudy and I read your appreciation of the *Meditations* with glowing eyes. What naturally pleased me so much was a fellow composer's insight into the work. "Phrase after phrase of Blow's theme is glimpsed like smooth rocks seen through the ripples", "At one point a voice…seems to shout in a desperate attempt at prayer, etc." Yes, indeed, but no one hitherto has expressed this so imaginatively…And then, of course, you write from inner knowledge having given so much of my music so splendidly. Now we await the Symphony that is to be mine in a setting that is really worthy of it. Trudy joins me in affection and gratitude. AB.[34]

That symphony *is* a remarkable work and Bliss was effusive in his praise of it and his thanks for its dedication. 'You have given me a splendid work, so varied and inventive…I am sure that no critic, who did not have the good fortune that I had, to follow its progress in the full score, could rightly judge your achievement. It is a big work, and full of fascinating detail…you were aware, I am sure, of the impact that this work made as you conducted it.'[35]

In a continuing friendship, and knowing that she looked out for up-and-coming talent, Bliss was so impressed with the young cellist,

Julian Lloyd Webber, that he wrote to recommend him to her: 'Can I bring to your attention, if you do not know him, a brilliant young cellist, Julian Lloyd Webber… I first heard him in the Prokofiev Concerto at the College, and yesterday he came up here with a friend at the piano, and played my own Concerto through by heart with absolute mastery. I was astounded!'

Gipps wanted to throw her hat in the ring when the Royal College of Music was looking to appoint a successor to Sir Keith Falkner on his retirement as Director in 1972. She asked if Bliss would be one of her referees. He wrote a serious and considered reply to her request saying that he would, of course, support her but, 'The Head of the RCM or any other musical academy ipso facto says goodbye to being an <u>artist</u>. He must be a full-time administrator struggling to raise money, to deal with the problems of the students, their parents, and especially the staff, many of whom are elderly and difficult, going to conferences and educational meetings, etc etc ad nauseam. I think it madness for you, with your fine talents, to submit yourself, unless it is entirely for financial reasons.'[36] He goes on to mention the 'sex difficulties, even to-day with a woman as judge, as senior doctors, as Cabinet ministers'. He urges her to think hard again but assures her of his support if she decides to apply. Happily, his advice was heeded.

1971 saw Bliss's eightieth birthday. In the Queen's Birthday Honours, he was given the singular honour of membership of the Order of Companions of Honour, an order limited to a maximum of sixty-five members. He received a letter from the Queen Mother's Private Secretary to 'convey to you Her Majesty's warmest congratulations on the Honour which you have received on the occasion of the Queen's Official Birthday.'[37] He also received a telegram from Buckingham Palace: 'my warmest congratulations on your 80th birthday, and my very best wishes, Elizabeth R'.

In May he received a letter from the headmaster of his old prep school, Bilton Grange, asking him for a composition to celebrate the school's centenary in 1973, and also in the hope that he would be able to attend the celebrations. Tim Fisher writes, enticingly, 'as you are looked on, without doubt, as our most distinguished old boy.'[38] Bliss had written by this, 'Well! Well!' It is a strange thing that however distinguished he might have become, the horrors of that youthful experience still hover in the mind. The commission never materialised, but here was another early life experience recalled.

Bliss's eightieth year was full of tributes, concerts, gifts and a general show of affection for his life of service as well as composer. Writing in the *Times* on 14 July, William Mann wrote that 'Anybody surveying the musical diary for this summer, and observing the quantity of concerts in honour of Arthur Bliss's 80th birthday scattered through these months might wonder when Sir Arthur's birthday actually takes place. The answer is August 2. On that evening the Proms will be giving their salute to Bliss: others, plenty of them…have to give their birthday concerts as and when…The Bruckner-Mahler Choir recently made a record of Bliss's *Pastoral*. The London Chamber Orchestra backed this disc with *A Knot of Riddles* sung by their first interpreter, John Shirley Quirk.'[39]

The day following his birthday, 3 August, a concert was given at the Victoria and Albert Museum by Philomusica. The first half included a specially commissioned work by Elgar Howarth to celebrate Bliss's birthday (complete with a 'happy birthday to you' woven into the texture at the end). After the interval the strings of the orchestra played Vaughan Williams's *Fantasia on a Theme of Thomas Tallis*, Elgar's *Introduction and Allegro*, and Bliss's own *Music for Strings* which Stephen Walsh in the *Times* described as 'one of the best string works by him or anyone else since the First World War.'[40] And while on the subject of this work, Bliss received a letter from Neville Cardus, the long-time music critic of the *Manchester Guardian* to say, 'More than thirty years ago I wrote these words about *Music for Strings*: "one of the finest works written in recent years…the canvas is filled out accurately and sonorously…the melody is fluid…the music is poetic or fanciful always, never just dexterous. The performance (in Manchester) was good enough to revere the genius of the composition." And, Sir Arthur, I have never used the word genius without a responsible sense of what the word means.'[41]

And so it went on. In the concert at the South Bank given by the London Chamber Orchestra Bliss was presented with a portrait commissioned by them from William Lennox Bisset which elicited this response from Bliss, 'When I feel downhearted I shall look at it and think what a formidable fellow I really am'.

The two major organisations with which he had been closely involved for many years, the Performing Right Society and the Composers' Guild made special gifts. At the Prom concert the PRS presented him with a Lyrita record of his works: *Melée Fantasque, Rout, Hymn to Apollo, Serenade,* and *The World is Charged with the Grandeur of God* conducted by Bliss himself, Brian Priestman and Philip Ledger. But perhaps even more touching than this was the Composers' Guild's two volumes of twenty-three short works written in Bliss's honour by a galaxy of his contemporaries including William Alwyn, Malcolm Arnold, Lennox

Berkeley, Benjamin Britten and many others. His old friend, the artist George Dannatt, gave him a painting using only the four colours of his *Colour Symphony*, purple, red, blue and green. They had some correspondence about the colours as far back as 1965 in which he wrote: 'instead of having one colour in mind, as it were, throughout the work, I had 4 distinct Ripolin ones (a commercial brand of paint), purple, red, blue and green. They are not my favourites, which incidentally are a primrose yellow, a Picasso blue (as seen in his beach picture) and dark green as used on old railway carriages (very beautiful) and gold.'[42]

Bliss's response to the gift of the 'Colour Symphony' painting was excited: 'Dear Giorgio, I have just unwrapped the painting and am filled with admiration for it, right at the first glance. I feel it is very much ME, and of course related to the Colour Symphony intimately. Trudy and I immediately tried it on the stair wall where it gets strong light from the big east window and where one passes it often going up and down the stairs...What a lovely thing it is to be 80! Love and grateful thanks from Arthur'.[43] This brings up the constant flow of gifts especially from the Dannatts to the Blisses. On one occasion Ann, whose nickname between them was 'Sly Pussy' (Trudy described her as having 'sly wit') sent a hammer, presumably to help with the hanging of pictures. Bliss responded with great excitement: 'Dearest of Sly Pussies, Your present was as usual <u>unimaginable</u>, and yet immediately straight to the point. When the hammer was revealed Trudy at once said "That's mine!" "No", I said, "It's <u>mine</u>!" Mine! No mine! Let go! I won't! Finally, the inscription settled it, and Trudy, baffled, released it. George's lovely painting does not need the fixtures, but some others, lying around, do....'[44]

That exclamation claiming that the painting is 'very much me' shows how much Bliss loved contemporary art, and with Dannatt's serious knowledge of music both as critic and practitioner they had much in common. Dannatt was an abstract painter (and collector) inspired by the St. Ives School modernists. Bliss found Dannatt's work moved him deeply, thus conversation and exchange of ideas was part of the natural flow of friendship which developed deeply over the years. We only need to remember the modernist design of Pen Pits to be reminded how important contemporary expression was to him. Bliss often visited the Dannatts' homes in London and their cottage called 'Hatch' on the edge of the Salisbury Plain, not far from Pen Pits. He found it a haven of peace especially after they had sold Pen Pits. He wrote to Dannatt about it after a week-long stay in 1972: 'Every time I come the beauty indoors and outdoors appeals to me more and more, and I become more aware of the two artists who have created it. Thank you again for the great privilege of using 58 (Hatch) for refreshment and work.'[45] Much earlier – a decade before – he had written a similar letter noting 'with pleasure additional interests – the opening vista across the road to the wooded hill, the new "action" painting in the kitchen, the beautifully and professionally cropped turf'. And later: 'Each time I am here I do a bit of work, George, by the aid of your piano – sections of *Tobias and the Angel* and the *Beatitudes* have been worked at here, and I shall do some of my new choral work (the *Golden Cantata*) this time too.'[46]

The work referred to in the first letter is the *Metamorphic Variations*, Bliss's last major orchestral work. Its genesis lies in a commission from the Croydon Arts Festival for their 1973 Festival. This was a major undertaking for Bliss, especially now he was in his eighties, and had suggested retirement as far back as 1963 – an impossibility for the creative artist, as he discovered quickly. As always, he looked for a stimulus to get his ideas moving for this commission. In this case Bliss clearly defined his idea for the work in a letter to Dannatt: 'Yes, the original idea of variation form for *my* new commissioned work *did* come from studying *your* visual variations *Tantris* mostly in your studio at EH or stacked in your music room.'[47] These were 'a series of abstract paintings which themselves were varied studies of the constant object'. Bliss wrote: 'I took the liberty of not only going into the Studio but of unwrapping the pictures piled in your music room and having a good study of them. Perhaps – indeed *most* probably – they helped me to complete the XVIth transformation (the *Polonaise*)....'[48]

Like the *Blow* variations, this new work is another fresh 'take' on variation form where three motivic ideas are subject to much greater transformation as the work progresses than normal variation treatment. This is partly what caused such problems in finding a suitable title for the work – something which wasn't settled until well after the work's first performance.

In August 1972, Bliss wrote to Dannatt to say 'I have finished the preliminary sketch of my/your and A's (the Dannatts were the dedicatees) new work. Is this forty minutes worthwhile? It is difficult to stand back at the moment to see it as a whole. Title – NOT Transformations or Transmutations I think. I have thought of the word Facets, but why not be traditional and simply call it *Symphonic Variations*'. Later in the same letter he responded to an idea from Dannatt about taping a conversation between them about the work. Bliss's response was typical: 'Your idea of taping conversations with me is really very intriguing – it would certainly make us all four laugh hereafter. Don't forget, if you bring in the analogy of Igor and Robert [Stravinsky and Craft], that it is held fairly widely that the latter did not only do the questioning but the answering too – so that puts the onus really on you.'[49]

What Bliss saw in Dannatt's series of paintings was a development of visual ideas with strong motivic images (*see* plate section for an example). Certain geometric shapes are features of all Dannatt's work but used in very different ways, colours, sizes, textures and relationships. Bliss found the idea of making a musical equivalent intriguing. Thus, his *donnée*.

He composed the work around three very different ideas which he described as a) a long lyrical cantilena for solo oboe, which opens the work; b) a two-bar phrase, first heard on the horns, and then on the strings; and lastly c) a cluster pattern of four semitones close together introduced by the woodwind. Of these 'A' is by far the most recognizable and is given most space and prominence in the opening *Elements*. The chordal theme (B) has echoes of Wagner's famous *Tristan* progression and, as Giles Easterbrook pointed out, the triptych of Dannatt paintings explored the interrelation of Tristan, Isolde and the fatal goblet. Hence, therefore, the three musical motifs and the concept of completely free development, transformation and exploration of the three motifs in a series of fourteen movements which Bliss gave descriptive titles including Ballet, Assertion, Polonaise, Funeral Procession, Cool Interlude, Dedication to GD and AD, and Affirmation. Two more movements, *Contrasts* and *Children's March*, which were omitted before the first performance leading Dannatt to remark to Bliss that 'You were quite right to cut out those two movements – not that I've heard them, but the work is the right length and balance as it is.'[50] In the end Bliss left it to the conductor to decide whether or not to include the two movements which are included as an Appendix. This caused a minor rumpus with Novello with an obviously irritated Bliss writing: 'Perhaps I have not made myself clear...the study score should be (with the new paging and rehearsal figures) be issued exactly as it was first performed at Croydon, i.e. with the 2 variations cut out. What I suggested to George Rizza (Managing Director of Novellos) was that these two cut-out variations should be issued later as a supplement...I have only suggested this because practically all the musicians who have seen the original score wanted their inclusion.'[51]

Another issue was the 'dedication' which, coming late in the work, and originally appearing unnumbered, meant that many questioned whether or not the whole work was actually dedicated to the Dannatts or just that section. Dannatt therefore suggested that Bliss should remove the two movements mentioned above and renumber the work giving the

Dedication its own movement number. One further 'difficulty' referred to by Dannatt in his lengthy post-premiere letter was 'getting over to the listener where the connecting "Interludes" of a few bars only, occur… Discussing and enthusing about your really tremendous score with VH (Vernon Handley – the conductor of the premiere on 21 April 1973), who confirmed my suspicion of some of the difficulties in it … he said that the "links" were the problem for the conductor… Why on earth should people, & non-musical people too, think that they ought to 'understand' an entirely new conception immediately?'[52]

Bliss's reply warmly noted that 'We shall really have to have a "hot line" between us – so frequently do missives come. I am immensely grateful for the comments on the music in your letter of 26 April – as Trudy says, in 50 years' time this will be a historic document on the work' (oddly, it is almost exactly this period of time that this book is being written). He went on to agree with another point raised in Dannatt's letter. Bliss's half-sister Enid, had immediately suggested that the work should become the subject of a ballet. Bliss replied that he would 'refuse appeals from ballet companies – one came the next day from Beryl Gray, Director of the London Festival Ballet – until such time as the work is so well known as a symphonic concert-piece, that the addition of 'legs' won't hurt it!'

An 'aside' in Dannatt's letter to Bliss on 10 June about hearing showed the effects of ageing beginning to tell. Dannatt wrote that whilst in Italy he went completely deaf in his left ear and concluded that 'I only mentioned my slight deafness because you have several times told me that you are a little deaf, and obviously you could not hear the pencil in the piano (removed in two minutes with Ann's help); and I realized then that my Hatch piano is regularly fed with pencils (or has been) in order to give you the idea for the scoring of the Scherzo!!'[53]

The final chapter in all this was finding a more descriptive name for the work, and in October 1974 Bliss wrote to Dannatt: 'May I pick your imaginative brain once more? I feel that our Variations need a title (like Elgar's) to distinguish it from a large number of contemporary works simply called Variations for Orchestra – Trudy suggests Croydon Variations, a good hard sound. Novellos suggest Fairfield Variations (rather a soft sound)… Have you any suggestions other than these that I can mull over – you are very good with the titles of your own paintings.'[54] Three days later Dannatt came up with a number of suggestions including the one Bliss chose: 'I thought you were right in wanting to call it "Transformations" because it is, in fact, surely, transformations on two* (Three despite what the short score says) themes… I should have thought (1) *Transformations* for orchestra or *Transformations on Two Themes* (I like the alliteration), or, arising out of that aspect of the work *Variations on Two Themes* or (3) *Metamorphic Variations: Metamorphoses*. You did say that the idea came to you from my constant painting of the same theme. These paintings were called the *Tantris* series (Reversal of Tristan – the golden cup, or bowl). Would (4) *Tantris Variations* appeal at all?'[55]

Finally came a letter on 4 November from Bliss to say 'I am <u>very</u> pleased with the title *Metamorphic Variations*. I am placing this note in the score: "I have added the word 'Metamorphic' to the title, because the three themes that constitute the opening section of the work, called *Elements* undergo a greater transformation during the progress of the work than the simple word 'Variations' implies.'[56] Joan Chissell, reviewing the first performance in the *Times,* felt that 'the underlying theme…would seem to be friendship, which explains why the idiom is so retrospectively romantic… always the composer seems to be drawing on a golden trove of personal memory.'[57]

The story of these Variations has taken us slightly forward in our timeline. Earlier in 1972, alongside writing the *Variations,* Bliss was asked for two short choral works. One was an *Ode to Sir William Walton,* written for his seventieth birthday celebration dinner at 10 Downing Street on 29 March (Edward Heath was Prime Minister), and premiered by the St. Margaret's Singers, directed by Martin Neary. The text was by Paul Dehn, who had collaborated with Walton for his second opera, *The Bear.* Bliss scored it for narrator, choir and three soloists singing from the choir. Neary remembered that Heath had devised an imaginative programme, aided by his Principal Private Secretary, Robert Armstrong (later Lord Armstrong of Ilminster, son of Sir Thomas Armstrong, Principal of the Royal Academy of Music) who wrote a special Grace set to music by Herbert Howells. After dinner, there was a musical feast, beginning with Bliss's *Ode,* for which Dehn had written an amusing script. Bliss responded by cleverly inserting numerous choral adaptations from Walton's most famous scores, including *Henry V* and *Belshazzar's Feast,* and some humorous pastiches of his own. After this Walton's own beautiful setting of *Set me as a seal upon thine heart* was sung. The evening ended with a performance of Walton's *Façade,* conducted by David Atherton. Heath described the performance of 'this precocious music to words by Edith Sitwell that had first made Walton famous' as bringing back 'all the glitter, the fun, and at the same time the hardness of the twenties'.

The other short choral piece was a *Prayer of St. Francis of Assisi*, written for the Orpington Junior Singers and directed by the indefatigable Sheila Mossman, who founded the girls' choir in 1949. Bliss wrote three pieces for the group: two in 1968 (a nursery rhyme for the youngest singers and *A Prayer to the Infant Jesus* for the main choir) and this *Prayer*, premiered in Bromley Parish Church on 11 June 1972, conducted by Jane Attfield as part of the Bromley Arts Festival (Mossman had died the previous year). Bliss treated these commissions with great respect for these expert young singers, and was inspired by St Francis's timeless plea for peace. 'Lord, make me an instrument of thy Peace, Where there is hatred, let me sow love....'. It is almost as if, at this late stage of his life, he is reflecting on his eighty years that had included two world wars, the loss of a brother, and the risible waste of it all. Writing for these young upper voices seemed to emphasize the need to encourage a new generation in new ways of thinking, and singing together was a perfect medium for the expression of hope for the future.

In July, for a second time, he was Roy Plomley's guest on the BBC radio programme *Desert Island Discs*, having last been in this studio in November 1959. Listening to this interview, in which one would expect a degree of light-heartedness, it is surprising to hear the haughtiness in Bliss's tone. It is almost as if he resents being asked personal questions on air that might give away more of himself than he wished. His choice of eight discs to 'take with him' to the island also seemed to have a touch of irony about them: his first choice was the call of the kookaburra, an Australian bird with a remarkable song sounding just like human laughter. As Bliss said, 'Laughter is a very healthy thing' and he would wish to be encouraged to laugh in the face of his adversity. Then he went straight on to a recording of Tom Lehrer called *The Elements*, listing all the known chemical elements at the time, but, as Bliss said, making fun of geology. This was designed again to make him laugh and to remember his wife, who was a keen geologist. The first serious choice was *Fair is my love* from his own *Serenade*, another tribute to his wife. Ravi Shankar playing an Indian Raga followed this, 'for between three and six in the afternoon as I sit under my palm tree'. The baying call of wolves followed this, 'for my self-protection, put on very loud in case I'm in danger'. His *Lambs* scherzo from *Meditations on a Theme by John Blow* followed as an antidote to the baying of the wolves.

Bliss next stated that he suffered from claustrophobia and he wanted to feel the comforting freedom of the immense spaces as described so colourfully in Borodin's *In the Steppes of Central Asia*. Finally, he chose *The Song of the Reapers* from his own *Pastoral*, reminding him of the lovely time he had in Sicily back in the 1920s with his wife. His favourite disc was *Fair is my Love*, his luxury was Field Glasses (he had chosen a telescope in his first programme), and his book was *The Swiss Family Robinson* by Johann David Wyss. This iconic novel about a family who is shipwrecked and manage to reach a desert island encouraged Bliss to feel that he would be able to learn many lessons on survival from the book. What is touching about the whole programme, despite the tone of voice, is the centrality of Trudy, a celebration of their mutually supportive lifetime partnership.

Throughout Bliss's life, Ralph Vaughan Williams was a huge musical force. He was the mature oak to all the saplings around him. He died in 1958 and was deeply mourned. For the centenary of his birth on 12 October 1972 Bliss was asked to unveil a blue plaque on 10 Hanover Terrace in London where he and his wife Ursula lived from 1953. This will have been a true act of homage to a much-loved friend and colleague with whom, all those years earlier, he had shared a house while writing *A Colour Symphony*.

Bliss's Indian summer, his final composing period, has been a revelation to me in the quality and inspiration which persisted despite his age and earlier thoughts of retirement. Even in the small-scale pieces there is now a feeling of benediction in the sound world. This is clearly evident in *Put thou thy trust in the Lord,* a supremely effective unaccompanied choral piece setting verses from Psalm 37 for the service in Westminster Abbey celebrating the Queen's Silver Wedding anniversary on 20 November. There is in this piece an avuncular hand on the shoulder (if etiquette allowed) to a much-loved monarch, and a musical style which has a rare warmth amongst his choral pieces.

Perhaps 'put thou thy trust' was an appropriate feeling, however, as Bliss was admitted to hospital for an operation for obstructive jaundice on 17 June. Trudy wrote to Gipps to say 'the operation was successful and, although he is very uncomfortable, there are no complications, and the doctors hope he may come home after two weeks.'[58] This was the start of a progression of ill-health which would end his life in under a year.

A major new project on which to focus his attention during 1971–2 was the semi-staging of *The Olympians* in an abridged version (but still in three Acts) in the Royal Festival Hall masterminded by the irrepressible Bryan Fairfax. The Australian dedicated himself to the performance of rarely heard or completely neglected works. He founded the Polyphonia Orchestra, a semi-professional group, to work with him, and intrepid they had to be as perhaps his most ambitious project was to give the world premiere of Havergal Brian's gargantuan *Gothic Symphony* in 1961. Although not quite as ambitious a project as this, Bliss's opera nevertheless proved to be a major undertaking and fell squarely into the kind of work deserving of an opportunity for reassessment even in a concert performance. Fairfax had already sought out and performed another of Bliss's neglected works, the *Serenade for Baritone and Orchestra* of 1921 in the Queen Elizabeth Hall on 19 March 1971. Realising and celebrating the strength of that work he looked to bring a new audience to Bliss's opera.

*The Olympians* was deemed too long as originally conceived, but the task of deciding how to shorten it was not an easy one. Bliss enlisted the help not only of his wife but of his trusty friend, George Dannatt. It would seem that it may possibly have been Dannatt who advocated the resuscitation of the opera, as Bliss's letter of 5 April 1971 refers to his 'most generous advocacy of my opera' but urging him not to waste time on it. Time *was* obviously spent, and a committee formed by the Polyphonia management the following month. Dannatt was asked to join them. In June Bliss wrote again but this time about the programme notes which Dannatt had offered to write. Bliss had to tactfully refuse this offer as 'what I did <u>not</u> know was that on their (Polyphonia Orchestra) staff they had a regular man, Michael Oliver, in charge of all their programme notes.'[59]

In August, Bliss wrote to Dannatt with three points of concern for the committee: finance, duration, and a request not to ask various key people, including Priestley, for money. He wants the finances broken down into core elements, and is deeply worried as to how to cut the opera to a manageable duration: 'It is easy to cut the libretto, but the score is quite another headache. If you have a vocal score, could <u>you</u> make any suggestions... Help me!'[60] Four days later a long screed arrived from Dannatt, very concerned at being asked to operate on a work that he did not know as well as he needed to in order to help in the way Bliss requested.

Novellos sent Bliss the records made of the live performance at Covent Garden in early September and he spent the next day listening and timing each act. 'The sound is of course <u>torture</u> to my ears, the singing often flat and in Diana's case hardly ever near her notes, while Rankl hurries along desperately, hating every minute of it...But that is all past history, and the only question is the duration.'[61] Here he found Novellos had under-timed each Act making shortening it even more crucial and yet more difficult. By this stage, though, Bliss was able to report that he had reduced both Acts I and II by about ten minutes, and with some other cuts the whole work was now about 1 hour and 52 minutes. His signing off to Dannatt showed his indebtedness to his friend: 'I abase myself before your aural ordeal and hope still to remain your affectionate friend, Arthur'.

A few days later, Fairfax weighed in with a letter to Bliss, remarking how helpful Dannatt had been in this process and offering two further suggestions for cuts. At that stage it seemed that all was now agreed upon while performing material was prepared and rehearsals got under way. Then comes a letter from Bliss to Dannatt in which he writes that 'I am literally at a loss to express what I feel when Trudy tells me that you both, and your mother, too, George, want to make donations to *The Olympians*.' So, finance and abridgement were successfully achieved and rehearsals got under way, which progressed to the memorably successful performance on 21 February (attended by both the Queen Mother and the Prime Minister). Happily, this performance is still with us through the recording made that evening.

As this was something of a 're-evaluation' occasion, this meant that it would either catch fire or return to oblivion. William Mann in the *Times* gave a very balanced view of the work when he wrote: '*The Olympians* inhabits just such a make-believe world of glamorous escape (as the romantic 1940s films), and Bliss's music – at its best, in the opening of the second act, still magically lovely, but often inventively unfocused, pleasant and vaguely appropriate noises that haven't found the right tune to dominate them – compounds the make-believe. *The Olympians* ought to have delighted large austerity-age audiences in 1949 and thereafter. But nowadays it seems merely to toy with the makings of music-drama. I don't see any of our opera companies spending thousands of pounds on a new production. But to hear the work in this concert performance was a pleasure.'[62]

The energy required over the past year to help bring this project to a successful conclusion was substantial and ill-health was sapping his reserves and so it was with some relief that he could turn his attention to a small *divertissement* for his half-sister Enid (Bliss-Morris), his father's late-in-life daughter from his third marriage. She decided, aged fifty-four, to marry a man a few years her senior called Thomas Frame-Thomson, her second marriage. Bliss's conundrum was a practical one, as he wrote to Marguerite Wolff: 'As Enid has practically <u>everything</u>, the present from the Bliss family raised a problem. It has now been solved by her wishing a special piece of music to be written by me, and recorded on cassette. I am thinking of a 'Wedding Suite' of a few short piano pieces. Now will <u>you</u> be a dear and play them. I thought of having them recorded in the same studio as you recorded my Sonata.'[63] An undated letter to

Wolff, presumably a few days later, thanked her for agreeing and stated that 'There will be 4 pieces in all – I send two of them, early efforts of mine (1913), which were published privately and have never been played. The two I would like you to learn are nos III and IV. The other two are very short pieces that I am copying out in mss and will send later.' After the recording in the Decca studios on 11 January 1974, Bliss wrote to thank her on the 17th for 'taking the trouble to learn and record my Suite for to-morrow's reception… a lovely piece of piano playing.'[64] The two early pieces were the third and fourth movements taken from *Valses Fantastiques*: Introduction – *Allegro Vivace*, and *Poco lento e molto espressivo*. The other two short movements were an opening, *Allegretto eleganto*, and a final *Moderato pomposo*, which was a transcription of *Enid's Blast* originally for trumpet and piano.

By way of a 'farewell' to Marguerite Wolff, two months before he died, he wrote thanking her for taking the trouble of travelling all the way to Sheffield to hear the second performance of the *Metamorphic Variations*. He ended his letter by saying 'I have heard quite a number of players tackle my Sonata by now – but no one with your particular panache – nor with, if I may say so, the added charm of your presence at the piano.'[65]

One of Bliss's last small choral pieces was *Mar Portugues*, a touching setting of a free translation by Alan Goodison of a poem by the Portuguese poet Fernando Pessoa. This poem was written in commemoration of the 600th anniversary of the Anglo-Portuguese Alliance, the oldest historical alliance in the world still in force. It was commissioned by Edward Heath, then Prime Minister, to celebrate the event and was sung before dinner in the grand surroundings of the Painted Hall at the Royal Naval College in Greenwich. Martin Neary conducted the first performance with the St. Margaret's Singers. The guest of honour was Marcello Caetano, the Portuguese President.

It was one of the Prime Minister's Private Secretaries, Tom Bridges, grandson of the former Poet Laureate, Robert Bridges, who suggested making an English translation of this Portuguese poem. It was at this point that an unusual and potentially tricky situation arose. Sir John Betjeman, who was Poet Laureate, was invited to make an English version. However, before this was done, Bliss received the translation by Goodison who worked in the Foreign Office. More difficult still was the fact that Bliss much preferred Goodison's translation to Betjeman's on the grounds that, as he diplomatically put it, it was more suitable 'for the purpose of a musical setting'. In the end both sets of words were printed on the menu for the evening. Heath said of the performance, 'In a setting of unsurpassed splendour, it all made for a magical evening. Under the splendid ceiling paintings of Sir James Thornhill, the augmented body of singers sang in two antiphonal groups, on each side of the staircase leading into the hall'. The evening started with a *Magnificat* for double choir by the seventeenth century Portuguese composer Dom Pedro da Esperança. This was followed by three English madrigals, and finally Bliss's *Mar Portuguese*. After the performance Bliss wrote to Neary that although his name was on the seating plan he couldn't bring himself to attend (along with several others) as a silent protest against the right-wing Caetano regime. He remarked that the Prime Minister had written to him saying that the performance 'sounded splendid and made a fitting conclusion to the musical part of the proceedings at dinner.'[66]

Bliss's final commission as Master of the Queen's Musick was to write music for the wedding of Princess Anne and Captain Mark Phillips on 14 November 1973. This consisted of a processional fanfare and interludes for the hymn 'Glorious things of thee are spoken' sung to the fine tune by C.V. Taylor called *Abbots Leigh*. He had continued writing a number of fanfares before this event including celebrating the 50th anniversary of the Croydon Symphony Orchestra on 15 May 1971 which he then revised and used as a greeting to the Santa Barbara Symphony Orchestra in January 1974. St. Paul's Cathedral was the setting for another impressive fanfare this time for the National Fund for Research into Crippling Diseases which took place on 18 October 1973. His final – and quite substantial – fanfare he called *Lancaster – Prelude* was written to mark the tenth anniversary of the Lancaster Concert series, receiving its first performance on 24 November 1974.

Earlier that year, Denis Forman of Granada Television asked Bliss if he would be the subject of a documentary that they would not broadcast but be part of Granada's Historical Record, where significant figures of the period talk about their work. This took the form of three sections: in the first, Bliss talks about his *Meditations on a Theme by John Blow*, which he regards as his finest orchestral work. He then discusses his music in a deeply personal way with Vernon Handley. Finally, his film music with Muir Matheson was discussed, and all this was filmed over some ten days in their house.

What comes over, despite his encroaching illness, is his sheer energy, and his unflagging memory for people, names and places. His eyes shine with interest and a desire to share thoughts. The energy is such that he dominates conversations, often bursting to get another point across. It is often difficult for others to get a word in edgeways. This very dominant personality and clear self-confidence is obviously what helped him to establish himself so quickly; it developed his position once people started to sit up and take notice of the young firebrand at the effective start of his composing career after the Great War.

It is difficult not to feel sorry for Vernon Handley in their substantial conversation as, straight away, Bliss puts him on the spot in the way a very much junior member of the profession (who Bliss nevertheless greatly admires) must have found difficult to answer negatively had he wished to do so. Bliss asks him about the sound of his music: 'Does that *sound* like me?', and then straight away: 'Is there a melodic line which is recognisably mine?' To the first, Handley cites dotted rhythms as being a hallmark of his style. To the second, rather diplomatically, 'It's not so much a recognizable line when you are being rhythmic and forcing the work along, but when you have one of your periods of repose, for instance in the last movement of the Violin Concerto, that's absolutely yours. Similarly *Green* and *Blue* in the *Colour Symphony*'.

Perhaps one of the most characteristic moments came next, when Bliss quoted a letter he had read of T S Eliot's, in which he writes: 'The artist concerned with originality may be considered as largely negative. He wishes only to avoid saying what has already been said as well as it can be before'. Bliss removes his glasses, leans forward, and glares at Handley with piercing eyes: 'See what I mean?' and then, said with an amused smile, 'Do I come up to that canon that I'm saying things which have been better said before or am I saying a little newer things in a little newer way? That's what one wants to feel, you see'. What can the poor young conductor say in the face of the elderly but fiery Master of the Queen's Musick? 'You are definitely saying newer things. The mood may not be very different from other composers, but the reason that one has to take time to come to your work is that you can't readily identify with your voice; one has to listen to quite a lot of the music to get to know it'.

Handley sits cleverly on the fence, but seems to say that Bliss does not have an easily recognizable voice. Bliss presses him: 'Well, what I want to know is what's wrong with the work? Are there works of mine that you have had a certain difficulty in putting over? Again, Handley cleverly puts the issue back to himself: 'Well, with me it will certainly be that if I don't understand it that's when it will be difficult to put over and so the two things collide there'.

The conversation moved on with Bliss admitting that he always had a problem with first movements and that Handley's difficulty in finding the mood of the first movement of the Cello Concerto was a symptom of this. Bliss concedes that there may be 'too many moods to make a whole'. Handley skilfully presents this as a return to his Classical roots: the first movement presents the argument and is therefore the hardest to compose. Bliss then reflects that 'I don't feel *au fort* that I'm a symphonic composer. I'm much happier in smaller forms'. He then cites the ballets and sets of variations which 'are small groups of movements knitted together. I have done symphonic movements in the three concertos but I find it more difficult to find myself spinning like a spider. I'm much more like a jackdaw that picks up all sorts of things which fascinate him and put them together'. Handley ripostes: 'Yes, but you *are* symphonic in procedure. With a movement you use developments all the time. I don't feel the *Meditations* is a set of variations as much as a symphonic whole'.

One or two other key points in the wide-ranging discussion saw Bliss remarking that 'the first thing I demand from music is flow.' Most emphatically he stated that 'I do demand enhancement of life which means that I must feel behind the music a great personality telling me something about an experience that I haven't had before. When I first heard Beethoven's Fifth, I came out of the Queen's Hall feeling taller in every way. That is the highest kind of music you can possibly get. I don't want to hear a lot of kettles being banged together and someone in falsetto singing something rather stupid!'

Finally, Bliss talked about inspiration that 'may come from words or, in my case, paintings.' This underlines the point made already that it was books he talked about at the end of his autobiography, not paintings. 'Something hits me and hits me in the shape of a very small phrase – a few notes or even a colour – three oboes or whatever it may be. Or it may come in a little rhythm. That rhythm grows like a seed and gradually begins to form and then you've got a page of notes down on paper and I think routine is necessary as you get to work at your piano or your desk every day'.

His discussion with Muir Matheson is very lightweight and follows the progress of his various films with which Matheson was involved. Two things emerged: one was that Matheson completely forgot *Seven Waves Away*. He could remember nothing about it even when Bliss (who was incredulous) reminded him of the plot. The other was Matheson asking Bliss which film pleased him most to which Bliss answered that it was *Things to Come*, his first which was most exciting. He commented that the film wasn't what H.G. Wells wanted as 'he thought that it would shake the government' perhaps as a warning of the imminent world crisis.

The undimmed mind was given one last considerable compositional challenge in the form of a commission from the Windsor Festival to celebrate the Quincentenary of St. George's Chapel, Windsor. Having written a short celebratory anthem, *Sing Mortals!* for the 1974 annual St. Cecilia Day service at the Musicians' Church, St. Sepulchre's, Holborn in London, he was very much attuned to the medium of choir and organ. But the cantata for Windsor was a major undertaking when he was tired, unwell and fighting the cancer which was eating away at him. As Trudy wrote, 'the following June (1974) Arthur became seriously ill and from then on, even after convalescence and partial recovery, there had to be fewer occasions that might tire him. He was not well enough, for instance, to go to a performance of a work that he knew would interest him, but he went in the morning and then wrote afterwards to George Dannatt: "October 21st 1971... Went to rehearsal of Henze's *Tristan* yesterday – was overwhelmed. I wish they had broadcast it. I crept away from the RFH feeling very small... Love, Arthur." '[67]

So, it is all the more remarkable that he managed to keep working on *The Shield of Faith* right to the end. On 30 August he wrote, 'I suspect that my last work, just completed before I went into hospital... will really be my last big opus' and this was prophetic as he didn't live to hear the first performance. For a text Canon Stephen Verney, one of the residentiary Canons at Windsor, chose a poem representative of each of the five centuries of the chapel's existence. It was an insightful choice of poems which in their sheer variety presented Bliss with the considerable problem of creating unity from such disparate poetic expression. William Dunbar's (1460–1520) poetic firework display, *The Lord is Risen*,[68] in which Christ defeats the dragon and the poetic lines tremble with energy – just Bliss's sort of text – comes first. Bliss loved this kind of literary electricity and in himself was not any less energetic despite his illness. George Herbert's (1593–1633) *Love* comes second, a complete contrast – lyrical but questioning with the subject feeling he is not worthy of heaven but growing to a gradual acceptance of the love which is so unsparingly offered. Extracts from Alexander Pope's *An Essay on Man* follow on sensitively from Herbert's essay on redemption, and Pope's opening 'Know then thyself' will have resonated with Bliss as it explores in one brief verse the life cycle of man. Bliss also said that 'we enter the region of scepticism. Is man a God, or Beast? Pope gives a scathing account of Man's life; there is no Shield of Faith here, only the cold comfort that God is wiser than we are.'[69] Tennyson's (1809–1892) *O yet we trust* from *In Memoriam* continues the subject of redemption in its opening words 'O yet we trust that somehow good Will be the final goal of ill'. Finally extracts from T.S. Eliot's (1888–1965) *Little Gidding* has that magical Walt Whitman-like sense of moving towards the unknown as we move into the present day. Eliot's inspired lines: 'We shall not cease from exploration And the end of all our exploring Will be to arrive where we started And know the place for the first time' describe in yet different terms growth of self-awareness and self-knowledge and acceptance of the redemptive power of faith – the theme of the whole cantata. The extract includes, too, the timeless lines: 'And all shall be well and All manner of thing shall be well'. One of the serious problems with Eliot's poem was getting his widow to agree that it could be used for this setting.

Bliss had never written a work before with such a considerable organ part,[70] but Dannatt had the inspired idea some time before to introduce him to Janacek's *Glagiolitic Mass* with its virtuoso organ part. In wanting to be able to use the organ to best advantage he spent a day exploring the chapel's instrument with Dr. Sidney Campbell, the organist. Campbell died on 4 June 1974 and so he, too, did not live to hear the completed work though Bliss acknowledged his advice with regard to registration (choice of organ stops) at the start of the score.

One of the ways Bliss found to move between disparate sections was to use soprano and baritone soloists, for whom he writes challenging roles. In order to move between Dunbar's and Herbert's poems, Bliss inserted an unaccompanied duet for the soloists using the Latin text *Gloria in excelsis Deo* which he winds down at the end to connect with the gentle organ introduction to Herbert's *Love*. This is an inspired setting, and one cannot help but muse on the repetition (three times) of the word 'Love,' as the choir enters, remembering the immense part true, devoted and constantly supportive love had played in his life. And to this extent, expression of faith and doubt, as this work obviously is in its choice of texts, undoubtedly Bliss is engaged here in a personal journey of retrospection however much he still faces forward. He has no way of knowing where that may lead – and there again we join Eliot in his line which could almost be Bliss's personal motto: 'We shall not cease from exploration'.

In earlier pages of this story there has been criticism of Bliss's vocal writing made from the experience of performing and recording it. But here, difficult though it undoubtedly is, the radiance of the writing simply propels a choir forward. His setting of *Love* has moments of ecstasy that are unique in his output and are surely summative. The pulsing energy of the Pope setting is redolent of his music for the stage, and is such a vivid contrast to the warmth of the previous movement that it is almost breathtaking. The thrusting regularity of the pulse in that movement is counterbalanced in Tennyson with a gently lilting compound time. The Eliot setting in the final movement changes texture again, with whole swathes of unaccompanied music for double choir. The *Scherzando* section is marked *quasi birdsong* and takes us back to the *Golden Cantata*, though here the organ's trillings underscore an intricate duet for two soprano parts like birds calling to each other. The final pages are magically cumulative. In the phrase 'When the tongues of flame are infolded into the crowned knot of fire...' he chooses to single out the word 'infolded' which he repeats, coming to a pause and suddenly we are in the ecstatic final bars where 'the fire and the rose are one'. The soprano soloist joins to sail over the choir to the words 'are one', the two soloists repeat the words and the choir gently joins for the final cadence. Bliss wrote of this as the 'Danteesque vision of the union of divine and human love.'[71]

It seems entirely appropriate that what was almost his final work should also celebrate his twenty-two years as Master of the Queen's Musick in being dedicated to Her Majesty the Queen 'by gracious permission'.

What seems to radiate from this work is hope that what these texts express may be something in which Arthur Bliss can believe. He left formal churchgoing behind decades earlier and we remember his conversion to Catholicism. His is surely a healthy agnosticism. But we also have his letter to William Alwyn of 15 January 1975, in which he stated that 'Belief should extend to the mystery beyond death. I am not convinced that this is the final shutting of the door.'[72]

Bliss's final work was commissioned by John Drummond as a short fanfare-like Prelude and Postlude for a BBC television series called *The Spirit of the Age*. George Dannatt, writing an overview of Bliss's music, noted that 'it gave him, in the last three months of his life, immense pleasure to write, rehearse and record – and never was the title of a last work more apposite to a composer who had, over so many years of creative life, expressed in his life and work The Spirit of the Age.'[73] Drummond wrote that 'He (Bliss) came to the studio to record it with the brass from the London Symphony Orchestra, and looked very frail. He died shortly afterwards. I felt his death keenly. He was the first really public figure to befriend me, and he had been immensely generous and kind over the years'.

The series was broadcast from 31 October 1975, but as Drummond admitted 'it failed to make the impact of earlier series. Was it the subject matter, or the fact that eight different presenters meant eight different kinds of programme and a much less homogenous result?' Be that as it may, it was little short of a miracle that, given his state of health, Bliss managed not only to write the music for this series, but that he also got to the studios to conduct just two months before his death.

Trudy remembered one last 'little expedition' that gave Bliss great pleasure. Charles Groves had recorded *Morning Heroes* with the Royal Liverpool Philharmonic Orchestra and John Westbrook as narrator. The recording company, EMI, sought Bliss's advice as to a suitable cover image for the record. He knew exactly what he wanted and, in the company of Bryan Crimp from EMI set off for the British Museum where there was a fifth-century Greek vase, brilliantly depicting Achilles with his sword and great crested helmet fighting, shield to the fore, all set to attack Hector. It was the perfect image.

By the beginning of March, Bliss was seriously ill. On the 27th he passed away peacefully at home. His ashes were interred in his mother's grave at Mortlake.

Two months later, on 20 May, there was a service of thanksgiving for his life and work in Westminster Abbey attended by representatives of both the Queen and the Queen Mother. The Prime Minister, Edward Heath, read the first lesson and David Willcocks gave the address. The music included Bliss's transcription of Bach's chorale prelude *Das alte Jahr vergangen ist* and his last anthem *Sing Mortals!* After the Dean's blessing trumpeters and trombonists from the Royal Military School of Music, Kneller Hall, played Bliss's *Fanfare for Heroes* of 1930. Also included in the service was the hymn tune *All my hope on God is founded* by his old friend Herbert Howells.

At the end of this long and extraordinarily fruitful life that was so richly lived, we ponder the question of mortality and immortality, seeking to judge whether Ruth Gipps, in her adulation of Bliss, was anywhere near the mark in her assessment of his music. We turn the mirror onto Bliss himself, reflecting on his warm words of encouragement to William Alwyn: 'Don't worry about the neglect of your music. One day the bell will ring, and when it does it will sound loud and clear.'[74] There is no doubt that Bliss's music has faded from the music-loving public's consciousness, and despite a spate of new recordings is not the household name that he was during his lifetime.

The *Times* obituary declared that Bliss was 'an internationally respected musician. He was a distinguished and fairly prolific composer of music... much of it durably outstanding, in most available genres.'[75] But some of those genres, including film, ballet and opera, are either ephemeral or require some certainty of success to recoup huge investment. A recent revival of *Miracle in the Gorbals* by Birmingham Royal Ballet was a resounding success, which should be followed by *Checkmate* and *The Lady of Shalott*: a contemporary public should find them equally powerful and engaging.

Bliss was not a composer of small-scale easy-listening music sought out by certain radio networks, and his idea of melody was angular, not hummable, and was not the kind to tease or annoy us as an earworm. His was, however, a melodic approach, and we need only think of the third movement of *Music for Strings* to cite a theme (a fugue before the scurrying finale) that sounded, re-sounded and developed becomes engaging, life-enhancing music that cries out for repetition. This comes out of one of the most soul-searching 'romances' of the period in the previous movement. Bliss's music is ripe for rediscovery. Bliss himself, as we have seen, was a heady mixture of self-promotion and reticence. George Dannatt's recollection of an evening together on New Year's Eve of 1973 was typical: Bliss brought an old recording of his *Discourse for Orchestra* to hear. 'After playing through this record and discussing aspects of the score, he said – in that charmingly insistent manner with which he would brush aside, too often, his own work – "Enough of Bliss, now let's hear something else", and, after a few suggestions, it became quite clear that what he wanted all along to hear had been the movement *Farben* (Colours) from Schoenberg's *Five Orchestral Pieces*.'[76] It is now for a new generation to say 'Enough of this, now let's hear some Bliss'.

# Endnotes

## Chapter One *The Curtains Open*

1 Robert Nichols *Such Was My Singing* (Collins, 1942) p.36
2 Arthur Bliss *As I Remember* (Thames Publishing, London 1970) p.3
3 Ibid. p.16
4 Ibid. p.16
5 Ibid. pp.16–17
6 Ibid. p.17
7 Ibid. p.17
8 Ibid. p.18
9 Ibid. p.19
10 Ibid. p.239
11 Ibid. p.102
12 Ibid. p.19
13 J.B. Hope Simpson *Rugby since Arnold* (Macmillan St Martin's Press 1967) p.143
14 Arthur Bliss *As I Remember* (Thames Publishing, London 1970) p.20
15 Ibid. p.20
16 Ibid. p.20
17 Ibid. p.21
18 Ibid. p.21
19 Ibid. p.23
20 Ibid. p.21
21 Ibid. p.22
22 Ibid. p.24
23 Ibid. p.25
24 Ibid. p.25
25 Ibid. p.27
26 Ibid.
27 Ibid. p.26
28 Ibid. p.28
29 Blythe, Ronald *The Penguin Companion to Literature* (ed. Daiches). Penguin, 1971. p.54
30 Bliss op.cit. pp.28–29
31 Ibid. p.29
32 Ibid. p.28
33 Bliss: *What Modern Composition is Aiming at* quoted in *Bliss on Music*: ed. Roscow (OUP, Oxford, 1991) pp.18–19
34 Ibid. p.19
35 Ibid.
36 Ibid. p.24
37 Bliss op.cit. p.47
38 Ibid. p.47
39 This quotation is from *Conversations with Eckermann: May 12, 1825* and quoted in Nichols' *Such Was My Singing* (Collins, London, 1942) p.15
40 Ibid.
41 Ibid. p.29

## Chapter Two *The Nation Arming*

1 Walt Whitman, *The Complete Poems* Penguin Classics, London, 2005 pp.305–306
2 Ibid., p.308
3 Op. cit. p.30
4 Ibid.
5 Ibid.
6 Ibid. pp.30–31
7 Chapman: *A Passionate Prodigality* Buchan and Enright, London 1933, 1965, 1985 pp.13–14
8 Taken from the *Field Service Pocket Book 1914* (Published by the War Office) The handbook details everyday military conduct in the field, and lays down the regulations and guidelines for marches, quarters, camp cooking, sanitation and water supply. There are chapters on orders and the means of communication, plus overseas operations, map reading and field sketching (the intelligence functions).
9 Chapman op.cit. p.16
10 Bliss op.cit. p.33
11 Bliss, op.cit. p.35
12 Ibid. p.32
13 Ibid. p.35
14 Ibid. p.36
15 Ibid. p.36
16 Ibid. p.39
17 Chapman op.cit. p.59
18 War Diaries for 13th Battalion, Royal Fusiliers
19 Bliss op.cit. pp.40–41
20 Bliss op.cit. pp.40–41
21 Ibid. p.45
22 Hugh Carey *Duet for Two Voices* (Cambridge University Press, 1979) p.91
23 Bliss op. cit. p.42
24 Letter from Howells to Bliss from Bath Villa, Lydney, Gloucestershire: 17 September 1918.
25 Letter from Bliss to his father from Guards Division, Base Depot. B.E.F. 25 September 1918.
26 Bliss op.cit. p.45
27 Ibid. p.45
28 Ibid. p.45

29 Ibid. p.46
30 Ibid. p.46
31 Ibid. p.46
32 Bliss op.cit. pp 47 and 49
33 Ibid. p.49
34 Ibid.
35 Bliss op.cit. p.51
36 Ibid.
37 Ibid. p.51
38 Ibid. p.52
39 Ibid. p.48
40 Ibid.
41 Ibid. p.52

## Chapter Three *The Diaghilev Effect*

1 Bliss op.cit. p.55
2 Ibid. p.54
3 John Drummond: *Speaking of Diaghilev* (Faber and Faber 1997, London) p.215
4 Ibid.
5 Ibid. pp.219–220
6 Quoted in *Arthur Bliss Music and Literature* edited Stewart Craggs (Ashgate, Aldershot. 2002) p.3
7 Bliss op.cit. p.56
8 Ed. Craggs op.cit. p.1
9 Bliss op. cit. p.71
10 Bliss pp.55–56
11 Ibid.
12 Letter from Vaughan Williams to the Carnegie United Kingdom Trust 15 December 1920 quoted in *Letters of Ralph Vaughan Williams 1895–1958*. Ed. Cobbe (OUP, Oxford 2008) p.127
13 H.E. Wortham: Arthur Bliss (The Sackbut April 1927 p.251)
14 Ibid. p.251
15 Ibid. p.252
16 Ibid.
17 Ibid. p.253
18 Quoted in Bliss op.cit. p.58
19 Ibid. p.58
20 Jeremy Dibble: *Charles Villiers Stanford: Man and Musician* (OUP, Oxford 2002) p.418
21 Quoted in Bliss op.cit. p.60
22 Stephen Banfield *Sensibility and English Song* (Cambridge University Press, Cambridge, 1985) p.368
23 Ibid. Quoting Bliss's lecture to the Society of Women Musicians. p.369
24 Ibid. p.369

25  Ibid. p.62
26  Ed. Gregory Roscow: *The Selected Writings of Arthur Bliss 1920–1975* (OUP, Oxford 1991) p.17
27  Ibid. p.18
28  Ibid. p.20
29  Ibid. p.21
30  Ibid. p.23
31  Lewis Foreman: *From Parry to Britten: British Music in Letters 1900–1945* (Amadeus Press, Portland, Oregon, 1987) p.120
32  Ibid. p.18
33  op.cit. p.254
34  Bliss p.60
35  Ibid.
36  Quoted in Bliss p.61
37  George Dannatt states this in his liner notes for CDA66137
38  Quoted in Bliss op.cit. p.63
39  Ibid. p.64
40  Ibid.
41  Ibid. p.65
42  Ibid. p.66
43  Giles Easterbrook, liner notes for Naxos 8.553383. 1995
44  Ibid. p.67
45  Edwin Evans: *The Musical Times*: 1 February 1923 p.97
46  Ibid.
47  Undated programme note quoted in *Arthur Bliss Music and Literature* Ed. Craggs (Ashgate, Aldershot 2002) p.13
48  Bliss op.cit. p.69
49  Ibid. p.69

**Chapter Four A Colour Symphony**

1  Bliss op.cit. p.73
2  Evans op.cit. p.20
3  Ibid. p.21
4  Ibid.
5  Ibid.
6  Ibid.
7  Michael Kennedy: *A Portrait of Elgar* (Oxford 1968) p.247
8  Ibid.
9  Bliss op.cit. p.71
10  Ibid. pp.71–72
11  Ibid. pp.73–74
12  Ibid.
13  *The Gramophone* 5, July 1971, p.236
14  Letter from Bliss to Scholes dated: 30 December 1923
15  Ed. Barry Still: *Two Hundred and Fifty Years of the Three Choirs Festival* (Three Choirs Festival Association: 1977) p.23
16  Letter from Bliss to George Dannatt dated 15 October 1970
17  Ibid.
18  Christopher Palmer, *Bliss* (Novello, 1976) p.7
19  Bliss/Dannatt letter op.cit.
20  Bliss, *As I Remember* op.cit. pp.74–75
21  Letter from Elgar to Bliss from Tiddington House, Stratford-upon-Avon 8 November 1928
22  Quoted in *Arthur Bliss Music and Literature*. Ed. Craggs (Ashgate, Aldershot, 1988, p.31
23  Michael Kennedy, *Portrait of Elgar* (OUP, London, 1968) p.247
24  *Arthur Bliss Music and Literature* op.cit. p.30

**Chapter Five *Love Via the Stage: The 'Volcanic Anglo-American'***

1  Constant Lambert: *Music Ho! A study of music in decline* (Faber, London 1934) p.34
2  Sam Ellis Bliss's New England: identity, interdependence and isolation: Doctoral thesis for Bangor University, 2011. p.10
3  Quoted in *Arthur Bliss Music and Literature* ed. Craggs. Paul Jackson *An American Interlude* (Ashgate, Aldershot. 2002) p.73
4  Ibid.
5  Banfield op.cit. p.370
6  Bliss op.cit. p.76
7  Patrick Mahoney *Sir Arthur Bliss in Santa Barbara* published in the journal *Noticias* (1971)
8  Bliss op.cit. p.76
9  Ibid. p.77
10  Ibid. p.77
11  Ibid. p.9
12  Quoted in Op. Cit. Ed. Craggs: Paul Jackson *An American Interlude* p.76
13  David Metzer: *The League of Composers: the initial years* (American Music Vol.15 No.1, Spring 1997) p.47
14  Bliss op.cit. p.78
15  Ibid.
16  Ibid. p.78
17  Personal e-mail from Paul Jackson to the author
18  Susan Borwick. *Notes*, vol. 56, no. 2, 1999, pp. 416–418
19  Letter dated 21 October 1924
20  Ibid. p.80
21  Ibid. p.81
22  Ibid. p.81
23  Ibid. p.82
24  Ibid. p.83
25  Ibid. p.84
26  Ibid. pp.84–5
27  Bliss, A. *Music in America*, in *Jazz in Print (1856–1929): An anthology of selected early readings in jazz history*. Hillsdale: Pendragon Press, (2002) pp.424–425.
28  Bliss op.cit. p.86
29  E-mail correspondence with the author 24 April 2020
30  Bliss op.cit. p.89
31  Typescript of BBC broadcast
32  Frank Howes *The English Musical Renaissance* (Secker and Warburg, London 1966) p.266
33  Ed. Craggs op.cit. p.6
34  *The Times* 9 September 1926
35  *Bliss on Music* Selected Writings of Arthur Bliss 1920–1975 (ed. Gregory Roscow. OUP 1991) pp.265–266
36  Ibid. p.264
37  Ibid.
38  *The Times* 28 January 1927

**Chapter Six *Towards* Morning Heroes: *1927–1930***

1  Bliss to Coolidge from 3 Redcliffe Square, London, 18 February 1927
2  Ibid.

3  Bliss to Coolidge from Santa Barbara, 31 July 1927
4  Ibid.
5  Bliss to Coolidge from 3 Redcliffe Square, London, 31 August 1927
6  Bliss op.cit. p.91
7  Bliss to Coolidge, from Amstel Hotel, Amsterdam, Monday 3 October 1927
8  W.H. Davies *Shorter Lyrics of the Twentieth Century, 1900–1922* (The Poetry Bookshop, London 1922) p.7
9  Ibid. p.10
10  Ibid. p.7
11  Giles Easterbrook *Note* in the score of the *Four Songs* (Novello and Co. Ltd, London, 1984)
12  Bliss op.cit. pp.45–46
13  Quoted in *Bliss on Music* op.cit. p.241
14  Ibid. p.240
15  Ibid.
16  Bliss op.cit. p.93
17  Ibid. p.93
18  *The English Musical Renaissance*: Frank Howes (Secker and Warburg, London, 1966) p.300
19  *Bliss's Pastoral*: the *Musical Times* (Vol.70, No.1035, May 1, 1929) p.406
20  Letter from Elgar to Bliss dated 9 May 1929 from Stratford upon Avon.
21  Bliss op.cit. p.96
22  Ed. Stephen Lloyd, Diana Sparkes and Brian Sparkes *Music in their Time: The Memoirs and letters of Dora and Hubert Foss* (Boydell Press, Woodbridge, 2019) p.85
23  Christopher Palmer booklet notes for Lyrita SRCD.225 1971
24  *The Times* 19 March 1930
25  Eric Blom *Music in England* (Pelican Books, West Drayton, 1942) p.267
26  *The Musical Times* Vol.71, No.1052 (1 October 1930) p.881
27  Ibid.
28  Bliss op.cit. p.96
29  Ibid.
30  *Bliss* Christopher Palmer (Novello, Borough Green, 1976) pp.21–22
31  Bliss op.cit. p.7
32  Bliss op.cit. p.97
33  *The Times* Friday 24 October 1930, p.12
34  Wood wrote 1927 but it should have been 1930
35  Sir Henry Wood *My Life in Music* (Victor Gollancz, 1949) p.259
36  *The Musical Times* Vol.71, No.1052 (1 October 1930) p.886
37  *The Musical Times* Vol.71, No.1054 (1 December 1930) p.1081
38  Ibid.
39  Ibid.
40  Arthur Bliss's *Morning Heroes*, *Monthly Musical Record*, October 1930, pp.289–91
41  Letter from Bliss to Susan Owen from East Heath Lodge, Hampstead, 27 March 1931
42  *Arthur Bliss Music and Literature* ed.Craggs (Ashgate, Aldershot, 2002) p.29

43 The author experienced a strange mental 'nudge' early one morning. For no reason at all Berlioz's *Symphonie Fantastique* came into my mind. It is not a work I had listened to for a long time and it is odd that it came into my head at that moment with no prompting. But when it led me to the connections detailed above it felt as if I was being pointed to it by a benign angel.

**Chapter Seven *Things to Come: New Paths***

1 Herbert Hughes: Preface to *The Joyce Book* (OUP, London, 1933) p.9
2 Banfield: *Sensibility and English Song* (Cambridge University Press, 1985) p.322
3 Bliss op.cit. p.100
4 Bliss op.cit. p.97
5 Ibid.
6 *The Times*, 20 February, 1933. p.8
7 Eric Blom, *The Musical Times* Vol. 74, No. 1083 (May 1933) p.424
8 Quoted in *Bliss on Music. Selected Writings of Arthur Bliss 1920–75* Ed. Gregory Roscow (OUP, 1991) pp.103–4
9 Wordsworth, *Intimations of Immortality* from *Recollections of Early Childhood*
10 McNaught, *A Short Account of Modern Music and Musicians* (Novello, London, 1938) p.49
11 Blom: Ibid. p.427
12 Bliss op.cit. p.101
13 Bliss op.cit. p.102
14 Ibid.
15 Lionel Tertis *My Viola and I* (Crescendo Publishing Company, Boston, USA, 1974) p.74
16 Ibid.
17 *The Musical Times* Vol.75. No.1093 (March 1934) p.214
18 Tertis op.cit. p.96
19 Ibid. p.217
20 Bliss op.cit. p.102
21 Tertis op.cit. p.77
22 Letter from Bliss to Boult dated 13 June 1933
23 Ibid.
24 Ibid.
25 Craggs, op.cit. p.234
26 Ibid. p.235
27 Ibid. p.239
28 Ibid. p.240
29 Bliss op.cit. p.103
30 Alan Powers: *Harmonious Mansions* Country Life August 29, 1985. p.560
31 Ibid. p.561
32 Ibid.
33 Bliss op.cit. p.104
34 Quoted in *Bliss on Music* op.cit. p.70
35 Ibid. p.87
36 Ibid.
37 Bliss op.cit. p.105
38 H.G. Wells *Two Film Stories* (London, The Cresset Press, 1940). p.9
39 Letter from Wells to Bliss headed 'Private' and dated 16 October 1934 from 47, Chiltern Court, Clarence Gate NW1 (Bliss Archive, Cambridge University Library)
40 Quoted in Roscow op.cit. p.32

41 Ibid. p.33
42 Quoted in *Arthur Bliss Music and Literature* op.cit. p.94
43 Ibid. p.95
44 Norman and Jeanne MacKenzie *The Time Traveller: The Life of H.G. Wells* (Weidenfeld and Nicolson, London, 1973) p.390
45 Ibid. pp.390–391
46 Giles Easterbrook: Liner notes for Chandos (CHAN9896) p.7
47 Quoted in *Arthur Bliss Music and Literature* op.cit. p.200
48 Bliss op.cit. p.106
49 Giles Easterbook op.cit. p.8
50 *The Times* 2 March 1936
51 Bliss: Introductory talk to a BBC Radio concert broadcast on 15 November 1950. Typescript in Cambridge University Library, printed in Roscow, ed., *Bliss on Music*, pp.190–191
52 *Bliss on Music* op.cit. p.62
53 Ibid.
54 Ibid. p.64
55 Ibid. p.64
56 Ibid. p.63

**Chapter Eight *Strings, Travel Guides and Checkmate***

1 Bliss op.cit. pp.107–108
2 Ibid. p.108
3 Ibid. p.107
4 Frances Donaldson *The British Council: The First Fifty Years*. (Jonathan Cape, London, 1984) p.1
5 *The Times* 12 August 1935
6 Bliss op.cit. p.109
7 *The Listener* was the BBC's own magazine published between 1929 and 1991.
8 Quoted in Roscow op.cit. p.105
9 Bliss op.cit. p.109
10 Roscow. op.cit. p.107
11 Ibid.
12 Ibid. (a reference to a German notion that England was a land without music. Actually, Oskar Schmitz reused the phrase 'Das land ohne musik' as the title of a book published in 1904, but taking his cue from an earlier publication by Carl Engel in 1866.
13 Ibid.
14 Ibid.
15 Ibid.
16 Ibid. p.13
17 Ibid. p.24
18 Bliss op.cit. p.11
19 Ibid. p.28
20 Roscow op.cit. p.39
21 Bliss op.cit. p.12
22 Roscow op.cit. p.43
23 Ibid.p.51
24 Ibid.p.55
25 Letter to Bridges Adams from East Heath Lodge, Hampstead. Undated.
26 Arnold Whittall in the *Musical Times* Vol.105/1453 March 1964 p.186
27 Quoted in Roscow op.cit. p.160
28 Ibid. p.61
29 Bliss op. cit. p.14
30 Ibid.
31 *Great Thoughts* January 1938 quoted in Roscow op.cit. p.62
32 Ibid.

33 Bliss op.cit. p.63
34 Roscow op.cit. p.64
35 Bliss op.cit. p.15
36 *Musical Times* Vol 78, No.1133, July 1937, p.649
37 Ibid.
38 *Musical Times* Vol 107, No 1482, August 1966, p.674
39 *Musical Times* Vol. 78, No 1132, June 1937, p.522
40 *The Times* 17 June 1937 (Paris Correspondent)
41 *The Times* 6 October, 1937
42 Kenneth Clarke, 'Ballet Décors', in *Gala Performance* (Collins, 1955), p.36
43 Dennis Arundell *The Story of Sadler's Wells* (Hamish Hamilton, London, 1965), p.212
44 *The Times* 28 January 1932
45 *The Times* 21 March 1932

**Chapter Nine *An American Interlude***

1 Bliss op.cit. p.17
2 Ibid. p.18
3 Ibid. p.19
4 Craggs op.cit. p.209
5 Ibid. p.208
6 Ibid. p.209
7 Michael Kennedy *Portrait of Walton* (OUP Oxford, 1989) p.101
8 Ibid. p.81
9 Susana Walton *William Walton Behind the Façade* (OUP Oxford 1988) p.65
10 Bliss op.cit. p.20
11 Quoted in Roscow, op.cit. p.74
12 *The Musical Times*, Vol. 103, No. 1437 (Nov., 1962), pp.761–762
13 Bliss on his Piano Concerto transcribed by David Wilby from a talk given to the Brighton and Hove Gramophone Society on 4 October 1959 and quoted in the Arthur Bliss Society Newsletter p.9
14 Bliss, op.cit. p.20
15 Craggs. Op. cit. p.13
16 Ibid.
17 Quoted in Craggs op.cit. p.15
18 *The New York Times* 11 June 1939
19 Letter from Bliss to Henn-Collins 15 June 1939
20 Letter from Henn-Collins to Bliss 16 June 1939
21 The other new works were Vaughan Williams's *Dives and Lazarus* and Bax's 7th Symphony.
22 Peter J. Pirie *The English Musical Renaissance* (Victor Gollancz, London, 1979) pp.61/162
23 Letter from Howard Bliss to Arthur Bliss 23 September 1943
24 *Gerald Finzi's Letters 1915–1956* edited by Diana McVeagh (The Boydell Press, Woodbridge, 2021) p.977
25 *The Times* 18 August 1939
26 Bliss op.cit. pp.20–121
27 Letter from Bliss to Elkus from East Heath Lodge, Hampstead dated 24 November but not giving the year which was possibly between 1936–38 but no later.
28 Bliss op.cit. p.23
29 Letter from Bliss to Koussevitsky 22 September 1939
30 Letter from Bliss to Koussevitsky 18 November 1939

31  Letter from Bliss to Koussevitsky 22 December 1939
32  Letter from Bliss to Elkus from 59 Hurd Road, Belmont, Mass. 7 October 1939
33  Bliss op.cit. p.25
34  Letter from Bliss to Elkus from Belmont. 7 November 1939
35  Letter from Robert Gordon Sproul to Bliss 28 August 1939
36  Bliss op.cit. p.26
37  Ibid.
38  Ibid.
39  Ibid. pp.126–127
40  Ibid.
41  Letter from Bliss to Coolidge from the Department of Music, University of California. 15 November, 1940
42  Letter from Bliss to Coolidge from 2632 Warring Street, Berkeley, Thanksgiving Day (28 November) 1940
43  Letter from Bliss to Coolidge from 2632 Warring Street, Berkeley, 31 January 1941
44  Ibid.
45  Letter from Bliss to Coolidge 9 April 1941
46  Craggs op.cit. p.1
47  Music and Letters Vol.23, No.4 (October 1942), pp.326–327
48  BBC Written Archives
49  Bliss op.cit. p.32
50  Ibid. p.33
51  Ibid. p.38
52  Bliss op.cit. p.40

**Chapter Ten** *The Dance Resumes: The BBC,* **Miracle in the Gorbals** *and* **Adam Zero**

1  Bliss op.cit. pp.41–142
2  Recollection of Nancy Farquharson quoted in *Bliss* (Illustrated Lives of the Great Composers), John Sugden (Omnibus Press, Speldhurst, Kent, 1997) p.69
3  Ibid. p.42
4  Ibid.
5  BBC script from the library of the University of California at Berkeley
6  Ibid.
7  Ibid.
8  Ibid.
9  Bliss op.cit. p.44
10  Ibid.
11  Craggs: *A Source Book* op.cit. pp.26–27
12  Bliss op.cit. p.48
13  Bliss op.cit. pp.149–152
14  Quoted in Craggs *Arthur Bliss Music and Literature* op.cit. p.253
15  Ibid.
16  Ibid. p.254
17  Bliss op.cit. p.159
18  Quoted in Nicholas Kenyon, *The BBC Symphony Orchestra 1930–1980* (BBC, London, 1981) p.182
19  Kenyon, op.cit. p.76
20  Mortimer op.cit. p.19
21  Ibid.
22  Craggs: *Arthur Bliss Music and Literature* op.cit. p.259
23  Ibid.
24  Ibid. p.260

25  Ibid. p.260
26  Bliss op.cit. p.58
27  Ibid. p.63
28  Ibid. p.64
29  Haskell *Gala Performance* op.cit. p.35
30  Kathrine Sorley Walker *Dance Chronicle* (Vol 21, No.2, 1998) p.234
31  Ibid.
32  Ibid. p.235
33  Clive Barnes *Ballet in Britain* (Thrift Books, Bungay, 1953) p.27
34  Arnold Haskell *Ballet* (Penguin Books, Harmondsworth, 1945) p.173
35  Arnold Haskell *Miracle in the Gorbals* (The Albyn Press, Edinburgh, 1946) p.9
36  Ibid. pp.12–13
37  Ibid.
38  Manville, Roger and Huntley, John *Technique of Film Music* (Focal Press, London, 1957) p.209
39  Quoted in John Sugden *Bliss* (Omnibus Press, London, 1997) p.72
40  Bliss op.cit. p.68
41  BFI Screenonline *Men of Two Worlds* (www.screeonline.org.uk/film/id/501093/index.html)
42  Helpmann *A Choreographer Speaks: New Theatre* magazine March/April 1947 Vol 3/10 p.3
43  Ibid.
44  Ibid.
45  Kathrine Sorley Walker *Dance Chronicle* (Vol 21, No.2, 1998) p.250
46  W. McNaught *Adam Zero: The Musical Times* vol.87, no.1239 (May 1946) p.55
47  Ibid.
48  quoted (extracted) from *When lilacs last in the dooryard bloom'd* Whitman *The Complete Poems* Penguin (London, 2005)
49  quoted in *The Sketch*, 1 May 1946, p.0
50  *Time and Tide*, November 20 1946

**Chapter Eleven** *Towards Grand Opera and Beyond*

1  Craggs (Bliss Source Book) op.cit. p.30
2  New York Times, 30 August 1953. p.5
3  Arnold Bax *Farewell my Youth* (Longmans, Green & Co., 1943) p.5
4  Transcribed from Pristine Audio CD PASC 460 (2016)
5  Quoted in Roscow (Bliss on Music) op.cit. p.86
6  The *Musical Times* Vol.156, No.1931 (Summer 2015) p.5
7  Frank Howes *The Cheltenham Festival* (Oxford University Press, London 1965) p.8
8  Ibid. p.9
9  quoted in Craggs op.cit. p.60
10  J.B. Priestley in conversation with Gareth Lloyd Evans in a BBC Radio 3 interview as an interval feature in a broadcast of excerpts from *The Olympians*, 21 February 1972
11  Bliss op.cit. p.70

12  J.B. Priestley radio interview op.cit.
13  Quoted in Bliss op.cit. p.171–2
14  Ibid. p.73
15  Priestley radio interview op.cit.
16  Craggs op.cit. p.71
17  Bliss op.cit. p.73
18  Both quotations The *Musical Times* Vol.113, No.1548 (Feb., 1972), pp.45 and 147
19  Priestley radio interview op.cit.
20  Ibid.
21  Ibid. p.65
22  The *Times* 30 September 1949
23  The *Times* 22 February 1972
24  Neville Cardus *Four Opinions on 'The Olympians'* (Opera Magazine, February 1950 vo.1/1) p.0
25  Harold D. Rosenthal, Ibid. p.3
26  Bliss op.cit. p.80
27  Ibid.
28  Ibid. p.181
29  Bliss op.cit. p.185
30  The *Times* 20 June 1949
31  Quoted in Roscow op.cit. p.188
32  Quoted in Craggs op.cit. p.216
33  Bliss op.cit. p.186
34  Ibid.
35  Ibid. p.186
36  Letter from John Ireland to Bliss from 14 Gunter Grove, London dated 2 July 1950
37  Edward Living The *Queen* magazine 10 March 1954
38  Letter from Howard Bliss, June 1950
39  Bliss op.cit. p.186
40  Donaldson op.cit. p.87
41  Ibid.
42  Ibid. p.88
43  Ibid.
44  Bliss op.cit. p.188

**Chapter Twelve** *Master of the Queen's Musick*

1  Bliss op.cit. p.89
2  Ibid. p.90
3  Bliss op.cit. p.91
4  Maurice Leonard *Kathleen: The Life of Kathleen Ferrier 1912–1953* (Futura, London, 1988) p.181
5  The *Times* 7 April 1952
6  The *Belfast Telegraph* Saturday 16 February 1963
7  Quoted in Roscow op.cit. p.216
8  John Amis *Amiscellany* (Faber and Faber, London 1985) p.209
9  Ibid. p.213
10  Bliss op.cit. p.92
11  Roscow. op.cit. p.90
12  Bliss op.cit. p.93
13  Bliss op.cit. p.93
14  Ibid. p.92
15  The *Times* 18 November, 1953
16  John Amis *Amiscellany* (Faber and Faber, London 1985) p.92
17  Transcript from BBC written archives quoted in Roscow op.cit. p.239
18  Christopher Palmer, *Bliss* (Novello, Sevenoaks, 1976) p.21–2
19  The *Times* 17 May, 1954
20  The *Times* 28 May, 1954
21  Ibid.
22  Cyril Ehrlich *Harmonious Alliance* (Oxford University Press, Oxford, 1989) p.25

23  Quoted in Sugden op.cit. p.95
24  Ibid. p.96
25  Bliss op.cit. pp.193–4
26  Ibid. p.94
27  Ibid.
28  *Musical Times* Vol. 96, No. 1348, (June 1955) p.305
29  Christopher Palmer *Aspects of Bliss* (*Musical Times* 112, 1971) p.743
30  Craggs op.cit. p.36
31  Ibid.
32  *The Times* Thursday 12 May 1855
33  Ibid.
34  Craggs op.cit. p.34
35  Letter from Howard Bliss dated 3 September 1950
36  Eric Blom *Music in England* (Pelican, London, 1947) p.267
37  Bliss op.cit. p.195
38  This and other such quotations are from the programme note written by Bliss for the premiere performance.
39  Frank Howes *The English Musical Renaissance* (Secker and Warburg, London, 1966) p.268
40  Ibid.
41  Quoted in Roscow op.cit. p.282
42  Letter to William Alwyn dated 15 January 1975. (Author's italics)
43  Ibid.

**Chapter Thirteen** *Musical Diplomacy, The Lady of Shallot, and Opera for Television*

1  Quoted in Bliss op.cit. p.201
2  Bliss op.cit. p.96
3  Ibid.
4  *The Times* 27 April, 1956
5  Ibid.
6  Ibid.
7  Bliss op.cit. p.99
8  Cyril Smith and Phyllis Sellick *Duet for Three Hands* (Angus and Robertson, London, 1958) p.87
9  Ibid. p.94
10  Ibid. p.98
11  Roscow op.cit. p.238
12  Manvell and Huntley *The Technique of Film Music* (London, 1957) quoted in Roscow op.cit. p.242
13  Ibid.
14  Quoted from the booklet notes for Marco Polo 8.223315 by the conductor Adriano.
15  *The Times* 10 May, 1958
16  Bliss op.cit. p.204
17  Ibid., pp.204–205
18  Ibid. p.206
19  quoted in Craggs op.cit. p.22
20  Booklet notes for FECD1904 (op. cit. 2005)
21  *The Times* 29 September, 1965
22  Bliss op.cit. p.206
23  Ibid.
24  Ibid.
25  Ibid.
26  Ibid. p.207
27  Letter from David Boyden to Bliss from 1208 Shattuck Ave, Berkeley. 24 February, 1957
28  Letter from Bliss to Boyden from 8, The Lane, London, 1 March 1957
29  Boyden to Bliss 3 May 1957
30  Boyden to Bliss 13 May 1957

31  Bliss to Boyden 19 May 1957
32  Ibid.
33  Boyden to Bliss 23 May 1957
34  Bliss to Boyden 23 June 1957
35  Quoted in Craggs op.cit. p.288
36  Bliss to Boyden 15 October 1957
37  Bliss to Boyden 8 December 1957
38  Plot summarized by Mark Shorer, San Francisco Ballet Silver Anniversary Programme, 24 May 1958
39  Christensen to Bliss, 8 May 1958
40  *San Francisco Chronicle* 26 May 1958
41  Ibid.
42  Charles Cushing to Bliss from 2239 Summer Street, Berkeley, 8 May 1958
43  Bliss op.cit. p.202
44  Ibid.
45  Ibid.
46  Ibid. p.203
47  Direct, or closely placed clashing of major and minor thirds
48  Quoted in Roscow op.cit. pp.248–9
49  Quoted in Craggs op.cit. p.296
50  Bliss op.cit. p.207
51  Bliss p.207
52  Ibid.
53  *The Times* 29 April, 1959
54  Letter from Bliss to Hassall dated 21 January 1960
55  Ibid.
56  Roscow op.cit. p.301
57  A long-running British science fiction television series begun in 1963 and still running.
58  *The Times* 18 May 1960
59  Ibid.
60  Letter from Hassall to Bliss dated only 'Friday' and assumed to be in 1960
61  Bliss op.cit. p.208

**Chapter Fourteen** *Unblessed Beatitudes*

1  Sugden op.cit. p.100
2  Ibid.
3  Letter from Sir Arthur Penn to Bliss 9 March 1960
4  Letter from Sir Arthur Penn to Bliss 10 May 1960
5  Letter from Bliss to Hassall dated 14 April 1959
6  Letter from Bliss to Hassall dated 5 August 1959
7  Letter from Bliss to Hassall dated 24 September 1959
8  Letter from Bliss to Hassall dated 12 December 1959
9  Letter from Bliss to Hassall dated 20 April 1960
10  Letter from Bliss to Hassall dated 23 July 1960
11  Letter from Bliss to Hassall dated 21 October 1960
12  Letter from Bliss to Hassall 12 January 1961
13  Letter from Bliss to Hassall 7 February 1961
14  Letter from Bliss to Hassall 4 March 1961
15  Letter quoted in Bliss op.cit. pp.209–210
16  *The Times* 18 May 1962
17  Ibid.
18  Bliss op.cit. p.212

19  *The Times* 26 May, 1962
20  Ibid.
21  *The Times* 5 September 1962
22  Letter from Herbert Sumsion to Bliss dated 10 September 1962
23  *The Times* 29 July, 1961
24  Quoted in the *Daily Telegraph* by Henry Raynor *Recollections for a Birthday* 19 July 1961
25  *The Times* 29 July 1961
26  Neville Cardus *The Venerable Square*, the *Guardian* 2 August 1961
27  *The Times* Ibid.
28  John Warrack *Mastering the Queen's Music*, the *Sunday Telegraph* 30 July 1961
29  Bliss op.cit. p.211–212
30  Bliss op.cit. p.212
31  *Bon Papa – an interview with Sir Arthur Bliss, Youth and Music News* July 1963
32  Quoted in Roscow op.cit. p.251–2
33  Roscow op.cit. p.256
34  Bliss op.cit. p.213
35  Bliss op.cit. p.213 (a translation from the French: 'The delicious and unfading pleasure of a useless occupation.')
36  George Dannatt, *Arthur Bliss: Cagtalogue of the Complete Works*: Introduction (Novello, London, 1980) p.23
37  *The Times* 12 July 1963
38  Giles Easterbrook liner notes for Hyperion CDA67188/9 (1998)
39  Quoted in Craggs op.cit. p.329
40  James Carroll, *Smithsonian Magazine* June 2006
41  Ibid.
42  Letter from Bliss to Hassall 30 August 1962
43  Letter from Bliss to Hassall 6 October 1962 It is likely
44  George Dannatt Introduction: *Arthur Bliss Catalogue of the Complete Works* Novello, London 1980) p.22
45  *The Times* 4 September 1963
46  Bliss op.cit. p.215
47  Bliss op.cit. p.11
48  Bliss op.cit. p.218
49  Ibid.
50  Ibid. pp.219–20
51  Quoted in Craggs op.cit. p.56
52  Bliss op.cit. p.221
53  Ibid. pp.222–223
54  *The Times* 19 February 1964
55  *The Musical Times* Vol.105, April 1964. p.283
56  Ibid.
57  Letter from Bliss to Crozier: 19 November 1963
58  Letter from Bliss to Crozier: 24 November 1963
59  Letter from Bliss Crozier

**Chapter Fifteen** *Australian Interlude and a Vision of Retrospect*

1  Bliss op.cit. p.225
2  Ibid. p.226
3  Ibid.
4  Ibid. p.228
5  Ibid. p.232
6  Ibid.
7  Ibid. pp.232–233
8  Ibid. p.234

9    Ibid.
10   Ibid. p.236
11   John Drummond *Tainted by Experience* (Faber and Faber, London, 2000) p.49
12   Ibid. p.49
13   Ibid. p.239
14   Ibid. p.239
15   Ibid.
16   John Drummond *Tainted by Experience* (Faber and Faber, London, 2000) pp.149–150
17   Drummond op.cit. p.206
18   Bliss to Alwyn, 4 February, 1973
19   Alwyn to Bliss, 7 February 1973
20   Ian Johnson *the Art of Film Music* (Boydell Press, Woodbridge, 2005) p.199
21   Quoted in Roscow op.cit. p.260
22   Ibid.
23   Letter from Bliss to Gipps dated 8 November 1967
24   Bliss to Gipps 10 June 1967
25   Bliss op.cit. p.90
26   Quoted in Roscow op.cit. p.264
27   Ibid.
28   Bliss op.cit. p.240
29   Bliss op.cit. p.241
30   Letter from Britten to Bliss 4 August 1966
31   A Breton Pardon is the feast day of a Patron Saint of a church at which an indulgence is granted, hence the origin of the word Pardon. Some locations attract considerable numbers of pilgrims. Each diocese and parish is known by its costume.
32   Ibid. p.243
33   Ibid. p.244
34   Ibid. pp.244–5
35   Ibid. p.245
36   Ibid.
37   Ibid. p.246
38   Ibid. p.274
39   John Amis *Amiscellany* (Faber and Faber, London 1985) p.266
40   Bliss op.cit. p.273
41   Ibid.
42   Ed. Diana McVeagh *Gerald Finzi's Letters 1915–1956* (Boydell Press, Woodbridge 2021) p.929
43   Letter from Bliss to Crozier: 28 January 1967
44   Letter from Bliss to Crozier: 31 May 1967
45   Letter from Bliss to Crozier: 13 November 1967
46   Waterhouse to Bliss: 4 August 1968
47   Waterhouse to Bliss: 6 August 1968
48   Waterhouse to Bliss: 23 August 1968
49   Robert Clarson-Leach *Marguerite Wolff adventures of a concert pianist* (Artmusique Publishing Co. London 1985) p.84
50   Ibid.
51   Ibid.
52   Ibid. pp.88–89
53   Ibid. pp.90–91
54   *The Guardian* 23 January 2011
55   Bliss to Wolff 4 August 1966
56   Bliss to Wolff 15 December 1967
57   Bliss to Wolff 30 October 1968
58   Bliss to Wolff 21 August 1969
59   *The Cambridge Hymnal* (Cambridge University Press, London, 1967) p.v
60   Ibid.

61   Ibid. p.ix
62   Memorandum noted by Denison dated 28 June 1966, quoted in Craggs op.cit. (Bliss Source Book) p.286
63   Ibid.
64   Ibid.
65   Ibid.
66   Michael Adeane to Bliss 23 July 1969
67   Bliss to Markarian, 1 March 1968
68   Elkus to Bliss 22 April 1968
69   Bliss to Elkus 30 July 1968
70   Elkus to Bliss 7 August 1968
71   Bliss to Elkus 24 September 1968
72   Bliss op.cit. p.275
73   Bliss to Elkus dated 21 December 1967, but in error, as it must have been 1968

**Chapter Sixteen** *The Curtains Close*

1    Bliss op.cit. p.275
2    Ibid. p.276
3    Ibid.
4    Ibid. pp.278/9
5    Letter from Carl Wuermer to Laton Holgren 24 November 1968
6    Ibid. p.279
7    Bliss op.cit. p.290
8    Bliss op.cit. p.276
9    George Dannatt: Introduction to Arthur Bliss Catalogue of Complete Works (Novello, London, 1980) p.25 footnote
10   Quoted in Roscow op.cit. p.271
11   Letter from Kathleen Raie to Bliss 17 December 1969
12   Which became Radio Three two years later in 1969
13   Radio 3 is the BBC's classical music station
14   Hansard 22 July 1969
15   Ibid.
16   Craggs op.cit. Introduction. p.4
17   *The Times* 28 June 1969
18   Interview with Sean Street of BBC Radio Solent in 1973 before Julian Lloyd Webber's performance of the Cello Concerto
19   Bliss op. cit. p.293
20   Quoted in Craggs op.cit. p.40
21   *The Times* 25 June 1970
22   Ibid.
23   *Composer* magazine, Summer 1966, issue 20, p.16
24   Bliss op.cit. p.280
25   Bliss op.cit. p.281
26   Roscow op.cit. p.274
27   Bliss to Kentner 9 September 1970
28   Roscow p.274
29   Ibid.
30   *The Times* 22 March, 1971
31   Letter from Bliss to Gipps 30 July 1952
32   Letter from Bliss to Gipps 2 June 1971
33   Ruth Gipps: *Meditations on a Theme, Composer* (Autumn 1971, No. 41) p.9
34   Letter from Bliss to Ruth Gipps 26 November 1971
35   Letter from Bliss to Ruth Gipps 29 May 1973
36   Letter from Bliss to Gipps 29 March 1972
37   Letter from Clarence House dated 15 June 1971

38   Letter from R.T. Fisher to Bliss dated 24 May 1971
39   *The Times* 14 July 1971
40   *The Times* 3 August 1971
41   Letter from Cardus to Bliss 27 June 1971
42   Letter from Bliss to Dannatt 8 September 1965
43   Bliss op.cit. p.282
44   Letter from Bliss to Dannatt 30 July 1971
45   Letter from Bliss to Dannatt 17 June 1972
46   Letter from Bliss to Dannatt 7 August 1962
47   Letter from Bliss to Dannatt 8 January 1973
48   Letter from Bliss to Dannatt 17 June 1972
49   Letter from Bliss to Dannatt 24 August 1972
50   Letter from Dannatt to Bliss 26 April 1973
51   Letter from Bliss to Novellos 27 October 1973
52   Ibid.
53   Letter from Dannatt to Bliss 10 June 1973
54   Letter from Bliss to Dannatt 26 October 1974. The Fairfield Hall was the location of the work's premiere.
55   Letter from Dannatt to Bliss 29 October 1974
56   Letter from Bliss to Dannatt 4 November 1974
57   *The Times* 23 April 1973
58   Letter from Trudy Bliss to Gipps 19 June 1974
59   Letter from Bliss to Dannatt 17 June 1971
60   Letter from Bliss to Dannatt 21 August 1971
61   Letter from Bliss to Dannatt 2 September 1971
62   *The Times* 22 February 1972
63   Letter from Bliss to Wolff 1 November 1973
64   Letter from Bliss to Wolff 17 January 1974
65   Letter from Bliss to Wolff 8 January 1975
66   I am grateful for the recollections of both the Walton *Ode* and *Mar Portugues* by Dr Martin Neary in private correspondence.
67   Bliss op.cit. p.286
68   Dunbar's title for this poem is *Done is a battell on the dragon blak*
69   Bliss's programme note for the work.
70   There is, of course, a substantial organ part in *The Beatitudes* but in that work it is part of an overall orchestral scheme.
71   Ibid.
72   Letter from Bliss to Alwyn 15 Janury 1975
73   George Dannatt Introduction to the Catalogue of Complete Works (Novello, London, 1980) p.28
74   Letter from Bliss to Alwyn 11 December 1972
75   *The Times* 29 March 1975
76   George Dannatt op.cit. p.30

# Bibliography

*This bibliography covers the principal publications referred to or quoted from. It does not include letters, articles in periodicals or newspaper extracts. All these are fully annotated in the notes on each page.*

Adriano: Booklet notes for Marco Polo 8.223315

Amis, John *Amiscellany* (Faber and Faber, London 1985)

Arundell, Dennis *The Story of Sadler's Wells* (Hamish Hamilton, London, 1965)

Banfield, Stephen *Sensibility and English Song* (Cambridge University Press, Cambridge, 1985)

Barnes, Clive *Ballet in Britain* (Thrift Books, Bungay, 1953)

Bax, Arnold *Farewell my Youth* (Longmans, Green & Co., London, 1943)

BFI Screenonline *Men of Two Worlds* (www.screenonline.org.uk/film/id/501093/index.html)

Bliss, Arthur *As I Remember* (Thames Publishing, London 1970)

Bliss, Arthur BBC script for *At Your Request* (Library of University of California)

Bliss, Arthur *Talk on his Piano Concerto transcribed by David Wilby* Brighton and Hove Gramophone Society on 4 October 1959, Arthur Bliss Society Newsletter

Bliss, Arthur, *Arthur Bliss's Morning Heroes, Monthly Musical Record*, (October 1930)

Bliss, Arthur. *Music in America*, in *Jazz in print (1856–1929): An anthology of selected early readings in jazz history*. Hillsdale: Pendragon Press (2002)

Blom, Eric *Music in England* (Pelican Books, West Drayton, 1942)

Blythe, Ronald *The Penguin Companion to Literature* (ed. Daiches). Penguin, 1971.

Borwick, Susan *Notes*, vol. 56, no. 2 (1999)

Carey, Hugh *Duet for Two Voices* (Cambridge University Press, 1979)

Chapman, Guy *A Passionate Prodigality* (Buchan and Enright, London 1933, 1965, 1985)

Clark, Sir Kenneth *Ballet Décors*, in *Gala Performance* (Collins, 1955)

Clarson-Leach, Robert *Marguerite Wolff adventures of a concert pianist* (Artmusique Publishing Co. London 1985)

Cobbe, Hugh (Ed), *Letters of Vaughan Williams 1895–1958* (OUP, Oxford, 2008)

Craggs, Stewart R. (Ed) *Arthur Bliss Music and Literature* (Ashgate, Aldershot, 2002)

Dannatt, George, Liner notes for Hyperion CDA66137

Dannatt, George: Introduction: *Arthur Bliss Catalogue of the Complete Works* Drummond, John *Speaking of Diaghilev* (Faber and Faber 1997, London)

Davies, W.H. *Shorter Lyrics of the Twentieth Century, 1900–1922* (The Poetry Bookshop, London 1922)

Dibble, Jeremy: *Charles Villiers Stanford: Man and Musician* (OUP, Oxford 2002)

Donaldson, Frances *The British Council The First Fifty Years* (Jonathan Cape, London, 1984)

Drummond, John *Tainted by Experience* (Faber and Faber, London, 2000)

Easterbrook, Giles *Note* in the score of the *Four Songs* (Novello & Co Ltd, London, 1984)

Easterbrook, Giles, Liner notes for Naxos 8.553383, 1995

Easterbrook, Giles: Liner notes for Chandos (CHAN9896) Evans, Edwin, *The Musical Times* 1 February 1923

Easterbrook, Giles: Liner notes for Hyperion CDA67188/9

Ehrlich, Cyril *Harmonious Alliance* (Oxford University Press, Oxford, 1989)

Ellis, Sam *Bliss's New England: identity, interdependence and isolation* (Doctoral thesis for Bangor University, 2011)

Foreman, Lewis: *From Parry to Britten: British Music in Letters 1900–1945* (Amadeus Press, Portland, Oregon, 1987)

Gipps, Ruth *Meditations on a Theme, Composer* (Autumn 1971, No. 41)

Gipps, Ruth Composer magazine, Summer 1966, issue 20

Haskell, Arnold (Ed) *Gala Performance* (Collins, London, 1955)

Haskell, Arnold *Ballet* (Penguin Books, Harmondsworth, 1945)

Haskell, Arnold *Miracle in the Gorbals* (The Albyn Press, Edinburgh, 1946)

Helpmann, Robert *A Choreographer Speaks*: *New Theatre* magazine March/April 1947 Vol 3/10

Hope Simpson, J.B. *Rugby since Arnold* (MacMillan St Martin's Press 1967)

Howes, Frank *The Cheltenham Festival* (Oxford University Press, London 1965)

Howes, Frank *The English Musical Renaissance* (Secker and Warburg, London 1966)

Hughes, Herbert: Preface to *A James Joyce Book* (OUP, London, 1933)

Johnson, Ian *The Art of Film Music* (Boydell Press, Woodbridge, 2005)

Kennedy, Michael *A Portrait of Elgar* (Oxford 1968)

Kennedy, Michael *Portrait of Walton* (OUP Oxford, 1989)

Kenyon, Nicholas *The BBC Symphony Orchestra 1930–1980* (BBC, London, 1981)

Lambert, Constant *Music Ho! A study of music in decline* (Faber, London 1934)

Leonard, Maurice *Kathleen: The Life of Kathleen Ferrier 1912–1953* (Futura, London, 1988)

Lloyd, Stephen, Sparkes, Diana and Sparkes, Brian *Music in their Time: The Memoirs and letters of Dora and Hubert Foss* (Boydell Press, Woodbridge, 2019)

MacKenzie, Norman and Jeanne *The Time Traveller: The Life of H.G. Wells* (Weidenfield and Nicolson, London)

Mahoney, Patrick *Sir Arthur Bliss in Santa Barbara* published in the journal *Noticias* (1971)

Manville, Roger and Huntley, John *Technique of Film Music (*Focal Press, London, 1957)

McNaught, William *A short Account of Modern Music and Musicians* (Novello, London, 1936)

McVeagh, Diana (Ed) *Gerald Finzi's Letters 1915–1956* (The Boydell Press, Woodbridge, 2021)

Metzer, David *The League of Composers: the initial years* (American Music Vol.15 No.1, Spring 1997)

Mortimer, Harry *on Brass* (Alphabooks, Sherborne, 1981)

Nichols, Robert: *Such Was My Singing* (Collins, 1942) Novello, London 1980)

Palmer, Christopher *Aspects of Bliss (Musical Times* 112, 1971)

Palmer, Christopher *Bliss* (Novello, 1976)

Palmer, Christopher, booklet notes for Lyrita SRCD.225 (1971)

Pirie, Peter J. *The English Musical Renaissance* (Victor Gollancz, London, 1979)

Poston, Elizabeth (Ed) *The Cambridge Hymnal* (Cambridge University Press, London, 1967)

Powers, Alan *Harmonious Mansions* Country Life August 29, 1985

Roscow, Gregory (Ed), *Bliss on Music* (OUP, Oxford, 1991)

Roscow, Gregory *The Selected Writings of Arthur Bliss 1920–1975* (OUP, Oxford, 1991)

Shirodkar, Marco: Booklet notes for FECD1904

Smith, Cyril and Sellick, Phyllis *Duet for Three Hands* (Angus and Robertson, London, 1958)

Sorley Walker, Kathrine *Dance Chronicle* (Vol 21, No.2, 1998)

Still, Barry (Ed), *Two Hundred and Fifty Years of the Three Choirs Festival, A Celebration in Words and Pictures* (The Three Choirs Festival Association, 1997)

Sugden, John *Bliss* (Omnibus Press, London, 1997)

Sugden, John quoting Nancy Farquharson in *Bliss (Illustrated Lives of the Great Composers*), (Omnibus Press, Speldhurst, Kent, 1997)

Tertis, Lionel *My Viola and I* (Crescendo Publishing Company, Boston, USA, 1974)

The *Field Service Pocket Book*, 1914 (The War Office)

Walton, Susana *William Walton Behind the Façade* (OUP Oxford 1988)

War Diaries for 13th Battalion, Royal Fusiliers

Wells, H.G. *Two Film Stories* (London, The Cresset Press, 1940)

Whitman, Walt *The Complete Poems* (Penguin Classics, London, 2005)

Wood, Sir Henry *My Life in Music* (Victor Gollancz, 1949)

Wortham, H.E. *Arthur Bliss* (The Sackbut April 1927)

# Index

À Becket Williams,
Christopher 188
Aber, Adolf 162
Addinsell, Richard 208, 214
Adriano (conductor) 226
Aldwych Theatre 65
Allen, Sir Hugh 59, 132, 193,
195, 196
Alwyn, William 196,
243, 251
Amis, John 54, 58, 184,
236, 240
Amsterdam 105, 230
Ankara 175, 225
Ansermet, Ernest 52, 53,
63, 132
Antheil, Georges 123
Aolian Hall, London 22, 65
Armstrong Jones, Anthony
272
Arne, Thomas 65
Arts Council of Great
Britain 227
Arundell, Dennis 166
Ashmansworth (Finzi's
home) 134
Ashton, Frederick 162, 210
Astor family 83
Atkin, Gabriel 35
Auric, Georges 54, 207
Australian Broadcasting
Commission 305

Bach, J S 17, 49, 53, 58, 156,
168, 190, 245, 272
Badingham Old Rectory,
Woodbridge 193
Banfield, Stephen 61, 83, 123
Barber, Samuel 190
Barbirolli, Sir John 173
Bare, June 162
Barnes, Clive 204
Barnes, London 10
Barr, Cyrilla 89
Bartlett, Ethel 237
Bartok, Bela 72, 82, 260
Bath Abbey 101
Bath War Hospital 44
Bath, City of 23, 44, 154, 190
Bax, Sir Arnold 21, 62, 116,
123, 151, 170, 174, 180,
213, 240
BBC 76, 131, 132, 142, 143,
145, 152, 154, 155, 157,
169, 187, 188, 190, 191,

193–201, 207, 212, 226,
241, 251, 253, 271, 273
BBC Chorus 144
BBC Concert Orchestra
239
BBC Northern
Orchestra 197, 238
BBC Scottish Symphony
Orchestra 197, 198
BBC Symphony
Orchestra 144, 145,
169, 197, 198, 208,
214, 246
Brains Trust 226
Broadcasting House
143
Commission of Violin
Concerto 238
Desert Island Discs 271
Doctor Who 276
Just a Minute 261
Light Music Festival
214
Memorial Concert radio
play 213
Music Advisory Panel
131, 132, 133, 148,
195, 209
Music Department 157
Music Department,
Manchester 198
Overseas Music
Department 186,
196, 198
Programme Committee
131
Radiophonic Workshop
276
The Listener 143,
152, 156
BBC Television Productions
275
Bebbington, Mark 8, 97
Beckwith, Arthur 22
Bedford College, London
(BBC) 188, 198
Beecham, Sir Thomas 11,
199, 235
Beethoven, Ludwig van 12,
14, 22, 53, 62, 96, 163, 190,
235, 241, 251, 272
Belinfonte, Paul 106
Bell, Vanessa 20
Belugi, Piero 266
Benjamin, Arthur 91
Bennett, Arnold 56

Benthall, Michael 201, 202,
205, 209
Berg, Alban 72, 169
Berkeley, Lennox 196
Berkeley, USA 179, 183, 186
Berkshire Festival, USA 177
Berlioz, Hector 20, 38, 121,
156, 245
Bernard, Anthony 74
Berners, Lord 62
Bilton Grange School 12,
13, 25, 35
Binney, Malcolm 206
Birmingham Town Hall 253
Birmingham University 247
Birmingham, city of 189
Bismark 187
Bliss Archive, Cambridge
University Library 8
Bliss, Sir Arthur
'American strain' 229
21 Holland Park 11
annual Christmas
card 107
aptitude for fanfares
151, 238
As I Remember 10, 95,
170, 184, 186, 228,
240, 248
attitude to faith 251
BBC memo 'The Case
for Live Music' 191
Berkeley lectures
on English Music
179–181
birth 10
characteristic disso-
nance 68, 100
Coaxing Caliban 194
compositional
periods 6
conducting style 5,
215, 243
Director of Music at
BBC 192–201, 213
discussing finales 255
early academic aptitude
12
early musical experi-
ences 12
energy in music 73
enfant terrible 6, 51, 64,
119, 172, 251
engagement and
marriage 94

experiments in sound
52, 53, 73, 87, 163
feelings about film
music 214, 258–259
Freedom of the
Worshipful Company
of Musicians 242
gassed in the First
World War 47
growth of romanticism
90
Hawthornden (first
house) 10
Hon. Fellow RCM
200–201
Hon. Fellowship
Pembroke College,
Cambridge 239
Hon. LL.D Glasgow
University 232
honours 168
interest in microscopes
15–16
interest in plants and
shrubs 232–233
knighthood 228
learning the viola 16
life at Cambridge 18–20
love of clocks 11
Master of the Queen's
Musick 151, 240,
241, 242, 247, 257,
260, 273
meeting with Trudy 93
melodic writing 99,
113, 238
notating music 88
Performing Right
Society Vice
Chairman 229
physical bearing 5
Pilgrim's Progress for
The Listener 152–157
Presidency of the LSO
260
purchase of 8 The Lane,
St. John's Wood 240
regular work schedule
146
relationship with Elgar
79, 110
signing up in 1914 and
various battalions he
was attached to 28
silver wedding
anniversary 227

songwriting 24
The Apostles 20
The Gods 18
Threefold Function
of Broadcast Music
paper 193–195
use of piano in
composition 146
views on Germans and
German music 22
visiting Professor,
Berkeley 177
Bliss, Barbara (Gatehouse)
7, 98, 102, 103, 124, 196,
199, 201, 227, 239, 265
Bliss, Elijah and Mary 10
Bliss, Enid 81, 239
Bliss, Ethel 48, 81, 85
Bliss, Francis (Frank, Bliss's
father) 10, 11, 20, 27, 32,
34, 42, 48, 49, 81, 83, 85,
103, 122, 176, 182, 229
Bliss, Francis Kennard 10,
12, 13, 17, 20, 31, 34, 35,
36, 37, 38, 39, 40, 80, 97,
98, 99, 101, 114, 115, 118,
121, 122, 126, 130, 151,
242, 245, 251, 261
Bliss, George 10
Bliss, James Howard 10, 12,
22, 31, 38, 81, 91, 95, 96,
124, 174, 175, 182, 182,
229, 243, 247
Bliss, Karen (see also Sellick)
98, 124, 167, 199, 201, 219,
227, 253
Bliss, Trudy 6, 8, 88, 95, 111,
122, 133, 134, 135, 142,
149, 156, 174, 177, 178, 179,
182, 186, 187, 188, 189,
192, 193, 195, 200, 201,
207, 212, 229, 232, 238,
239, 254, 255, 256, 267,
270, 271, 272, 274, 277,
305, 306
author 212, 213, 232
broadcasting 200,
212, 214
Bliss Charitable Trust 7
Bloch, Ernest 264
Blom, Eric 112, 125, 126,
128, 247
Bloomsbury Group 20, 51
Blow, John 67, 179, 247,
248–250
Blunden, Edmund 175
Bolshoi Ballet 270
Bonavia, Edward 119, 185
Boosey, Leslie 243
Borwick, Susan 89
Bosch, Hieronymous 250
Boston Symphony Orchestra
90
Boston, USA 88, 89, 100,
177, 178
Boult, Sir Adrian 6, 58, 59,
74, 131, 132, 133, 144, 145,
149, 151, 157 172, 174, 177,
178, 183, 186, 198, 199,
200, 215, 257
Bournemouth Symphony
Orchestra 243
Boyce, William 180
Boyd, Stephen 259
Boyden, David 264, 265,
266, 267
Bradley, F.H. 9

Brahms, Johannes 17, 19, 22,
62, 88, 125, 126, 128, 172
Brain, Alfred 59, 92
Brain, Dennis 92, 237
Brewer, Herbert 74
Bridge, Frank 184
Bridges, Robert 105
Bridges Adams, William
and Nancy 158, 159, 160,
162, 165, 183, 193, 227
Brighouse and Rastrick
Band 197
Bristol, city of 154, 186, 187
British Academy 8
British Council 148, 158,
162, 168, 170, 173, 174,
183, 191, 199, 212, 225,
230, 253
Executive Committee
212
Music Committee 212
British Film Institute 208
Britten, Benjamin 79, 115,
180, 198, 206, 222, 237,
243, 249, 276
Brook, Peter 220, 239
Brooke, Harold 107, 218
Brooke, Rupert 16, 49, 263
Brooklyn, Long Island 19
Browne, W Denis 18
Brueghel, Pieter 250, 269
Brussels 168, 260, 267
Buckingham Palace 228,
229
Bullock, Sir Ernest 232
Burn, Andrew 7
Burnley 155
Burra, Edward 201, 202, 205
Bush, Alan 192, 237
Busoni, Ferrucio 17, 173
Butterfield, William 15
Byrd, William 154, 179, 180

Calvert, Phyllis 223
Cambridge 35, 65, 117, 193
Cambridge Festival Theatre
166
Cambridge University 16,
36, 45, 98, 173, 271
Cambridge University
Library 8
Cambridge University
Madrigal Society 238
Cambridge University
Music Club 271
Camden Studios (BBC) 241
Campoli, Alfredo 213, 214,
243, 254, 258
Canadian Broadcasting
Corporation 171, 191
Carducci, Giosuè 123
Cardus, Neville 224
Carey, Hugh 35
Carlyle, Jane Welsh 212, 232
Carlyle, Thomas 212, 232
Carnegie Hall 172
Carnegie Trust 55, 56
Carnegie, Andrew 55, 83
Carpentaria, USA 239
Carpenter, Nettie 22
Carrington, Dora 147
Carta, Hubert 201
Cartier, Rudolph 274
Cary, Joyce 207
Casals, Pablo 88, 155, 157
Chandler, Raymons 215
Chandos Records 141
Chaplin, Charles 82, 92

Chapman, George 115
Chapman, Guy 29, 30, 32
Chappel, William 166
Chappell music publishers
141
Chelsea Barracks, London
45, 46
Chelsea, London 161, 215
Cheltenham Festival 214,
215
Chisholm, Eric 156, 196
Chopin, Frederick 91, 203
Christiansen, Lew 265,
266, 268
Christie, Agatha 9, 215
Churchill, Sir Winston 275
City of Birmingham
Symphony Orchestra 189,
226, 247, 253
Clark, Edward 196
Clark, Kenneth 165, 201
Clark, Robert 8
Coates, Eric 243
Cohen, Harriet 213
Colum, Padraig 123
Commonwealth War Graves
Commission 46
Concertgebouw 58
Conservatorio Benedetto
Marcello (Venice) 104
Coolidge String Quartet 184
Coolidge, Elizabeth Sprague
88, 89, 103, 104, 105, 123,
183, 184
Copa Films 259
Copland, Aaron 77
Cornford, Frances 65
Cornwall 156, 233
Coronation of HM Queen
Elizabeth II 238
Couperin, Francis 62
Covent Garden (Royal
Opera House) 204, 209,
211, 220
Cradley Rectory,
Herefordshire 15
Craggs, Stewart 184
Craigenputtock, Scotland
232
Crichton, Ursula 173
Crimp, Bryan 173
Crisp, Clement 162
Crystal Palace Festival 156
Cunard, Lady Maud 199,
200
Curtis School of Music,
USA 89
Curwen publishers 56
Cushing, Charles 269
Czecho-Slovak Radio
Symphony Orchestra 226

D'Indy, Vincent 248
Da Vinci, Leonardo 124
Daily Mail, The 64, 194
Daily Telegraph, The 62, 188
Dale, Benjamin 132, 189
Damrosch, Walter 62
Dance Chronicle, The 210
Dannatt, George 77, 78, 80,
220, 227, 261
Dante Alighieri 210
Darnbrough, Monica 7
Davidov, Vladimir 271
Davies, Agnes 10
Davies, W.H. 102, 106
Davies, Walford 154
Dawson, William 93

Day Lewis, Cecil 237, 241,
247, 248, 273
De Falla, Manuel 21
De la Mare, Walter 70, 71
De Montford Hall, Leicester
239
De Valois Studio 166
De Valois, Dame Ninette 12
De Valois, Ninette 160, 165,
166, 167, 210
Debussy, Claude 14, 19, 32,
49, 51, 52, 53, 61, 67, 88
Decca Records 140, 141
Delage, Maurice 54
Delius, Frederic 52, 80,
159, 249
Denham Studios 140, 141
Dent, Edward 13, 17, 23, 35,
36, 41, 49, 98, 219, 225
Desert Island Discs 5
Diaghilev, Sergei 21, 43, 51,
52, 63, 159, 201
Dickinson, Thorold 207, 208
Dods, Marcus 226
Donaldson, Frances 148,
230
Dostoevsky, Fyodor 202
Dowland, John 179, 180
Draper, Charles 59
Drummond, Sir John 52
Drury Lane Theatre,
London 21
Dudley, Earl of Leicester
158
Dunnett, Roderick 219, 276
Dunstable, John 179
Dvorak, Antonin 130
Dyson, Sir George 5, 14, 25

East Heath Lodge,
Hampstead, London 110,
147, 158, 187
Easterbrook, Giles 7, 68,
106, 141, 142, 206
Eastman School of Music,
USA 89
Edinburgh Festival 227, 257
Edinburgh University
208, 258
Edmunds, Chris 196
Ehrich, Cyril 243
Eichheim, Henry 87, 90, 92
El Greco 203, 205
Elgar, Lady 22, 42
Elgar, Sir Edward 15, 16,
22, 31, 32, 41, 52, 56, 74,
77, 78, 79, 80, 99, 107, 110,
117, 159, 180, 197, 216, 241,
243, 245, 250
Elkus, Albert 8, 84, 177, 178,
179, 180, 181, 186, 190
Elkus, Jonathan 8
Elliot, Ursula 188, 196
Ellis, Sam 82
Engel, Carl 89
Epstein, Jacob 124
Eton College 14
Evans, Edwin 69, 72, 104
Evesham (BBC) 18

Faculty of Arts Gallery,
London 91
Fairey's Band 197
Fairfax, Brian 224
Falkner, Keith 148
Farquharson, Maurice and
Nancy 187, 189, 200
Fedricks, Bill 236

Feeney Trust 247
Ferrabosco, Alfonso 255
Ferrier, Kathleen 233, 234, 235
Festival of Britain 227
*Film Dope* magazine 259
Finzi, Gerald 105, 134, 135, 175, 176, 189, 245, 261
Fletcher, Frank Morley 92
Fletcher, John 108
Foden Motor Works Band 158, 197
Fonteyn, Margot 162
Foot, Robert 193
Foreman, Lewis 8, 132, 199
Foss, Dora 110, 170, 171
Foss, Hubert 110, 129, 130
Fouquet's Restaurant, Paris 123
Fragonard, Jean-Honoré 111
Frankenstein, Alfred 269
Fraser, Claud Lovat 56, 61, 69, 134
Fraser, Grace 56, 134, 159
Frend, Charles 169

Gainsborough Pictures 226
Garland for the Queen, A 238, 240, 242
Garrick Club 220, 271
Gatehouse, Michael 265
Gatehouse, Richard 201
Gatehouse, Susan 239
George, Lloyd 199
Gershwin, George 77, 210
Gertler, Mark 147
Gibbons, Orlando 179, 180
Gibbs, Armstrong 58, 59, 196
Gieseking, Walter 168
Gilels, Emil 168, 270
Glasgow Grand Opera Society 156
Glasgow University 232, 258
Glasgow. City of 156, 201
Gloucester Cathedral 76, 243
Gloucestershire Echo, The 215
Goddard, Scott 58, 172
Godfrey, Sir Dan 56. 243
Goehr, Walter 198, 199
Goethe, Johan Wolfgang von 24
Gonville and Caius College, Cambridge 17
Goodwin, Felix 90
Goossens, Eugene 21, 22, 62, 74, 77, 88, 123, 178, 183
Goossens, Leon 103, 128, 172, 189, 254
Gordon, Alexie 212
Gould and Company publishers 18
Grace, Harvey 113, 119
Grainger, Stewart 223
Granada Television 250
Granville-Barker, Harley 96
Graves, Sir Cecil 193, 195, 199
*Great Thoughts* magazine 160
Grenadier Guards 5, 45, 46, 49, 258
Griller Quartet 227, 228
Gropius, Walter 140
Grotian Hall, London 106

Groves, Sir Charles 225
Gudounov, Boris 254

Hadley, Patrick 193
Hadow, Henry 56
Haig, Field Marshal 32
Haileybury College 10
Hallé Orchestra 157, 198
Halliwell's Film Guide 226
Hammersmith Musical Society 57
Hampstead 111, 128, 147, 168, 187, 188, 189, 215, 263
Handel, George Frederic 13, 155, 255, 271
Hardy, Thomas 95, 96, 105, 175, 233
Harland, Julia 207
Harland, Peter 134, 135
Harold Brooke Choir 107
Harris, Roy 77, 92
Harvard University 93, 179
Haskell, Arnold 204
Hassall, Christopher 263, 264, 266, 268, 273, 274, 275, 276, 277
Heifitz, Jascha 170
Heine, Heinrich 216
Helpman, Robert 162, 201, 202, 204, 205, 209, 210, 211, 219
Hely-Hutchinson, Victor 157, 200
Henderson, Roy 112
Henkel, Lily 23
Henn-Collins, Panda 173
Hepworth, Barbara 147
Herbage, Julian 197, 198
Hess, Myra 57, 148, 189, 190, 234
Heward, Leslie 58, 59, 189
Heyter, Sir William 257
Heyworth, Peter 221
Hill, Alfred 201
Hindemith, Paul 72, 130, 236, 255
Hitchcock, Alfred 259
Hodgson, Ralph 25
Hoffman family, Santa Barbara 93, 94
Hoffman, Bernard and Irene (Trudy's uncle and aunt) 94
Hoffman, Gertude (Bliss's mother-in-law) 88
Hoffman, Ralph (Trudy's father) 93, 122, 233
Hoffman, Trudy (Bliss's future wife) 93
Hoffman, Walter (Trudy's brother) 193
Holbrooke, Josef 54
Holland Park, London 11, 22, 48, 81
Hollywood 138
Hollywood Bowl 190
Holme Valley Male Voice Choir 156
Holst, Gustav 21, 52, 62, 66, 67, 69, 123, 151, 159
Homer 11, 115, 116, 198, 216, 233
Honneger, Arthur 25, 54, 61, 64, 98, 132, 137, 206
Hope-Wallace, Philip 211
Hopkins, John 238
Household Cavalry (State Trumpeters) 272

Howells, Herbert 21, 41, 42, 43, 49, 50, 53, 55, 56, 70, 74, 76, 77, 97, 123, 261
Howes, Frank 99, 109, 147, 215, 250
Hughes, Herbert 123, 215
Huxley, Aldous 251
Huxley, Julian 225, 226

International Composers Competition 168
International Composers Guild 89
International Society for Contemporary Music 72, 98, 196
Inverewe gardens, Scotland 233
Ireland, John 62, 74, 97, 123, 228
Isle of Wight 225

Jackson, Paul 8, 88
Jackson, Sir Thomas 15
Jacob, Gordon 196
James, Henry 75
James, Ivor 59
Jeremy, Raymond 22
John, Augustus 123
Johnson, Basil 14, 229
Johnson, Ben 108
Johnson, Dr Samuel 258
Johnston, James 220
Joyce, Eileen 169
Joyce, James 72, 123, 124
Julliard School of Music 89

Kabalevsky, Dmitry 270
Kandinsky, Wassily 165
Karsavina, Tamara 159
Kaufman and Connelly 93
Keats, John 49
Keller, Hans 100
Kelly, Sir Gerald 239
Kenilworth Castle 157
Kennedy, Michael 80
Kensington, London 25, 95, 215
Kenyon, Sir Nicholas 197
Kerr, Deborah 223
Kharkov 253, 256
Khatchaturyan, Aram 270
Kiev 253, 256
King Edward VII
King George V 208, 238
King James II 248
King's College, Cambridge 13, 35,
Kipling, Rudyard 45
Kitchener, Lord 32
Kitchener's Army (or 'New Army') 28, 45
Knightsbridge Barracks, London 46
Kodaly, Zoltan 72
Korda, Alexander 136, 138, 139, 140, 141, 169
Korda, Vincent 140
Koussevitsky, Serge 90, 176, 178
Krein, Michael 214
Kremlin, Moscow 254, 270
Kruschchev, Nikita 257, 270, 271
Kutcher String Quartet 128

Lake Mohonk, USA 84

Lambert, Constant 82, 123, 162, 169, 179, 193, 211
Le Corbusier 140
League of Composers 87, 89
Lebrun, Albert 162
Leeds, City of 156
Léger, Fernand 140
Leicestershire Choirs 239
Leigh, Vivien 206
Leningrad 253, 256
*Les Six* 54, 61, 72
Letour, Celestine Adrienne 10
Lewis, Anthony 247
Lewis, Wyndham 61
Li Po 83, 84, 115, 118
Library of Congress, Washington 89, 104, 184
Lilburn, Douglas 201
Lister, Moira 259
Liszt, Franz 17, 168, 172
Lloyd Evans, Gareth 220
Lloyd, Stephen 169, 170, 207
London 90, 92, 95, 101, 103, 106, 107, 110, 115, 122, 133, 136, 159, 165, 169, 174, 175, 182, 183, 187, 189, 190, 200, 207, 213, 229, 239, 240, 253, 256, 267
London Film Symphony Orchestra 169
London Gazette 32
London Light Orchestra 214
London Philharmonic Orchestra 149, 208, 214
London Symphony Orchestra 16, 112, 140, 141, 208, 235, 259, 260, 273, 305
Los Angeles 82, 181
Los Angeles Philharmonic 92
Louisville, Kentucky 261
Luck, Rupert 42
Lyric Theatre, Hammersmith 56, 57

MacDowell Colony for Artists 86
Mackenzie, Norman and Jeanne 140
Madrid 229, 231
British Institute 230
Mahler, Anna 168
Mahler, Gustav 22, 62
Mahoney, Cynthia (Bliss's half-sister) 81,85
Mahoney, Patrick (Bliss's half-brother) 81, 85
Maier, Guy 90
Makower, Ernest 148, 149, 162, 174
Malvern Hills 15
Manchester, City of 157, 189, 237
Mann, William 223
Markova, Alicia 166
Marsh, Edward 263
Mason, James 223
Matheson, Muir 141, 169, 208, 226, 259
McKnight Kauffer, Edward 161, 165, 166
McNaught, William 127, 128, 210, 220
Memorial Theatre, Stratford-upon-Avon 57
Mendelssohn, Felix 92, 155

Mengelberg, Willem 58, 59
Menin Gate, The 260
Menzies, William Cameron 139
Messiaen, Olivier 101
Mew, Charlotte 106
Mewton-Wood, Noel 175, 225, 235–238
Meyer, Robert 212
Meyerbeer, Giacomo 162
Meyerstein, Edward 51
Miekle, Robert 80, 120, 121, 245, 246
Milford, Robin 196
Milhaud, Darius 25, 54, 61, 72, 183, 264
Millay, Edna St Vincent 182
Milnes, Robert 7, 149, 213, 214, 255, 257
Milton, John 210
Ministry of Information 207
Mission to Seamen 253
Moeran, E.J. 123
Moger, Gladys 65
Moiseiwitsch, Benno 198
Monteaux, Pierre 88, 98, 99, 100, 177
Montecito (Santa Barbara) 85
Montgomery, Peter 196
Montreal 177, 186, 187
Moore, G.E. 20
Moore, Gerald 254
Moosehead Lake, Maine USA 177
Morley College, London 199, 236
Morley, Thomas 179, 180
Morning Post, The 132
Morris, R.O. 79, 95, 161
Morrison, Elsie 241
Mortimer, Fred 158
Mortimer, Harry 158, 197
Mortlake, London 10
Moscow 253, 254, 255, 256, 257
Moscow Conservatoire 270
Moscow News 270
Moscow State Symphony Orchestra 257
Mossolov, Alexander 25
Mozart, W.A. 17, 125, 126, 128, 260, 272
Munsh, Charles 208
Murray, Earl 266
Museum of Performance and Design, San Francisco 8
Music and Letters 185
Musica Britannica 248
Musical Mirror, The 82
Musical News and Herald 139
Musical Standard 56
Musical Times, The 72, 107, 109–110, 113, 119, 125, 126, 130, 147, 162, 210, 214, 246, 247
Musicians' Benevolent Fund 151
Myers, Rollo 188

Nash, John 61
Nash, Paul 61, 133, 134
National Brass Band Festival 157

National Gallery Concerts 190
New College, Oxford 148, 257
New Queen's Hall Orchestra 69
Newcastle upon Tyne 156
Newman, Ernest 66, 85
New York 10, 83, 86, 93, 94. 100, 173, 183, 184, 186
World's Fair 168, 170
New York Herald 62
New York Philharmonic-Symphony Orchestra 173
New York Stadium 190
New York Times 173, 212
Nichols, Basil 193, 195
Nichols, Robert 9, 24, 44, 61, 106, 107, 108, 109, 115, 118
Nicholson, Ben 135, 147
Nicholson, Harold 148
Nietzsche, Friedrich 64
Nikisch, Arthur 58, 59
Nisbet, Ulrich 91
Norfolk and Norwich Festival 110, 113, 156
Norland School, Holland Park 12
Norton, Frederick 65
Novello, Ivor 263
Novello, publishers 23, 107, 142, 220, 267
Novo-Dievitchy Monastary, Moscow 254

Observer, The 70
Olivier, Laurence 239
Opera magazine 224
Orbita, SS 94
Ord, Boris 58, 59, 238
Orient Express, The 257
Ormandy, Eugene 178
Orr, C.W. 123
Owen, Susan 120
Owen, Wilfred 80, 115, 116, 118, 120, 121, 263
Oxford 132, 148, 190
Oxford and Cambridge Boat Race 12
Oxford University Press 110

Paganini, Niccolo 246
Palais Royale, Paris 123
Palmer, Christopher 78, 112, 115, 242, 245
Pancoast, Lillie 10
Paris 160, 162, 163
Paris Conservatoire 20
Parry, Sir Hubert 17, 31, 59, 235
Pascal, Gabriel 206, 207
Pattison, Lee 90
Pearl Harbor, Japanese attack 193
Pears, Peter 237
Pembroke College, Cambridge 17
Pen Pits 133–135, 166, 193, 207, 232, 239, 240
Pen Selwood 133
Performing Right Society (PRS) 229, 242, 243, 253, 263
Philadelphia Orchestra 99, 100
Philadelphia, USA 88
Philharmonic Quartet 22
Phillips, Montague 196

Phillips, R.A. 230
Phoenix Theatre, London 170
Picasso, Pablo 83
Pirie, Peter 174
Piston, Walter 77
Playfair, Nigel 56
Plumley, Roy 5, 271
Poliziano, Angelo 108
Pooley, Elizabeth 7
Portsmouth Guildhall 243
Poulenc, Francis 54
Poussin, Nicolas 266
Power, Sir John 162
Power, Tyrone 259
Powers, Alan 135
Priestley, J.B. 61, 111, 152, 214, 216–220, 222, 223, 225, 227, 263
Prince Andrew 273
Prince's Theatre, London 204
Princess Margaret 272
Prior Park, Bath 23, 43, 44, 45
Pro Arte String Quartet 183, 184
Prokofiev, Sergei 132, 163, 206
Promenade Concerts 69, 100, 140, 169, 175, 189, 205, 241
Providence, Rhode Island 83
Puccini, Giacomo 54
Pudney, John 241
Purcell, Henry 57, 62, 179, 180, 235, 271

Queen Elizabeth I 158
Queen Elizabeth II 238, 271
Queen Mother, HM 238
Queen Victoria's Diamond Jubilee 11
Queen's Hall Orchestra 92
Queen's Hall, London 17, 58, 100, 112, 120, 122, 169, 175, 235

Rachmaninov, Sergei 91, 172, 208
Radcliffe College, Massachussets 93
Radio Times, The 169, 194, 197
Rankl, Karl 220
Ravel, Maurice 11, 14, 19, 20, 21, 62, 90, 210, 272
Ravinia Park, Chicago 177, 190
Rawsthorne, Alan 180, 193
Raybould, Clarence 198, 208, 254
Reading, Lord 254
Reed, Henry 233, 238
Reed, W H 16, 74
Reeves, George 106
Reis, Claire 87
Reiss, Thelma 148
Remoortel, Edouard van 259
Renoir, Pierre-Auguste 178
Riddle, Frederick 130
Rignold, Hugo 235
Rimsky-Korsakov, Nikolai 99
Robertson, Rae 238
Rome 230, 234, 247

Ronald, Landon 16
Rootham, Cyril 229
Roscow, Gregory 276
Rosenthal, Harold 224
Rostal, Max 214
Roussel, Albert 123
Royal Academy of Dramatic Art (RADA) 201
Royal Academy of Music (RAM) 133, 142, 189, 235
Royal Academy, The 239
Royal Albert Hall, London 17, 208, 241, 273
Royal Birmingham Conservatoire 8
Royal College of Music (RCM) 17, 20, 21, 25, 58, 59, 66, 67, 95, 200, 208
Royal Festival Hall 236, 238, 246, 253, 258
Royal Fusiliers, 13th Service Battalion 28, 29, 30, 38
Royal Institution 125, 136
Royal Military School of Music, Kneller Hall 208, 272
Royal Opera House, Covent Garden 204, 209, 211
Royal Philharmonic Orchestra 101, 226
Royal Philharmonic Society 112, 242, 271
Royal Scottish Academy of Music 232
Royal Shakespeare Company 158
Royal Societies Club 74
Roze, Raymond 65
Rubbra, Edmund 261
Rubens, Peter Paul 266
Rubinstein, Arthur 130, 168
Rugby School 13–16, 27, 35, 254
Russell, Bertrand 20
Russia 21, 52, 137, 187, 253, 255, 257, 270
Russian Ballet (Diaghilev) 63

Sachse, Wilhelm 16
Sackbut, The 57
Sackville-West, Edward 198
Sadler's Wells Ballet Company 165, 201, 211, 219
Sadler's Wells Theatre 163, 166
Sale, Richard 259
Salle Gaveau, Paris 54, 58
Salter, Lionel 141, 214, 275
Salzburg Festival 72, 149, 151, 277
Salzburg, city of 154, 215
Salzedo, Leonard 87
San Francisco 84, 85,92, 94
San Francisco Ballet Company 264, 269
San Francisco Chronicle 269
San Francisco War Memorial Opera House 269
Santa Barbara 8, 85, 87, 91, 92, 93, 94, 95, 103, 108, 111. 182, 187, 229
Sargent, Sir Malcolm 112, 149, 166, 241, 246, 271
Sassoon, Siegfried 35

Satie, Eric 90
Saunders, Max 201
Savile Club 189, 225
Sawyer, Mairi 233
Scanes, Sybil 106
Scarlatti, Domenico 168
Scherchen, Hermann 98
Schnabel, Artur 169, 261
Schoenberg, Arnold 17, 21, 53, 72, 79, 82, 87, 125, 169, 181, 272
Scholes, Percy 75, 76
Schubert, Franz 194
Schumann, Robert 168
Schumann, William 77
Schwarz, Rudolf 253
Scriabin, Alexander 22
Sellick, Christopher 253, 305
Sellick, Karen (Bliss's daughter) 7, 31, 305
Sellick, Phyllis 211, 213, 238, 254, 255, 256, 257
Selwyn College, Cambridge 17.
Serkin, Rudolf 169
Service, Robert 40
Sessions, Roger 123
    String Quintet 264
Shakespeare, William 16, 31, 118, 245, 272
Shankar, Ravi 272
Sharp, Cedric 22
Shaw, George Bernard 16, 205
Shepherd, John 8
Shirodkar, Marco 262
Shoreham, Sussex 28, 29, 30
Shorer, Mark 262
Shorer, Suki 270
Shostakovich, Dmitri 255, 257, 270
Sibelius, Jean 190, 237
Simenon, Georges 215
Sinding, Christian 159
Smetana, Bedrich 130
Smith, Cyril 148, 211, 213, 238, 254, 255, 256
Smith, John 8
Smith, Matthew 124
Smith, William Overton 264
Smyth, Ethel 235
Sneddon, Bill 8
Society of Women Musicians 21, 61, 144, 242
Solomon, Cutner 129, 168, 171, 172, 173, 175, 233
Solomon, J.J. 77
Somerset 133, 136, 166, 170, 239
Sorley Walker, Kathrine 201, 202, 210
Sousa, John Philip 11
Spain/Spanish idioms 226, 230
Spencer, Edmund 210
Spender, Natasha 192
Spender, Stephen 137, 189
Spenser, Edmund 111
Sproul, Robert 181
St Basil's Cathedral, Moscow 254
St Paul's Cathedral 70
Stainer and Bell publishers 18
Standard Oil Company 10, 71

Stanford, Sir Charles 17, 20, 32, 59, 60, 61, 74, 95, 221, 271
Starkie, Walter 230
Steinway & Son 173
Stokowski, Leopold 88, 98, 99
Strauss, Richard 21, 22, 52, 72, 221, 250
Stravinsky, Igor 21, 43, 51, 53, 54, 59, 61, 63, 64, 68, 70, 71, 78, 79, 82, 83, 90, 91, 99, 100, 123, 125, 132, 151, 163, 177, 181, 205, 211, 242, 272
Sugden, John 243
Sullivan, Sir Arthur 65
Sutherland, Joan 241
Symons, Arthur 123
Szymanowski, Karol 98

Tallis, Thomas 179
Tausky, Vilem 239
Tchaikovsky International Piano Competition 257, 270
Tchaikovsky, P.I. 15, 172, 174, 204, 209, 271
Temple, Frederick 15
Territet, Switzerland 15
Tertis, Lionel 17, 128, 129, 130, 131, 233
Thalben Ball, George 273
Thatcher, Reginald 133, 193, 195
The Lane (No.8), St John's Wood 240, 255
Theocritus 108, 233
Thompson, Randall 264
Thompson, W.W. 198
Three Choirs Festival 76
Thursfield, Anne 51
Thurston, Frederick 65, 128, 130
Tillett, Emmie 257
Time and Tide 211
Times, The 32, 60, 61, 100, 101, 112, 118, 125, 143, 151, 165, 166, 169, 175, 222, 223, 226, 235, 240, 242, 246, 254, 258, 260, 262, 274, 277
Tippett, Sir Michael 198, 199, 237, 260
Toscanini, Arturo 151, 155, 163, 173
Tovey, Donald Francis 92
Turner, Harold 162
Tye, Christopher 179

University of California, Berkeley 8, 84, 87, 177, 181, 182, 186, 190, 263, 264, 266, 267, 68, 269

Valencia 230
Valentine, Gunner Moses 34, 52
Van Dieren, Bernard 123, 124, 125, 126
Vancouver 84
Vanderbilt family 83
Varèse, Edgard 87
Vatican, The 96
Vaughan Williams, Ralph 18, 27, 56, 62, 67, 78, 79, 80, 82, 109, 112, 117, 151, 161,

165, 166, 170, 179, 180, 240, 261, 271
Venetian String Quartet 104
Venice Festival (Coolidge) 103
Verdi, Guiseppe 16
Vic-Wells Ballet 160, 165
Vienna Philharmonic Orchestra 149
Vyvian, Jennifer 254

Waddell, Julia 134
Wadsworth, Edward 56, 61, 135, 190
Wadsworth, Fanny 56. 190
Wagner, Richard 44, 159, 190
Wales 152, 154, 155
Walter, Bruno 151, 169
Walton, Sir William 51, 123, 129, 165, 170–171, 180, 193, 197, 205, 206, 238, 240, 243, 250, 256, 263
Walton, Susana 171
Warlock, Peter 123, 179
Warrack, Guy 201
Warrell, Arthur 154
Watkinsons's School, Orme Square, London 12
Watson, Sydney 148
Webern, Anton 72
Weelkes, Thomas 180
Weingartner, Felix 151
Weldon, George 225
Wellington Barracks, London 45
Wells, H.G. 82, 136, 137, 138, 139, 140, 141, 142, 143, 206
Welsh, James 201
Western Orchestral Society 243
Westminster Abbey 238, 253, 258, 271, 272
Westminster Gazette 51
White, Robert 179
White, Roderick 91
Whitelaw, Robert 16
Whitman, Walt 27, 29, 115, 117, 118, 211
Whittall, Arnold 159
Widdicombe, Gillian 241
Wigmore Hall 57, 128, 236
Wilbye, John 179, 180
Wilcox, Herbert 239
Wilder, Thornton 209
Williams, Caroline 8
Wilson, Sir Steuart 18, 57
Wilson, W.N. 13
Wingates Temperence Band 155, 157, 158
Witts, Richard 214
Women's Royal Naval Service (WRNS) 201
Wood, Charles 17
Wood, Sir Henry 69, 90, 113, 118, 140, 142, 175, 205, 243
Woolf, Virginia 20
Wordsworth, William 126
Worshipful Company of Musicians 242
Wortham, H.E. 57, 58, 63
Wotton, Sir John 112
Wright, Kenneth 157, 186, 187, 188, 198, 273
Wylie, Elinor 182

Yeats, William 49
York Bowen, Edwin 97
Young, Ernest 22
Ypres 260, 263
Ysye International Competition for Pianists 168

Zorian String Quartet 237

BLISS WORKS
A Child's Prayer 102
A Colour Symphony 6, 41, 52, 56, 69, 74, 75–80, 81, 87, 88, 100, 107, 110, 120, 126, 145, 243
A Salute to Painting 239
A Song of Welcome 241, 242
A Wedding Suite (piano) 19
Adam Zero 201, 209–211
Angels of the Mind 6
Arr. Pergolesi La Serva Padrona 57 (score missing)
Arr. Purcell Act Tunes and Dances 57
Aubade for Coronation Morning 238
Baraza (Men of Two Worlds) 214
Birthday Fanfare for Sir Henry Wood 205
Birthday Song for a Royal Child 273
Caesar and Cleopatra 205, 206
Cantata: Mary of Magdela 263
Cello Concerto 176
Cello Concerto 6
Checkmate 79, 142, 159–166, 177, 201, 202, 249
Christopher Columbus 226
Clarinet Quintet 120, 125–128, 129, 130
Concerto for Piano, Tenor and Percussion 90
Concerto for Piano, Tenor voice, Strings and Percussion 57
Concerto for Two Pianos and Orchestra 90, 237
Conquest of the Air 158, 169–170
Conversations 63–65
Discourse for Orchestra 261–263
Edinburgh Overture 258
Fair is my love (song) 272
Fanfare for a Political Address 151
Fanfare for BBC's In Dominion 152
Fanfare for Heroes 151
Fanfare: Service of the Order of the Bath 258
Faster than Sound 206
Four Songs 106, 107
France Arises (Présence au Combat) 206
Fugue for String Quartet (lost) 41
Hymn to Apollo 100, 101, 102
Incidental music for As You Like It 56

Incidental music for *The Tempest* 65, 85
Intermezzo (piano) 18
Introduction and Allegro 99, 100, 101, 199
Kenilworth 156, 157
Madam Noy 50, 51, 52, 56, 58, 73
March: The Phoenix-Homage to France, August 1944 208
Masks (piano) 90, 91
May-Zee (piano) 18
Meditations on a Theme by John Blow 67, 79, 247–252, 253, 259, 260, 262, 275
Mêlée Fantasque 69, 70
Men of Two Worlds 207, 208, 226
Metamorphic Variations 6
Miracle in the Gorbals 166, 201–205, 209, 214
Morning Heroes 40, 78, 80, 99, 105, 107, 108, 110, 111, 113–122, 126, 127, 129, 159, 171, 200, 222, 242, 250, 252, 260, 263
Music for Strings 147, 148, 149–151, 167, 176, 177, 178, 179

Narcissus and Echo 166
Night Club Scene (from *Adam Zero* arr. for piano) 211
Oboe Quintet 103, 104, 128, 190
Pastoral (choral work) 79, 105, 107, 108, 109, 110, 111, 115
Pastoral (clarinet and piano) 39, 58
Peace Fanfare for Children 208
Piano Concerto 170–176, 222, 225, 233
Piano Quartet in A minor 23–24
Piano Quintet 54
Piano Sonata 175, 236
Processional 238, 241
Rhapsody (1919) 55, 56, 57, 106, 166
Rhapsody for piano (lost) 24, 40
Rich or Poor (song) 102
Rout 56, 57, 59, 61, 63, 69, 72, 73, 82, 83, 106, 166
Salute to the RAF 258
Salute to the Royal Society 273
Seek ye the Lord 253

Serenade 111, 112, 114
Seven American Poems 182, 185
Seven Waves Away (film) 259
Simples (song) 124
String Quartet (1914) 22–23
String Quartet (MS c.1929) 90
String Quartet in B flat, No.1 55, 227
String Quartet No. 2 227–228
String Quartet No.1 (1941) 183
Suite for Piano (1916) 18
Suite for Piano (1925) 96, 97
The Ballads of the Four Seasons 83–84, 87
The Beatitudes 115, 170
The Beggar's Opera 239
The Enchantress 233–235, 237
The First Guards 258
The Hammers (song) 25
The Lady of Shalott 263, 264
The Lady of Shalott 8
The Olympians 54, 111, 216–224, 226, 228, 233, 266, 277
The Shield of Faith 6

The Tramps (song) 40
The Women of Yueh 86, 87
Theme and Cadenza 214
Things to Come 136–143, 151, 158, 164, 169, 177, 198, 206, 275
Three Jubilant and Three Solemn Fanfares 208
Three Romantic Songs 70
Tis time, I think, by Wenlock town (song) 24
Tobias and the Angel 263, 273–277
Toccata (piano) 96
Two Interludes 89
Two Nursery Rhymes 65, 73
Two Studies for Full Orchestra 66–69
Valses Fantastique (piano) 19, 23
Viola Sonata 120, 128–131, 233
Viola Sonata 17
Violin Concerto 176
Violin Concerto 238, 242, 243–247, 258, 272
Violin Sonata 41, 42, 43, 
Welcome the Queen 241